# The Military Family

# The Military Family

## A Practice Guide for Human Service Providers

Edited by
James A. Martin, Leora N. Rosen,
and Linette R. Sparacino

*Foreword by Gary L. Bowen*

Westport, Connecticut
London

**Library of Congress Cataloging-in-Publication Data**

The military family : a practice guide for human service providers / edited by James A.
Martin, Leora N. Rosen, and Linette R. Sparacino ; foreword by Gary L. Bowen.
    p. cm.
Includes bibliographical references and index.
ISBN 0–275–96540–6 (alk. paper)
    1. Families of military personnel—United States.   I. Martin, James A. (James
Ashworth), 1946–   II. Rosen, Leora N.   III. Sparacino, Linette R.
UB403.M54   2000
355.1—dc21      99–055036

British Library Cataloguing-in-Publication Data is available.

Library of Congress Catalog Card Number: 99–055036
ISBN: 0–275–96540–6

First published in 2000

Praeger Publishers, 88 Post Road West, Westport, CT 06881
An imprint of Greenwood Publishing Group, Inc.
www.praeger.com

Printed in the United States of America

The paper used in this book complies with the
Permanent Paper Standard issued by the National
Information Standards Organization (Z39.48–1984).

P

In order to keep this title in print and available to the academic community, this edition
was produced using digital reprint technology in a relatively short print run. This would
not have been attainable using traditional methods. Although the cover has been changed
from its original appearance, the text remains the same and all materials and methods
used still conform to the highest book-making standards.

# Contents

# Tables and Figures

**FIGURES**

# Foreword

In their edited volume *The Military Family: A Practice Guide for Human Service Providers*, James Martin, Leora Rosen, and Linette Sparacino make an important contribution to understanding military families. The chapters testify to the resiliency of military families across a variety of contexts and life course events and suggest ways that human service practitioners in both the military and the civilian sectors can help military families negotiate the evolving and interdependent worlds of work and family life. The reviews of literature and reports of data across chapters show that the majority of military families, including the children and youth in these families, successfully handle the many adversities and positive challenges associated with life in an organization in which family needs and demands are often secondary to those of the organization.

A particular contribution of this volume is its focus on military families within a life course perspective. Proponents of life course theory recognize the importance of social-historical and cultural influences on family structure and interaction. Chapters in the volume strike at the heart of how organizational and operational dynamics in the military services play out in the lives of military families and their children. These dynamics include the outsourcing and privatization of many support functions from the military sector to the civilian sector. As a consequence, the volume is directed to civilian human service providers who will assume a larger role in the future as a formal support system for military families.

Proponents of life course theory assume that families must be understood in their developmental context. This developmental context includes an appreciation for both structural shifts in the family system over time, including the timing and sequencing of family statuses, as well as individual development. Chapters are included that focus on the young enlisted family, the senior military wife, and military retirement. As described in these chapters, military families may face pressure points in balancing work and family demands at certain intersections of the work and family life cycle. Chapter authors suggest a number of strategies by which human service professionals can help military families anticipate and manage the intersection of work and family demands at critical junctures in the life course.

The volume's focus on children in the military is particularly appreciated, including chapters on young children, adolescents, and the adult children of military parents. Prior books on military families have either neglected or given little attention to the situation and needs of children growing up in the shadow of the military. Given that many of these children and youth attend civilian schools and access human services in the civilian sector, civilian service providers should find these chapters informative in their attempt to understand the situations and experiences of children growing up in military families.

Illuminated from the backlight of life course theory, the chapters offer a risk and resilience perspective in examining military families. This risk and resilience perspective is implicit in the context of models that focus on family stress, coping, and social support, as well as models that focus on the nature of family-environment fit in which family needs and competencies are examined within the context of community resources and demands. From this perspective, family adaptation and resiliency are enhanced in situations where families are able to balance situations and conditions that challenge them with protective factors that buffer these influences or positively affect their coping behavior. As community assets, both military and civilian human service providers play a potentially important role in helping military families manage risks that challenge their adaptation and develop and access protective factors that promote the capacity of the family system and its members. Several chapter authors point to the centrality of the unit chain of command as a first line of support for military families and as a critical link between military families and the human service delivery system. In addition, several chapter authors stress the importance of human service providers working to strengthen informal sources of support for military families, including their connections with extended family, friends, work associates, and neighbors.

In the context of the many changes that have taken place in the U.S. military over the last decade, including higher operational demands for active duty members, greater challenges in the recruitment and retention of service members, radical shifts in the human service delivery system, and a perceived decline in families' informal connections and sense of community, Martin and colleagues' contribution to the military family literature is timely. They have succeeded in providing military and civilian human service providers with a guidepost for understanding military families on the threshold of the 21st century and for increasing the effectiveness and efficiency of their interventions on behalf of these families. *The Military Family* should be required reading for human service professionals who assist in the care and treatment of military families and their children.

Gary L. Bowen
School of Social Work
The University of North Carolina at Chapel Hill

# Acknowledgments

We are very grateful to the individual authors whose contributions have made this book possible. We would like to acknowledge the support provided by the Walter Reed Army Institute of Research, particularly Col. Robert Gifford who originally suggested this book, LTC Kathy Knudson who supported the development of the initial chapters, and Dr. Joel Teitelbaum who provided some of the initial information for the book. We are grateful to Col. Gregory Belenky for offering workspace for the editors to meet. We are especially grateful for the editorial comments and technical assistance provided by Dr. Susan Turkel Dr. Joseph Rothberg and Ms. Rhona Martin. In addition, their encouragement and good humor helped sustain this work.

# Introduction

The United States military is often thought of as a reflection of our society; so, too, is the military family. As the various authors in this book highlight, there are unique differences between military members and their families and the general population. These include a number of demographic differences (they are younger, there are more minority members, and there is a higher proportion of two-parent families in the military) related to current recruitment and retention patterns. There are also differences related to the unique nature of military service and military family life. There are frequent periods of family separation associated with the military members' deployment for training or military operations. In addition, military members and their families are typically stationed great distances from extended family, and overseas assignments are common. Despite these and many other differences, the military family is first and foremost an American family. Military families share all the life course issues that challenge families in our society—raising children, coping with financial problems, managing career and family, dealing with marital problems including domestic violence, and transitioning into retirement. However, the military family faces challenges not shared with their civilian counterparts; these challenges set them apart and make them different. Dealing with these challenges sometimes involves personal and family sacrifices not well understood or appreciated by civilian society. Such misperceptions, and a corresponding lack of appreciation for the rigors of military family life, may result in a lack of empathy and understanding and a corresponding lessening of public support for military families.

In the past the military services often closed ranks and attempted to provide for the needs of their own members and their families with minimal outside assistance. They adopted the "we take care of our own" philosophy. In reality, seldom was the military equipped to meet the needs of all its members and their families. Some, specifically junior enlisted families, were even denied selected family benefits, for example access to on-base housing. Those in a career status believed that these benefits of service had to be earned and that junior enlisted members, and by extension their families, were not yet entitled to these benefits.

The adoption of an All-Volunteer Force concept in 1973 and dramatic changes in global military threats have produced corresponding changes in the nature of military service and service life. The return of American military forces from overseas, base closures at home and abroad, military reorganizations, and substantial overall personnel downsizing have all had a powerful impact on the military and the nature of military family life. Part of this downsizing has been possible because of Department of Defense outsourcing and privatization initiatives, including various military community human service functions. Human services for military family members are now increasingly being provided by civilians, either via contract providers working in on-base military facilities or from sources in the civilian community by way of fee-for-service arrangements with compensation based on traditional earned benefit and/or entitlement models. In the context of this shift in the provision of human services, it is essential that civilian human service providers have basic knowledge of and experience with military family life in order to serve this population adequately. This book provides civilian human service providers with some of this basic information—a "101" course in military family studies. This book is intended to encourage civilian providers to involve themselves in the provision of services to military members and military families and to proactively engage the military community in this process.

Space considerations prevent us from going into all of the unique aspects of the individual service branches and all of the associated family life issues that evolve over the military family life course. As editors, we have provided what we believe are useful chapters focused on some of the more common and basic issues. We hope that civilian human service providers will treat these chapters as a "necessary but not sufficient" introduction to the military family and the many challenges in military family life. We hope the reader will be encouraged by these discussions and will use this book as a foundation for further study. These chapters are intended to convince the reader that efforts to better understand the military family are necessary and important for successful engagement with this population.

A number of historically momentous events, and social change that has affected the military family in ways that are especially noteworthy, have influenced the development of what is a relatively sparse professional literature on the military family. Many of these same historical and social forces continue to shape the military family to the present day. Ruben Hill wrote one of the earliest books on the military family in 1949. Hill's book dealt with the U.S. military family of World War II—a time when millions of men served in a draft status, many for prolonged periods in combat units in Europe or the Pacific. At that time, most American families were connected to the military in some way through a father, son, husband, brother, uncle, aunt, or close friend. The central issue for military families at that time, dealt with in much detail by Hill, was the adjustment associated with prolonged separations and the corresponding reunion. Often the context was that a man left his family to serve as a soldier, and then two or three years later returned to his family as a civilian.

As Tom Brokaw (1999) has noted in his book, *The Greatest Generation* going into military service and often to war was a fundamental fact of military life in this period of American history. Today relatively few Americans experience this separation from home and family or the corresponding risks associated with military training and operational deployments. For those who serve in our armed forces, and for their families, some of the fundamental experiences of military duty and family life have not substantially changed from those experienced by earlier generations of military families. Separation and reunion experiences, as documented in Hill's book, are still as relevant today as they were in World War II. As described here in Chapter 8, "Wartime Stress and Family Adaptation," and Chapter 10, on "Marital Adjustment During Deployment," today separations and reunions are both wartime and peacetime issues for military families. For those individuals serving in the reserve components, as noted in Chapter 2 "The Citizen Soldier," transitions between civilian and military life have become increasingly important issues for reservists and national guardsmen who now make up more than 50 percent of the *uniformed component* of the total force.

The next book of importance was not written about the military family, but for the military family—or at least certain members. In 1942 Nancy Shea wrote *The Army Wife*. This was a self-help book for young women who had married or were about to marry Army officers. This book provided information on protocol and etiquette for the young officer's wife, and it may be characterized as the militarization of the rigid sex roles of the 1940s and later in the 1950s and 1960s in the context of the "two for one" career pattern. It is noteworthy that at that time the term "military wife" was commonly used to refer only to officers' wives. For the most part, as described in Chapter 1, which traces some of the historical roots of the current military family, enlisted wives were typically discounted.

Change over the past 30 years is especially evident in the military's concern regarding the needs of young military families and the special issues that confront these families as described in Chapter 3. Nevertheless, senior wives remain important to the military, and the question of their role in the military community is explored in Chapter 5 within the context of two studies of senior Army wives. While these data are limited to samples of Army spouses, the editors have added an exhibit that provides linkage to senior spouses in the other military service branches.

In the mid-1980s two landmark books on the military family were published. Edna Hunter edited the first book. Gary Bowen and Dennis Orthner edited the second book. These two important books were published at a time when the All -Volunteer Force had been in effect for almost a decade, and the number of military family members had increased dramatically. Old attitudes born of the adage "if the military wanted you to have a wife they would have issued you one" were being replaced with a growing sense of responsibility on the part of the military for the needs of family members. Both books detail the special stresses of life confronting military families, issues such as separations and frequent relocations. These issues continue to affect military families, as described in Chapter 4, "Coping with the Unique Demands of Military Family Life." This chapter draws on more than a decade of research conducted since the early 1980s and highlights both the issues as well as some of the important interventions that have emerged over this period. Chapter 6 looks at an important issue for many military spouses—their own efforts to secure and sustain employment (and for some spouses developing and maintaining careers) within the unique constraints of a military lifestyle. Chapter 7 deals with career service members and their families as they eventually face transition from their military careers into civilian life. Employment and career issues are themes that are carried across these two chapters.

Family violence has become the focus of a great deal of attention throughout our society in the past two decades. While spouse and child abuse are not necessarily more prevalent in the military than in the civilian world, dealing with these issues in the context of military life requires specialized knowledge of the population being served and the specific programs and interventions developed for this purpose. The chapters on child and spouse abuse provide an overview of the military services' family advocacy programs, and they represent an important resource for civilian human service providers. A third chapter in this section, on the military's support programs for new parents, provides an example of family advocacy prevention initiatives taking place within the military service branches.

The scope of the present book goes beyond that of previous books. It deals not only with special issues affecting military families, but in addition it also addresses issues that affect all military families across the life course. While the editors have not organized the book using a life course format, this social science concept has influenced our thinking. Where appropriate and practical, we have used this conceptual model in the presentation of the needs and life experiences of military families. For example Chapter 14 deals with children's issues, Chapter 15 with adolescents, and Chapter 16 with the adult children of military parents—a unique group of adults in our society, many of whom have spent a considerable part of their formative years living in military communities in Europe or the Far East.

In preparing this book, we hope that we have been able to bring the military family to life so that civilian human service providers can better understand the life conditions and experiences of current and future military families. Chapters in this book describe the challenges of military family life and highlight the resiliency that exists among individuals, and families and within a unique institutionally based community. We hope that human service providers will positively identify with these truly American families and recognize the importance of their service and sacrifice to our nation. We also hope that this book provides the requisite knowledge and supports the adoption of the necessary promilitary-family attitudes necessary to encourage civilian practitioners to offer their services to this population.

James A. Martin, Leora N. Rosen, and Linette R. Sparacino
Washington, DC
May 30, 2000
In honor of Memorial Day

## REFERENCES

Bowen, G. L. & Orthner, D. K. (1989). *Organization Family: Work & Family Linkages in the U.S. Military.* Westport, CT: Greenwood Publishing Group.

Brokaw, T. (1998). *The Greatest Generation.* New York: Random House.

Hill, R. (1949). *Families under Stress: Adjustment to the Crises of War Separation and Reunion.* New York: Harper & Row (reprinted by Greenwood Press, Westport, CT, 1971).

Hunter, E.J. (1982). *Families under the Flag: A Review of Military Family Literature.* Westport, CT: Greenwood Publishing Group.

Shea, N. (1966). *The Army Wife* (4th ed.). New York: Harper & Row.

**Part I**

# The Culture and Conditions of Military Family Life

# Chapter 1

# Today's Active Duty Military Family: The Evolving Challenges of Military Family Life

*James A. Martin and Peggy McClure*

## INTRODUCTION

In a fundamental sense, "the military family" has existed throughout time and across all military forces. It is best represented by the women and children who have marked their lives by long periods of husband and father absence. Terms such as "waiting wives" and "camp followers" reflect their historical status and challenging experiences. Today, spouses and children of active duty men and women service members continue to share the challenges and hardships of military service and the associated demands of military family life. Duty demands and the conditions of military family life, including long and often unpredictable duty hours, relatively low pay and limited benefits, frequent separations, and periodic relocations (sometimes to foreign countries and cultures), remain the major stressors of military family life.

An additional stressor that is often overlooked by the public during periods of relative peace, but never by the military family, is the inherent danger associated with military service—danger intrinsic to all military training and military operations. Military service has always produced widows and orphans. While most of Americans recognize the dangers inherent in places like Kosovo, and many can still recall the dramatic television coverage of the Persian Gulf War, most Americans are less likely to remember the other major combat deployments since 1980. These include the Panama invasion (1989) that resulted in 23 combat deaths and the peacekeeping mission in Somalia (1992-1994) where 30 U.S. soldiers lost their lives in combat. Between 1992 and 1998 more than 70,000 American military personnel served peacekeeping duty in Bosnia, Serbia and other parts of the Baltic region and many more continue to serve in that region of the world. Thousands more continue to serve in Korea and the volatile Persian Gulf region.  Excluding the Persian Gulf War (where there were relatively few combat casualties but where subsequently thousands of service members contracted a range of medical conditions known collectively as Gulf War Illness), there have been more than 380 combat deaths and more than 800 military members wounded in action between 1981 and 1997 (Dyhouse, 1998a, p. 26).  In addition, terrorist attacks have killed 313 military personnel during this period in Beirut, Lebanon, and Dhahran, Saudi Arabia (Dyhouse, 1998b, p. 23).

The numerous conflicts in the last decade of the twentieth century reminds us that the world is a dangerous place and that American military forces can be called on at any time to deploy to hostile locations around the globe.  Meanwhile, today's military family members, like those who came before, continue to share a disproportionate burden for family life while experiencing the universal tradition of waiting, worrying, and, for some, grieving.  Civilian human service providers engaged in roles that involve service and support to military families can take pride in knowing that their efforts contribute to the well-being of these families and therefore our nation's military readiness.

## COMPARING THE PAST WITH TODAY'S ALL-VOLUNTEER FORCE

Except for wartime periods, the United States has relied on a small, primarily volunteer military to ensure its security and national interests.  Drafts were used in periods of national emergency where much larger forces were required.  However, the experiences of the Vietnam era soured most Americans on the concept of conscription.  Likewise, as a result of their personal experiences in Vietnam, many senior military leaders came to believe that maintaining a world-class military requires a highly trained and well-motivated professional force—an *All-Volunteer Force*.  In 1973 the United States initiated the development of this new military (Janowitz & Moskos, 1979).  Since the adoption of the All-Volunteer Force concept, the U.S. military has experienced a number of dramatic changes.  These include changes in the composition of the force, duties and career experiences, entitlements of service, and even change in the nature of the military community.  Table 1.1 provides a summary comparison of today's All-Volunteer Force with yesterday's military.

Table 1.1
A Comparison of the Pre- and Post-All-Volunteer Military

| Points of Comparison | Prior to the All-Volunteer Force | The All-Volunteer Force Period |
|---|---|---|
| The People | • Married officers and enlisted members treated as if single.<br>• Limited ethnic-racial and gender diversity.<br>• A force representative of the larger society, reflecting its culture and values. | • Primarily a married force.<br>• Diversity the norm.<br>• A force increasingly less representative of the larger society and less identified with the normative culture and values. |

**Table 1.1 (continued)**

| Points of Comparison | Prior to the All-Volunteer Force | The All-Volunteer Force Period |
|---|---|---|
| **Their Duties and Career** | • A long history of guarding America's coasts, and exploring and settling its frontiers.<br>• Lengthy, frequent postings to remote and/or foreign areas—a large overseas garrison force.<br>• Duty and personal life often one and the same. Considerable tolerance for professional mistakes and personal misconduct. | • Operations around the globe.<br>• Rapid deployment from home station and a focus on being "trained and ready" now! Lack of time predictability and frequent absences.<br>• A perception of a "zero-defect" duty and personal life environment. |
| **Their Entitlements** | • Rank has its privilege and "earned" benefits the norm.<br>• Limited recognition of families. "If they wanted you to have a family, they would have issued you one."<br>• From meeting basic life needs on the frontier to a form of "welfare capitalism." | • Growing concern over equity and fairness. A focus on entitlements for service.<br>• Profamily values and "family well being" a leadership focus.<br>• Multiple programs and services to enhance recruitment, retention, and readiness. Emphasis on privatization of programs and services. Well-being a personal responsibility and self-help the norm. |
| **The Military Community** | • From frontier post to the military "company town."<br>• Social control requires "singles" inside the gates.<br>• Rank provides on-base family housing and a corresponding economic advantage. The development of large on-base housing developments and corresponding military community facilities. | • From "company town" to "military hometown."<br>• From barracks to dorms to off-base apartment living.<br>• Owning property an important economic advantage. Concern about deterioration of on-base housing—the development of a military "ghetto." Privatization of community functions. |

Source: Adapted from Twiss and Martin, 1998.

### The People: Demographic Changes

*Size of the Force.*  Since the end of the Cold War in 1989, the Department of Defense has experienced budget cuts, base closures, return of forces from western Europe and the Pacific region, rebasing of forces within the continental United States, and substantial military and civilian personnel reductions.  For example, the number of active duty personnel decreased from more than 2 million in 1975 to a level of 1.4 million members in 1999.  As a result of the 1999 conflict in Serbia, this downward trajectory seems to be on hold as the president and the Congress debate the issue of necessary military size and structure for the 21st century.  This debate will no doubt continue into the next administration and there is every likelihood that there will continue to be economic pressure to continue cutting the size of the armed forces.

Even in an era of budget surpluses, there are some daunting and expensive challenges associated with maintaining a military force capable of an active worldwide presence, while at the same time embarking on a necessary program of modernization in preparation for 21st century military threats (Gansler, 1998).  The challenge of maintaining today's relatively small, highly skilled military force raises serious budget issues.  The armed forces are experiencing severe personnel problems in both the recruitment and retention of qualified personnel.  In a period of prolonged economic prosperity and corresponding low unemployment, it is likely that any politically acceptable solution to these problems will require a significant increase in personnel expenditures in both recruitment incentives and broadly defined pay, allowances, and other quality-of-life benefits.

*Increasing Percentage of Married Personnel.*  Although the majority of senior military members were married during the period prior to the adoption of the All-Volunteer Force concept, the frequent turnover of single, young men under conscription effectively limited the overall number of married military members.  While today's all volunteer military is much smaller, the complexity and technology of modern warfare increase the need to retain trained personnel in second and subsequent enlistments.  This results in a force composed of a higher proportion of members in the midlevel enlisted ranks—individuals who are older and therefore more likely to be married and with children.

Today, the percentage of married members differs by branch of service, with the greatest difference occurring in the most junior ranks.  For example 45 percent of Air Force junior enlisted members are married as compared to only 26 percent of junior enlisted Marines.  Although rates do vary by rank and service, the overall result of recent recruiting and retention trends is an increase in the proportion of married military members (Segal & Segal, 1999).  In 1973, 51 percent of the active force was married; by 1997, 58 percent was married.  Most of this growth represents enlisted marriages.  In fact, during this period, the percentage of married officers actually declined from 84 percent to 73 percent.  Table 1.2 highlights the distribution of married military members by  their

Table 1.2
Percentage of Married Active Duty Members by Pay Grade
(Total: 829,988 Married Active Duty Members)

| Service Branch | Entry Level E1-E4 | Mid-Grade Level E5-E6 | Senior-Grade Level E7-E9 | Junior Officers O1-O3 | Senior Officers O4-O6 | Service Total |
|---|---|---|---|---|---|---|
| Army | 32 | 78 | 86 | 59 | 89 | 57 |
| Navy | 31 | 76 | 88 | 60 | 87 | 58 |
| Air Force | 45 | 80 | 87 | 65 | 89 | 66 |
| Marine Corps | 26 | 76 | 88 | 57 | 92 | 46 |
| Total | 33 | 78 | 87 | 61 | 89 | 58 |

Source: Data from the Defense Manpower Data Center, 1997.

branch of service and by rank in 1997. As a result of these demographic changes, the Department of Defense and each of the military services have placed considerable emphasis on developing family programs and services, many focused on young enlisted families. These initiatives are typically referred to as part of the concept of "quality of life" (Defense Science Board, 1995).

Family members now outnumber active duty members—there are 1.4 million active duty military members and more than 2 million family members of active duty military personnel (Defense Manpower Data Center, 1998). Today, military leaders continue to consider family issues critical to the recruitment, the readiness, and the retention of military personnel (Segal & Harris, 1993).

*Early Entry into Parenthood.* Although most recruits are single when they enter military service, many marry before the end of their initial enlistment, and they tend to start having children early. This is in contrast to their civilian peers who typically pursue education and employment opportunities and who increasingly defer marriage and family until their mid- to late twenties (Newman & Newman, 1999). The problems facing young, junior enlisted families are well documented (Dougherty, 1999; Burke & Moskos, 1996; Segal and Harris, 1993; Peterson, 1992). These families are at the bottom of the pay scale, and they are typically inexperienced in dealing with the stresses of marriage, parenthood, and military life. Surveys suggest that, compared to senior enlisted personnel and officers, junior enlisted members are less satisfied with military life, feel the military is not a good place to raise children, are generally less satisfied with their marriages, and are more likely to blame the military for their problems (Dougherty, 1999).

*Female Service Members and the Male Spouse.* In the past two decades the percentage of women among U.S. military personnel has increased significantly—from 1.6 percent in 1973, to 8.5 percent in 1980, to 11.8 percent in

1993 (Maisels & Gormley, 1994). In 1998, almost 14 percent of active duty personnel were women (DMDC, 1998). The individual service branches differ in percentages of active duty women, ranging from 17 percent in the Air Force to 5 percent in the Marine Corps (DMDC, 1998). While the overall number of active duty personnel has been decreasing, the overall percentage of active duty women in the armed forces is still growing. Furthermore, the increasing numbers of military "jobs" open to women ensure an even larger active duty percentage. For example, almost all Air Force jobs are now open to women, and the Navy has opened most shipboard assignments to women.

Currently, 47 percent of active duty women are married (DMDC, 1998). A little more than half of these (54 percent) are in dual-military marriages. This means that the other 46 percent are married to civilians. Anecdotal evidence indicates that civilian husbands tend to be socially isolated, and as military spouses the military community often overlooks them. Alt and Stone (1990) suggest that the social role of a man who "stays home" or who "follows a woman" is suspect, especially in the military, which continues to emphasize traditional masculinity to such a large degree. On some installations, traditional "wives" clubs have started to welcome civilian husbands, renaming their organizations "spouse clubs." A recent study, which interviewed civilian husbands of service members, indicated that this trend is far from universal. Most would agree that the military has a long way to go before these spouses are fully integrated into the military community (Stander, McClure, Gilroy, Chmoko, & Long, 1998).

*Dual-Career Families.* With the increase in the number of women in the military, there has been an increase in the number of dual-career military marriages. This is partly explained by the fact that the work place is a primary locale for meeting potential marriage partners (Segal & Segal, 1999). In 1992, almost 8 percent of military members were in such marriages (DMDC, 1994; Military Family Clearinghouse, 1995 [using 1992 DMDC data]). Whether in uniform herself or employed in the civilian sector, the traditional military wife who devotes herself full time to homemaking and support of her husband's career as hostess and volunteer worker is less and less common. Like their civilian counterparts, military spouses are increasingly seeking employment outside the home as a source of additional income and personal satisfaction.

Military leaders recognize that the military must consider the needs of the working spouse in order to retain career personnel. Two areas of particular concern are childcare and spouse employment opportunities. Military members are routinely transferred to new locations every two to three years. This makes it very difficult for any spouse to develop or maintain a career. Often their status as a military spouse makes it difficult for them to find even reasonable employment. Segal and Harris (1993) note that underemployment is a significant problem for civilian spouses of military members. The Task Force on Quality of Life in the Military (Defense Science Board, 1995) recommended that improving services to help spouses find employment should be a high priority for the Department of Defense.

Even though the military has outperformed many civilian employers in providing affordable, quality childcare, the costs are still prohibitive for many military families, and the demand for childcare in military communities far exceeds the current supply. In addition, there is also a need for longer and more flexible hours to accommodate the needs of dual-military and single parents (Stander et al., 1998).

*Changes in Family Structure.* In many ways the military community experiences the same trends occurring in the larger society. Not only are traditional roles within the family changing, but other civilian trends such as increasing divorce rates are evident among military families as well. It is difficult to obtain accurate statistics on divorce in the military, partly because many couples with troubled marriages leave the service before they divorce. This makes it particularly hard to compare military and civilian divorce rates. Nevertheless, it appears that divorce among military couples has increased, as it has in the civilian population. One subjective indicator of this is that divorce has become more "acceptable" in the military. For example, divorce is no longer perceived as a stigma that may ruin an officer's career. Another indicator of the increase in divorce is the number of active duty members who are single parents—99,000 active duty military members or 7 percent of military personnel in all the services. Table 1.3 provides percentages of active duty members by rank and branch of service who are single parents. A high percentage of military personnel who divorce also remarry. While there are no current data, earlier research indicates that when children are involved, stress in these blended families is high, as is the likelihood that the second marriage will fail (White & Booth, 1985).

Table 1.3
**Percentage of Active Duty Members Who Are Single Parents (Total: 99,000 Single Parents)**

| Service Branch | Entry Level E1-E4 | Mid-Grade Level E5-E6 | Senior-Grade Level E7-E9 | Junior Officers O1-O3 | Senior Officers O4-O6 | Service Total |
|---|---|---|---|---|---|---|
| Army | 11 | 11 | 9 | 6 | 7 | 10 |
| Navy | 5 | 8 | 7 | 3 | 3 | 6 |
| Air Force | 4 | 8 | 7 | 4 | 3 | 6 |
| Marine Corps | 3 | 6 | 8 | 3 | 3 | 4 |
| Total | 7 | 9 | 8 | 4 | 3 | 7 |

Source: Data from the Defense Manpower Data Center, 1997.

Many believe that military life puts a great deal of stress on marriage, and therefore military couples may be at especially high risk for divorce. The separations and reunions that accompany major deployments are thought to be major sources of marital strain. However, evidence to support a strong association between deployment and divorce is lacking. Researchers have found that fluctuations in divorce rates in the military may have more to do with the availability of legal resources than with deployment status (Durand, 1992; Teitelbaum, 1992). As Bell and Schumm (1999, p. 7) explain, "some courts do not allow a military couple to finalize a divorce if one or both partners are overseas; the overseas partners might not receive a fair hearing unless they were present to voice their side of the story." The evidence to date indicates that most military couples do cope with stresses of separation and reunion and that those who are not able to sustain their marital relationships have marriages that were typically at risk before the deployment (Bell & Schumm, 1998). A self-selection process is likely as well. That is, couples who cannot cope with the stresses of military life may leave the service. It is difficult, if not impossible, to actually track these families, making any statement on percentages very questionable and potentially misleading.

Longer life expectancy in our society has had an impact on family structure. Today, more and more adult children are caring for their elderly parents, often while they are still raising their own children. The military is becoming more sensitive to the fact that increasing numbers of personnel have such eldercare responsibilities. Many of these military members are senior in rank. Senior military women, especially those who are single, often find this an especially challenging issue. The Department of Defense and the individual services have initiated and implemented a few programs designed to assist families caring for older relatives. At present, however, the bulk of programs and services in the military are directed toward the needs of families at earlier stages of the life cycle (Parker, Martin, & Hendrickson, 1996).

### Their Duties and Career

Since the inception of the All-Volunteer Force concept in 1973, a continuous debate over the nature of military service (and lifestyle) as either a "calling" or an "occupation" has existed (Moskos, 1988). While this contrast may be an oversimplification, most would agree that the adoption of the All-Volunteer Force concept has been associated with an occupational model of military service. Recent calls for changes in military compensation (Stroup, 1999) that will reward performance, as well as the traditional compensation based on rank and length of service, represent this continued trend toward an occupational (or employment) model of military service. This model has both direct and indirect effects on the military family and their well-being. This includes potential changes in family member expectations about the demands of duty and service life and corresponding perceptions regarding fairness of current pay and benefits as compensation for meeting these demands.

There is a perception among some military leaders that the move toward an occupational philosophy of military service has resulted in many entering service members not developing a sufficient identification with the military during their initial term of service.  It is common to hear leaders describe these first-term service members as retaining a view more akin to a wage-based employee—"when it gets too demanding, I will just leave and find something else to do."  Many first-term service members do just that.  Other leaders attribute first-term personnel losses to the "Glick effect" (Newman & Newman, 1999), what might be called a lack of persistence in today's youth.  Whatever the cause, rates of enlisted personnel who leave military service before completing their first term (three to four years) have remained in the 30 percent range for all branches of service across the entire 25-year period of the All Volunteer Force (General Accounting Office, 1997).  Today, these attrition rates are as high as they have ever been, suggesting that for many junior enlisted service members, the balance of demand versus benefit from service life just is not worth the effort—especially over the long haul.  Among those who are married, young military wives often share the same perception that the sacrifices associated with a military lifestyle are too great, especially the long and demanding duty days and all too frequent and sometimes lengthy family separations.

There is no doubt in the minds of most military leaders that the conditions of military service, especially time spent away from home on training exercises and actual deployments, and the unpredictable garrison duty hours, are prime factors in the decision to leave military service.  For many young men and women, a very strong civilian economy provides an attractive alternative—even for those who must suffer the consequences of "quitting" before they have completed their voluntary military contract.  Many military leaders experience these same pressures on their family life.  In recent years, some of the best and brightest leaders have chosen to end their military careers prematurely in order to better meet their family needs and desires.

### Entitlements: Pay, Allowances, and Other Benefits of Service

Military pay has always been low, particularly for those in the most junior enlisted ranks.  Even with the adoption of the All-Volunteer Force concept, pay has remained low by comparison with civilian standards (Maze, 1999).  Military members, especially those in the middle to senior enlisted grades, have viewed themselves as not very well compensated, and junior enlisted families are often considered "low-income" households (Twiss & Martin, 1998).  On January 1, 1999, military members received an across-the-board 3.6 percent pay increase. While this increase was large enough to match the growth in private-sector salaries and more than twice the current rate of inflation (Maze, 1999), this pay raise needs to be considered in the context of the estimated (1998) 13.5 percent gap between private sector income and military pay and benefits.  While there is an indication that the president and Congress will add at least another 4 percent in 2000, with even slightly higher percentages for middle to senior enlisted members and some officers (Maze, 1999), those at the bottom of the rank structure remain in what can be considered low-income jobs. In these circumstances, and combined with typically poor money management skills, many junior enlisted members with families will continue to face an economic struggle.

In the past, the military services have tried to offset low pay with various nonmonetary benefits—housing, medical care, commissary, and exchange (shopping) privileges on base. Today, military members perceive many of the nonmonetary benefits associated with military service as inadequate, noncompetitive with civilian sector benefits, and rapidly eroding. Medical care, housing benefits, and various community services are perceived by many to be less today than they were just a generation ago (Maze, 1999). The Joint Chiefs of Staff have described these concerns, along with low military pay and deteriorating retirement benefits, as major threats to military recruitment and retention. There have been efforts to respond to these challenges. For example, two recent Secretaries of Defense (Secretaries Perry and Cohen) have focused public attention on quality of life initiatives and they have emphasized the connection between family well-being and overall military readiness.

Despite an apparent awareness of the importance of family factors to military readiness, there are other powerful political and economic forces at play today. With a national policy still willing to commit military forces to a broad array of crises around the globe, and a defense budget that must fund a major new investment in 21st century weapons systems, something has to give. In this case the likely losers are programs in the various personnel categories of the defense budget, including what we have come to define as basic quality-of-life programs.

The Department of Defense has been a leader in the national movement toward privatization of what are considered inherently nongovernmental functions (Hassket, 1997). Many of these initiatives are related to the Clinton-Gore administration's National Performance Review Act and the associated initiatives for "reinventing government" (GAO, 1998). The over-arching objectives are to reduce the size of government and to enhance performance in the services government provides to its citizens. In some cases, the purchase and/or contracting out of functions, including a broad range of human services, seems to have resulted in cost savings, as well as some improvement in the range and quality of the services delivered (Hassket, 1997). Unfortunately, most recognize that the initial cost savings associated with privatization are typically a result of the competition inherent in the selection process (Hassket, 1997). It is still not clear that these cost savings can be maintained across time and with subsequent competition without a diminishment of services or overall service quality. For the military, there is another lingering and obviously more pressing issue: Will this reliance on the private sector for these quality-of-life services negatively affect the psychosocial "connection" between members and their families, and the military as an institution? Many believe that the military's direct and observable role in providing human services does make a difference in developing and sustaining a sense of connection and corresponding commitment to the military institution (Bowen, 1998). Clearly the last chapter has not been written on the issue of privatization, especially in the context of the provision of human services to military members and their families.  Unfortunately, as current human services infrastructure is given up or lost in Department of Defense privatization initiatives, it may be impossible to revert back to previous human service delivery arrangements, even if it proves to be an important morale, cohesion, and *esprit de corps* factor.

While the All-Volunteer Force concept provided a very successful military force for the Persian Gulf War battlefields, it remains to be seen if an All-Volunteer Force can be sustained in the 21st century.  It is not just the issues of the size of the active duty military force required to meet U.S. defense needs (including its commitments around the globe) or providing adequate pay and allowances for this force that will determine the fate of the All-Volunteer Force concept.  Leaders must also examine DOD's ability to support and to sustain military families in a world where the demands of military service and the corresponding sacrifices required by members and their families are likely to increase, not decrease.  While recruitment may be driven by opportunity factors — including training and initial compensation—retention will be most heavily impacted by overall quality of life—especially one's family life.  Quality of life in this context means more than just benefits and services.  Compensation cannot overcome all dissatisfaction with military quality-of-life considerations, in particular the amount and frequency of family separations.  Unless we have a force of sufficient size (or a corresponding reduction in our overseas commitments) to provide for a deployment schedule that allows for a reasonable family life, poor morale and retention will be nagging problems for all service branches.

### Their Community

The descriptions of the many hardships associated with family status represent the historically "negative" aspects of military family life—the "sacrifice" part of the phrase "a life of service and sacrifice."  For some, specifically the wives of officers and more senior noncommissioned officers, military family life is sometimes exciting and often enjoyable.  In modern times, many senior military families have lived in exceptionally attractive and comfortable government housing on military installations around the globe.  Often, these military communities contained "within their gates" many of the facilities and services found in a typical (if not idealized) small American town (Martin & Orthner, 1989), and these communities and this lifestyle represented the military's version of "welfare capitalism" (Twiss & Martin, 1998).  Even for families living outside the gates (overall only about 30 percent of military families actually live on base), worldwide U.S. military installations have provided a "hometown" with basic services available to all regardless of rank.

In recent years, a small amount of on-base housing has been made available to the most junior enlisted families, those not previously eligible for housing (Twiss & Martin, 1997).  Unfortunately, the quality of this housing has not been universally good (Defense Science Board on the Quality of Life, 1995), and at some installations government housing, especially for the most junior-grade military families, has come to represent the worst aspects of America's experience with public housing (Twiss & Martin, 1998). Since much of this military family housing stock was built almost 50 years ago, the prohibitive life-cycle costs associated with major renovation and safety upgrades will likely result in more units demolished that new units built.

Approximately 70 percent of military families now live in civilian communities and receive some form of military housing allowance (Defense Science Board, 1995; Twiss, 1999). In urban areas, military families typically compete with local civilians for scarce, often expensive, and sometimes marginally adequate or safe rental properties. In these locations, junior enlisted families are especially disadvantaged. In more rural areas of the country, housing costs may be noticeably lower, but adequate housing often entails a substantial commute to and from the military installation. The prohibitive economics of owning more than one vehicle and the lack of reliable public transportation in these rural communities creates an isolating effect for the lowest in rank, typically the youngest military families with the fewest resources. In many of these rural locations, junior enlisted personnel compete with other low-income families for housing in trailer park communities.

Securing safe, adequate, and affordable housing is one of the most pressing military family issues (Twiss & Martin, 1997). It represents an important goal and, at the same time, a major frustration for the Department of Defense. The problem of providing adequate housing for the entire force (married and single members) has become more acute during the 1990s, even with substantial reductions in the size of the U.S. military during this time frame. Optimistically, defense officials say that it will take more than a decade to overcome these problems, if at all (Cox, 1999).

Whatever the hardships of life on or off the installation, there is a tradition (and an expectation among many) that the military provides support for its members and their families—"we take care of our own." While formal installation services and programs are important and appreciated, it is the informal community that actually seems to matter the most in sustaining this cultural tradition. Research indicates that military families, like their civilian counterparts, are more likely to look for assistance from their informal networks of support—their friends and relatives (Bell, 1993; Bell, Schumm, Segal, & Rice, 1996). Neighbors bringing baked goods to a family moving in next door, friends looking out for each other's children, and spouses comforting and supporting each other while their military partners are away are just some examples of the informal exchanges that are thought to contribute to a sense of community among military families. An earlier study of people retiring from the military noted that what many respondents said they would miss most about being in the military is being part of the military community and the corresponding sense of belonging that they experienced while they were in the service (McClure, 1992). While this may be true for those looking back after a career of military service, there is little evidence that this sense of community is prevalent among the majority of current active duty families. In fact, there is concern that this sense of connection may be eroding, if not missing altogether, in the lives of many military families (Bowen, Martin, Mancini, & Nelson, 1999).

There is reason to believe that some of the demographic trends and organizational changes discussed so far in this chapter create real challenges for military communities as the Department of Defense heads into the next decade. Especially relevant are: the continued expansion of privatization initiatives across all aspects of military life; the housing crisis and increasing dispersion of military families throughout surrounding civilian communities—sometimes into socioeconomic and racially segregated areas; base closures and corresponding consolidation of installations into megabases with increasingly diverse populations and multiservice presence; and the tendency of policy makers to pay attention to physical facilities and formal services without considering other aspects of installation life that often contribute to strengthening informal ties among members and their families. Clearly, a better understanding of quality-of-life factors and their influence on readiness and retention is necessary. Leaders also need to give more consideration to the concept of "community" and what this concept means for the future military.

While some changes are inevitable, military leaders need to take a closer look at the implementation and the possible second-and third-order effects that may result from various quality-of-life policy changes. Even if these changes are inevitable, how they get implemented and the identification of possible moderating factors are critical tasks for the Department of Defense, each service, and even local installation-level leadership. The concept of "military community" must be revisited and updated for a twenty-first century military.

## SOME ENDURING ISSUES AND THEIR CONSEQUENCES FOR FAMILIES

### "Duty First"

The concept of "duty" often gets restated or interpreted by many members of the military as meaning "duty first." Members are socialized in the philosophy of "service before self," and there is a common expectation that military service requires personal sacrifice, which includes family sacrifice. The conditions of military life, including the demands associated with military training, extremely long and often unpredictable duty days, the realities of operational deployments and even combat, have historically been perceived as requiring a total commitment to the military—typically a commitment to one's unit, the unit's mission, and its members. This is the very essence of the concept of military unit cohesion (Manning, 1991).

As Segal (1986) pointed out, both the military and the family are "greedy institutions" often requiring enormous amounts of time and energy from its members. Today, more than ever, men and women in uniform view family life as a competing priority. While personal and family sacrifices for the sake of duty are understandable under certain conditions, many military members and their spouses question what constitutes the necessity for such sacrifice. Fairness and a sense of equity in sharing unpleasant duties or difficult assignments have always been important in the military. Today, long duty hours and frequent deployments have some members and their families believing that they are not being treated fairly or that too much is expected from them. Some view the entire system as overloaded. In the wake of both downsizing and a proliferation of peacekeeping and peacemaking missions in the 1990s, even senior leaders have openly questioned whether the armed forces are being asked to do too much. "We are stretched too thin" is a common phrase used across the ranks from private to commanding general.

### "An Unlimited Commitment"

The concept of "an unlimited commitment," referring to the possibility that military members could conceivably be asked to sacrifice their lives for their country, is deeply rooted in military tradition. Most members and their spouses accept this philosophy as a condition of service. What they object to is extending this philosophy to include policies and especially unit leadership practices that seem to devalue the importance of personal and family time. Members complain about training that seems unnecessary or, in the worst cases, is not efficiently managed. For example, a unit may be deployed overseas for an exercise, only to have to wait an extra week for the shipment of required equipment, or a member arrives at a training school only to find out that for "administrative reasons" classes will not begin for another week. At every level of the military, from the smallest work group all the way to the halls of the Pentagon, military members and their spouses are looking (and hoping) for leaders, and corresponding leadership policies and practices, that respect the value of "their" time, especially family time. Good military leaders know that the duty demands they make on their subordinates need to be reasonable, equitably shared, and whenever possible, predictable. When they are not, military members and their spouses begin to contrast their lives in the military with what they see in the civilian community—life as it is experienced by relatives, friends, and neighbors, as well as family life portrayed in the popular media. When military members perceive that they possess marketable skills in an economy actively recruiting qualified workers, these options become very compelling. When they begin to compare the various economic advantages in many civilian professional fields they often become even more uncertain about their decision to remain in uniform. This is also true for the military spouse who is staying at home typically shouldering the enormous burden and responsibilities for maintaining a stable and satisfying family life while the military member is away.

### Balancing Duty and Family Life Demands

Morale and retention considerations require that military leaders be good stewards of members' time and supportive of the needs and desires associated with family life.  Military members and their spouses also share responsibility for balancing duty demands and family life.  As noted earlier, a condition of voluntary service is the acceptance of "service before self" as a guiding philosophy.  This means that there will be times when duty requirements must take priority over personal and family needs and desires and that members may be required to deploy.  They may miss important family events.  In exceptional times, such as war or other important military operations, they may not be available even for a family crisis.  This has been true for soldiers, sailors, Marines, and airmen throughout military history and it will continue to be a reality of future military service.

What this *does not* mean however; is that military members and their families are helpless.  Finding balance in military family life requires learning to use available time wisely.  For example, do I really need to hang around the unit at the end of the duty day to "shoot the bull" or play pool in the dayroom with buddies?  Is a trip to the bowling alley for a beer with the other unit members after work really necessary *today*?  As a leader, do I need to go into the unit to check things on Saturday and Sunday—*every weekend*?  Am I really so important to the unit that I cannot take leave and enjoy some time off (vacation days with my family)?  Is this, from the perspective of my wife's or my children's needs, the right time to volunteer for a desired assignment or military school?  Could this school or training experience be put off until a later date?  At some point in time, the question may even be, "From a family perspective, is reenlistment (or, for the career service member, is retirement) the right choice now?"

Family members share in this responsibility for managing time wisely and openly addressing important career decisions.  They need to participate in some of the hard choices required to balance military service life and family life.  The point is, there are always choices.  Across each stage of the military life course, there are things that the member and member's spouse can do to better manage the conflict between duty and career demands.  There are steps that family members can take to enhance their own and the family unit's resiliency in the face of military life demands.  Developing effective time management skills is an important example and setting priorities is an example of necessary skills that must be learned to successfully meet the challenges of military life.  Building and sustaining a personal and family network of peers, other friends, and family is another critical skill.  A key to success is involvement in both formal and informal unit-based and community-based (either military or local civilian) activities that provide an opportunity to develop supportive personal and family relationships.  These opportunities range from joining a neighborhood playgroup for young children to participating in a local church social activity.  Becoming a member of a unit-family support group is always an important step.  For some spouses support networks include peers at work.  While participation may take many different forms, becoming imbedded in a reciprocal manner in a diverse and dense array of supportive relationships is critical for successful survival as a military family member.  In the context of a military career, these reciprocal relationships help military family members develop the resources and critical skills that allow them to continue healthy personal and family life when the military member is away—either on a temporary deployment or an unaccompanied overseas tour of duty.  These resources and skills include the development and maintenance of interpersonal relationships, as well as very practical things such as money management or getting car or home repairs accomplished—skills in living that promote family functioning and contribute to personal self-esteem.

## EFFORTS TO ENHANCE MILITARY FAMILY QUALITY OF LIFE

Albano (1994, p. 283) points out that the military's relationship with its families can be characterized by "a shift from neglect to concern, from informal mechanisms and implied obligations to a formal, institutionalized policy response; and from locally determined, piecemeal, ad hoc, reactive measures to federally funded, comprehensive, planned services."  Based on her well-referenced overview of this history of military recognition of family concerns, Albano believes that these trends will continue in the future (Albano, 1994, pp. 293-298).  While there are many current examples of these trends, specifically the Air Force's development of an integrated services delivery model for family advocacy programs, the development of New Family Support Programs, and a reemergence of interest in voluntary aspects of community support (Bowen et al., 1999), there are other trends to consider.  For example, the privatization of military family programs and the associated costsavings are now used as examples of the way DOD needs to do business in the future (Hembre, 1998).  Whether one subscribes to this view or not, the reality of federal downsizing includes the Department of Defense and military quality-of-life programs and services.  As noted earlier, and restated here for emphasis, many of these initiatives have taken place and continue to happen in the absence of data on possible second- and third-order effects of these changes on the sense of institutional identity with the military that is thought to be important for member well-being and military operational success (Manning, 1991).

### Leadership and Organizational Attitudes and Actions

Most military leaders are sensitive to the needs of families.  Most recognize that aspects of family life have a tremendous impact on the morale and well-being of military members.  Leaders, even at the small unit level, recognize that family readiness is related to overall unit readiness.  Military education for leaders, officer and noncommissioned officers alike, across all command levels, now incorporates information and promotes discussion of how family issues affect recruitment, retention, and readiness.  Within the context of downsizing and privatization initiatives, each of the military services still supports an array of human service programs aimed at enhancing family well-being and promoting family resiliency.  Military communities still offer a variety of services designed to prepare, support, sustain, and restore family functioning associated with both normal aspects of family life, and the unique and often stressful experiences associated with military duties and career demands. Today, these formal activities are being complimented by new efforts to promote a sense of informal "community" among military members (Bowen et al., 1999). A search of the subject "military family" on any Internet World Wide Web search engine will document the extent of these formal and informal efforts. There are now numerous DOD, service-specific, and even installation- and unit-specific web pages that contain valuable family information. In addition, there is a rapidly growing number of informal military family support web pages as well as military women and military spouse pages that contain family-related information and opportunities for "cyberspace" connections to other military family members. There are even web pages for military teens and "former military brats." In many ways, these pages on the Internet represent the military community of the future—a community of relationships not bound by geographic limits—a military community without fences and gates.

### Today's Social Contract between the Military and Its Members and Their Families

Simply stated, the military services are trying to recruit and retain "a few good men" and women. In the case of retention, this often means retaining families. The military services offer members considerable opportunity for both personal development and technical training. Leaders recognize the importance of quality of life, including family life. At the same time, leaders recognize that many of the demands of military service (and military family life) are as real today as they have been throughout military history. As discussed earlier, military service still requires this concept of "service before self" and willingness, if called, to make enormous personal and family sacrifice. For a few, this sacrifice can be life itself. In response to this willingness to subject oneself voluntarily to this heightened degree of social control, and a willingness to give of oneself in service and sacrifice, military members and their families expect that they will be able to live a decent lifestyle, one at least comparable to their civilian contemporaries. They expect, should the service member be injured or killed as part of military service, that the member's family will be cared for by what we refer to in military memorial services as a "grateful nation." This is the essence of the social contract that exists between the government and military members, including military family members. It is a sacred contract. It is in the context of this relationship that policy makers and military leaders need to consider the requirements for broadly defined quality of life for military members and their families. Changes to quality of services such as military housing, medical care, or retirement benefits for military members all speak to this sacred contract. Every effort must be made to guard against actions that diminish this relationship.

## SUMMARY AND IMPLICATIONS

This chapter offers the civilian human service provider a framework for understanding the enduring realities of military life for service members and their families.  It highlights the demanding nature of military duties in the context of stressful events such as operational deployments, including combat, as well as the stress associated with day-to-day life in the military across the life course of a military career.  The evolving conditions and benefits of military service, including recognition and benefits associated with rank and career status, have been discussed.

While initially only families of career officers received recognition, families have always been present in military society, and these families have always shared in the hardships of military life.  In modern times, and especially since the adoption of the All-Volunteer Force concept in 1973, there has been a dramatic institutional recognition of the military family, including first-term, junior enlisted families.  This has not occurred without some debate.  There are some thoughtful leaders who are concerned that current military family policies, especially family benefits, encourage early marriages and promote premature family development.  There are some who retain the earlier view that benefits, like those associated with family status, should be entitlements earned by time in service and a demonstrated career commitment.

This chapter has illustrated the continuing tensions that exist between the demands of duty and the demands of family life.  This is an enduring tension associated with military service.  It is important that human service providers understand that this is a tension that most commanders and other subordinate leaders know well, many from their own personal life experience.  Most commanders and subordinate leaders consciously try to provide and protect family time for their unit members.  They do this while recognizing that unit demands do come first and that members and their families make many personal and family sacrifices in the name of their commitment to duty and service.  The chapter highlights that there are things that individuals and families can do to manage personal and family time more effectively.  Understanding this message and developing the requisite attitudes and habits are among the most important yet difficult life adjustments new military families have to make in their adaptation to military life and a military career.

Civilian human service providers will play an increasingly important role in the future delivery of broadly defined health and social services to military members and their families.  Contracted civilian employees, contracted services, other forms of privatization, fee-for-service arrangements, and even military-civilian community partnerships in the delivery of services will continue to evolve.  The military's tradition, one that has never been fully successful, of "caring for our own," has and will continue to move from a form of institutional social welfare capitalism as seen in the concept of the "company town" to a model where individual employees choose from among an offering of employee benefits packages designed to meet an array of personal needs, desires, and family types.  In most cases these services will come from the local community and from professionals who typically will not have personal experience in the military. Service providers may have very little professional preparation for serving military populations. The authors in this book have sought to help fill this knowledge gap. We hope that this book will provide a core knowledge base to enhance the delivery of human services to this truly unique group of American families. We also hope that this book will encourage human service providers to recognize and value the important contribution they can make to the well being of military families and the our nation's security.

## REFERENCES

Albano, S. (1994). Military recognition of family concerns: Revolutionary War to 1993. *Armed Forces and Society, 20*(2), 283–302.

Alt, B., & Stone, B. (1990). *Uncle Sam's brides: The world of military wives.* New York:Walker.

Bell, D. B. (1993, August). Army support for families during Operation Restore Hope at Fort Drum, New York. Paper presented at the Army Community Service Directors' Training, Alexandria Bay, New York.

Bell, D. B., & Schumm, W. R. (1998, May 7). Supporting the families of Army peacekeepers: What we learned from two recent deployments. Paper presented at the Fourth Annual Joint Service Family Readiness Matters Workshop, Portland, OR.

Bell, D. B., & Schumm, W. R. (1999). Family adaptation to deployment. In P. McClure (Ed.), *Pathways to the future: A review of military family research* (pp. 109–133). Scranton, PA: Military Family Institute of Marywood University.

Bell, D. B., Schumm, W. R., Segal, M. W., & Rice, R. E. (1996). The family support system for the MFO. In R. H. Phelps & B. J. Farr (Eds.), *Reserve component soldiers as peacekeepers* (pp. 306–408). Alexandria, VA: U.S. Army Research Institute for the Behavioral and Social Sciences.

Bourg, M. C. (1995). Male tokens in a masculine environment: Men with military mates. Paper presented at the American Sociological Association, Washington, DC.

Bowen, G. L. (1998). Effects of leader support in the work unit on the relationship between work spillover and family adaptation. *Journal of Family and Economic Issues, 19,* 25–52.

Bowen, G. L., Martin, J. A., Mancini, J. A., & Nelson, J. P. (1999). *Community capacity in the United States Air Force.* Fairfax, VA: Caliber Associates.

Burke, S. C., & Moskos, C. C. (1996). Family readiness: Applying what we know and highlighting what we need to know. *Military Family Issues: The Research Digest, 1*(1), 1–4.

Cox, M. (1999, February 15). Private fix for housing woes. *Army Times,* p. 10.

Defense Manpower Data Center (DMDC). (1994). *The 1992 surveys of officers and enlisted personnel and their spouses: Overview and executive summaries.* Arlington, VA: DMDC.

Defense Manpower Data Center (DMDC). (1997). *The 1996 surveys of officers and enlisted personnel and their spouses: Overview and executive summaries.* Arlington, VA: DMDC.

Defense Science Board on the Quality of Life. (1995). *Report of the task force on quality of life.* Washington, DC: Office of the Secretary of Defense, The Pentagon.

Department of the Army. (1997). *Army demographics: Demographic profile as of 7 Feb 97*, Working Draft. Washington, DC: Office of the Deputy Chief of Staff for Personnel.

Dougherty, L. (1999). Transition into the military: Issues for the junior enlisted and junior officer members and their families. In P. McClure (Ed.), *Pathways to the future: A review of military family research* (pp. 67–86). Scranton, PA: Military Family Institute of Marywood University.

Durand, D. B. (1992, August). The redistribution of responsibilities and power in Army families following Operation Desert Shield/Storm reunions. Paper presented at the Section on Sociology of Peace and War at the 87th annual meeting of the American Sociological Association, Pittsburgh, PA.

Dyhouse, T. (1998a). Newest generation of war vets emerge from Persian Gulf. *VFW Magazine, 85*(6), 20–27.

Dyhouse, T. (1998b). Fighting terrorism American style. *VFW Magazine, 85*(4), 20–25.

Gansler, J. S. (1998, September-October). The revolution in business affairs—The need to act now. *Program Manager*, pp. 30–33.

General Accounting Office (GAO/NSIAD-97–39) (1997). *Military attrition: DOD could save millions by better screening enlisted personnel*. Washington, DC: GAO.

General Accounting Office (GAO/AIMD-98-159). (1998). *The Results Act*. Washington, DC: GAO.

Hassket, G. (1997). Privatization: Let the buyer be aware. *Military Family Digest, 2*(1), 1–5.

Hembre, J. (1998, January-February). NCMA Hosts Deputy Secretary John Hembre at east coast educational conference. *Program Manager, 27*(1), 44.

Janowitz, M., & Moskos, C. C. (1979). Five years of the All-Volunteer Force. *Armed Forces and Society, 5*, 171–218.

Kerner-Hoeg, S., Baker, S., Lomvardias, C., & Towne, L. (1993). *Operation Restore Hope. Survey of Army spouses at Fort Drum, New York: Survey methodology and data book*. Fairfax, VA: Caliber Associates, Inc.

Manning, F. J. (1991). Morale, cohesion, and esprit de corps. In R. Gal & A. D. Mangelsdorff (Eds.), *Handbook of military psychology* (pp. 531–558). London: John Wiley & Sons, Ltd.

Martin, J. A., & Orthner, D. K. (1989). The "company town" in transition: Rebuilding military communities. In G. L. Bowen & D. K. Orthner (Eds.), *The organization family: Work and family linkages in the U.S. military* (pp. 163–177). New York: Praeger.

Maze, R. (1999, January 18). Upping the ante on 2000 pay increase. *Army Times*, p. 3.

McClure, H. M. (1992). *Alienated patriots: A sociological portrait of military retirees*. Unpublished doctoral dissertation, University of California, Berkeley.

Military Family Clearinghouse. (1995). *Military family demographics: Profile of the military family*. Arlington, VA: Military Family Resource Center.

Military Family Resource Center. (1998). *Profile of the military community: 1997 demographics*. Arlington, VA: Military Family Resource Center.

Moskos, C. C. (1988). Institutional and occupational trends in armed forces. In C. C. Moskos & F. R. Wood (Eds.), *The military: More than just a job?* (pp. 15–26). Washington, DC: Pergamon-Brassey's.

Newman, B. M., & Newman, P. R. (1999). *Development through life: A psychosocial approach* (7th ed.). Pacific Grove, CA: Brooks/Cole.

Parker, M. W., Martin, S., & Hendrickson, K. (1996). Elder-care: An issue that's "come of age" for military families. *Military Family Issues: The Research Digest, 1*(2), 15–16.

Peterson, M. (1992). *1991 survey of Army families II: Final summary.* Unpublished manuscript U.S. Army Research Institute for the Behavioral and Social Sciences, Alexandria, VA.

Segal, D. R., and Segal, M. W. (1999).   Changes in the American armed forces: Implications for military families. In P. McClure (Ed.), *Pathways to the future: A review of military family research*  (pp. 1–10). Scranton, PA: Military Family Institute of Marywood University.

Segal, M. W. (1986). The military and the family as greedy institutions. *Armed Forces and Society, 13*(1), 9–38.

Segal, M. W., & Harris, J. J. (1993). *What we know about Army families* (Special Report 21). Alexandria, VA: U.S. Army Research Institute for the Behavioral and Social Sciences.

Stander, V., McClure, P., Gilroy, T., Chmoko, J., & Long, J. (1998). *Military marriages in the 1990s.* Scranton, PA: Military Family Institute of Marywood University.

Stone, B. D., & Alt, B. S. (1990). *Uncle Sam's brides: The world of military wives.* New York: Walker.

Stroup, T. G. (1999, February 10). Skewed military pay scales. *The Washington Post,* p. A22.

Teitelbaum, J. M. (1992, April).   ODS and Post-ODS divorce and child behavior problems.  Paper presented at the Office of the Secretary of Defense Family Research In-progress Review, The Pentagon, Washington, DC.

Twiss, P. (1999).   The future of U.S. military housing.   In P. McClure (Ed.), *Military families in the year 2005: A review of military family research* (pp. 35–66). Scranton, PA: Military Family Institute of Marywood University.

Twiss, P. C., & Martin, J. A. (1997). *Quality of life and shelter: A history of military housing policy and initiatives since the adoption of the All-Volunteer Force concept (1973-1996)* (Report One: MFI Technical Report 97-3).   Scranton, PA: Military Family Institute of Marywood University.

Twiss, P. C., & Martin, J. A. (1998). *Quality of life and shelter: A history of military housing policy and initiatives since the adoption of the All-Volunteer Force concept (1973-1996)* (Report Two: MFI Technical Report 98-1).   Scranton, PA: Military Family Institute of Marywood University.

White, L. K., & Booth, A. (1985). The quality and stability of remarriages: The role of stepchildren. *American Sociological Review, 55*(3), 689–698.

# Chapter 2

# The "Citizen-Soldier" and Reserve Component Families

*Josephine G. Pryce, Dorothy Ogilvy-Lee, and David H. Pryce*

## INTRODUCTION

Significant changes have occurred in the organization and missions of our armed forces during the last 25 years. Many of these changes are having a major impact on military families and the human services that support them (Knox & Price, 1995). During this period, the U.S. military has undergone a transition from being an overwhelmingly active-duty force to what is now referred to by the Pentagon as the "total force" (Armed Forces Information Service, 1993). The total force concept relies heavily on reserve components made up of Army and Air National Guard and Army, Navy, Marine Corps, and Air Force Reserve units.

    The Army National Guard is the oldest U.S. military organization, with a history of continuous service dating from 1636, preceding the first national military force by about 150 years (Knox & Price, 1999). The Guard provides trained organizations for war or other national emergencies under its federal mandate. To be ready for domestic emergencies within home state boundaries is a constitutional state role that the Guard has that other reserve components do not. All reserve components are primarily composed of civilians who perform part-time military duty, commonly referred to as "citizen-soldiers." Over 15 million citizen-soldiers are currently serving, comprising over half of the total armed forces. These reservists have over 2.5 million immediate family members (U.S. Department of Defense, 1996; 1997).

    Almost half of the reserve component is 30 years of age and younger, with about 30 percent of the remaining group being 31 to 40 years of age and about 20 percent in the 41 to 50 age range. Around 6 percent of reserve component members are over 50 years of age (Armed Forces Information Service, 1997). As in the active component, service members are either enlisted or officers. With few exceptions, enlisted members are required to have a high school education and officers a college education. Pay is higher for officers than for enlisted personnel and continues to be so throughout the course of a military career.

The citizen-soldier traditionally trains one weekend per month and one continuous two-week period annually—an average of 39 days a year. Such training is designed to prepare augmentation organizations and individual manpower for the active force, for which reservists receive pay and some military benefits. With the transition to the total force, active-component manpower has been dramatically, and some would say drastically, reduced by about 50 percent since the mid-1980s, while the strength of the reserve-component has remained relatively constant (Knox & Price, 1999). Current national policy relies heavily on the reserve components, requiring frequent activation and subsequent deployments of National Guard and reserve organizations and individual service members in support of national policy around the world (Fogleman, 1997a; 1997b; U.S. Navy, 1998; Weaver, 1998). "Everyone is in the pool," said Brig. Gen. Pat O'Neal, a deputy commander of the U.S. Army Forces Command. "They are all eligible to go. That's the change" ("Slimmer Army," 1998). The new reliance on citizen-soldiers is a fundamental policy shift that carries with it profound implications for human service providers.

The total force policy dramatically impacts the traditional occupational role and personal lifestyles of citizen-soldiers and their families. The National Guard and reserve are now eligible to be called up as the need is identified and deployed across the country or anywhere in the world, at any time throughout the year. No longer will active-duty personnel necessarily be first in line to meet mission needs. Indeed, the reserve components have certain organizations that are essential to success but are seldom found in the active-duty force. Combat service support functions such as civil affairs, prisoner-of-war handling, morgue or graves registration, water purification, and laundry and bath are examples of this. National Guard and Reserve units have served throughout the world in recent years, including the Persian Gulf War. More reservists have been called to duty for service in the former Yugoslavia than were in service throughout the Vietnam War ("Slimmer Army," 1998). During 1997, 25 percent of Army soldiers serving in Bosnia were from its reserve components (U.S. Army, 1998). Weaver (1998) remarks that the average part-time Air Guard aircrew member currently performs duty 80 to 120 days away from home annually. Currently, reserve components are undergoing far more calls to active duty and subsequent deployments than at any time since World War II.

International missions ranging from military contingencies and training to humanitarian and civic assistance are another new role for the National Guard. The Army National Guard has undertaken such activities in approximately 70 countries. These activities range from taking needed resources to hospitals and children's centers to building playgrounds and repairing homes. These missions not only provide training for Guard members but also promote the United States' image across the world (U.S. Army, 1997).

In addition to the reserve component's expanding global role, the National Guard has traditional state military responsibilities. The National Guard's state mission requires that soldiers be ready for deployment in response to natural disasters and civil disturbances as state governors may direct, providing personnel, and equipment, and time. They are charged to fulfill these responsibilities even though their own family members may be involved in the disaster or crisis. A recent addition to National Guard responsibilities is to train to respond to weapons of mass destruction such as chemical, biological, and nuclear attacks within the United States. This responsibility involves teams of National Guard members who will train for and deploy to the crisis, make assessments, and advise authorities in security, logistics, reconnaissance, medical support, air support, and communications (Wolfe, 1998).

The combined effect of increased mobilizations and deployments and the unusual number of recent natural disasters have taxed the resources of the reserve component. Increased and extended absences from home and family, potentially dangerous and tedious duty, and disruption in civilian employment are challenging the total force policy and raising questions that remain unanswered. This trend of mobilization and deployment is unlikely to change in the near future. The challenges are stark reality to all reserve component families.

## THE NEW MILITARY FAMILY BRINGS NEW CHALLENGES

The reorganization of the U.S. military has not only reshaped the role of the reserve component but has also effectively redefined the military family. Any contemporary discussion of military family issues must include the families of the National Guard members and reservists' families. The challenges that they face must be understood from their perspectives and experiences.

Citizen-soldier families are being confronted with increasing absences of the service member and lengthening deployments. This is a major change for families whose service members were only a few years ago, absent but one weekend a month and a couple of weeks in the summer. The nature of the separations has changed from purely training exercises to dangerous or hazardous missions in underdeveloped countries.

Reserve-component families are challenged by disruption of the service members' civilian employment and differences in pay between their civilian and military jobs. Just how long employers and families will support such financial and emotional disruptions are legitimate questions as yet unanswered (Ledford, 1998).

American communities are challenged as well by the total force policy. National Guard and reserve organizations are located primarily in civilian communities. Police officers, school teachers, fire fighters, dentists, engineers, sanitation workers, lawyers, accountants, medical providers, state troopers, university professors, mental health professionals, and cooks compose this force. The absence of these individuals from these positions may adversely impact the services normally available within the community. During the Persian Gulf War, some small communities were left without a medical provider while their local doctor served overseas. The prospect of casualties bears particularly ominous portents for community-based reserve component units.  An Army Reserve unit from Pennsylvania lost 22 personnel to one SCUD missile attack during the Persian Gulf War (Knox & Price, 1999).  The loss was devastating not only to individual families but also to the whole community.

## TRADITIONAL MILITARY CULTURE AND THE CITIZEN-SOLDIER FAMILY

Challenges faced by citizen-soldier families are somewhat different than those of the active component.  Understanding the stresses these families experience is important to meeting their human service needs and to providing support for them.

A growing body of literature addresses military families and the way in which military duty affects their lives.  Most of the literature on military family life and issues has focused on the active duty military family, and until recently, little attention has been given to reserve-component families (Griffith, 1989; Knox & Price, 1995; 1999).  This leaves an important gap to fill if these families are to receive education and support that has been shown to mitigate the stressors associated with military life.  Human service providers can contribute to Guard family well-being through their knowledge and support of the National Guard Family Program.  This system has been so successful that the Army has made the National Guard the leading agency in implementing family assistance and support programs for all reserve and active duty Army families who are not located near their own unit or active Army installation.  Understanding this model program will greatly assist human service providers in meeting the needs of citizen-soldiers of all armed forces branches.

### Military Cultural and Organizational Paradigm Shifts

A brief review of traditional military culture and its relationship to the military family is necessary to understand the limited resources that the military offers for family support.  It also contributes to understanding why family independence and self-sufficiency is emphasized in the context of promoting reciprocal support among military families.

Prior to World War II, the U.S. military was predominantly male and single.  Traditions and rituals dominated the military culture and wives and children were uncommon.  During the Cold War, the military transformed itself from a professional "brotherhood of arms" to an occupational or career model, and the number of military families grew (Bowen, 1982).  High-level military policy makers were typically unaware of the need for formal family support.  First- and second-line military leaders were also unaware of these needs.  Consequently, little formal family support existed during this period.  On military installations, active-duty family members were gradually provided support in the form of subsidized housing, medical care, entertainment, recreation, and tax-free shopping within the exchange and commissary systems.  These benefits and services were provided to reservists only in the unlikely and uncommon circumstance that they were officially called to active duty.

In 1973 the military became an "All-Volunteer Force." The "total force" policy (comprised of active duty members, reserve component members, and government civilian employees) emerged as military leaders, stung by disappointment in Vietnam, made sure that the U.S. military would never again be used in foreign armed conflict without the activation of significant numbers of reserve military forces. The total force policy was to ensure commitment of the American citizenry to support of its military in any extended commitment, such as the conflict in Bosnia, as military members would come from both the active and reserve components (Knox & Price, 1999). Gen. Dennis J. Reimer, while serving as the Chief of Staff of the Army, described the total force as not about supplements or replacement by the Guard but rather a "seamless" force created by combining elements of the reserves and active Army (U.S. Army, 1998). An example is the deployment of 147 personnel from the Virginia Army National Guard's 3d Battalion, 116th Infantry Regiment (Light) to Bosnia. In addition to traditional infantry combat patrol duty, these citizen-soldiers responded to local crises by using their civilian skills, they repaired a computer system, engineers and carpenters redesigned bridge positions, and X-ray technicians responded to medical emergencies (Calvert, 1998).

The total force policy and the shift to a military force based on an occupational model of military service required increased attention to military family issues. In the absence of a draft, recruitment and retention had to be more family-focused, as research demonstrated family influence on both (Orthner et al., 1987; Vernez & Zellman, 1987; Burnam et al., 1992). If military strength was to be maintained, family matters had to be taken into consideration. In the ensuing years, family attitudes toward military service, especially spouse attitudes, were identified as influencing whether or not a service member stayed in the military for any length of time.

In 1983, the U.S. Army circulated *The White Paper* (U.S. Army, 1983) that proclaimed a change in its regard for families. In essence, it said that Army families were important to readiness and retention, and that they would be provided support. The goal of this support was to mitigate the stress of military life. In the next few years all the armed forces branches significantly increased policies and plans implementing structured military family support centers and formal programs that are in place today on military installations.

In 1986, a similar document, the National Guard Family Program, was published (U.S. Army & U.S. Air Force, 1986). It echoed the 1983 document by reaffirming that military families were important to citizen-soldier readiness and retention. The National Guard policy statement was visionary in that it called for a partnership to be developed between the National Guard and its family members to lessen the distress of military life (Ogilvy-Lee, 1997a). That partnership has led to a different focus and provision of human services and support for Guard family members, as well as for all citizen-soldier families.

The military family member knows that the mission is the focus of military life. Families are expected to make necessary sacrifices and to understand that the military mission must come first.  This demand requires adaptation and self-sufficiency on the part of military families.  This has traditionally been called having the "right stuff" (Wolfe, 1979).  With the implementation of the total force and resulting increases in deployments, expectations of reserve component families have become the same as those of the active-component family.  They are expected to adapt, adjust, and be equally committed to the mission, without the support systems provided on active-duty bases and installations.

### Military Family Literature

Literature on military families and lifestyle largely focuses on issues affecting readiness and retention of service members and adaptation of family members to the demands and stress of military life.  Specific stressors have been identified that affect both active and reserve component families.  These include frequent mobilization and deployments, frequent family separations due to absences of the military member, and life-threatening hostile environments; add to these the ongoing conflict between meeting personal and family needs and low military pay (Martin & Ickovics, 1987; Teitelbaum, 1991).

Military family members typically identify separations, deployments, and reunions as the most stressful of issues affecting their lives (Vernez & Zellman, 1987).  Separation places a great strain on family development and marital relations, as the spouse remaining in the home becomes solely responsible for family integrity and adaptation.  The strain on children is also a concern.  These issues have been identified as one of the most important reasons for leaving military service.  Grissmer and Kirby (1985) found that one-third of reservists reported leaving service because of conflicts with family and encroachment on personal time.

A previously identified issue for reserve component families is the differential between civilian pay and military pay and conflicts with civilian employment (Grissmer & Kirby, 1985; Moskos, 1987).  Increased frequency and duration of deployments strain the relationship with employers who have come to expect employees' military absences of two weeks a year.  When mobilization and deployment disrupt civilian employment, their civilian income normally ends, and families must content themselves with living on military compensation, which may be less, in some cases much less, than their civilian income.  Upward mobility, promotions, work opportunities, selected work hours, and impact on vacations are sources of continuing stress in civilian employment.  This combination of stressors is a major issue for the reserve component and contributes to varying levels of commitment to military service by citizen-soldiers and their families.

Varying levels of commitment may be influenced by the fact that reservists, in contrast to active-duty personnel, reside primarily in communities where military installation support and networks of military peers and families are not found.  Consequently, a military-focused network of social support for managing the demands and difficulties on service members and their families, as called for by the National Guard Family Program, may not be in place. This is not to suggest that no social support system is available to these families. Civilian personal and familial relationships may provide some level of social support.

A less-attended theme in the literature is the influence of the pervasive "right stuff" philosophy on help seeking. This line of thought implies that those who have it (the right stuff) do not need any assistance or support to cope with the demands and stresses of military life. This perspective has been an inhibitor to the use of human service programs or social services, especially psychological counseling or social support, by military members or their families (Brown, 1993). Use of such services or programs has been widely perceived by service members as having an adverse impact on a military career. Since the development and fielding of effective family support programs, military leaders, service members, and their families have gained a more appropriate understanding of help seeking. Families can be prepared to cope with military-related stress through anticipation, education, and preparation. They can, and should, use social programs and services when necessary (Knox & Price, 1995).

An issue closely related to help seeking is confidentiality. Confidentiality is limited in a military human service setting because of issues that may affect the mission. Service members' performances are, by necessity, subject to review by their commander. The impacts of culture and tradition and the limits of confidentiality are factors in the use of human services by military members and their families even in a changing military culture.

A finding highlighted in recent military family literature, and especially prevalent in work published after the Persian Gulf War, suggests that family preparation for separations and deployments, and family support and network connections between military families made a difference in the wartime coping abilities of families (Knox & Price, 1995). Military family literature since the Persian Gulf War has also suggested that preparation of service members and their families prior to deployment has made a difference in the wartime coping abilities of families (Knox & Price, 1995).

Psychoeducational programs, such as the Army's *Operation R.E.A.D.Y.* (Resources for Educating About Deployment and You), address planning and preparing for deployments, emotional adjustment, coping skills, using social support during separations, and adjustments during reunions. These factors are found to make a difference in the coping abilities of families (Figley, 1993; Peebles-Kleiger & Kleiger, 1994). Teaching reservists and family members to anticipate and plan for the demands of military life mitigates the stressors that families have identified as central to military service (Price & Hornig, 1993). These programs emphasize using human services as a resource to help families cope. Military support for this type of education for reservists and their family members is derived from a partnership philosophy of unit readiness being equivalent to family readiness. Families need to be prepared to adapt to military demands with self-sufficiency and support.

## FAMILY SUPPORT PROGRAMS AND THE RESERVE COMPONENT

Family support and family readiness have become central to the reserve component as citizen-soldiers are currently serving about 13 million "man-days" a year in augmenting the active component (Weible, 1998).  Support for families can be provided and obtained in a variety of ways that acknowledge stress, validate family sacrifices, develop family networks, foster mutual aid, and encourage reciprocal connections between and among these military families.  The goals of these family support initiatives are to prevent problems through education and planning and to facilitate development of social support networks, problem solving, and self-sufficiency among military families.  For reserve component families, developing and maintaining a military family support network is often hampered by geography, that is, the distance between the home and the military unit location.

One of the positive outcomes of the Persian Gulf War was the implementation and utilization of National Guard Family Assistance Centers (FACs) by both active and reserve component families (Brown, 1993).  Family support grew in visibility and impact, reinforcing the philosophy of having active family assistance for support in both peacetime and war.  The National Guard's success in the rapid establishment of FACs and successful delivery of services further validated its pioneering role in the evolution of family support within the total force.

### The National Guard Family Program

The Department of Defense funded the National Guard Family Program (NGFP) in 1987.  The goal of this program was to educate and to facilitate the adaptation of National Guard personnel and their families to military demands and duties (Ogilvy-Lee, 1997a).  The philosophy underlying this program was visionary.  It incorporated a partnership perspective between the National Guard and its families.  The NGFP responded rapidly during the Persian Gulf War when the total force demands on the reserve component were put to the test.  The NGFP set up over 470 Family Assistance Centers across the nation to meet the needs of thousands of National Guard and reservist families, as well as active component families who lived at a distance from military installations.  Much needed services were provided to all military families, regardless of service branch,.  Often this took place through the efforts of family member volunteers.

Over 13 years old, the NGFP is a model for mutual support and self-sufficiency among military families, clearly exhibiting a partnership philosophy.  The NGFP relies on family member volunteers, interested volunteer civilians, retirees, and local community resources.  The program has a national director.  Every state and territory has a Family Program Coordinator.   The self-sufficiency and mutual support model has proven to be most effective given the likely prospect of declining budgetary emphasis on military family support programs. The program is decentralized, with each state having a program tailored to involving Guard families and meeting their needs, especially during mobilization and deployment. State family programs receive broad guidance from the national director (Ogilvy-Lee, 1997a). The program has been designed to promote self-definition within the state, taking into consideration important differences such as population, size, geography, resource availability, and different command priorities (Ogilvy-Lee, 1997b). It is expected that variations in state programs will reflect the impact of the specific environments in which these state-level programs meet family needs. For example, Oregon has no active military installations. Alabama, on the other hand, has several from which to draw some support for reserve component families. What works in Alabama would not work in Oregon.

State coordinators have an annual leadership and program meeting and attend the Annual National Guard Family Conference. In 1998, approximately 600 volunteers and paid staff, representing the NGFP across the 54 states and territories, attended the national conference workshops and planning sessions. While the NGFP is decentralized and relies on a self-help model, the program provides ongoing training for coordinators and volunteers. Recognizing limited budgets, this program has assumed responsibility for generating participation, sharing, activities, support, assistance, and resources for military families largely through its volunteers.

Through program education and activities, service members and families are offered orientation and annual updates on the National Guard, especially military-specific matters, deployment preparation and mobilization, and identification of available benefits, entitlements, and services. They are encouraged to participate in local family support groups (FSGs) to mitigate stress and network with other National Guard and reserve families. Family members are encouraged to anticipate the need for readiness for deployment through preparation and involvement in FSGs, by attending unit information briefings, by making time for classes and workshops for adults and children, and by using their Family Assistance Centers. Volunteer activities may involve programs targeted for Guard youth such as Guard-sponsored summer camps. Volunteers frequently organize fund-raising events, unit picnics, and holiday events.

### Psychoeducational Programs

One of the trends in National Guard and reserve family support programs has been the use of psychoeducational curricula and programs. These have been used to educate families on military policies and anticipation and preparation for deployment and reunion. These training programs educate participants on the emotional and psychological stresses of military life and how effective individual coping strategies and social support can mitigate distress. The curriculum and programs are designed to address issues affecting service members and their families.

### Operation R.E.A.D.Y.

One of the best examples of this type of program was mentioned earlier. *Operation R.E.A.D.Y.* was developed following the Persian Gulf War and is being used extensively by the National Guard Family Program. This curriculum has several components and is intended for use by the military in briefings, by family members, and by human service workers. As Knox and Price (1995) illustrate, families, especially young families with little military experience, may fail to understand the importance of anticipation and preparation for deployment, particularly those deployments that may occur suddenly. Lack of preparation may result in financial difficulties, ignorance of military benefits or community resources, inability to maintain contact with the military member, and little or no community support.

*Operation R.E.A.D.Y.* provides a multimedia resource library of materials that may be used to educate military families about the practical and emotional challenges of deployments, separations, and reunions (Knox & Price, 1995). The materials were developed from various interventions and programs used by both the active and reserve components throughout the Persian Gulf conflict (U.S. Army, 1991). The materials used focus on all types of families from single military members, single parents, dual-career couples, to military spouses. They even include content for children. The materials are organized in a "train the trainer" format for easy use by professionals and nonprofessionals. The format encourages family members to become participants in the training. All parts of the curriculum contain evaluation materials, which can be used for reports and feedback to military communities and commanders. Regardless of who delivers the materials or organizes the program, support of commanders at all levels is essential. This support is the key to success of family support and quality-of-life programs (U.S. Army, 1993; Walker, 1994). The enlightened commander who leads by persuasion and example will succeed with his or her organization's family support program. Authoritarian approaches do not work when there is no rule to compel compliance and certainly not with family member volunteers.

### The Army Family Readiness Handbook

The conceptual framework for *Operation R.E.A.D.Y.* is found in the *Army Family Readiness Handbook*. This handbook provides background material for active component and reserve component users (Price & Hornig, 1993). The psychoeducational model uses a "prevention and wellness" perspective. It is designed to promote self-sufficiency and mutual support among military families (Unger & Powell, 1990). The handbook provides guidelines for educating families on the stress of military life. It highlights effective coping strategies that can be used by commanders, military personnel, and family assistance center staff and family members. The conceptual framework emphasizes the partnership between the military and family members, with the goal of self-sufficiency and interdependence among military families. A central feature of the handbook identifies leadership support throughout the military hierarchy as necessary to family involvement, especially in a program run by volunteers. Family members are encouraged to become trainers, using the *Operation R.E.A.D.Y.* materials, or to assist with the training. Family members are told that the primary ownership of the program is theirs.

The curriculum consists of four training modules with sections tailored to family structure. It focuses on preparation for deployment and separation (predeployment), reunions (postdeployment), and the tasks associated with implementing a Family Assistance Center. The final module addresses advanced training in organizing and implementing a Family Support Group.

*Predeployment Module.* Deployments are recognized as one of the primary stresses for military families. For reservists the stress may be exacerbated due to inexperience with military life. The predeployment curriculum identifies ways in which soldiers and families can prepare for separations (Price, 1993a). It identifies financial and practical planning, legal planning, especially wills and obtaining power of attorney for caregivers of children or elderly parents, making family care plans, insurance, property, and emotional stress and various coping strategies for adults and children. The module encourages families to anticipate separations as part of military life and take care of these issues well before deployment occurs. The curriculum reinforces the importance of anticipatory coping for the inevitable deployment and planning for it. It teaches soldiers and families that planning will reduce stress and facilitate adjustment and coping during deployments. This is particularly true with planning for the financial aspects of deployment separations. A different budget will be required for the family, and each adult member must be prepared to implement it.

The predeployment curriculum is tailored to specific groups including single soldiers, single-parent soldiers, married soldiers and spouses with or without children, and dual military career couples with or without children. The curriculum may vary in the amount of time of presentation and audience participation in developing individual deployment plans for families.

*Postdeployment Module.* The content of this curriculum addresses soldier, family, and community preparation for homecoming and reunion (McCleskey & Price, 1993). The curriculum identifies issues that are known to impact the successful reunification of service members with families and community. The first part of the training is delivered at the service members' deployment location prior to their return home. Families participate in the training in their own communities. A second training session is held for both the soldier and his or her family together. The goal of this curriculum is to facilitate military family members developing realistic expectations of each other and to help all family members understand the transition process that accompanies reunion. Families are taught to identify and to understand readjustment stress and to learn to use specific coping strategies known to mitigate the stress often associated with reunion. In addition to normalizing the reunion stress, family members and soldiers are taught to identify readjustment problems that may become chronic. In particular, participants are taught to become knowledgeable about the symptoms of acute situational stress and how to access mental health assistance. The goal is to prevent the development of subsequent distress and/or the development of posttraumatic stress disorder.

Both the predeployment and postdeployment training sessions consist of about eight hours of instruction and are supported by training videos and work-books for children. The training is organized to address the unique differences of the reservist military family. The Virginia Army National Guard in preparing their soldiers and families for an eight-month deployment to Bosnia successfully used both predeployment and postdeployment training programs.

*Family Assistance Center Module.* FACs are organized and implemented as temporary assistance centers during reserve component mobilization and de-ployment, or activation for state emergencies. These centers provide families with information, resources, referrals, and support (Price, 1993b). The FAC is a one-stop multiservice center and is operated by military or civilian staff mem-bers and family and civilian volunteers. The FAC is an important element of services to reservist families. During the Persian Gulf War, several hundred FACs were established across the United States. The National Guard alone op-erated 471 centers nationwide. Altogether, FACs served more than a quarter of a million family members during the war, meeting many human service needs. The centers are set up to supplement existing human services on military instal-lations when large deployments occur and to provide services in communities where no other military services exist for military families. The State Area Command (state-level headquarters of the Army National Guard) is responsible for resourcing and operating FACs.

The FAC curriculum module trains military members and volunteers in the operating procedures of the center and how to partner effectively with military and civilian organizations. The array of human services delivered in these military social service centers include advice on military benefits and entitle-ments, financial and legal assistance, and in some situations medical and mental health referrals.

Because the personnel who operate the FACs are seldom-trained human service professionals, one of the FAC's essential activities is to develop partner-ships with civilian social service providers to whom family members may be referred. The FAC is an essential component of family support for reservist families as increasing numbers of National Guard members and reservists are being deployed in the total force military. In communities where there is no military installation nearby, linkages with other human service providers and social services are a critical part of FAC operations in order to provide problem solving and emotional support to reservist families. The FAC education cur-riculum addresses how to set up and run a FAC on a military installation (an active-duty model) and how to establish and operate a FAC in a civilian com-munity (a reserve component model).

*Family Support Group Module.* Family support groups and organizations vary in their presence and degree of involvement of family members throughout the reserve components. This is due, in part, to family member time constraints, to lack of resources to support such groups, and to the fact that many reservist families have existing support from family and friends in their home communities. Current experience shows that family support networks may be more feasible than groups per se. During the Persian Gulf War, family support groups were found to be effective in reducing stress for reservist families where they were organized on the principle of talent and interests and not primarily on the rank of the military spouse. In fact, where spouse rank determined family support group leadership, group effectiveness deteriorated. This is less of a problem for reservist families whose focus tends to be meeting human needs and who balance their military experience with their lives in civilian communities. Family support groups are especially important to younger and more inexperienced military family members and their children, many of whom are learning to cope with the new experience of separation and deployment.

The advanced family support group training module promotes organizing "grassroots" support among reservist families. The module identifies rank orientation as a problem in a support group and encourages organization based on the interests, talents, and needs of members. Interested individuals are provided training in communication, being a volunteer and managing volunteers, identifying information and referral resources, organizing and implementing programs for family members and children, encouraging self-sufficiency, and connecting families to social services when needed. The module provides members with training literature to create support groups with the goal of family members providing each other mutual support (White, McCleskey, & Price, 1993).

## HUMAN SERVICE PRACTICE WITH CITIZEN-SOLDIER FAMILIES

Knox and Price (1999) identify several principles or recommendations for human service work with citizen-soldier families. The challenges of coping with the demands and stresses of military life come from numerous sources. Success in human service work relies on an ecological systems approach to assessment, problem solving, and coping (Hepworth, Rooney, & Larsen, 1997). These same principles apply to all citizen-soldier families regardless of armed forces branch.

### Adopt a Person/Family-in-Environment Approach

Human service providers must strive to understand the military hierarchical culture and its requirements of military personnel and families. Rank is one defining feature of the military culture and may reflect education, income, access to resources, as well as level of responsibility. It is important to understand military norms and beliefs in relation to families and how they may affect delivery of services, as well as to develop an understanding of where the citizen-soldier and family fit in the military setting in which the service member works. It is important to note where the reservist does his or her duty, either in the community, close to home, or at some distance. The needs of a family who must support the absence of the citizen-soldier for one or two nights a month for military training will be different from one who does not.

### Individualize the Citizen-Soldier and Family

Reservist families have varying commitments to the military. In part that depends upon the importance of the service member's job to the family, either as a career choice or as a means of supplemental income. It is important to individualize and understand the level of commitment and attachment to the military environment. Reservist families may effectively balance their allegiances to home, community, and to military demands, or they may not. Regardless of commitment level, enlightened human service workers can help families access the resources they need.

### Respect the Limits of Military Confidentiality

Confidentiality has limitations for military personnel and their families. Information gathered for the purpose of human services may be reviewed by military officials based upon their perceived need and the information's relationship to the military member's duties. In all human service contact, the military member and his or her family must be reminded of the limits of confidentiality. This is most important regarding sensitive issues such as sexual orientation where a military member may be punished or discharged from the military. Human service workers must maintain confidentiality where that is possible. They must be prepared to inform the client of the limits of confidentiality and make appropriate referrals to nonmilitary counselors when needed.

### Establish a Safe Environment for Communication

Military rank can be an inhibitor to open and honest communication, especially in counseling sessions. Leaving rank outside of the counseling environment is ideal, but it is important to recognize that this is very hard to do for individuals with a high attachment to their military position. This may be particularly true for upper-ranking officers and senior noncommissioned officers for whom issuing commands is the norm. The human service worker must strive to understand this and address it in a context safe for the client. The worker must negotiate how to talk about rank before it becomes a problem and facilitate the client's adjustment to a very different environment for problem solving.

### Understand Developmental Issues and Conflicts

Military duties that bring separations to families disrupt normal developmental processes and may leave conflicts unresolved. Families can be taught to share an understanding of what the absence of the military member means to each family member especially in relation to special occasions such a birthdays, special school events, or graduations.  It is important to help families anticipate these possibilities and plan for them.  It is possible for families to talk openly and honestly about developmental issues and conflicts.  Human service workers can help families recognize when communications are failing or strained beyond coping resources and normalize seeking help to improve the situation.

### Support the Limits of Self-Determination for Military Families

Reservist families face many challenges with increasing separations and deployments.  Their ability to adjust and cope depends heavily on their developmental stage as a family and their level of commitment to military structures or imperatives.  It is important to understand where the family is in relation to that commitment and determine if there are conflicts regarding the situation.  Self-determination is limited in this context and may inhibit the ability to cope.  For reservist families, having the support of family and friends is important to keeping a positive perspective.  Support from other citizen-soldier families may help to normalize developmental issues and conflicts and provide opportunities to share insights and coping strategies.

### Advocate for Prevention and Intervention without Stigma

While there has been an important shift in thinking regarding the strain of military life and the importance of system support for families, concerns remain about the impact of the use of social services by military families.  There is still a certain stigma attached to using mental health services.  Human service workers can normalize the strain of military responsibilities and facilitate the use of social services by families as a form of self-reliance and self-sufficiency.  Human service workers may also work with the military hierarchy, especially unit commanders, to help them understand how to support families' use of needed services.

### Know and Use Military Resources

Self-education about military resources is critical to effective human services that meet citizen-soldier family needs.  Self-education means reading military newspapers and other local publications that highlight military family issues. Newspapers such as *Army Times, Air Force Times, and Navy Times* address family issues and concerns in each issue.  Newsletters such as *The Military Family* and the *National Military Family Association* address ongoing issues and policies that affect families and identify contact persons.  The Military Family Resource Center (MFRC) is a clearinghouse for research articles, papers, books, pamphlets, technical reports, journal articles, and program materials.

There are several on-line networks on the Internet, which can help social service providers stay informed on current issues. The Navy's Lifeline site is a prime example <www.LIFELines4qol.org>. There are also a growing number of program materials, such as *Operation R.E.A.D.Y.*, that are user friendly and available to human service workers for the development of programs for military families. These program materials are especially important to reservist families who may not live in or near a military community but desire to create group support for themselves. They may also be used to help families understand the military hierarchy, benefits and entitlements, and how to access military resources.

The National Guard State Family Program Coordinator (SFPC) located in every state and territory can be a valuable resource for human service providers. The SFPC's function is to facilitate adjustment and coping, as well as use of family support and military resources by citizen-soldier families. They collaborate and network with human service providers to meet families' needs in their local communities. Sending the SFPC a letter of introduction, outlining expertise and interest in providing assistance to the program, is a good way for human service providers to initiate the contact.

The local reserve unit commander is another key military resource. It can be invaluable to develop a working relationship with the commander and immediate staff as part of the community of support for citizen soldier families. Human service providers can educate commanders as to their expertise and how they can support family readiness in their communities.

## SUMMARY AND IMPLICATIONS

The U.S. military is in the process of dramatic change. This change involves the reduction in size of all branches of the active duty armed forces. More responsibilities, both local and global, are being placed on the reserve components. Defense policy makers are striving to establish a fully integrated, seamless force of both active and reserve components—a total force. This new level of reliance on the reserve component is unprecedented and presents both opportunity and challenge.

Citizen-soldiers and their families are being asked to do more with less. In recent years, reservists have been sent to do the nation's defense work all over the globe. With these deployments have come family separations and the myriad stressors that accompany such separations. The military establishment cannot provide human service support to these citizen-soldiers and their families who live in every neighborhood in the nation. Civilian human service providers will be asked to fill the need. Here, too, is opportunity and challenge for human service workers. It will not be easy, but it must be done.

# REFERENCES

Armed Forces Information Service. (1993). *Defense 93: Almanac issue.* Alexandria, VA: American Forces Information Service.

Armed Forces Information Service. (1997). *Defense 97: Almanac issue.* Alexandria, VA: American Forces Information Service.

Bowen, G. L. (1982). *Family patterns of U.S. military personnel.* Springfield, VA: Military Family Resource Center.

Brown, R. W. (1993). Military family service centers: Their preventive and interventive functions. In F. W. Kaslow (Ed.), *The military family in peace and war* (pp. 163–172). New York: Springer.

Burnam, M. A., Meredith, L. S., Sherbourne, C. D., Valdez, R. B., & Vernez, G. (1992). *Army families and soldier readiness* (Technical Report R-3884-A). Santa Monica, CA: Rand Arroyo Center.

Calvert, B. R. (1998). Virginia infantrymen return from "troll duty" in Bosnia. *National Guard, 52*(7), 16–19.

Figley, C. R. (1993). Weathering the storm at home: War-related family stress and coping. In F. W. Kaslow (Ed.), *The military family in peace and war* (pp. 173–190). New York: Springer.

Fogleman, R. R. (1997a, February 3). The (Air) Guard's role in global engagement. Paper presented at All Adjutant Generals Conference, Washington, DC.

Fogleman, R. R. (1997b, February 17). The (Air Force) Reserve's role in global engagement. Paper presented at the Reserve Officers Association, Washington, DC.

Griffith, J. (1989). *Survey of Army families: Spouses of the Army National Guard and U.S. Army Reserve soldiers.* Rockville, MD: Westat, Inc.

Grissmer, D. W., & Kirby, S. N. (1985). *Attrition of nonprior-service reservists in the Army National Guard and Army Reserve* (Report R-3267-RA). Santa Monica, CA: Rand.

Hepworth, D. H., Rooney, R. H., & Larsen, J. A. (1997). *Direct social work practice: Theory and skills* (5th ed.). Pacific Grove, CA: Brooks/Cole.

Knox, J., & Price, D. H. (1995). The changing American military family: Opportunities for social work. *Social Service Review, 69*(3), pp. 479–497.

Knox, J., & Price, D. H. (1999). Total force and the new American military family: Implications for social work education. *Families in Society, 80*(2), p. 128.

Ledford, T. (1998, September 14). Employers feeling work crunch: Some businesses struggle when reservists called up. *Army Times,* p. 20.

Martin, J. A., & Ickovics, J. R. (1987). The effect of stress on the psychological well being of Army wives: Initial findings from a longitudinal study. *Journal of Human Stress, 13*(3), pp. 108–115.

McCleskey, K., & Price, D. (1993). *Postdeployment training.* Alexandria, VA: U.S. Army Community and Family Support Center.

Moskos, C. C. (1987). *The sociology of the Army reserves: A preliminary assessment* (ARI Research Note 87–82). Alexandria, VA: U.S. Army Institute for the Behavioral and Social Sciences.

Ogilvy-Lee, D. (1997a). *The National Guard Family Program: 1997 Update.* Information paper, National Guard Bureau Family Program Washington, DC.

Ogilvy-Lee, D. (1997b). *The National Guard Family Program Annual Review.* Washington, DC: National Guard Bureau Family Program.

Orthner, D. K., Early-Adams, P., Devall, E., Giddings, M., Morley, R., & Stawarski, C. (1987). *The Army Family Research Program: Community satisfaction and support programs.* Athens: University of Georgia.

Peebles-Kleiger, M. J., & Kleiger, J. H. (1994). Reintegration stress for Desert Storm families: Wartime deployments and family trauma. *Journal of Traumatic Stress,* 7(1), p. 173.

Price, D. H. (1993a). *Predeployment training.* Alexandria, VA: U.S. Army Community and Family Support Center.

Price, D. H. (1993b). *Family assistance center.* Alexandria, VA: U.S. Army Community and Family Support Center.

Price, D. H., & Hornig, S. (Eds.). (1993). *The Army family readiness handbook.* Alexandria, VA: U.S. Army Community and Family Support Center.

Slimmer Army depending on reserves for Bosnia duty. (1998, May 25). *The New York Times,* p. A8.

Teitelbaum, J. M. (1991). Impacts of ODS family stressor, supports, and coping among spouses of active duty soldiers deployed to the Persian Gulf. In *Family policies and programs: Persian Gulf conflict,* Appendix A. (pp. 1–27). Washington, DC: Department of Defense.

Unger, D. G., & Powell, D. R. (1990). *Families as nurturing systems: An introduction.* Prevention in Human Services, 9(1), pp. 1–17.

U.S. Army. (1983). *The White Paper* (DA PAM 608-41). Washington, DC: U.S. Army.

U.S. Army. (1991). *The yellow ribbon: Army lessons from the home front, Desert Shield–Desert Storm.* Fort Leavenworth, KS: Combined Arms Center.

U.S. Army. (1993). The Army family action plan X (Circular 608-93-1). Washington, DC: U.S. Army.

U.S. Army. (1997). Army National Guard fiscal year 1997—posture statement. Washington, DC: National Guard Bureau.

U.S. Army. (1998). The White Paper, One team–one fight–one future: For the common defense. <HYPERLINK http://www.hqda.army.mil/ocsa/ot_text.htm.>

U.S. Army & U.S. Air Force. (1986). *National Guard Regulation No. 600-12. Air National Guard Regulation No. 211-1.* National Guard family program. Washington, DC: National Guard Bureau.

U.S. Department of Defense, Defense Manpower Data Center (1996, September). *Military personnel by branch of service.* Washington, DC: Department of Defense.

U.S. Department of Defense, Defense Manpower Data Center (1997, September). *Military personnel by branch of service.* Washington, DC: Department of Defense.

U.S. Navy. (1998). Naval reserve force strategic plan. <www.ncts.navy.mil/Navresfor/data/pages/stratei.hmtl.>

Vernez, G., & Zellman, G. L. (1987). *Families and mission: A review of the effects of family factors on Army attrition, retention, and readiness.* Santa Monica, CA: Rand Corporation.

Walker, P. (1994, September 19). Former leaders say Army needs to prove it cares. *Army Times,* p. 16.

Weaver, P. A. (1998). A time of change. *National Guard,* 52(8), pp. 16–21.

Weible, J. (1998, May 4). Reserve affairs gains acting chief: New assistant secretary puts improving the lives of reservists on top of his list. *Army Times,* p. 20.

White, L. B., McCleskey, K., & Price, D. H. (1993). *Family Support Group (Advanced Training in Team Building, Problem Solving and Communication).* Alexandria, VA: U.S. Army Community and Family Support Center.

Wolfe, C. (1998). Guarding the homeland. *National Guard,* 52(5), pp. 16–19.

Wolfe, T. (1979). *The right stuff.* New York: Farrar, Straus, & Giroux.

# Chapter 3

# The Special Case of the Young Enlisted Family

*David S. Wolpert, James A. Martin, Lea M. Dougherty, Barbara Janofsky Rudin, and Susan Kerner-Hoeg*

## INTRODUCTION

Young enlisted military families represent a uniquely vulnerable population. Typically these young couples are newly married and many are beginning families. They are often away from home and extended family for the first time. Many of these couples face economic stresses and associated issues such as difficulty obtaining adequate and affordable housing, or locating affordable and satisfactory childcare. This chapter describes the presence of these junior enlisted families within the military and the demographic variations across the services. The chapter discusses the adult and family developmental challenges faced by these young couples within the context of military service duty demands and the challenges of military family life. Issues associated with financial management, housing, spouse employment, childcare, family separations, and military duties are considered. The chapter provides pragmatic suggestions for human service providers working with these young military families.

The typical new recruit in today's All Volunteer Force is a single, never married. high school graduate with no dependent children, who has never committed a serious criminal offense, and who does not have a history of serious drug or alcohol abuse, mental illness, or other disqualifying medical condition. Most enlistees enter the military within a year or two after high school graduation. Some have tried college or trade school; others have been employed, mostly in unskilled and low-paying jobs. For many, military service is seen as an opportunity to transition into adulthood, to develop personal and technical skills, and to gain work experience that will be valuable in subsequent civilian life. Some young men and women enlist in military service because of the immediate monetary incentive; others are looking for funds to use later for college or advanced technical training. Only a small percentage of new recruits enter enlisted service with the specific goal of a military career.  While this is a profile of the typical new recruit, there are obvious variations among the thousands of young men and women who enter military service yearly.  Waivers are granted for a number of conditions, and increasingly military recruiters find it necessary to seek these less qualified individuals to fill the ranks.  This is a recruitment trend that is likely to continue in the context of a healthy economy where jobs are plentiful and in a culture where young adults and their parents increasingly view military service as an undesirable entryway into adulthood and the world of work.

## A PROFILE OF THE ARMED FORCES

Recent data from the Defense Manpower Data Center (DMDC), reported by the Military Family Resource Center (1998), provides a picture of the similarities and the differences among and between the services.  Almost 85 percent of current service members are in the enlisted ranks.  Of these, more than 50 percent are in the category of "junior enlisted"—the bottom enlisted pay grades of E1 through E4.  These E1 through E4 enlistees are typically young men and women serving their first four-year enlistment.  The percentages of junior enlisted service members differ by branch of service—ranging from 39 percent of the Air Force, 42 percent of the Navy, and 45 percent of the Army, to 62 percent of the Marine Corps.  Approximately 35 percent of enlisted soldiers, sailors, Marines, and airmen/airwomen are from minority groups.  African Americans comprise 22 percent of the enlisted force and Hispanics 7 percent.  Women comprise almost 14 percent of the total enlisted force.  The percentage of enlisted service members age 20 or younger in each service provides insight into the differences among the services' missions.  Almost 30 percent of Marine Corps enlisted members are 20 or younger, while only 18 percent of the Army, 16 percent of the Navy, and 12 percent of the Air Force are this young.  The Air Force and Navy require a high density of technically skilled individuals capable of operating increasingly sophisticated weaponry.  In contrast, the Marine Corps and Army, while employing high-tech weapons and needing skilled members, still rely on the "soldier" as their primary instrument of combat.  This equates to a need for large numbers of young men (and women in some military occupational specialties) capable of performing the physically and mentally challenging requirements associated with the primary soldier tasks of ground combat operations.

While most young men and women are single when they enter the military, most eventually marry.  Today, more than half of all military members are married.  The percentages of married junior enlisted service members range from 45 percent in the Air Force to 26 percent in the Marine Corps.  In both the Army and the Navy approximately 31 percent of junior enlisted personnel are married.  This means that at any point in time there are approximately 212,000 junior enlisted members coping with the demands of military service life while simultaneously attempting to meet the responsibilities of marriage.  For over 100,000 of these young military couples, the challenge also includes parenthood.  In 1997, junior enlisted service members were the parents of over 160,000 children age five and under.  In addition to the married junior enlisted service members, almost 28,000 additional junior enlisted service members are single parents, comprising 11 percent of the Army, 5 percent of the Navy, 4 percent of the Air Force, and 3 percent of the Marine Corps.

Many young men and women who enter military service fail to complete their first enlistment—typically four years of service. Attrition rates (an unexpected discharge from military service) have averaged more than 30 percent for the past two decades (GAO, 1997). While there are a variety of reasons for these premature losses, many enlistees are separated for a "lack of motivation" or for other negative behaviors (e.g., drug or alcohol abuse), resulting in a separation decision by the member's commander (GAO, 1997). While there are some differences among the services in their retention standards, junior enlisted members serving on active duty are recognized by each of the services as an important component of a well-trained, highly motivated, conscientious military.

## CHALLENGES CONFRONTING YOUNG MEMBERS AND THEIR FAMILIES

There are a number of challenges that all military families face but which may be most difficult for new enlisted families. Some of the most pressing concerns of young enlisted families include financial management, housing, spouse employment, childcare, and separation from extended family.

### Financial Management

One of the most difficult challenges for military families is the management of their finances. Across the enlisted ranks pay is low. The demands associated with military duties and lifestyle make it difficult for members to hold down a second job. For a variety of reasons, which are discussed in Chapter 6 of this book, spouses often find that it is difficult to obtain employment. This issue is compounded for young families because military pay for junior enlisted service members is even less adequate, especially for families with children. When faced with managing finances and living on a budget for the first time, many young service members and their spouses find themselves unprepared for this task. To exacerbate this situation, military members often find it easy to make purchases on credit, and these young families are often an easy target for lenders with high interest rates. Pre-approved credit card applications frequently arrive unsolicited in the mail. Even the military exchanges and military clubs offer easy and automatic credit. As a result, it is not uncommon to find junior enlisted members who are having their wages garnished for outstanding debts, a situation that only creates other family problems and stresses. A common concern for unit leaders is the number of "letters of indebtedness" that cross their desks each month and the amount of leadership time required to address the financial problems of their subordinates.

An average 31 percent of Air Force junior enlisted service members and 40 percent of Navy junior enlisted service members report having problems paying their bills every other month (Caliber Associates, 1996; 1997; 1998). Results of military community needs assessment surveys demonstrate the requirement for financial management assistance for junior enlisted families. Classes and coun-seling in financial management can help young families learn how to budget and to make appropriate financial decisions. This is a critical skill for both the mili-tary member and the nonmember spouse, especially when the young service member is deployed and the spouse must assume primary responsibility for managing the family's finances. Increasingly unit leaders are recognizing the importance of personal and family financial management skill training as part of unit readiness preparations.

### Housing

While military members are entitled to housing, this typically equates to a barracks room or, for some sailors, living space on board ship. Married mem-bers must usually find housing in the local civilian community—fully 70 percent of married military members and their families reside in civilian housing. This percentage is even higher among junior enlisted members. Historically, "rank has its privilege," and junior enlisted families are generally not provided either on-base housing or sufficient financial resources to afford adequate and safe off-base community housing (Twiss & Martin, 1998). The junior enlisted member's current entitlement to married housing benefits (typically a housing allowance that includes a differential by area housing costs) is a good start toward correct-ing this problem but is only a recent development. Junior enlisted families living in off-base housing typically pay more than their housing allowance covers. Driven by finances, some live in unsafe neighborhoods, while others reside far from the installation where housing is more affordable. For example, of those junior enlisted families who live off base, 65 percent of Navy families and 53 percent of Air Force families live more than 15 minutes travel time from the installation (Caliber Associates, 1996; 1997; 1998). The 15-minute travel time is a standard typically related to alert requirements. The problem of locating affordable, safe, and convenient housing is often compounded by the fact that most junior enlisted families have only one vehicle. If this vehicle must be used by the military member for transportation to and from duty, the spouse is left at home without transportation. Unless the military member leaves work to pro-vide transportation, the nonmember spouse may not have a reliable way to get to his or her civilian job, the grocery store, or the doctor.

### Spouse Employment

A third challenge confronting the junior enlisted family is the desire or need for the nonmember spouse to work. A full 53 percent of Navy and 55 per-cent of Air Force civilian spouses of junior enlisted service members report be-ing employed (Caliber Associates, 1996; 1998). Though these percentages are relatively high and would seem to tell a good story, a variety of issues and situa-tions unique to the military can affect the type of work available to these spouses. Many spouses of first-term military members are young and have few job skills, limiting the kinds of jobs for which they are eligible. Many spouses who do have skills and/or experience have had to give up secure employment to follow military members to their initial or follow-on assignments.  There are job assistance services both on and off base to help spouses find employment, but local employer biases against nonpermanent military residents can be difficult to overcome.  Because military spouses are subject to relocation, employers often view military spouses as poor candidates for employment—especially for a career position.  For many spouses of junior enlisted members, employability may also be contingent on where they live and their ability to obtain reliable transportation.

### Childcare

Another concern for junior enlisted families with working spouses, dual-military couples with children, and single parents is the availability of affordable, quality childcare.  A total of 51 percent of Navy junior enlisted and 48 percent of Air Force junior enlisted have one or more children living in the home (caliber Associates, 1996; 1998).  Childcare is available on most military installations on a rank-correlated sliding fee scale.  Childcare costs for the junior enlisted family, however, can represent a large percentage of the family's income.  Costs at military childcare facilities are based on total family income, and the additional salary from the nonmember spouse may push the family into a higher income bracket, resulting in higher childcare costs.  If the family does not live on or close to the installation, it may not be feasible to use military childcare.  These families are reliant on childcare that is available in their community, which is often more expensive than military childcare and may not always be high quality or safe.  In addition, civilian childcare providers are not generally prepared to handle the unpredictability of a military member's duty requirements.  For the first-term family, especially single parents and the dual-military couples with children, affordable, safe, quality childcare that allows flexibility is extremely important but can be difficult to find.

### Separation from Extended Family Members and Friends

The challenges of military family life are often most difficult to manage when the young military family is geographically separated from their extended family and friends who would normally provide a natural support system during stressful times.  For example, when the military member deploys (or is otherwise away from home because of military duties), the nonmember spouse is often left isolated and reliant on neighbors, spouses of other unit members, or co-workers if help is needed.  Civilian spouses overwhelmingly report that they go to their member spouse first for support (80 percent), followed by a friend (58 percent), or another family member (47 percent).  Since their network of friends is typically very sparse, the absence of the member's support and the distance from extended family may put the spouse and family at risk (Caliber Associates, 1997; 1998).

Although modern technology provides a variety of effective ways of communicating with friends and loved ones back home (phone, fax, and, to an increasing extent, e-mail), extended family members are typically unable to be present to provide immediate, tangible support when things go wrong (e.g., the car breaking down or a child getting sick) or to share in happy events (e.g., the birth of a child or a promotion).  Often, for the first time, the young service member and spouse must juggle the many responsibilities of day-to-day living on their own, when in the past they may have been able to rely on extended family or friends for guidance and assistance.

## STRESSORS CONFRONTING YOUNG ENLISTED MEMBERS AND THEIR FAMILIES

These challenges to daily life are often intertwined with stressors that are specific to the military: demands associated with military duties, deployments and other military-related family separations, and relocation.

### Duty Demands

There are certain unique military requirements that must be balanced with family expectations.  Although these requirements apply to all military members, they often add a considerable additional burden on the young first-term enlisted member and his or her family.  The military member is considered "available for duty" seven days a week, 24 hours a day, 365 days a year.  There are recalls to duty, alerts, training requirements, exercises and extra duties.  It is normal to be at work before sunrise and frequently to work more than an eight-hour day.  A full 53 percent of Navy junior enlisted respondents and an average of 40 percent of Air Force junior enlisted respondents report working more than 40 hours per week (Caliber Associates 1996; 1997; 1998).  There may be periods of shift work that require the member to work at night or on rotating 12-hour shifts.  Working 40 hours a week is the exception rather than the rule in the military, and there is no overtime pay compensation.  To exacerbate the stress, many jobs for first-term enlisted members are physically demanding and can often place them directly in harm's way.

Because of duty demands and the operational credo that "the mission comes first," there is often very little personal time for military members to be with their families.  To further compound the difficulties of time management, there are numerous required unit functions that occur outside normal duty hours that conflict with family life.  For example, unit leaders may expect members to participate in off-duty unit-sponsored social or recreational activities, designed to enhance unit cohesion and organizational *esprit de corps*.  From the unit leader's perspective, this is time well spent, but it is additional time away from the family.  In 1996, over 52 percent of married junior enlisted Navy respondents indicated that their job interfered with their family life to a moderate or great extent (Caliber Associates, 1996).  For married junior enlisted Air Force members, 40 percent responded that unpredictable work schedules interfered to a moderate or great extent with their ability to meet family responsibilities.  Over 34 percent of the same group responded that being kept at work beyond normal hours created the same problem (Caliber Associates, 1997; 1998).  These time demands make it difficult, if not impossible, for junior enlisted military members to take on a frequently needed second job to help the family financially. Conversely, on the rare occasion that the young enlisted member does get permission to take on a second job, there is even less time available for the family.

Another aspect of duty stress is the "fishbowl" effect of being in the military. Under the Uniform Code of Military Justice (UCMJ) the service member may be severely punished for behaviors that may not be considered offensive or even constitute criminal activity in the civilian community. Violations of courtesy (not saluting), bouncing a check, or not cutting the grass in installation housing can result in some sort of repercussion. While none of these behaviors would come to the attention of a civilian employer, in the military they are behaviors that could result in some type of punitive action being taken by the member's commander. In addition, the military has strict regulations against drug use and severe punishments for driving under the influence of alcohol (DUI) and other alcohol abuse. As has been highlighted in recent news stories, fraternization with a subordinate and relationships between officers and enlisted can be grounds for severe punishment. For a military member, an adulterous relationship can result in criminal prosecution. Military members are subject to maintaining their residence and their conduct, including their family members' conduct, to military standards. Families living on a military installation can lose their housing privileges as a result of the misconduct of one of the family members. The service member and his or her family members must never behave in such a manner that brings embarrassment to the military. Together, these factors create a "fishbowl" effect.

### Duty-Related Deployments and Separations

Other major military-specific stressors are deployments and duty-related separations. Military members live with the possibility of being deployed at a moment's notice. This can range from a two-day local training exercise to a prolonged mission halfway around the globe. For those in the Navy and Marine Corps, six months sea duty is standard. In a 1996 Navy survey, over 25 percent of junior enlisted service members reported being away from home for more than 180 days during the past 12 months (Caliber Associates, 1996). Army soldiers and Marines may be in the field for days or weeks of training or deployed for months on a peacekeeping mission. Air Force members are increasingly being deployed for short operational activities, although many are now experiencing six-month deployments in support of peacekeeping and other humanitarian missions around the globe. Although 60 percent of junior enlisted Air Force respondents reported being away from home fewer than 14 days during the past year, an average of 25 percent reported being away from home between 14 and 90 days during that same period (Caliber Associates, 1997; 1998). Even in so-called peacekeeping roles, there is the reality, more often for those in the Marines and the Army, of being directly in harm's way. For family members waiting at home, there is the uncertainty of not knowing exactly where the service member is, whether or not there will be consistent lines of communication, and when he or she will return.

These separations create a number of problems for all military members and their families.  They are especially acute for the first-term young military family.  Often there is no extended family nearby to lend support, and returning "home" to be with extended family is often not an option.  This can be more of a problem when the young military family is stationed overseas and the service member is deployed.  Not only are these families new to the military and away from their extended families, but they must learn to cope with a different culture and language.  They may find it difficult to become comfortable in the communities outside the installation.  These families often remain isolated and unhappy during their entire overseas tour.

If the service member is a single parent or part of a dual-military couple with children, there is the added stress of finding someone reliable to take care of their children during their deployment.  While stationed in the United States, this task sometimes falls to the member's parents or other extended family members.  Overseas, it is much more difficult to work out satisfactory arrangements.  For junior enlisted members overseas, desirable arrangements (such as flying family members in to care for children) are typically unaffordable.  Single parents and dual-military couples must develop a Family Care Plan and in it clearly designate who will take care of their child or children while they are deployed or away on temporary duty.  They must also obtain a power of attorney for their caretaker to act for them while they are deployed.  Experiences during the Persian Gulf War brought home the importance of having a reliable and adequate childcare plan.

Separation places the burden of responsibility for the day-to-day running of the family squarely on the shoulders of the spouse who remains at home (or for single parents and dual-military couples, on their designated childcare provider).  The at-home spouse must cope with emergencies such as car problems, house repairs, illnesses, or injury as well as the many normal daily household problems.  In addition, family financial management and the provision of a healthy environment for rearing and disciplining children are the responsibilities of this spouse.  Often the smooth execution of these responsibilities requires that the spouse have a power of attorney.  This document must have been completed prior to the member's departure.

Deployments and separations interfere with the service member's ability to obtain and to maintain a second job to supplement the family income.  The job is often lost when the member deploys.  A job held by the civilian spouse may also be jeopardized by the added burden of managing the family alone during deployment, or the inability to pay for childcare to replace the childcare previously provided by the deployed service member.

## Relocation

A third duty-related stressor for many young first-term families is relocation associated with the service members' first assignment or their reassignment to a new installation.  This may be the first time the young couple has lived away from home and extended family and from the support systems they have always had.  Relocation is more difficult when the first assignment is overseas and the family must adjust to both a new culture and a new language. Relocation can create financial problems. There are usually out-of-pocket moving expenses that are not reimbursed by the military. For example, 39 percent of junior enlisted Air Force families found that their unreimbursed moving expenses were higher than they expected (Caliber Associates, 1997; 1998). Many military members take an advance on their military pay to help offset relocation expenses. Their regular paycheck is then reduced until the advance is paid back. Relocation requires good planning and often tests a young couple's money management skills.

Some families will encounter a local cost of living at their new duty station that is higher than what the military reimburses. This high cost of living may require choices and compromises on housing quality and safety. It may require the nonmember spouse to seek employment outside the home or the service member to consider taking on a second job. For the Navy, 9 percent of junior enlisted respondents, and for the Air Force, 8 percent of junior enlisted respondents reported having a second job (Caliber Associates, 1996; 1997; 1998). Moving upsets the young family's balance. Although there is support offered to relocating families by the services, many families are unaware of the programs and services or do not live close enough to the installation to take full advantage of them.

Table 3.1 offers a summary of some of the important issues discussed in this chapter. The table also reminds the human service provider that the military family, even the young first term family, often has a number of certain strengths.

Table 3.1
**First Term Military Family Issues**

| Issue | Potential Strengths | Potential Weaknesses |
|---|---|---|
| **Financial Management** | Commissary, exchange, medical care, and support services help reduce cost of living. | • Limited, fixed income.<br>• Pre- and post-enlistment debts.<br>• Lack of money management skills. |
| **Housing** | Access to government quarters or the provision of a housing allowance helps ensure adequate housing. | • Government housing may be substandard.<br>• Civilian housing costs may exceed housing allowance resulting in inadequate, substandard, and/or unsafe housing and/or housing a great distance from the installation.<br>• There are significant costs associated with setting up a first household. |
| **Spouse Employment** | Spouse employment may supplement family income, and work relationships may provide a source of social support. | • Often the only available and/or accessible job is low level, low wage and provides little or no career opportunity.<br>• Available employment may not cover expenses of working (i.e., childcare, transportation, etc.). |
| **Child-care** | Quality childcare is usually available on the installation. | • Childcare costs create a financial burden.<br>• Childcare hours may not correspond with duty hours. |

**Table 3.1 (continued)**

| Issue | Potential Strengths | Potential Weaknesses |
|---|---|---|
| Extended Family | Couple can make their own decisions without excessive extended family interference. | • Couples are often making own decisions for the first time.<br>• There may be no extended family support available for emergencies. |
| Duty Demands | The military member has the opportunity to learn a work ethic, a sense of personal responsibility, and gain technical skills. | • Duty hours are often more than 8 hours/day, individuals may work rotating or 12-hour shifts (military duty is 24 hours a day/7 days a week), and this often interferes with family time.<br>• The military expects high standards of personal and family member conduct and exerts a variety of social control mechanisms on personal and family life. |
| Deployment/ Separation | There is considerable support available from military installation agencies and unit family support groups. | • A spouse may not have adequate experience for being totally responsible for running a household on his or her own.<br>• A spouse may have a limited personal support network. |
| Relocation | New assignments provide opportunity to see new places and meet new people. | • All moving costs are not covered by military allowance, causing financial hardship.<br>• Moving is stressful, especially for those with limited experience in moving and setting up a household. |
| General Issues | Many young couples are resilient and possess a sense of adventure. | • Spouse and military member are going through a multitude of personal and marital life adjustments all at one time.<br>• Military duties and duty demands can be very stressful.<br>• Couples do not have the benefit of extended family and long-time friendships as sources of immediate support. |

## SUMMARY AND IMPLICATIONS

Service providers should become familiar with the many military-sponsored programs and services available to service members and their families to assist in their successful transition into military life. Formally, there are the programs and services offered by the services' Family Centers; Morale, Welfare, and Recreation; sponsorship programs; and installation newcomer orientation programs. Informally, each military unit (or unit spouse organization) may have a welcoming guideline. Each branch of the military has an aid society (Army Emergency Relief, Navy and Marine Corps Relief, and the Air Force Aid Society) that offers assistance in times of emergency. Many of these agencies have special services and assistance targeted to the young military family.

Every sizeable military installation has a Family Center that offers a variety of programs and services. These include financial management, spouse employment assistance, family life education, relocation assistance, and information and referral. The chaplains and mental health providers on base offer services and support to young families. There are special programs targeted to reducing some of the stresses of being a young family in the military. The New Parent Support Programs offered by each of the services focus on first-time parents (see chapter 13 for a detailed description of these programs) and are designed to assist young (often at-risk) parents in learning parenting skills. Each service also has a Family Advocacy Program that offers a variety of services to prevent family violence (see chapters 11, 12, and 13 for descriptions of these services).

Within the local civilian community there may also be programs and services that could benefit the young, first-term military family, especially if where they live makes it difficult for them to use the services offered on the installation. Spouses may need or desire referrals to local civilian resources that provide education, training, or employment. Some young military families are eligible for food stamps; Women, Infants, and Children (WIC) program; or even public assistance.

It is important for service providers to be sensitive to the potential ambivalence from these young military families about accepting assistance from military and civilian human service agencies. Despite all of the available services and programs offered on or near almost all military installations, the young family is often reluctant to take advantage of them for fear of the effect of seeking help on their careers. It is important to recognize that many family issues are unique to the military. There are numerous programs and services provided by the military and the community to address them. The context in which these services are provided (e.g., a caring approach and an understanding of the demands of military life) is the key to successfully helping these young families adjust and thrive in the military.

## REFERENCES

Caliber Associates. (1996). *1996 Navy Needs Assessment Survey*. Washington, DC: United States Navy.

Caliber Associates. (1997). *United States Air Force Community Needs Assessment*. Washington, DC: United States Air Force.

Caliber Associates. (1998). *United States Air Force Community Needs Assessment*. Washington, DC: United States Air Force.

General Accounting Office (GAO). (1997). *Military attrition: DOD could save millions by better screening enlisted personnel* (GAO/NSIAD-97–39). Washington, DC: GAO.

Military Family Resource Center. (1998). *Profile of the military community: 1997 Demographics*. Arlington, VA: Military family Resource Center.

Twiss, P.C., & Martin, J.A. (1998). *Quality of life and shelter: A history of military housing policy and initiatives since the adoption of the All-Volunteer Force concept (1973-1996)* (MFI Technical Report 98-1). Scranton, PA: Military Family Institute of Marywood College.

# Chapter 4

# Coping with the Unique Demands of Military Family Life

*Leora N. Rosen and Doris B. Durand*

## INTRODUCTION

The military life stresses discussed in the previous chapter are not unique to junior enlisted families and affect military families at all stages of the life cycle to a greater or lesser degree. Changes in military family policies and the changing nature of military service described in Chapter 1 have had an impact on military family members' subjective experience of certain life stressors and quality-of-life issues in the military. This chapter describes the changes that have occurred over the past decade in spouses' perceptions of military-specific stressors, the resources and supports provided by the military to help sustain families as they confront these stressors, and spouses' overall satisfaction with military family life. Data for this chapter come from five Army family surveys conducted in the 1980s and 1990s. In addition, it includes comments made by spouses as part of the qualitative data gathered in these large-scale studies.

This chapter examines changes and consistencies over the past decade in some of the common stresses experienced by Army spouses as a result of the demands of service life. It examines stress mediators, particularly the informal social supports that ameliorate some of these stressors and enable spouses to cope. Certainly not all military spouses react in the same way to these unique military lifestyle demands. For example, while for many spouses the frequent relocations are highly stressful, for some moving is enjoyable. Research results must be interpreted in the light of these individual differences, even when reporting on some of the most stressful aspects of military life. While these data are specific to Army spouses, there are many aspects of military family life that are shared by all military spouses regardless of their unique service affliation.

This chapter is based on data from two main groups of studies: the first is the Army's Unit Manning System Family Health Study, a longitudinal study involving two waves of data collection from 1985 to 1986. The second is the Survey of Army Families, a series of cross-sectional studies of the entire Army conducted in 1987, 1991, and 1995 under the sponsorship of the U.S. Army Community and Family Support Center. The chapter also includes information from other studies conducted in response to specific events or problems. Because the overwhelming percentage of "military spouses" are women, the presentation of data from these studies will focus primarily on the "traditional" military family—the male military husband and the female civilian spouse.

The five primary surveys presented in this chapter are summarized in Table 4.1. For ease of reading, they will be referred to in the text of this chapter by the year each study was initiated: 1985 and 1986 for the two-phased Unit Manning System Family Health Study and 1987, 1991, and 1995 for the three Surveys of Army Families.

**Table 4.1**
**Studies Contributing to This Chapter**

Study Name:  Unit Manning System Family Health Study (UMS I).  Date: 1985
Sample:  Participants included wives of soldiers from 12 battalions participating in the Unit Manning System Field Evaluation.  Survey questionnaires were mailed to approximately 3,000 wives, and a total of 945 subjects returned completed questionnaires representing a 33% return rate.

Study Name:  Unit Manning System Family Health Study (UMS II).  Date: 1986
Sample:  The second survey included all those who participated in the first survey plus spouses from an additional battalion.  The overall response rate at time 2 was 40%, with 1,148 spouses returning completed questionnaires.

Study Name:  Survey of Army Families (SAF I).  Date: 1987
Sample:  In SAF I, 20,272 questionnaires were sent to a random sample of civilian spouses of active duty Army soldiers worldwide.  The overall response rate was 67% adjusting for undeliverable questionnaires.

Study Name:  Survey of Army Families (SAF II).  Date: 1991
Sample:  In SAF II, 8,000 questionnaires were sent to Army spouses residing in the United States, Alaska, Korea and Panama, but not to those in Europe, who were surveyed separately.  A total of 3,006 spouses returned questionnaires, representing a response rate of 37%.

Study Name:  Survey of Army Families (SAF III).  Date: 1995
Sample:  In SAF III, survey questionnaires were mailed to 33,000 spouses of active duty soldiers.  This included an over sampling of male spouses and Army spouses in Europe (USAREUR).  The response rate was 48%, with a total of 12,561 spouses participating in the study.

There have been many changes in military life since the Unit Manning System Family Health Study was conducted in 1985 to 1986. For example, the number of military families stationed overseas has decreased and the number of military deployments has increased. Nevertheless, a number of important military life issues and their consequences have remained constant. For example, families remain concerned about issues such as finances and insufficient family time.

## THE STRESS AND SATISFACTION OF MILITARY LIFE

This chapter considers seven areas that are thought to be important influences on stress and satisfaction associated with military family life—mission-related stress, financial well-being, housing and community, military community services, spouses' unit, family support activities, and the military (Army)–family interface. Each of these areas has received varying degrees of attention in the surveys presented in this chapter. Typically, they are considered core components of overall military family quality of life.

### Mission-Related Stress

The term "mission-related stress" refers to the specific stresses related to the military mission, namely separations due to field duty, deployments, unaccompanied overseas tours, frequent relocations, and the dangers of combat. In the 1985 study, these stressors were found to contribute significantly to increased psychological distress among Army spouses. For example, husbands' deployment was associated with elevated symptoms of depressed mood among these spouses (Rosen, Carpenter, & Moghadam, 1989).

*Separation.* Although military families have always been subject to separation, since the Persian Gulf War Army families (as well as families in the other services) have been vulnerable to an ever-increasing number of soldier absences. In the *Army 1997-98 Green Book* (West, 1997, p. 13) Togo West, then Secretary of the Army, noted: "Last May, worldwide deployments reached their highest mark in the Army's 222 year history. More than 33,300 active and reserve component soldiers and civilians performed more that 1,200 missions in 100 countries. These included operational missions, multinational exercises, and humanitarian and peacekeeping operations."

Despite the increase in the number of deployments over the past decade, it is noteworthy that the proportion of spouses reporting severe stress as a result of separation has actually decreased from 17 percent in 1985 to 6 percent in 1995. In all the studies during this period, however, many spouses wrote comments about separation experiences filled with a sense of loneliness, anxiety, and depression. During separations, most spouses described themselves as solely responsible for maintaining the household, caring for children, and resolving family problems. There were, however, some positive comments, with a number of spouses saying that separations provided an opportunity to develop greater independence.

*Perceived Dangers Associated with Military Training and Combat.*  One of the very real changes affecting spouses over the last decade is how the media can bring the immediate (if not live) action of combat into their lives.  Many spouses were "glued" to their television sets during the Persian Gulf War watching CNN coverage of military activities in the Gulf region while they were actually taking place.  Some spouses actually found the coverage too upsetting to watch.  One consequence of such coverage is the increased degree of fear spouses have for the well-being of their loved ones.  For example, 73 percent of the spouses surveyed during the Gulf War (1991) reported severe stress associated with their concern that their spouses would be sent to a place where actual combat could occur.  This can be compared to 46 percent of spouses who expressed these same concerns in 1986, a period when there was no combat.

Training exercises are also an important contributor to stress among spouses.  The absence of the service member combines with the possibility of accidents during training.  In the 1985 survey, 21 percent of spouses experienced severe stress over concerns about their husbands' safety at work.  This is considerably lower than the percentage experiencing concerns about combat.

*Relocation.*  Relocation is a fact of life for most military families, and the military understands that one of the most significant stressors associated with relocation is the length of time that families have to wait for permanent housing.  According to the 1987 study, almost half of families surveyed had been waiting three months or more for permanent housing.  Typically, military families may make several moves as part of moving to a new military base.  For enlisted families relocation often involves going from guest quarters to a series of apartments before they find one that they can afford or that meets their basic needs.  During this time, considerable costs may accumulate.  The 1987 survey found that 51 percent of families had unreimbursed moving costs of $500 or more, while 12 percent had unreimbursed costs of $2,000 or more.

Military relocation services typically include premove destination information, lending closets, temporary lodging, relocation counseling, and orientation briefings.  The 1991 survey found that 60 percent of spouses were satisfied with the relocation assistance they had received from the military.  This sense of satisfaction contributed greatly to overall satisfaction with Army life (Rosenberg, 1995).

The reaction of wives to constant mobility is an important determinant of their level of stress.  Not all spouses found relocation to be a negative experience.  Some survey respondents said moving did not bother them—they had adjusted and enjoyed seeing new places and meeting new people.  One comment writer was disappointed that they hadn't moved enough, another noted that moving around drew their family together since they had to rely on each other, and some felt relocation was one of the benefits Army life had to offer.  However, a similar number found moving stressful and worried about selling the house or transporting furniture.  A few spouses also felt moving disrupted their children's education and friendships.

*Housing and Community.* In the 1985 study, 42 percent of the spouses in this sample lived in on-post government housing, 41 percent lived off post in rented houses or apartments, and 17 percent lived in homes that they were purchasing in the civilian community. Several women in the survey wrote comments expressing dissatisfaction with housing. Many expressed concern about the insufficient on-post housing and long waiting lists.

Since that time, housing has undergone some significant changes. This includes the closure of many bases in Europe and a number of bases in the United States, all forcing the relocation of thousands of military families. In response to congressional and Department of Defense concerns for lower-ranking families, more on-post housing has been made available to junior enlisted families. Because there has not been an overall expansion of housing resources, more senior service families now have to live off post. According to the 1995 survey, 34 percent of spouses reported that they lived on post in government housing, 34 percent rented off post, 23 percent were buying their own homes, and 7 percent lived in off-post government housing. This represents an overall decrease in on-post housing since 1985, but there has been an increase in home ownership. This is important, in the light of a finding from the 1991 survey, which showed that home ownership contributes greatly to satisfaction with housing. A full 88 percent of those who were purchasing their own homes in 1991 were satisfied with their housing compared to 68 percent who lived on post and 49 percent who lived off post in rented or government housing. Satisfaction with housing had a significant influence on the psychological well-being of spouses in the 1985 study (Rosen, Carpenter, & Moghadam, 1989). Overall satisfaction with housing, however, has changed little since the 1985 study.

A major source of dissatisfaction in the 1985 and 1986 studies was spouses' assessment of the cost of off-post housing. In their view the high cost aggravated the housing problem by straining the family budget. Again, financial burdens were viewed as the heaviest for junior enlisted families, especially those junior enlisted families' forced to live in civilian housing in high-cost areas of the country. Data are not available from the earlier studies on the percentage of spouses who were concerned with the cost of housing. In the 1995 survey, however, one-third of spouses were greatly concerned about the cost of housing, and 24 percent were moderately concerned.

Regarding community and neighborhood, many spouses in the 1985 and 1986 studies expressed dissatisfaction with their geographic location. Typically, they were bothered by distance from friends and family and the high cost of living. Many preferred to be closer to an urban area in order to enhance spouse employment opportunities. Those who enjoyed where they were living discussed the friendly community or proximity to extended family members. For some, being far from home made adjustment to military life more difficult. Several spoke of the cost of traveling home or keeping in touch by telephone. Those close to home and extended family appeared much happier. As before, the high cost of living at certain post locations aggravated what spouses considered to be an insufficient income.

Over the past decade there has been little increase in severe stress related to maintaining contact with extended family members, but there has been some increase in moderate levels of stress. In 1985, for example 9 percent of spouses reported severe stress associated with their difficulty maintaining contact with their own extended family. By 1995, 12 percent expressed severe stress. In 1985, 14 percent expressed moderate stress concerning difficulty maintaining contact with extended family. By 1995 this had increased to 24 percent.

*Financial Well-Being.* Concerns about financial matters were found to contribute significantly to spouses' overall psychological distress in the 1985 study (Rosen, Carpenter & Moghadam, 1989). Spouses described precarious family financial positions—running out of money before the end of the month, living "paycheck to paycheck," and having little or no savings. Enlisted and first-term wives were especially anxious, and the high cost of living at some posts exacerbated these problems.

A decade later (1998), the financial status of soldiers and their families was still a problem. In 1995, many spouses reported that they had to use means other than their husband's military paycheck to keep their families fed and clothed. Within the last two years, 20 percent of these families had used the Women Infant, and Children program (WIC); 14 percent used free or reduced-price school lunches; 12 percent needed to use Army Emergency Relief (AER) financial assistance; and 4 percent needed food stamps. Furthermore, 64 percent of employed spouses in the 1995 study said that they worked because their family needed money for basic expenses.

*Job Security and Benefits.* When the 1985 study was conducted, well over half of the respondents were satisfied with their husband's job security in the military, and many commented that job security greatly alleviated the stress of military life. In addition, one-third of these spouses were satisfied with Army pay and allowances. Since that time there have been major changes in military job security and benefits. After the end of the Cold War, the Army reduced the size of its active component by 36 percent, the reserve component by 33 percent, the Army National Guard by 20 percent, and Department of Army civilians by 37 percent. This translates into a loss of 620,000 soldiers and civilian employees (West, 1997, p. 15). Similar downsizing has occurred in the other services.

Although a major portion of the planned downsizing of the Department of Defense has been accomplished, many spouses remain quite concerned that their families will be affected by future personnel reductions. In the 1995 survey one-fourth of all spouses expressed serious concerns regarding the possibility of involuntary separation. This was down from 37 percent in 1991.

In 1991, job security and benefits were the top reasons given by Army spouses for wanting to stay in the Army. Fifty percent of spouses said that security and stability were reasons for remaining in the Army, while 33 percent gave retirement benefits and 36 percent cited medical care as reasons. Only 19 percent gave current military pay and allowances as a reason. This may indicate a downward shift from 1985, when well over half of spouses were satisfied with job security in the Army, and a third were satisfied with pay and allowances.

Though half of the 1985 respondents indicated satisfaction with retirement benefits, this decreased the following year to 38 percent, dropping to a level more in line with that of 1991.

### Military and Other Community Services

*Childcare.* Finding suitable, affordable day care is a persistent problem for military families. A total of 70 to 80 percent of parents with children use some form of childcare. Overall, the most common type of childcare used is an unlicensed baby-sitter. Employed parents, however, are more likely to use in-home licensed care, on-post day care, or preschools. According to the 1987 study, 8 percent of parents of infants and toddlers, and 11 percent of parents of preschoolers used day care on post. This was similar to 1995 data in which 11 percent of parents with children four years or younger used on-post day care. The 1991 study indicated a slightly higher usage (14 percent).

Satisfaction with Army day care has increased over time. In the 1987 study, 58 percent of parents were satisfied with the quality of on-post day care, compared with 60 percent in 1991, and 67 percent in 1995. Satisfaction with availability of care has been consistently lower than satisfaction with quality. An average of 49 percent of spouses were satisfied with availability in 1987 compared with 46 percent in 1991, but in 1995 this had increased to 58 percent. Satisfaction with drop-in care also improved from 39 percent in 1987 and 36 percent in 1991 to 44 percent in 1995. Satisfaction with the cost of care, however, has not improved; it was 46 percent in 1987 and 44 percent in 1995. No data on cost are available for 1991. The authors of the SAF I report based on the 1987 study noted that a great disparity existed between officer spouse views and enlisted spouse views. Only 42 percent of enlisted spouses were satisfied with the cost of day care, compared with 60 percent of officers' spouses.

*Other Military Community Services and Programs.* The Army, like the other service branches, provides an array of services and programs to active-duty members and their families. For example, the Army Community Services (ACS) program includes spouse employment counseling, relocation assistance, financial counseling, information and referral services, and even assistance with tax preparation. Availability of specific programs varies from post to post. Usage of ACS programs has increased over the past decade. According to the 1987 study, 55 percent of spouses had used ACS programs at their current location, while in 1995 66 percent of spouses had used such programs. This increase may be due to the expansion in the number and availability of programs rather than an increase in the use of specific programs. Some usage has decreased, for example the ACS information and referral program, and the financial counseling program.

The Army and other service branches provides Morale, Welfare, and Recreation (MWR) programs such as library services, sports, and various recreational services. Usage of these services and programs has decreased over the past decade, especially the use of library services. Consumer services such as the commissary and PX are used consistently by virtually everyone.

SAF I (1987) reported that overall 80 percent of users of ACS programs were satisfied. However, by 1995 only 58 percent of respondents reported being satisfied. Since there was no apparent change in the nature of these programs over this period, one possible explanation for this drop in satisfaction may be increased customer expectations. When weighing overall satisfaction with community services, survey respondents who wrote comments were divided in their opinions. Some felt the services were "unbeatable," run by "caring people who can help you with any problem you may have," and "make being in the Army worthwhile." Others complained that agency workers were "rude and uncooperative" and that "the hardships of Army life weren't compensated by free services."

### Health Care

Health care is seen as an important military benefit, yet medical care for the military has changed drastically over the past 10 years. In 1985 most active-duty military family members were receiving their medical care from military health care providers in military medical facilities. Today, a great deal of the required medical care for family members is provided by contract employees working in military medical care facilities, or the care is provided in the civilian sector as part of the military's new TRICARE program—a focused effort to partner military and contracted civilian health care resources into a program that offers military members and their families, as well as retired members and their families, a choice between "managed care" using a combination of military and civilian health care providers in a health maintenance format and a more traditional (but more expensive for the consumer) open fee-for-service care.

Despite the changes in health care services between 1985 and 1995, all three SAF studies indicated that 90 percent or more of spouses had used Army medical facilities at their current location, and, furthermore, satisfaction with the quality of care appears to have increased over this period. In 1985, only 35 percent of spouses were satisfied with the quality of medical care, while in 1987, 47 percent were satisfied. In 1991 and 1995, 61 percent and 57 percent respectively were satisfied with medical care.

Satisfaction with treatment by doctors and support staff appears to have remained the same over the years, with over half of all spouses expressing satisfaction. On the other hand, satisfaction with certain aspects of access to care (for example, getting appointments and hours of operation) appears to have decreased, which is consistent with the known reductions in the availability of military health care facilities. It is yet to be seen how family members will view the new TRICARE program. Initial reports suggest that there is considerable dissatisfaction with access, cost, and overall quality of care under this new program.

The most frequent complaint about medical care from the written comments of these earlier surveys was the way patients were treated by hospital staff members. Typical comments referred to "uncaring," "condescending," and "incompetent" staff. Some spouses felt that they were treated impersonally as if they were "nobodies" or "not human." The quality of care was described as "incomplete," "rushed," and "substandard." Others, however, were enthusiastic about the quality of military medical care. As one woman said: "I don't think I could've gotten better care in a civilian hospital, no how, no way."

Trouble obtaining appointments was another problem that was frequently mentioned in the comments, especially by working women. Spouses complained of long waiting periods, which included long waits in the emergency room.

The 1991 study reported a strong correlation between global satisfaction with medical care and the Army way of life and noted that "medical care has a more significant impact on general satisfaction with the Army way of life than almost any other program or service" (Rosenberg, 1992). This corroborates findings from 1985 (Rosen, Carpenter, & Moghadam, 1989).

## THE SOLDIER'S UNIT

### Leadership

Army leadership support and concern, particularly at the small unit level, was found to be significantly related to spouses' satisfaction with Army life (Rosen, Carpenter, & Moghadam, 1989). Unfortunately, satisfaction with leadership has tended to be low. In the 1985 and 1986 studies, only 27 percent to 30 percent of spouses expressed satisfaction with leadership in the soldier's unit. Lack of concern for the individual soldier was associated with leaders' failure to encourage their soldiers on the job and with a lack of effort to secure promotions, heavy job demands, and a general lack of consideration for the soldier's welfare. These concerns included soldiers being poorly fed when out in the field or not getting a break after an arduous field exercise. Poor leaders were defined as incompetent, out of date, lacking flexibility or common sense, caring only for themselves and their careers, showing little appreciation for the soldiers' efforts, and practicing favoritism. This contributed to negative attitudes toward the Army as a whole.

Disrespect toward spouses by unit leaders was also specifically mentioned. Several spouses quoted unit leaders as saying, "if the Army wanted the soldier to have a wife, they would have issued him one." This phrase can be interpreted as a sign of disrespect for military families and no doubt was seen as disrespect by these women. From their perspective, this negative attitude toward families intensified during soldiers' absences.

Satisfaction with leadership appeared to have increased slightly in the 1991 and 1995 studies. A total of 37 percent of spouses in the 1991 study and the

1995 study were satisfied with the leadership of officers, and 39 percent to 40 percent were satisfied with the leadership of noncommissioned officers.

### Work Hours and Time Management

Another area of great concern to spouses is the time their husbands spend on the job. A large number of respondents in the 1985 and 1986 studies complained about their husbands' long duty hours and excessive time away from home for training. They described the long hours as "the pits," precluding "a healthy home life." Only 25 percent were satisfied with spouse's duty hours. In addition, only 17 percent to 21 percent were satisfied with the unit-training schedule. In 1995, 56 percent of spouses reported that they would not know when their husbands would be able to leave work at the end of the duty day; 49 percent reported that their husbands would often be unexpectedly kept at work beyond normal duty hours, and 28 percent noted that their important plans had to be canceled due to the soldiers' unpredictable work schedule. This situation has certainly not improved and may even have worsened; in 1987, 39 percent of spouses said that the soldier seldom came home when expected at the end of the duty day. The 1987 study found that uncertainty about the soldier's work schedule contributed significantly to lower psychological well-being among Army spouses (Rosen & Moghadam, 1991).

Perceived disorganization within the unit was another area of concern ascribed to poor leadership. This perception was linked to information dissemination and work policies. Units were perceived to be disorganized because they were "always saying one thing, doing something else and in general keeping the wives pretty confused about field time, duty hours, time off, etc." Inflexible time-off policies, having to work late, and doing menial chores or no chores during the workday was seen as inefficiency on the part of the units.

## FAMILY SUPPORT GROUPS

The Army has been aware, at least since the Vietnam War, of the importance of informal support networks among Army spouses as a source of assistance, particularly during deployments. The UMS studies found that social support from other spouses within the soldier's unit buffered military spouses against the stress of soldier absences due to field duty and that support from nonunit wives was not as effective as support from spouses within the company or battalion (Rosen & Moghadam, 1990).

The Army attempted to institutionalize this support after the Persian Gulf War by mandating that all units establish volunteer-led Family Support Groups (FSGs). Prior to this mandate, the development of these groups received a great deal of impetus during the 1980s Unit Manning System experiment, which was designed to foster cohesive units with strong support systems (Rosen & Moghadam, 1989a). Following the Persian Gulf War, the Army Center for Lessons Learned stated that FSGs play a central role in sustaining families by providing social and emotional support before, during and after family separation (Teitelbaum & Rosenberg, 1996).

Research has shown that a large percentage of spouses actively participate in FSGs when soldiers are deployed. As expected, when the deployments are over, the participation rate drops off. In 1995 just about half (52 percent) of the survey respondents reported that their soldiers' units had an FSG, which is consistent with findings from earlier studies conducted after the Gulf War. However, in these earlier studies, only 66 percent of those who had FSGs said that these were active, compared with 74 percent in 1995. Of those 1995 respondents who reported their FSG as active, 42 percent said it was doing a good job in supporting families. This is slightly lower than the proportion of spouses during the Gulf War who thought that their FSGs were performing well.

While data indicate that participation in FSGs can be an important source of social support mediating stress, there are a number of factors that have a negative effect on the FSG's ability to provide support and to sustain itself. Among these factors are service member's rank, the feeling that FSG participation is forced on spouses, and the use of the FSG as a gossip mill.

In the 1985 study, most informal friendships within the unit occurred between women whose soldier-husbands were of similar rank (Rosen & Moghadam, 1989b). This is understandable because most people feel comfortable among those they perceive as their social equals. However, the hierarchical structure of the Army is a potential source of difficulty for the effective running of an FSG in which spouses married to soldiers of vastly different ranks must come together voluntarily to give and receive informational, emotional, and instrumental support. Lower ranking spouses can be made to feel inferior and have their opinions disregarded. One officer's wife quoted the highest-ranking wife in her support group as saying, "This is not a democracy. What the major's wife says goes." In the interviews we conducted, feelings of intimidation were expressed by some junior enlisted wives. For example, one junior wife stated that she didn't know any officers' wives since she "was not on their social level." Another enlisted wife commented that officers' wives look at enlisted men's wives as if "we're better than you and make you feel out of place." These feelings are apparently fairly common and appear to reflect husbands' attitudes and beliefs about fraternization as illustrated by the comments of a junior enlisted wife who reported "some officers tell their sergeants not to associate with the lower ranks."

A second problem was the perceived forced nature of the participation in FSGs—an issue often raised by respondents from the 1985 and 1986 studies who wrote comments. This problem was particularly evident among senior enlisted wives and officers' wives. One officer's wife reported that she was told by the colonel and lieutenant colonel's wives that if she did not support battalion functions it would reflect on her husband's evaluation report. The wife of a master sergeant was told that her husband would be replaced if she didn't participate. Today, the official rule is that a spouse's participation cannot be reflected in a service member's evaluation, although some wives still believe that what they do or do not do will have a bearing on their husband's career. During a deployment to Bosnia, one commander's wife said: "I don't think it would hurt my husband's career if I didn't participate." Another commander's wife in the same group said: "If you're not involved, you're ostracized."

A third factor that may hamper participation in the FSGs is the concern that these meetings serve as a way of pipelining information about family problems back to those in command. Several officers' wives noted that this is a belief on the part of junior enlisted soldiers who "refuse to allow their wives to attend." There is some indication that this type of distrust inhibits horizontal bonding. Several comment-writers stated their reluctance to confide in other spouses in the soldier's unit for fear that the information would somehow harm his career. As one wife wrote: "I made a sincere effort to make time to join our present FSG, boy, was that a huge mistake. There were NCO's wives who loved to gossip. I will never again trust anyone in our support group. I am keeping to myself. So much for 'Family Support.' "

Factors such as these, whether real or perceived, seem to be effective barriers to participation in the FSGs, despite the fact that the FSGs offer the best potential source for both vertical and horizontal support among spouses. One wife revealed how rewarding the FSGs can be when they work successfully: "We have a strong and great FSG program. I am very active and I feel this helps with the stress factor while our husbands are gone. I love the FSG. It's about time the Army started caring about the families."

## FAMILY LIFE IN THE ARMY

In the 1985 study, the level of dissatisfaction with the kind of family life that one can have in the Army was similar across all rank groups. According to those who chose to write comments, Army-related stresses took their toll on the family in several ways.

### Family Time

Insufficient time the soldier spent with the family forced spouses with children to play two roles. Comment-writers expressed anger and frustration at having to be both mother and father—"and not get paid for it!" One bitter wife stated: "I never wanted to become a single mother and I didn't marry to be alone." Some observed the emotional stress, noting their children were lonely and worried about their fathers. "The frequency and the irregularity of field duty seems to rob our family of the continuity our son needs," added another mother.

Spouses felt that the soldiers also suffered. "Husbands do miss an awful lot of milestones in their children's lives." The following comment from a 1985 study respondent highlights the conflict that many soldiers face in meeting both their military and parental demands: "The Army in general gives you what you need (a house, paid medical) but in between the lines is what most people will give up ten years of service for—never being home for the firsts in your child's life—having your four year old daughter ask for an 'all the time daddy' for Christmas." Soldiers may be unavailable not only physically but also emotionally. Even when they do get time off, "they're too tired to do anything."

### Marriage

The quality of many marriages seems to suffer. Spouses feel the Army is not conducive to a strong family and that military attitudes have considerable impact on marital stability. One spouse wrote, "I can foresee lots of families falling apart if some (Army) attitudes toward the men and their families don't change." Marital problems and the perceived high divorce rates in the armed forces were viewed in the studies to be a result of long hours and separation, financial stress, and frequent moves. "I'm sure the long hours and little pay have a lot to do with all the divorces"; "I have seen several marriages end due to the stress of not enough money and the long working hours seven days a week. The stress is sometimes more than we can bear."

Spouses want to see their soldiers more often and share more quality time with them. They feel it is important to spend time together as a family. The anxiety of those living far from family and friends is further compounded. Some spouses noted not only the impact of scheduling on their families but the emotional carryover as well: "I feel that military life has caused most of our marital problems. My husband is under so much pressure from his superiors. Depending on what happens at work causes his mood swings at home."

Several spouses expressly blamed the Army and its policies for marital breakup. Even spouses who noted that it was possible to maintain a good marriage within the military, and that military life could even draw some couples closer, admitted that sustaining a marriage within the Army was very difficult. Many spouses observed that newlywed couples were especially vulnerable: "If couples didn't have a good marriage to begin with, it couldn't survive the Army."

### The Army-Family Interface

Research has shown that soldiers' and spouses' perceptions of the fit between Army life and family life is a major determinant of spouses' overall satisfaction with Army life, with soldiers' and spouses' desire to remain in the Army, and with soldiers' personal morale. Results of the 1985 and 1986 studies indicate that spouses' attitudes toward whether or not soldiers should stay in the Army had a significant effect on actual reenlistment (Moghadam, 1990). These attitudes were primarily influenced by the Army-Family Interface. Similar results were obtained in the Operation Desert Storm Family Health Study (Rosen, Westhuis & Teitelbaum, 1993). Factors used to assess the Army-Family Interface include perceptions of the Army's concern for families, the kind of family life one can have in the Army, and the extent to which the Army shows respect for spouses. Spouses' perceptions of the Army-Family Interface are strongly influenced by satisfaction with small-unit leadership, and satisfaction with soldiers' work schedule.  Furthermore, spouses' satisfaction with soldiers' work schedules has been shown to have an impact on soldiers' personal morale (Rosen, Moghadam, & Vaitkus, 1989).

Paralleling empirical research on the impact of the family on the soldier's ability to do his job, many spouses also recognize the relationship between happy home lives and effective soldiers.  Comments from several spouses offer corroborating evidence of the relationship between the Army-Family Interface and the soldier's personal morale: "A soldier that does not have peace of mind and is having so many family problems due to not being able to be home enough is not happy or confident in his work, and if that lacks, he is not giving his most."

The attitude that a unit has toward a soldier's family can determine whether or not the soldier is satisfied with his job, which in turn impacts on his performance at work.  The morale, care, well-being, and values of family members have not been shown enough importance at the unit level, thereby decreasing the effectiveness of the modern fighting force.

Comments from several spouses suggest that the family seems to be an active influence in the soldier's career decision.  Many wrote that they look forward to living a "normal life" and being "a real family" when they leave the Army.  Several spouses gave the negative impact on their families as the main reason they wanted their husbands to get out.  "They lose a lot of hard-working people," one spouse noted, "because of the way the Army fools around with the family."

Even with the Army's increased emphasis on families over the last decade, little appears to have changed in how spouses perceive support and concern by Army leaders for families.  This is true despite an overall decrease in perceptions of the Army's demands on families and a decrease in perceived day-to-day stress.  The higher levels of satisfaction expressed by spouses in 1991 (where 43 percent of the respondents said that they were satisfied with the Army's concern for families) probably reflect the enormous effort made by the Army to support families during the Persian Gulf deployment.  In the 1985 and 1986 surveys only 32 percent of the spouses felt this way about the Army's concern for families.  In addition only 27 percent of the 1985 sample and 23 percent of the 1986 sample felt satisfied with the respect the Army shows spouses.  This can be contrasted with the 43 percent of the 1991 respondents who felt this way about the Army's respect for spouses.

Perceptions of the kind of family life you can have in the Army do appear to have increased over the past decade.  In 1995, more than one-half of the spouses (57 percent) said that they were satisfied with the kind of family life one can have in the Army.  This is in contrast to the 44 percent who felt this way in the 1985 survey and the 36 percent who felt this way in 1986.

### Global Satisfaction with Army Life

Over the past decade, despite some fluctuations, on the average about two-thirds of Army spouses have said they would be satisfied if their husbands made the Army a career.  The percentage of spouses who express satisfaction with the Army way of life is lower than the percentage of spouses who would be satisfied if the soldier made the Army a career.  However, this percentage may be increasing.  For example, in 1985 42 percent of the spouses surveyed were satisfied with the Army way of life, and in 1995, 61 percent were satisfied with the Army as a way of life.

In 1985 and 1986 studies, most comment-writers concluded they were satisfied with their military lifestyle and were proud to be a part of it.  These spouses were proud to be able to overcome the hardships posed by military life.  They consider themselves "the backbone of the Army," with the toughest job in the Army—helping their husbands to be effective soldiers and taking on all the responsibilities demanded by running a household.  Several spouses found it "rewarding" and a "quality way of life"; they were eager to raise their children in the Army.  "It was during our years as civilians that my family found living day to day terribly stressful."  Yet many that expressed general satisfaction prefaced their comments by conceding that Army life was very difficult and took a lot of adjustment.  Even spouses who expressed overall satisfaction were not totally enthusiastic.  They considered Army life "not bad" or merely "okay."  However, while many spouses expressed serious reservations about particular aspects of military life, they did not regret the decision to live in a military setting and were basically satisfied with the Army way of life.  Only a small proportion of comment-writers wrote that the costs outweighed the benefits.

## SUMMARY AND IMPLICATIONS

Human service providers need to understand the various stressors that confront military families across the military family life cycle.  Providers also need to be knowledgeable of the sources of support that have been established by the military to assist families.  Often the task of linking families to these supports will be the most helpful thing that the civilian human service provider can do to assist a military family.  This chapter has highlighted some of the most common stressors and those sources of support typically available to the military family.

Military family members are required to make many sacrifices, and while most are prepared for this, some spouses experience considerable stress related to the uncertainties, dangers, disruptions, and separations associated with being married to a service member.  Despite the increase in the number of deployments over the past decade, separation-related stress seems to have decreased among Army spouses, yet separations remain one of the most difficult aspects of military family life.  Concerns about the dangers of combat have remained fairly constant, except immediately following the Persian Gulf War, when they were somewhat higher than usual.

Social supports can be an effective way of helping spouses cope with stress. Many formal and informal support systems have been set in place by the military specifically to assist spouses in coping with military life stress and to improve the overall quality of military family life. Among these are unit-based FSGs, which are designed to help spouses cope with the stress of deployment separations. About half of all spouses are aware of the existence of FSGs associated with their soldier's unit, and two-third to three-quarters of FSGs are very active. However, only 40 percent of spouses seem to feel that they do a good job.

The Army provides a variety of installation-level human services and various recreational programs. Utilization of specific human services tends to be low, although there has been an overall increase in the number of family members who have used Army programs and services over the past decade. This may be due to the increase in the variety of services available. However, overall satisfaction with services appears to have decreased over the past decade.

In addition to the support and recreational programs, the Army provides access to health and dental care. Overall satisfaction with the quality of care has increased over the past decade, although there has been a decrease in satisfaction with certain aspects of availability of care. This is an area of concern, because health care contributes greatly to family members' overall satisfaction with Army life. In addition, the Department of Defense has instituted TRICARE, a major change in the way health care is delivered. It will be important to see how military families accept this program.

Studies have repeatedly found that a key to positive morale for soldiers and their families lies in strong, effective, caring leadership. The Army's emphasis on the importance of leaders' concern for families may be having an effect, in that satisfaction with small-unit leadership appears to have increased slightly over the past decade, although there is much room for improvement. The most tangible evidence that the unit cares about the soldiers' family life is in the scheduling of predictable time for families to be together. This signals the acceptance by leaders of the family as an important and necessary part of the soldier's life, contributing toward well-being and enhanced military job performance. There does not appear to have been any improvement in this domain over the past decade, and it is even likely that things may have gotten worse. This issue is not unique to the Army. News accounts of Air Force pilots' decisions to leave the service continually emphasize the issues of time away from family and the lack of predictability in their duty schedules. "Family time" is obviously a critical issue for all military families.

Perceptions of the Army's concern for families and respect for spouses have not changed dramatically over the past decade, except during the Gulf War when concern was higher than usual, reflecting the huge increase in the Army's efforts to help families at that time. However, satisfaction with the kind of family life one can lead in the Army has increased over time, as has satisfaction with the Army way of life. Two-thirds of spouses have consistently said they would be satisfied if their husbands made the Army a career. Thus, despite decreases in job security and benefits packages over the past decade, and despite no improvement in the family time problem, global satisfaction with Army life has increased, and the desire to remain in the Army has remained the same. This may partly be due to the fact that new incoming soldiers and their families have reduced expectations regarding job security and benefits compared with soldiers and families of a decade ago, and they may be satisfied with less. It may also be related to increased satisfaction with domains of Army life that have a significant impact on global satisfaction, such as childcare and quality of medical care. The Army of today may attract a more resilient type of Army couple because of the increased expectation that soldiers will be sent on deployments at the present time as compared with a decade ago.

However, from the Army's perspective, there are clearly important areas that have not improved at all, or where the majority of spouses are still dissatisfied despite small improvements. Among these are satisfaction with the Army's concern for families, the respect shown to spouses, and the amount of time soldiers are allowed to spend with their families. These domains are unlikely to improve through human service or recreational programs, and are much more likely to be tied to small-unit leadership and operational tempo which reflects policies and decisions at higher levels of leadership. As the Army and the other services try to do more with less, the quality of family life even for the most resilient families may be sacrificed.

## REFERENCES

Coser, L. (1974). *Greedy institutions: Patterns of undivided commitment.* New York: Free Press.

Griffith, J. D., Stewart, L. S., & Cato, E. D. (1988). *Annual survey of Army spouses and families in 1987.* Alexandria, VA: U.S. Army Community and Family Support Center.

Moghadam, L.Z. (1990) *The reciprocal nature of work and family: Perceptions of the work/family interface and its impact on Army reenlistment behavior.* Ph.D. dissertation, University of Maryland, Department of Sociology, College Park, Maryland.

Rosen, L. N., Carpenter, C. J., & Moghadam, L. Z. (1989). Impact of military life stress on the quality of life of military wives. *Military Medicine, 154*(3), 116–120.

Rosen, L. N., & Moghadam, L. Z. (1989a). Can social supports be engineered? An example from the Army's Unit Manning System. *Journal of Applied Social Psychology, 19*(15, part 1), 1292–1309.

Rosen, L. N., & Moghadam, L. Z. (1989b). Impact of military organization on social support patterns of Army wives. *Human Organization, 48*(3), 189–195.

Rosen, L. N., & Moghadam, L. Z. (1990). Matching the support to the stressor: Implications for the buffering hypothesis. *Military Psychology, 2*(4), 193–204.

Rosen, L. N., & Moghadam, L. Z. (1991). Predictors of general well being among Army wives. *Military Medicine, 2*(156), 357–361.

Rosen, L. N., Moghadam, L. Z., & Vaitkus, M. A. (1989). The military family's influence on soldiers' personal morale: A path analytic model. *Military Psychology, 1*(4), 201–213.

Rosen, L. N., Westhuis, D. J., & Teitelbaum, J. M. (1993). Life events, social supports, and psychiatric symptoms among spouses of soldiers deployed to the Persian Gulf during Operation Desert Shield/Storm. *Journal of Applied Social Psychology,* *23*(19), 1587–1593.

Rosenberg, F. R. (1992*). Spouses of reservists and national guardsmen: A survey of effects of Desert Shield/Storm,* Unpublished manuscript, Walter Reed Army Institute of Research, Washington, DC.

Rosenberg, F. R. (1995). *Survey of Army Families II, November, 1991: A multivariate analysis of CONUS results.* Washington, DC: Department of Military Psychiatry, Walter Reed Army Institute of Research.

Segal, M. W. (1986). The military and the family as greedy institutions. *Armed Forces and Society, 13*(1), 9–38.

Teitelbaum, J.M. & Rosenberg, F. (1996). *Comparative analysis of the Survey of Army Families III with the Survey of Army Families II: Report to the U.S. Army Family and Community Support Center.* Washington, D.C.: Department of Military Psychiatry, Walter Reed Army Institute of Research.

West, T. (1997, October). America's Army meets the new millennium. *Army 1997-98 Green Book, 47*(10), 13–16 (Association of the U.S. Army).

Chapter 5

# The Role of the Senior Military Wife—Then and Now

*Doris B. Durand*

## INTRODUCTION

Based on personal life experiences as the spouse of a senior military officer and a subsequent empirical study examining role perceptions for senior officer and enlisted wives, this chapter provides a perspective on the evolving role of senior wives in military society. I became a military wife in the early 1960s and remained one until my husband retired after 24 years of active duty. I was completely integrated into the military way of life. I was unquestionably part of what Hanna Papanek (1973) referred to as the "two person career," a pattern where formal and informal demands are placed on both members of a married couple, but only one spouse, generally the man, is employed by the institution. My role in support of my husband's career was explicitly spelled out in Nancy Shea's book, *The Army Wife* (1966): "As a wife you have a most important role in your husband's Army career. His work will reflect his life at home, your attitude toward the Army, your interest in his duty, and your adaptability. It is your responsibility to create the right background for your husband and your ability to do so can make a subtle, but important contribution to his advancement" (Shea, 1966, p. 1).

I followed Shea's guidance by belonging to the Officers' Wives Club (OWC) and attending every commander's wife's coffee. I worked at the local military community thrift shop to help raise funds for military social welfare activities on base, and prepared cookies and casseroles for unit gatherings. I believed that if my husband were to get promoted, I had to do what the Army expected of me. During the period of my husband's military career it was not uncommon to have a comment about the wife's achievements, or lack thereof, included in the military member's annual efficiency report, a practice that is no longer accepted by the Department of Defense.

As the years of service went by, I noticed that some wives were not so able and some wives were not so willing to participate in the job of "officer's wife."

Accommodations were gradually made for this change. For example, because so many wives were working, what had been the standard morning coffees for unit wives were moved to evenings. As these changes occurred, I often wondered what was happening to the concept of commitment to the Army wife's role that had been part of my early life experiences as a military wife.

In 1990, some years after my husband's retirement, I had the opportunity to participate in a research project focused on Army families' adaptation to wartime deployment. Because of my own experiences, I was interested in learning more about the topic of spouse commitment and service in support of husbands' careers. While I found similarities between today's Army wives and those of my era, I also found many differences.

Today, wives do not routinely join Officers' Wives Clubs. In fact, many installations no longer have separate Officers' Clubs. Many wives do not attend unit coffees, nor do they do volunteer work in their military community. Many of today's military spouses are women working or going to school, and they do not feel an obligation to participate in military community activities. Because almost 70 percent of military families now live in civilian housing off the installation, if these women participate in any community activity, it is typically in the civilian rather than military community.

While participating in this research project, I repeatedly heard from military spouses, "The Army is his job, not mine." In 1991, the year of the Persian Gulf War, the *Survey of Army Families* (Rosenberg, 1995) reported that about half of its respondents were employed, either full time or part time, and only about 10 percent participated as volunteers in either military or civilian community organizations. These data provide a strong indicator that the role of the military wife, as I had experienced it several decades earlier, has indeed changed. Wives no longer have the same type of commitment to the organization (in this case the Army) that I had known earlier. This raised the question, "What impact does this change in service and commitment have on the Army and its way of life—if any?

Today's Army (as well as the other service branches) is a highly deployable force responding to worldwide missions. Today's military life style includes the risk of injury or death of the service member, geographic mobility, frequent separation of the service member from the rest of the family, and sometimes residence in a foreign country (Segal, 1988, p. 82). Who provides support to military families during these stressful episodes? In the past, it was the military wife who was the source of care and comfort for other, often more junior, military spouses.

In 1994, I undertook a study specifically designed to examine the role of today's senior military spouse. How different is today's role from the one with which I was familiar? I knew that there had been monumental societal changes with corresponding impacts on women and their roles in both the family and society. Clearly, there had been an emergence of an egalitarian gender ideology precipitated by the women's movement of the 1960s, an increase in the labor participation rates of women, a rise in their educational levels, and a shift in fertility patterns.

## AN EMPIRICAL STUDY OF OFFICER AND SENIOR ENLISTED WIVES

To assess the role of contemporary military wives, I conducted interviews with two groups of wives—those who were new to the Army and those who had been associated with the military lifestyle for a number of years. In order to broaden the scope of my investigation, I included both senior officers' wives and senior enlisted wives. The senior enlisted wives are important both because of their numbers in the military family population and because these women have traditionally also served an important leadership role in military communities.

The study described here of senior enlisted wives used a self-administered questionnaire, covering a wide range of subject matter. Information collected included: (1) demographic data; (2) wives' perception of an "Army wife" role; (3) clarity/ambiguity of the Army wife role; (4) perceptions of the Army's and husbands' expectations for wives' behavior; (5) commitment to the Army and the Army community; (6) alignment with the "two-for-one" career pattern; and (7) wives' satisfaction with their current lives.

Questionnaires were distributed to wives at selected Army training schools where they were in residence with their student husbands. (Many active-duty women students inquired why I was not interested in their family situations. I told them I was only looking at the traditional Army family at present, but agreed that those female soldiers who have civilian husbands, dual-military couples, and single parents were important groups for further research). These active-duty military husbands were at Army schools for the various career branches, for example, Infantry, Signal Corps, and Medical Service Corps. Husbands were of different ranks. Officers ranged from newly commissioned second lieutenants to senior colonels. Noncommissioned officers ranged from master sergeant to sergeant major. For the purpose of this chapter, officer wives and enlisted wives are discussed separately.

### SENIOR SPOUSES

The Army Officer's Guide (Crocker, 1990, pp. 215–216, 228) gives a description of the schools that military officers typically attend as they progress in an Army career. Table 5.1 describes officer professional development schools. Professional development education for noncommissioned officers is less centralized and typically occurs at either the installation or major command level. The exception is the Sergeants Major Academies, the capstone of enlisted military education.

#### Officer Spouses

There were 308 officer wives who responded to the study questionnaire administered in 1994. It should be remembered that not all wives join their husbands during these educational assignments. For a variety of reasons, mainly because of children's school needs and/or their own employment, many wives

remain at their current home.  The respondents in this study represent a convenient sample and cannot be considered a representative sample of all officer
wives or even representative of the wives who joined their husbands at these
schools.  Fifty-one percent of the wives were married to lieutenant colonels and
colonels; 34 percent were married to captains and majors; and15 percent to
lieutenants.  The average age of the wives was 33.  They had fewer than two
children on average.  Ninety percent of them had completed education beyond
high school, and 11 percent had graduate degrees.  In contrast to most married
women in the United States, the majority of these wives were not employed.
Fewer than 15 percent of these wives were working full-time; 15 percent were
working part time.  There are a number of possible explanations for the low rate
of employment.  Because these women were with their husbands at these training schools, which lasted between six weeks and nine months, few of them
would find it convenient or feasible to actively pursue work for such a short
period of time.  It is also possible that these women were full-time homemakers
before going to the schools and never intended to work or look for work.

**Table 5.1**
**Education and Training Phases for Officers and Senior Noncommissioned Officers
in the U.S. Army**

| |
|---|
| *Lieutenant Phase*.  This phase starts upon entry to active duty and lasts until promotion to captain at about three and a half years of service.  It includes attendance at the branch officer basic course.  This is a course to prepare newly appointed commissioned officers for their first duty assignments. |
| *Captain Phase*.  This phase runs from about three and a half years to eleven years of commissioned service.  Attendance at the advanced course for their branch is the normal expectancy for most officers.  This instruction prepares them fully for assignments pertaining to command and for duty as staff officers at the battalion and brigade level. |
| *Major Phase*.  This phase runs from about the eleventh year to the eighteenth year of service.  Approximately 50% of each year group of Army officers (each service has a different school) will attend the Command and General Staff College (CGSC) at Fort Leavenworth or a comparable Command and Staff College at another service.  Instruction deals with command and staff responsibilities for large units of the armed forces and with many other vital matters of major commands and staffs. |
| *Lieutenant Colonel Phase*.  This phase starts at about the eighteenth year of service and runs until about the twenty-second.  Highly capable officers are selected by a Department of Army (DA) centralized selection board for battalion command or project management duties during this phase.  About 15% to 20% of the eligible officers will attend the Army War College (AWC) or another senior Service College during this phase.  The purpose of these studies is to prepare officers for highest level command and staff duties. |
| *Colonel Phase*.  This phase starts about the twenty-second year of service and lasts for the remainder of the officer's career unless he or she attains general rank. |
| *Senior Noncommissioned Officers*.  Each of the military services operates some type of senior-level Noncommissioned Officers Academy.  Leadership education at lower enlisted ranks is typically provided at local installation and/or major command-level First Sergeant and Primary Leadership Development Courses. |

*The Military Wife Role.*  In the questionnaire, I asked the wives: "Do you think there ever was a special role for the wife of an Army officer?" and "Do you think there is a role for the Army wife today?"  Ninety-four percent of the wives thought there had been a special role for Army wives in the past. Most wives (85 percent) thought there is still a role today.

Some wives objected to the term "Army wife."  Others objected to an "Army wife role."  As one wife stated: "I would never call myself an Army wife anymore than the wife of an executive from IBM would call themselves an IBM wife.  I participate and enjoy many activities that are associated with an Army post because I chose to as a person and to support my family.  I feel an obligation to do my share.  I do resent the expectation that Army wives come attached to their husband's jobs."

Over 50 percent of these women were clear about what they thought was expected of them in the so-called Army wife role.  Only 36 percent agreed with the statement: "I am often uncertain of exactly what is expected of me as an Army wife"; 51percent disagreed.  As would be expected, because rank is strongly correlated with number of years in the Army, role ambiguity decreased as the rank of the husband increased.

*The Army's and Husband's Expectations.*  If wives believe there is a role, what do they think is expected of them in that role?  Specifically, what do they perceive the Army expect and what do they perceive their husbands expect?  Looking back on my own experiences as an Army wife, what my husband expected me to do was actually the same as what the Army expected me to do.  That same congruity exists among today's wives.  I used the list of duties that Shea had discussed in 1966 in her book *The Army Wife*, to which I added some things that officers' wives today may think are important for them to do—for example, going to work.

As highlighted in Table 5.2, today's wives perceive that the Army expects them to do a great deal.  Note that today's military wives also believe the Army has expectations about how they should conduct their private lives.  Over three-fourths of these women thought that the Army expects them to take good care of their children.  Almost one-third think the Army expects them to cook for their husbands.  The latter finding brought to mind a class I attended in 1970s for student aviators' wives.  We were told that we were responsible for getting up at 0400 hours (4:00 am) to prepare breakfast for our husbands before they hit the flight line.  The message was clearly stated: if a man had not been fed and crashed, it would have been the wife's fault for not keeping him properly nourished.

Table 5.2 looks at the specific activities and wives perceptions of what their husbands expect, what the Army expects, and whether this is very important to them.  The data demonstrate that today's wives do not perceive that their husbands expect them to participate in Army activities to the same degree that they perceive that the Army does.  On the other hand, these wives see their husbands as expecting a great deal of them at home.

What is interesting about these data is the lack of congruity between the perceived Army's expectations, the perceived husband's expectations, and what the wives rated as "very important" activities.  For example, 92 percent of the wives perceive that the Army expects them to attend Army functions with their husbands. A similar number (88 percent) perceive that their husbands expect this of them. However, only 36 percent of these women rated going to Army functions as one of their "very important" activities. On the other hand, 35 percent of these women rated going to work as "very important" to them and 45 percent perceived that their husbands expected this of them. Only 9 percent perceived that the Army expected this of them.

**Table 5.2**
**Officers' Wives' Perceptions and Ratings for Military Family Life Activities**

| Activity | Does the Army expect this of you? | Does your husband expect this of you? | Do you rate this activity as "very important"? |
|---|---|---|---|
| | Percentage yes | Percentage yes | Percentage yes |
| Taking good care of your children | 77 | 92 | 89 |
| Attending religious services | 21 | 36 | 53 |
| Keeping your home neat and clean | 40 | 76 | 52 |
| Preparing meals for your husband | 31 | 68 | 48 |
| Attendance at Army Functions with your husband | 92 | 88 | 36 |
| Going to work | 09 | 45 | 35 |
| Being a member of a Family Support Group | 64 | 50 | 26 |
| Attendance at Army/unit functions for wives | 81 | 61 | 20 |
| Entertaining of other Officers or dignitaries In your home | 54 | 65 | 19 |
| Leading a Family Support Group | 50 | 33 | 18 |
| Participating in civilian community activities | 22 | 12 | 17 |

**Table 5.2 (continued)**

| Activity | Does the Army expect this of you? | Does your husband expect this of you? | Do you rate this activity as "very important"? |
|---|---|---|---|
| | Percentage yes | Percentage yes | Percentage yes |
| Volunteering in youth activities | 19 | 10 | 13 |
| Belonging to the Officers' Wives' Club | 45 | 17 | 07 |
| Volunteering at ACS and Red Cross | 20 | 02 | 05 |

It is important to note the differences, based on the husband's school setting, in the wives' perceptions of the Army's expectations; the husbands' expectations; and the importance of various activities to the women themselves. One might expect that with all the societal changes previously mentioned, the younger officer wives would view others' expectations differently from the older wives and that they would rate many activities as less important in their own life view.

When wives' perceptions of what the Army expects were examined, there were only two Army activities where the three groups differed. The Army War College (AWC) wives perceived the Army as having greater expectations for them to be members of Family Support Groups (FSGs) and for them to entertain other officers and dignitaries. In addition, the AWC wives perceived that their husbands expected more of them when it came to belonging to the Officers' Wives' Club (OWC), FSG, and entertaining in the home. These expectations are in line with what has been traditionally expected of senior wives (seniority based on husband's rank); the more senior care for the more junior, guidepost charities, and extend hospitality to all.

Among the nontraditional activities, it was the younger officer wives who were significantly more likely to perceive their husbands expecting them to work than the wives at Command and General Staff College (CGSC). Interestingly, there was no significant difference between the younger wives and those at AWC. This finding can be attributed to the fact that the majority of younger wives had no children and were able to work. On the other hand, the majority of the AWC wives had children who were in their late teens or older, so these wives were most likely expected to work to contribute toward college tuition costs and other family expenses. The CGSC wives had younger children who were in school and they were not expected to work. The younger wives viewed working as more important to them than did the wives at CGSC or AWC. This seems to reflect the changing societal values—it is now a good thing for wives to work.

*Commitment to the Army.* Commitment, as defined in this study, has both a behavioral component and an attitudinal component. The behavioral component elicits an exertion of effort on behalf of the organization (Mowday, Porter, & Steers 1982, p. 27) that is participation in Army activities and programs. The attitudinal component comprises an identification with the goals and values of the organization, a strong desire to remain in the organization, and the closing out of possible alternatives (Backman, 1981, p. 260)—in other words, a preference for Army activities, programs, and services over civilian ones.

Considering the lack of congruity between perceived organizational expectations and the wives' assessment of those expectations as not being of great importance to them, one might wonder if these wives are no longer committed to the Army and no longer committed to supporting and fostering their husbands' careers. To estimate the extent of behavioral commitment, wives were asked, "Do you participate in your unit's Family Support Group (FSG)?" Participation in FSGs was selected as the main measure of behavioral commitment because FSGs are considered by Army leaders as essential to the deployment requirements of today's Army.

Based on survey data that assessed commitment to the Army, these wives did not appear to be behaviorally committed to the Army, but they were attitudinally committed. Fifty-seven percent of these wives reported that they usually did participate in FSGs. Significantly more senior wives reported participating than younger wives. Forty-four percent of those women that participated said they participated as leaders of an FSG. Twelve categories of persons were identified as possible leaders for FSGs, including the commander's wife, junior officers' wives; senior NCOs' wives, and the wives of enlisted soldiers. Only 26 percent of wives stated they believed that the commander's wife should take charge of FSGs, while almost an equal number (25 percent) chose any wife in the unit who wanted to, regardless of her husband's rank. These data provided another indication that things had changed from earlier periods when the commander's wife automatically served as the group leader. Although the commander's wife was not formally designated as the leader, these earlier Army wives were well aware of the "shadow chain of command" where wives "wore" their husband's rank.

The second component of the attitudinal commitment measure assessed wives' desire to remain associated with the Army and the Army community. These women were asked: "If your husband left the Army tomorrow, how would you feel?" They had five choices ranging from "very happy" to "very sad." Forty-one percent of these women reported that they would be sad to leave the Army compared to 14 percent who said they would be happy to leave. The largest percentage (44 percent) were unsure how they would feel. This probably reflects the impact of downsizing and reduction of benefits on morale of soldiers and their families. What was surprising was the fact that the AWC wives had the largest percentage (20 percent) that would be happy to see their husbands leave the Army compared to 11 percent of CGSC wives and 15 percent of the younger wives. Many of these senior wives seemed to feel that they had done their 20 years. They appeared ready for something different. Many of these women may have been negatively affected by the reduction in senior command positions available for their husbands. Many had envisioned their husbands as a brigade or division commander, but now those dreams were not to be realized as the number of opportunities for these senior command positions diminished as a function of overall Army downsizing.

The third component used to measure attitudinal commitment had to do with the wives' preference for military activities, programs, and services versus those of the civilian community. These women were asked about friendships, children's education, grocery shopping, and religious services with a variety of response options.

The preferences shown in Table 5.3 indicate that with the exception of schools and religious activities, these women overwhelmingly preferred what the military provided to them. Today's Army wife appears to enjoy the military way of life over a civilian-based life. As one wife related: "I enjoy the closeness of the Army community. I'm a real people person and the life we've chosen gives me an opportunity to be with and help other people. I get a real feeling of satisfaction volunteering in our community. I can see the results of our efforts. I dislike being taken advantage of and I think it's time the Army looks at compensating some volunteer work."

*Commitment to Husband's Career.* A strong attitudinal commitment to the Army versus a weaker behavioral commitment shows a shift away from the two-for-one career pattern to which earlier wives had been so intimately tied. If wives exhibit a weak commitment to their husbands' careers, that would be further evidence of an ineffectual two-for-one career pattern.

This study examined wives' commitment to their husbands' careers by looking at several survey items. These included: their desire to attend unit events; their willingness to make changes to help their husbands advance; doing a great deal to further his career; understanding the demands of his job; working as a team; and positive attitude to their husband's being in the Army. These data suggest that most wives (74 percent) are committed to their husbands' careers.

**Table 5.3**
**Officers' Wives' Preferences for Military or Civilian Friends, Programs, and Services (N= 308)**

| | | | |
|---|---|---|---|
| **Living arrangements**: | On-post 63% | Off-post 37% | |
| **Friends**: Army 60% | Civilians near post 12% | People back home 28% | |
| **Medical care**: Military 53% | CHAMPUS 26% | Civilian 20% | |
| **Education**: DOD Schools 32% | Public schools 31% | Private schools 37% | |
| **Religious activities**: On-post 43% | Off-post 45% | None at all 12% | |
| **Grocery shopping**: Commissary 84% | Civilian grocery stores 16% | | |

It is important to remember, however, that the women in this study were the ones who had accompanied their husbands to these schools, thus already showing a high degree of commitment.  There were no significant differences among the officer wives at the different schools regarding commitment to their husbands' careers.  There was a strong relationship between the wives' commitment to their husbands' careers and their commitment to the Army.  The importance of this relationship held for all wives, regardless of husband's rank or the school setting.

*Career versus Family.*  Contemporary officer wives expect equality within the family unit.  When asked, just over one-third of the wives agreed with the statement, "The husband should be head of the family."  Likewise, when asked how much they agreed with the statement, "A man should expect his family to adjust to the demands of his job," a similar number disagreed.  Over three-quarters of the wives agreed with the statement, "When family needs conflict with my husband's job, the needs of the family should come first," and over four-fifths agreed that, "Both a husband and wife should share equally in the responsibilities of child care."

Only during the last 25 to 30 years has there been a significant endeavor to do research on military families.  We do not know how women would have responded to these statements decades ago, but based on my own experiences and those of my Army peers, I believe that the percentages would have differed greatly.

### Stepping in as Needed: Senior NCO Spouses

As surely as the role of the senior officer's wife has undergone transformation, there has been a corresponding transformation in the role of the senior noncommissioned officer (NCO) wife.  At one time there was a clear distinction between officer wives and the wives of NCOs. This distinction is slowly disappearing.

In times past, officers and enlisted personnel represented separate and unequal classes.  The Continental Army had no tradition to imitate other than that of its rival, Great Britain.  Consequently, it is not surprising that a pseudoaristocratic officer class developed, which was organizationally and socially separate from the enlisted or "serving class."  This provided the beginnings of an American military aristocracy, which would blossom into a full-blown, powerful caste system and remain firmly entrenched well into the 20th century.

If we look back at the role noncommissioned officers' wives played during our country's early years, we discover that the numbers of enlisted wives were minimal and the few who were in some way associated with the military were laundresses, there to wash and mend soldiers' clothing.  According to Goldman, until World War II, "military wife" was synonymous with "officer's wife" since few enlisted men were married, and if married, their families were of little concern to the military (Goldman, 1976, p. 119).

Today, NCO wives represent the majority of military wives.  With such a visible presence and officers' wives no longer totally committed to the earlier "officer's wife" role, NCO wives are stepping in to perform the roles that used to be the purview of senior officer wives.

To examine the inroads that senior NCO wives have made into their voluntary leadership roles, I conducted a comparative study of the most senior NCO wives whose husbands were attending Army schools for senior NCOs with officer wives whose husbands were attending a senior Army leadership school. This study compared the 134 wives in attendance with their husbands at the Army's Sergeants Major Academy with the 60 officer wives in attendance at the Army War College. The comparison was based on social demographics of age, ethnicity, and education and on their perceptions of expectations for them by the Army and their husbands. As with the earlier study, these respondents do not represent the population of Army NCO or officer wives. They are samples of convenience.

*Demographic Analysis.*   There were significant differences between the wives' groups in age, ethnicity, and educational attainment. The senior NCO wives were younger, more racially and ethnically diverse, and less well educated than the senior officer wives. The average age for wives at the AWC was 42 years of age and at the Sergeants Major Academy (SGMA), it was 38 years. At the AWC 98 percent of the wives were white compared to only 59 percent at SGMA. At the SGMA 13 percent were African-American, 10 percent Hispanic, 10 percent Asian and 8 percent other. All of the wives of the AWC had at least a high school education with 71 percent having completed college. Eighty-eight percent of the SGMA wives had a high school diploma or better and 22 percent had a college degree.

*Perceptions of Army's Expectations.*   I was interested in how the two groups differed in their perception of the Army's expectations of them as wives of military members. I was also interested in their view of these expectations and the extent to which they felt they were able to fulfill these expectations. The questions asked of the wives were similar to those described in the previous section on senior officer wives, and the two groups were compared.

Overall, there was substantial agreement between the two groups on their perceptions as to what the Army expected of them as military wives. The major difference between the AWC and SGMA wives was the higher expectation experienced by the SGMA wives in home and family responsibilities (e.g., keeping their homes clean, preparing meals, and taking care of children). These findings are consistent with the traditional view that a wife's role is to support her soldier husband and to provide care for their families.

What is most interesting in this study is that there were no apparent differences between the AWC and SGMA wives on what they perceived as expected of them in support of Army community and unit activities. Two notable findings are a lack of differences in perceived expectations for being a member of a Family Support Group and responsibility for entertaining officers and dignitaries in the home. In these two areas, AWC wives were expected to perceive greater responsibility. NCO wives did feel that they were expected to attend Army functions, that they were to volunteer for community activities, and most important that they had a responsibility to take charge of family Support Groups. Traditionally the commander's wife was expected to take charge of social and support activities in the Army community regardless of whether these activities involved officer and enlisted wives. It was always the custom that the NCO wife could, and should, support enlisted wives, but they seldom took charge when officer wives were involved.

Today NCO wives perceive a shared responsibility. Some officer wives (15 percent) continue to believe that the commander's wife should always be in charge of FSGs, but almost double that percentage (27 percent) believe that FSGs can be run by any wife in the unit who wants to regardless of her husband's rank. Among senior NCO wives, 47 percent agree that any wife in the unit who wants the job should take charge and only 12 percent think it should be the commander's wife. Current official policy dictates that the commander can appoint anyone to be in charge of a unit's FSG; no longer does leadership automatically fall to a commander's wife. Within our sample 37 percent of the SGMA wives served as leaders within their husbands' unit FSG.

When we examined wives' perceptions of their husbands' expectations for their participating in Army activities or family activities, there was a significant difference between the two groups of wives concerning family activities and little difference regarding their participation in Army activities. Army officers expect their wives to entertain officers and dignitaries in their homes, whereas few NCOs expect this of their wives.

When women evaluated what was important to them, the differences between the wives was apparent once again when home activities were discussed. NCO wives rated keeping their homes neat and clean and preparing meals as significantly more important to them than the perceptions provided by officers' wives. However, with only one exception, being a member of the FSG, the NCO wives did not differ significantly in their evaluation of Army activities as important to them.

The actual differences between officer and NCO wives were not readily apparent in wives' self-perceptions. The major difference in this sample was that the NCO wives believed that the Army and their husbands expected them to place more emphasis on home responsibilities. They did feel a responsibility to participate in Army activities and, in many instances, assumed responsibilities no longer taken on by officers' wives.

## SUMMARY AND IMPLICATIONS

The role of the Army wife is evolving from what it was in the 1960s and 1970s. Wives acknowledge the Army's expectations, and those expectations have not appreciably changed over the years. What seem to have changed are the wives' ability and/or willingness to meet the organizational expectations for the role of military wife.

Today women expect greater equality in their marital relationships. If a wife truly wants a career, she may forsake living together with her husband for a commuter marriage, or she may insist that her husband leave the Army on her behalf, sometimes even at later stages of his career and/or their marriage. In some cases, this is when opportunities may be opening for her. Many wives do not expect to "renounce ambition for themselves rather than being ambitious only for their husbands" (Friedan, 1963, pp. 355–356). Even if a wife is not career-minded, there appears to be a limit on how much she is willing to sacrifice for the Army. Husbands' careers are important, but it appears that family is even more important for today's Army wife. Some "two-for-one" couples continue to exist, but service providers must be mindful that in many instances, the profamily emphasis may be in conflict with the Army's demands.

Human service providers who have prior military experience will be aware that "what we are is not what we were" (Weibles, 1998, p. 12). This is true for both officer and NCO wives. Service providers who have had no military experience must recognize that their clientele will be composed not only of those military members and spouses from today's military, but there will also be some older individuals from this earlier era. Interventions must be attuned to the confusion many women of this earlier generation must feel in this changed environment.

The military as an institution does not incur the same obligation from spouses today as it did formerly. Perhaps as wives see pay levels not keeping pace with civilians', as they see the military benefit package dwindle, and as they see job security disappear in an era of downsizing, they do not experience sufficient rewards associated with fulfilling the military's expectations. Community agencies no longer can find a sufficient complement of volunteers among officers' wives to assist them in meeting their service or program goals. While it used to be officers' wives who were the backbone of community volunteers, today's military community programs must rely heavily on volunteers from among enlisted and noncommissioned officers' wives, and sometimes from the retired population that lives in the local civilian community. Recently I completed a study of volunteer activities throughout the Army (Durand, 1997). I found that those who are volunteering do so to help others and their communities. However, such a small percentage of wives, both officer and enlisted, actually volunteer that program needs are often not being met.

These research results are relevant to the other services as well. Military wives, in general, have been impacted by the societal changes of the last three decades. They are not as inclined as before to meet others' expectations; they have expectations of their own. Wives are invested, however, in the military lifestyle, in their husbands and families, and in themselves. It is through these channels that service providers can elicit an identification that will invoke positive results for assisting military spouses or eliciting their support for programs and activities.

## NOTES

A Family Support Group is a company- or battalion-affiliated organization of officer and enlisted soldiers and family members that uses volunteers to provide social and emotional support, outreach services, and information to family members prior to, during, and in the immediate aftermath of family separations (deployments, extended tours of temporary duty, and field training exercises). The main objective of the FSG is to ease the strain and alleviate possible traumatic stress associated with military separation for both family and soldier. The purposes of wives' clubs usually encompass such worthwhile goals as: to organize and sponsor educational, charitable, cultural, and social activities; to provide information of interest to members; and to foster ideals of charity and fellowship in keeping with those of the U.S. armed forces (Crossley & Keller, 1993, p. 200).

## REFERENCES

Andersen, M. L. (1993). *Thinking about women: Sociological perspectives on sex and gender* (3rd ed.). New York: Macmillan Publishing Company.

Backman, C. W. (1981). Attraction in interpersonal relationships. In M. Rosenberg & R. H. Turner (Eds.), *Social psychology: Sociological perspectives* (pp. 235–268). New York: Basic Books, Inc.

Crocker, L. P. (1990). *Army officer's guide.* Harrisburg, PA: Stackpole Books.

Crossley, A., & Keller, C. A. (1993). *The Army wife handbook: A complete social guide.* Sarasota, FL: ABI Press.

Durand, D. B. (1997). *An assessment of burnout among Army volunteers and the implications for soldier and family readiness and quality of life.* Washington, DC: The Walter Reed Army Institute of Research.

Friedan, B. (1963). *The feminine mystique.* New York: Dell Publishing.

Goldman, Nancy L. (1976). Trends in family patterns of U.S. military personnel during the 20th Century. In *The social psychology of military service* (pp. 119–134), N. Goldman & D. Segal (Eds.).Beverly Hills: Sage Publications.

Mowday, R. T., Porter, L. W., & Steers, R. M. (1982). *Employee-organization linkages: The psychology of commitment, absenteeism, and turnover.* New York: Academic Press.

Papanek, H. (1973). Men, women, and work: Reflections on the two-person career. *American Journal of Sociology, 78*(4), pp. 852–872.

Rosenberg, F. R. (1995). *Survey of Army Families II, November, 1991: A multivariate analysis of CONUS results.* Washington, DC: Department of Military Psychiatry, Walter Reed Army Institute of Research.

Segal, M. W. (1988). The military and the family as greedy institutions. In C. C. Moskos & F. W. Wood (Eds.), *The military: More than just a job?* (pp. 79–98). Washington, DC: Pergamon-Brassey's International Defense Publishers, Inc.

Shea, N. (1966). *The Army wife* (4th ed.). New York: Harper & Row.

Weible, J. (1998, July 13). The new military: It's a far different force than a generation ago. *Army Times,* pp. 12–14.

Chapter 6

# Military Spouse Employment: Challenges and Opportunities

*Theresa J. Russo, Lea M. Dougherty, and James A. Martin*

## INTRODUCTION

Women have been making important contributions to military efforts throughout history. Mayer (1996) discusses the wives and workers of the American Revolution who were known as "camp followers." Coffman (1986) enhances this picture of the late 18th and early 19th century "employed" military spouses, with descriptions of their struggles under extreme hardships to keep families together during periods of war and peace, and throughout the exploration and settlement of America's western frontier. In her book, *Women of the Regiment: Marriage and the Victorian Army*, Trustram (1984) highlighted what might be considered an early example of military spouse employment as she described the struggles and the contributions associated with the status of the wife of an English soldier during the Victorian era. These military spouses were cooks, seamstresses, and nurses, as well as wives and mothers, and they deserve recognition for their important place in U.S. military history.

Today, women accompany U.S. service members to locations throughout the United States and numerous countries around the globe. As more and more women seek employment and career opportunities as members of the Armed Forces, traditional military spouses have been joined by civilian male spouses of female service members. In addition, there are increasing numbers of dual-career couples serving in the Armed Forces (Military Family Resource Center, 1998). Today, spouse employment is recognized as an important quality-of-life issue for the Department of Defense (Military Family Resource Center, 1998). It is an issue that reflects the changing nature of American society and what has become the most diverse military in the world.

## Changing Roles and Expectations

Presently it is common, if not expected, that a woman will seek employment outside the home (Tingey, Kiger, & Riley, 1996; Scarville & Bell, 1993; Myers, 1991).  This is true for married and single women.  Meeting family and work responsibilities can be very stressful for women because both of these roles demand a great deal of time, energy, and commitment.  Families are much "greedier" for women than for men.  Traditionally, women are expected to make the majority of personal sacrifices in order to meet the demands of the family (Segal & Harris, 1993).  As a result, women experience more role conflict and interference from work to family and family to work than do men (Duxbury, Higgins, & Lee, 1994; Crouter, 1984).  Many life cycle and personal factors influence employment status.  Women who do not have children or who have older children, as well as women who have a higher level of education and women with more work experience, are more likely to be employed outside the home (Scarville & Payne, 1995; Bowen, Orthner, Zimmerman, & Meehan, 1992).  While women with younger children may choose to stay home because of the parenting demands, many other women choose to remain at home because of the difficulties associated with locating quality and affordable childcare.

Despite the conflict between work and family roles, the majority of women wants or need employment outside the home.  The attempt to balance work and family life is a challenge for any woman but may be particularly challenging for a military spouse, who has the additional task of adapting to the demanding aspects of military life.  These demands include frequent relocation, sometimes to overseas or rural areas; unpredictable work hours for the military member; and frequent separations due to military training and operational requirements.  This demanding lifestyle makes locating and maintaining employment difficult for military spouses.  It is no surprise that even in today's economy, where a period of record employment opportunities is reported (Jowers, 1998), military spouses lag behind their civilian counterparts in work force participation (Scarville & Bell, 1993).

## Unique Aspects of Being a Military Spouse

There are many professions where the "call" or requirements of work take precedence over day-to-day personal and family life.  Typically, this occurs in professional work life and in what may be considered career employment associated with skilled and semiskilled jobs.  What is unusual in the military is the level of commitment and dedication to service that is expected of all service members, even the most junior military members.  For many, especially junior enlisted service members, there is little personal control of duty requirements.  This includes a lack of personal control over when one comes and goes to and from work and a similar lack of control over required periods of time spent away from home associated with military training and operational deployments.

For civilian spouses of service members, their own work or career typically comes second. Many military spouses must function in their work-life and career almost as if they were single. The more junior the rank of the service member, the less control he or she has over this obligation of service. Because of these seemingly all-encompassing demands, many refer to the military as "a greedy institution." As indicated earlier the family is also a "greedy institution" demanding time and energy from family members (Segal, 1986). Therefore, in many military marriages, family life responsibilities are likely to fall predominantly on the nonmilitary partner.

Military leaders realize that retaining a military member often requires an active effort to retain the family. The military looks to retain service members (and their families) who are committed to the military, although some leaders interpret this to mean the families who do not present problems or complaints. However, it is becoming increasingly hard to find these ideal military families. Today, military spouses are more independent and less likely to view themselves as just an extension of the military member (Styles, Janofsky, Blankinship, & Bishop, 1990). Spouses are concerned with how they are treated by the military. Many feel that their actions as spouses should be independent of the military member; however, they believe that the military, as an institution and as an employer, should be supportive of families' needs and provide families with the services and programs necessary to cope with the demands of today's military lifestyle. These increasing expectations for employer accommodation are in line with the perception that military service has become more of an occupation and less of a vocation (Moskos, 1977).

### Dual Careers (Joint-Service) and the "Trailing" Male Spouse

According to data provided to the Military Family Resource Center (1998) by the Defense Manpower Data Center, approximately 6 percent of military members were in joint-service marriages in 1997. Percentages differ by gender and by branch of service. Overall, 22 percent of military women are married to another service member while only 4 percent of military men are married to women serving on active duty. The Air Force has the highest percentage of both women (27 percent) and men (6 percent) married to another service member.

Overall, there is a greater percentage of joint-service marriages within enlisted ranks than within the officer corps. The highest percentages of the total for joint service marriages are found in the pay grades E1 through E4 (35 percent) and E5 through E6 (39 percent). Approximately 12 percent of joint service marriages are senior enlisted members, 8 percent are lieutenants and captains, and 5 percent are more senior officers. Joint-service couples are especially challenged with balancing work and family responsibilities because of the demanding nature of their occupations and the institution to which they belong. Women in these marriages, similar to married women in civilian professional positions, often experience more role conflict between home and work than the men in these joint-service marriages, resulting in higher work stress (Bowen et al., 1992).

### The Civilian Male Spouse

When we consider the increasing number of employed women balancing work and family responsibilities, we cannot overlook male civilian spouses, the husbands of women serving in the military. As described above, the nature of military life makes it difficult to balance work and family responsibilities. Civilian men in these marriages face many of the same "trailing spouse" issues as civilian women married to military personnel. These couples confront frequent relocation, separation from the military member, and long and unpredictable work hours. However, they are a very small subgroup in an organization with a strong tradition of the male being the military member and the female being the "dependent spouse." Therefore, civilian husbands may not benefit from the same support systems as civilian wives (i.e., officer's wives' clubs and other social organizations primarily focused on women as members) and they may face contempt for their supportive role in a traditionally male-dominated culture.

Scarville and Bell (1993) noted that civilian husbands are significantly different from civilian wives regarding their demographic characteristics and their employment activities. These civilian husbands are likely to have higher educational levels, and many have prior military service experience. Most are employed full time or are seeking full-time employment. Perceived as distinctively different from civilian wives and present in far fewer numbers, they are often excluded from policy and political discussions of spouse employment issues. The following case example demonstrates the challenges these spouses face in today's military.

Ed has his degree in education and holds a teaching certificate. He is married to Lori, a nurse in the Navy. The only teaching position that Ed has been able to locate at their current location requires him to commute about 40 minutes each way. Part of the position requires Ed to be involved in extracurricular activities at the school—usually after school and evening hours. Often he doesn't get home until late in the evening. Lori often has night shift duty, so sometimes they don't see each other for days. Ed has found it difficult to establish any friendships at their current location since he is usually not available to participate in functions for officer spouses since they typically occur in the early evening. Most of the spouses he has met are female rather than male. This isolation from a suitable peer group makes it very lonely for him when his wife is deployed.

### The Military's Interest in Spouse Employment

The Department of Defense has a number of reasons for being interested in the issue of spouse employment (for both male and female spouses). These factors include the importance of employment and career opportunities for the economic well-being of military families, as well as employment as an important source of life satisfaction for many spouses. Leaders have come to recognize that spouse satisfaction with military life is directly associated with military member retention decisions (Segal & Harris, 1993; Scarville, 1990). In addition, the demand for safe and adequate community childcare associated with both spouse employment and the presence of joint-service couples represents an important spouse employment issue for the military.

## SOME BENEFITS OF EMPLOYMENT FOR MILITARY SPOUSES

### Employment as a Financial Necessity

In both the civilian and military sectors, more families are becoming or desire to become dual-income families. Approximately 65 percent of military spouses are in the labor force (Military Family Clearinghouse, 1995). Spouse employment is important for many reasons, although the need for a second income to meet financial obligations and to achieve a more comfortable lifestyle is typically at the top of the list for most couples (Scarville & Payne, 1995; Military Family Clearinghouse, 1995).

Many families face the financial challenge of beginning military service and family life simultaneously. A junior enlisted service member earns slightly more than minimum wage (Rand, 1998). At the same time, he or she may be newly married with young children. The financial costs during these early life cycle stages are a challenge for any family, particularly families with low annual incomes. It is not surprising then that more than one-third of both male and female soldiers (primarily enlisted personnel) married to civilian spouses have experienced at least one month over the past 12 where they have lacked money to pay their bills (Bowen et al., 1992). The addition of a second income can help alleviate these financial problems. The difficulty is that many of these young civilian spouses lack the necessary skills and training for employment other than in minimum wage jobs that often fail to offset the costs associated with childcare or the transportation expenses of going to and from the job.

### An Opportunity to Enhance Family Quality of Life

Spouse employment creates quality-of-life opportunities for some military families that they could otherwise not afford. It is often debated in U.S. culture whether the need for a dual-income family is truly a financial "necessity" or just allows a standard of living that is valued in our culture. For many families, there is no question that a second income is a financial necessity. Without a second income they are unable to meet the basic needs for shelter, food, health care, and so on. For other families a second income provides quality-of-life opportunities that would not otherwise be available. These opportunities vary from buying a stereo system, owning a home, taking a family vacation, paying for children's college, and contributing to a retirement fund.  The value placed on these quality-of-life opportunities varies from family to family, but generally this additional income enhances a family's standard of living and provides a more comfortable lifestyle.  In some cases, spouse employment will sustain a family's well-being at an even more basic level.  Military families are no different from civilian families in their needs, desires, or aspirations.  The extra income from spouse employment may also provide some of the resources necessary to cope with the stressors and expenses that are inherent in a military lifestyle.

### Opportunity to Enhance Personal Well-Being

The spouses of officer personnel tend to focus on the intrinsic rewards of employment.  In a recent survey, for example, many reported their primary reasons for working outside the home as "independence/self esteem" (55 percent) and "always planned to have a career" (51 percent) (Military Family Clearinghouse, 1995).  Education facilitates employment as well as the intrinsic values of independence and self-esteem.  These factors become core motivations for seeking a job or a career outside of the home.  The spouses of officers are more likely to have a higher education level, and it is not surprising that these women more frequently report these reasons for working than do enlisted spouses.  This does not imply that these women do not value the social relationships that often come from the work environment.  Most find these relationships supportive, especially during times when their husbands are deployed.

While it is a challenge in any dual-career marriage to meet the needs of both spouses, military spouses need and expect their active-duty service members spouses to recognize and appreciate their efforts (Thomas, Albrecht, & White, 1984).  Balancing work and family can be particularly difficult if one of the spouses' careers is as demanding as a military one.  Military members believe their spouses should be able to build and maintain a career (Scarville & Bell, 1993).  A military lifestyle does not always facilitate this opportunity.  For example, being employed and having a social support network of friends and family is important to women who successfully adapted to separations due to deployment (Wood, Scarville, & Gravino, 1995).  A study of adaptation during the Gulf War (Rosen, Westhuis, & Teitelbaum, 1994) found that wives who were employed may not have had the time to cultivate support from within the Army community.  This does not mean they do not have support systems.  In some cases these women establish support networks outside the military community, typically in their work and personal life environments.  The following example highlights this observation.

Kelly and Jim have been married for 23 years.  They have two teenage sons, Paul and Mark.  Jim is two years from retirement from the Air Force.  They have been at their current location for two years, have developed a number of friendships with their civilian neighbors, and have decided to retire in this community.  Kelly has been working in the childcare center on base while she was taking classes for a degree in medical technology. She has one more year to finish.  Work and school have added to her network of friends in the local area.  Jim just received permanent change of station (PCS) orders, and Kelly has decided to stay at their current location with their sons until Jim retires in order to keep her job and finish her degree.  The family is now facing the challenge of having to split the family up in order to meet Jim's military obligation and at the same time to promote opportunity and growth for Kelly and the children.

## SOME BARRIERS TO SPOUSE EMPLOYMENT

### Education and Training Issues

Military spouses often face two difficult issues when seeking employment. They either find themselves lacking the necessary training and education (underskilled) or find the employment opportunities to be below their training and education level (underemployment) (Scarville & Bell, 1993).  Because of their young age, many enlisted military spouses have not completed high school. Few have any post–high school job training or technical education that would prepare them for semiskilled or skilled employment.   The lack of this employment preparation means that they must enter the job market focused on minimum wage, service industry jobs.  In many cases these spouses are living in civilian communities near military installations, and because they are not living on the military installation they are unaware of some of the potential job training and employment skill training opportunities available locally from federal, state, county, and community resources.

Scarville and Bell (1993) discussed underemployment with regard to working fewer hours per week than desired, being overeducated for a position, and not fully using job skills.  Factors of race, education, and length of time at the current location are also associated with underemployment.  More enlisted wives than officers' wives reported feeling underemployed because of their skill training (Scarville & Bell, 1993).  This may be because officers' wives are able financially to wait until a more suitable position is available rather than take a position for which they are overqualified.  In addition, proportionately more enlisted wives are in jobs that have lower skill requirements (Scarville & Bell, 1993).

A factor facilitating underemployment is that service sector jobs, which require less skill, are a growing segment of the labor market (Scarville & Bell, 1993).  These types of positions are typically less intrinsically rewarding but may be initially satisfying for a younger spouse new to the work force.  They are not likely to satisfy a spouse with advanced education or technical skills, or women who have work experience in a skilled position.  In contrast, spouses in more professional and semiprofessional positions were less likely to report underemployment, possibly because these types of positions require higher education and training levels (Scarville & Bell, 1993).  However, these positions may be more difficult to find, particularly for military spouses stationed at installations away from major population centers.   The following vignette highlights this issue:

Kate is 35 years old and has been married to Tom, a staff sergeant in the Marine Corps, for 14 years. They have three children, twelve, ten, and seven. They have traveled a great deal with the Marine Corps, just moving to their seventh location. Kate had started college but quit after one year so she could marry Tom. Now that her children are older and childcare won't be such an issue she would like to find a job. Because she has no work history, training, or qualifications she is finding her choice of available jobs fairly limited. Their current assignment is in a relatively rural area of the country. This location does not provide opportunities to pursue more education or training.

## The Impact of Military Duty Requirements on Spouse Employment

Family adaptation to a military lifestyle has received considerable research attention. Factors such as long and unpredictable work hours, frequent relocation, and deployments create a stressful lifestyle (Knox & Price, 1995; Segal & Harris, 1993; Schumm, Bell, & Tran, 1994). These factors, unique to a military lifestyle, make it difficult for many spouses to secure and sustain employment. The irregularity and unpredictability of a service member's work hours make it difficult to plan on that person for help with childcare and other family and household responsibilities. Military spouses typically find the primary burden of family life responsibilities falling on them. Without a partner to share in family life responsibilities, many military spouses find it difficult to secure employment outside the home.

### Childcare Responsibilities and Resources

Childcare concerns are often a source of great stress for working parents, particularly mothers since they tend to take on the major responsibility for the household, including childcare arrangements. The expansion and use of childcare facilities has facilitated increasing participation of women in the labor market during this century (Blau & Hotz, 1992). A study of spouse employment and childcare among military families found that the demand for childcare is related to the earnings of the military spouse (Lakhani & Hoover, 1994), and that the expense of child-care is a significant barrier to employment for military spouses (Scarville & Bell, 1993; Scarville & Payne, 1995).

Child-care is obviously more of a concern for families with younger children than families with older children, therefore junior enlisted and junior officer families have the greatest need. Lakhani and Hoover (1994) found that officers' wives are able to pay more for childcare than enlisted wives because of their husbands' higher income and because they are more likely than enlisted wives to be employed in professional occupations. As a result, officers' wives are more likely to use the child development centers on base, which tend to be more costly, whereas enlisted wives are more likely to use family day care homes. The implication is that due to various factors such as the quality of the facility and materials available to children, the training of key staff, and the developmentally appropriate curriculum, child development centers tend overall to provide a higher quality of care than family day care homes. It is very stressful and disconcerting for working women to place their children in a childcare arrangement they are not satisfied with (Tingey, Kiger, & Riley, 1996). Many women choose, due to the lack of adequate and affordable childcare alternatives, to remain at home.

### Structural Employment Barriers

Structural issues such as geographic location, availability of transportation, attitudes of employers toward military, and salary are potential barriers toward spouse employment (Scarville & Bell, 1993). Spouses typically have very little control over these barriers. Employer attitudes can be especially difficult to overcome. Many employers are resistant to hire and train a person, particularly for a professional or semiprofessional position, if they believe that person will only be in the job for a short period of time (Scarville & Bell, 1993). Associating a potential employee with the military often creates the perception of instability, thus causing employers to shy away from hiring this person. This is a common experience for many military spouses who seek employment in the civilian community.

Barriers such as availability of transportation exist for many military families, particularly junior enlisted families (Military Family Clearinghouse, 1995). Many military installations are not located in communities with public transportation systems. For most military families, especially enlisted families, the costs associated with purchasing, operating, and maintaining a second car to get the spouse to and from work often outweighs the potential income they will make at that job. The following vignette provides an example of the situation in which military spouses find themselves with regard to access to employment:

Margaret, 22 years old, is married to Joe, a junior sergeant in the Army. They have been married four years and have two children, ages two and three months. They have been at their current location, a small town near a large mid-west military base, for almost two years. Margaret is a beautician but is having difficulty with transportation issues so she can take a job near the installation. Margaret and Joe only have one car and they live off post, so it is difficult for her to get to a place of employment without buying another car. Margaret's job would require her to work late afternoon and evening hours, which presents a difficulty with childcare. Joe is often not finished at work in time to pick up the children before the day care closes, and the cost for two children in day care would be more than half of Margaret's income. Although she would like to work, Margaret doesn't see how she could manage to work out all of these details.

### Relocation as a Barrier to Job Advancement and Careers

Relocation is difficult in any dual-career family. Often in relocation, one spouse becomes the accompanying spouse and is faced with the challenge of locating employment opportunities. This can have personal and career implications for the accompanying spouse. Their sense of self may be diminished because they feel helpless to influence their own lives as "trailing spouses." They are lacking the support systems and connections that the other spouse experiences from their new employment situation (Bayes, 1989). Scarville and Payne (1995) identified the potential for these spouses to become "discouraged workers," those that would like a paid job but are not employed and do not continue to look for employment. The inability to find satisfying work, lowering career goals, or feeling diminished professionally are major stressors for an individual (Bayes, 1989). In addition, the loss of income after a move can be detrimental to a family. Some military families reported losing as much as 10 percent to 20 percent of their family income in the first year after a move (Warner & Little, 1988). Bowen (1989) found that when a spouse of a service member is employed, the family seems to adjust better to relocation, in spite of the problems associated with continuing a spouse's career without interruption. The following vignette provides an example to the impact of relocation on military spouses:

Alison has been married to Sam for 10 years. Alison and Sam have two children, ages seven and four. They met in college and both have four-year degrees. Sam is a helicopter pilot and a major in the Army. Allison's degree is in economics and after several short PCS moves for Sam to complete officer training and flight school, she realized finding a job at each location was difficult. Alison decided to start a framing business so she could move her business with her. It provided her with the flexibility to be with her children, and she did not have to seek out childcare with each PCS move. The challenge and frustration Alison faces with her business is that with each PCS move she must start over. It usually takes Alison six months to a year to establish a clientele and advertise her business; just as her business begins to grow and flourish over the next two to three years she finds it is time to pack up and relocate. The family is faced with a reduced income each time the family moves, and this adds additional stress on both Alison and Sam.

## THE ASSOCIATION BETWEEN SPOUSE EMPLOYMENT AND READINESS AND RETENTION

### Recent Research Findings

Military family research has demonstrated that retention is affected by spouse support (Segal & Harris, 1993). Research has found that spouse support is affected by spouse employment. It is not just whether the spouse is employed, but whether the employment situation (type of work, hours, pay, etc.) meets expectations (Segal & Harris, 1993). For example, spouses who are underemployed, discouraged workers or unemployed are likely to be dissatisfied with the military lifestyle, thus affecting their spouses' retention in the military (Scarville, 1990). In addition, a spouse's dissatisfaction with the military is likely to affect a service member's overall morale, which will then affect the individual readiness of the military member (Segal & Harris, 1993). There are also data that suggest that spouse employment may better prepare families to deal with deployments by providing them with additional financial resources (Scarville & Bell, 1993).

### Special Implications for Dual Military Couples

For dual-military couples, retention is affected by the perception of each spouse's career intention. The military will either retain both or lose both service members depending on the effects of policies and programs for either spouse (Lakhani & Gade, 1991). Dual-military couples with children face even more of a challenge balancing work and family responsibilities. For example, their dependent care plans appear to be slightly less satisfactory than other married couples (Pliske, 1988); they more frequently miss alerts and are late for work more often (Burnam, Meredith, Sherbourne, Valdez, & Vernez, 1992). However, the continued improvement of policies regarding childcare will help retain dual-military couples (Schumm, Bell, Rice, & Sanders, 1996). Retention of these service members should be more desirable than replacing them with less experienced ones who are not yet married or have children.

## CURRENT ACTIONS AND FUTURE OPPORTUNITIES

Lakhani (1994) discussed home basing as one of the newest service initiatives. Home basing is defined as the relocation of a larger number of military personnel from outside of the continental United States (OCONUS) to the continental United States (CONUS). These changes should be accompanied by greater duration at each PCS location. The idea of home basing military members (for a suggested six to eight years) may have many benefits, including greater opportunity for spouse employment (Lakhani, 1994). Under these conditions of employee stability, employers may be more willing to invest in hiring and training military spouses. A longer period of time for employment would allow employers to recover their training costs and at the same time allow spouses to advance their careers resulting in higher earnings and benefits (Lakhani, 1994). This stability may increase retention of dual-military couples because home basing will increase the likelihood of the co-location of couples. Home basing has not yet become policy for the military. With the implementation of downsizing, families seem to be moving more frequently rather than less frequently. In the long term, downsizing and the associated consolidation of military functions in a smaller number of installations may work to create the same effect—home basing and a lowering of many spouse employment barriers.

## SUMMARY AND IMPLICATIONS

Spouse employment has and will continue to be an important yet difficult challenge for the Department of Defense. The "priority of military service" will not change. In fact, the nature of future military structure and function will likely increase the overall work or duty demands, the unpredictability of duty requirements, and the amount of time spent away from family. If the DOD is to be successful in supporting spouse employment opportunities, it will come from many efforts including education and training encouraging the employment of spouses by the private sector and developing adequate and affordable child care resources.

The Department of Defense and the individual services need to continue to support adequate spouse employment opportunities. Successful implementation of these opportunities for spouse employment will require local installation efforts to hire spouses in both appropriated and nonappropriated activities, and from partnerships with local community employers that encourage job training and employment opportunities for military spouses. Spouses themselves must take a variety of self-help initiatives. Table 6.1 highlights many of these macro to micro spouse employment initiatives.

**Table 6.1**
**Employment Initiatives**

| Area | Department of Defense | Installation | Self-Help |
|---|---|---|---|
| Education and Training | Provide job training<br><br>Create partnerships with colleges and technical schools for education and training for military spouses<br><br>Establish programs to provide scholarships, grants, and loans for education and training<br><br>Create policies for home-basing that support training and employment opportunities | Work with local community and business leaders to create positive attitude about military spouses<br><br>Create partnerships with local colleges and technical schools to provide education and training for military spouses<br><br>Support spouse job referral programs | Develop an optimistic attitude<br><br>Take advantage of educational and training opportunities<br><br>Set realistic goals for education and training |

**Table 6.1 (continued)**

| Area | Department of Defense | Installation | Self-Help |
|---|---|---|---|
| Spouse's Military Requirements | Create policies that allow some flexibility to meet family demands<br><br>Create policies that value families like joint domicile for dual-military couples | Create command and unit climate committed to family support, including support for spouse training, education, and employment | Work with unit and command to create flexibility for family demands |
| Childcare | Build/increase size of childcare centers and set affordable rates<br><br>Establish and monitor policies for quality home-based child care | Operate centers so they provide quality childcare and required operating hours | Utilize the various childcare services available on the local installation |
| Relocation | Create policies to make homebasing possible | Provide effective sponsorship for all new families | Make an effort to learn about the new community |
| Jobs | Establish policies and programs that encourage military and civilian partnerships | Establish mechanisms to create positive community attitude about military spouses as employees<br><br>Facilitate opportunities for spouses to create employment-related support networks | Have optimistic attitude<br><br>Actively pursue possibilities<br><br>Create and access employment-related support networks |
| Transportation | Create policies and programs to form community partnerships for public transportation | Create community partnerships for helping families access public transportation and financing for vehicles<br><br>Institute programs for financial counseling | Utilize public transportation and financing of vehicles<br><br>Become informed consumers before making vehicle purchase or prioritize finances |

Human service providers must consider both the burden and the value of spouse employment among those military family members in their client population. Encouraging spouses to develop realistic expectations and to build their own employment-related support network is critical. For many, gaining required basic education and job training will be a necessary first step. Many military bases and most local civilian communities offer numerous volunteer employment opportunities. Not only do these positions provide valuable job training and experience, but they are also often a stepping stone into a paid position. Many of these volunteer organizations provide some childcare reimbursement. For some spouses, starting a home business maybe worth exploring. While an alternative, home businesses are not always as simple as they first appear, and a spouse considering this step needs to have a good source of expert advice and guidance. Many military bases offer some of this supportive guidance through their various family service organizations. Whatever a spouse's personal situation, an important aspect of entering and maintaining employment is the establishment of a support network of friends and peers who will encourage and sustain these employment efforts.

## REFERENCES

Bayes, M. (1989). The effects of relocation on the trailing spouse. *Smith-College Studies in Social Work, 59*(3), 280–288.

Blau, D. M., & Hotz, V. J. (1992). Special issue on childcare. *Journal of Human Resources 27*(1), 1.

Bowen, G. L. (1989). *Family adaptation to relocation: An empirical analysis of family stressors, adaptive resources, and sense of coherence.* Alexandria, VA: U.S. Army Research Institute for the Behavioral and Social Sciences.

Bowen, G. L., Orthner, D., Zimmerman, L. I, & Meehan, T. (1992). Family patterns and adaptation in the U.S. Army. (ARI Technical Report 966). Alexandria, VA: U.S. Army Research Institute for the Behavioral and Social Sciences.

Burnam, M. A., Meredith, L. S., Sherbourne, C. D., Valdez, R. B., & Vernez, G. (1992). *Army families and soldier readiness* (Technical Report R-3884-A). Santa Monica, CA: Rand Arroyo Center.

Coffman, E. M. (1986). *The old Army: A portrait of the American Army in peacetime* (pp. 1784–1898). Oxford, England: Oxford University Press.

Crouter, A. C. (1984). Spillover from family to work: The neglected side of the work-family interface. *Human Relations, 37*(6), 425–442.

Duxbury, L., Higgins, C., & Lee, C. (1994). Work-family conflict: A comparison by gender, family type, and perceived control. *Journal of Family Issues, 15*(3), 449–466.

Jowers, J. (1998, September 7). Enjoying a robust market: Strong employment climate embraces military spouses. *Army Times*, p. 18.

Knox, J., & Price, D. H. (1995). The changing American military family: Opportunities for social work. *Social Service Review, 69*(3), 479–497.

Lakhani, H. (1994). The socioeconomic benefits to military families of home basing of armed forces. *Armed Forces and Society, 21*(1), 113–128.

Lakhani, H., & Gade, P. A. (1991). Career decisions of dual military career couples: A multidisciplinary analysis of the U.S. Army. *Journal of Economic Psychology*, *13*(1), 153–166.

Lakhani, H. A., & Hoover, E. (1994). *The interrelationships of child-care use, spouse employment, army satisfaction, and retention in the U.S. Army*. Alexandria, VA: U.S. Army Research Institute for the Behavioral and Social Sciences.

Mayer, H. A. (1996). *Belonging to the Army: Camp followers and community during the American Revolution*. Charleston: University of South Carolina Press.

Military Family Clearinghouse. (1995, June). Military family demographics: Employment profile of military spouses. Paper presented at Department of Defense Spouse Employment Policy Forum.

Military Family Resource Center. (1998). *Profile of the military community: 1997 Demographics*. Arlington, VA: Military Family Resource Center.

Moskos, C. C. (1977). The all-volunteer military: Calling, profession, or occupation? *Parameters*, *7*(1), 41–50.

Moskos, C. C. (1990, August). Army women. *The Atlantic Monthly*, 71–78.

Myers, L. W. (1991). Military stress: Work involvement and perceived job performance. *National Journal of Sociology*, *5*(1), 63–79.

Pliske, R. M. (1988). *Families and readiness: An examination of the 1985 Department of Defense Survey of Enlisted Personnel* (Research Report 1490). Alexandria, VA: U.S. Army Research Institute for the Behavioral and Social Sciences.

Rosen, L. N., Westhuis, D. J., & Teitelbaum, J. M. (1994). Patterns of adaptation among army wives during Operations Desert Shield and Desert Storm. *Military Medicine*, *159*(1), 43–47.

Scarville, J. (1990). *Spouse employment in the Army: Research findings* (Research Report 1555). Alexandria, VA: U.S. Army Research Institute for the Behavioral and Social Sciences.

Scarville, J., & Bell, D. B. (1993). Employment and underemployment among army wives. Paper presented to 54th Annual Conference of the National Council on Family Relations, Orlando, FL.

Scarville, J., & Payne, G. (1995). Trends in Army spouse employment. Paper presented at the Department of Defense Policy Forum on Spouse Employment: Creating Opportunities for the 21st Century, Alexandria,VA.

Schumm, W. R., Bell, D. B., Rice, R. E., & Sanders, D. (1996). Trends in dual military couples in the U.S. Army. *Psychological Reports*, *78* (3, part 2), 1287–1298.

Schumm, W., Bell, D. B., & Tran, G. (1994). *Family adaptation to the demands of Army life: A review of findings*. Alexandria, VA: U.S. Army Research Institute for the Behavioral and Social Sciences.

Segal, M. W. (1986). The military and the family as greedy institutions. *Armed Forces and Society*, *13*(1), 9–38.

Segal, M. W., & Harris, J. J. (1993). *What we know about Army families* (Special report 21). Alexandria, VA: U.S. Army Research Institute for the Behavioral and Social Sciences.

Styles, M. B., Janofsky, B. J., Blankinship, D., & Bishop, S. (1990). *Investigating family adaptation to Army life: Exploratory site visit findings*. Alexandria, VA: U.S. Army Research Institute for the Behavioral and Social Sciences.

Thomas, S., Albrecht, K., & White, P. (1984). Determinants of marital quality in dual-career couples. *Family Relations*, *33*(4), 513–521.

Tingey, H., Kiger, G., & Riley, P. J. (1996). Juggling multiple roles: Perceptions of working mothers. *The Social Science Journal*, *33*(2), 183–191.

Trustram, M. (1984). *Women of the regiment: Marriage and the Victorian army.* Cambridge, England: Cambridge University Press.

Warner, J. T., & Little, R. D. (1988). Permanent change of station moves, spousal earning losses and reemployment. Paper presented at Eastern Economic Association meetings, Boston, MA. Cited in W. R. Schumm, D. B., Bell, & G. Tran. (1994), *Family adaptation to the demands of Army life: A review of findings.* (ARI Report 1658). Alexandria, VA: U.S. Army Research Institute for the Behavioral and Social Sciences.

Wood, S., Scarville, J., & Gravino, K. S. (1995). Waiting wives: Separation and reunion among Army wives. *Armed Forces and Society, 21*(2), 217–236.

# Chapter 7

# Military Retirement and the Transition to Civilian Life

*David S. Wolpert*

## INTRODUCTION

Members of the armed forces who retire after 20 or more years of service face a number of stresses and challenges as they move through the transition from military to civilian life. Good preretirement planning, especially in the areas of employment, spouse employment, relocation, finances, and medical care, can greatly reduce stress and lead to a more positive postretirement civilian life. For the civilian human service provider it is important to understand the unique circumstances of military retirees and their families and the challenges associated with the role transition from active duty to civilian life. Military members and their families come to this important midlife transition with numerous strengths and weaknesses that the civilian provider must address when working with this special population.

There will be almost 2 million military retirees by the year 2000 living in the United States and many countries throughout the world (Snyder, 1994). These retirees are at varying stages of their lives and have a wide variety of families that they live with or support. Those families for whom this transition has been fairly recent bring a variety strengths and weaknesses with them when they seek assistance for life problems. For example, a military retiree has experienced frequent moves during his or her career, so spouses and children have learned to set up house and make new friends, but often they have been the "outsiders." These families may be very comfortable with the civilian community, or they may have spent a career insulated within the military community and have not developed many civilian relationships. Now they must establish a whole new life in a nonmilitary community. The service member may relish the decreased pressure and a new challenge, but some service members may become depressed because they are home with unfamiliar responsibilities and a significant loss in status. In general, the retiree spends much more time at home with the family. Being home may be a welcome change, but the retiree may also feel like a stranger who has intruded on someone else's established routine. In most cases, the military retiree will start a second career. This may be the time when the retiree's spouse pursues a career and many family roles change.

Typical military retirees are faced with many critical decisions in the transition to the civilian world. Actions taken while still on active duty to prepare for this transition may affect how well they and their family adapt to this new environment and this new life stage. For the civilian human service provider, understanding the history, background, and many issues involved with military life experiences will enable the provider to place his or her services in a more informed context.

Military retirement is quite unique. Although there are other examples of retirement from public service organizations (e.g., police and fire departments) after 20 or more years of service (YOS), the military mission and lifestyle creates a distinct set of issues for those who retire from active military service. In most cases, the military retirement benefit allows members to retire at a relatively early age. Members know precisely when they will be retirement eligible. As a result, they have the possibility to plan for and pursue a second career in the civilian world. If they do not pursue a second career, then members can expect a potentially lengthy, postmilitary life.

This chapter discusses retirement in general, and specifically military retirement and preretirement planning within an historical context. It examines military retirement within the theoretical framework of role transitions to explain the potential problems service members may encounter in making the transition to the civilian job market. Finally, the chapter reviews previous and current programs and services offered by the military and other agencies to assist with the general retirement preparations. The chapter ends with a discussion of issues for civilian human service providers to consider when they deal with recent military retirees and their families.

## BACKGROUND: SOME IMPORTANT TERMS AND HISTORICAL CONCEPTS

### Retirement

There is no single definition of retirement, and often the definition used, either separately or in combination, suits the user's purpose. The *Oxford English Dictionary* (1979) first speaks of "falling back, retreating, or receding from a place or position" and second of "withdrawal from occupation, office, or business activity." (This latter definition is at the core of most definitions of retirement.) Atchley (1976) sees retirement as being employed less than full time while collecting a retirement pension earned through prior years of service as a job holder. A third alternative is the employer definition, as in the case of the military retiree who may not meet the first two definitions but is considered retired by the military.

## History of Retirement

It is generally agreed that retirement is a relatively new phenomenon, which is an outgrowth of the Industrial Revolution (beginning in the middle of the 19th century). Until then, not enough surpluses were created to support noncontributers or nonworkers, so everyone had to work. It should be noted that in many cultures support was provided to those who contributed spiritually to the community (e.g. priest, rabbi and/or scholar) but whose tangible contributions may have been limited or nonexistent. Prior to the written word, the older members of the community were the purveyors of history, culture, and knowledge. They were essential in maintaining the continuity of the community. With the advent of the written word, this role for the elders was no longer as important, and their status declined. In the nomadic hunter/gatherer societies, how diminished capabilities were dealt with varied from culture to culture. Sometimes when a person's ability to work deteriorated because of age, accident, or illness, the amount of resources he or she received from the community also decreased. Ultimately, in some cultures, when a person's utility totally disappeared, they were left behind to die (Baum & Baum, 1980). The rootedness of an agricultural society may have been more conducive to withdrawing from work. When the owner of the land became less able to perform the day-to-day labors, those tasks were relegated to his children or others. Of course, this was the exception rather than the rule, and it certainly was not retirement as we know it today.

Another function of retirement, since the advent of the Industrial Revolution, has been to trim the number of workers in the general labor force or in a particular labor setting. For example, the federal government goes through periodic reductions in force (RIFs) using retirement (either encouraged or involuntary) as one way to make those reductions. Retirement also is a way of coping with fluctuating levels of unemployment and providing a more or less respectable form of unemployment in the United States (Busse & Kreps, 1964). The ability to retire workers into a living situation supported by pensions allows younger workers either to enter the labor force or to advance in their current positions. In a technological society retirement allows for those with the most current training to move through the employment stream.

The broad government pensions of today evolved from a social security system developed by Bismarck for Germany in 1888. The intent was to provide a minimum stipend for older workers after their removal from the labor market. As the other European countries adopted this format, the mandatory retirement age was generally set at 65. This was the age when it was felt the ability to perform effectively on the job had markedly declined, but there is no other obvious justification for this age, and it appears to have been rather arbitrary. Nevertheless, life expectancy was not much beyond that age at the end of the 19th century.

Almost 50 years after Bismarck, in response to the devastating unemployment in America caused by the Great Depression, the United States adopted the Social Security Act of 1935. This legislation included a pension plan with contributions made by both the employee and the employer. This was the watershed for retirement and pension programs in this country. It evolved into a near universal source of retirement income covering over 90 percent of those currently in the labor market. The development of private pension plans was stimulated during World War II because they were a mechanism for deferring taxes on profits by the employer and a way to decrease and defer taxes on income for the employee. As a result, private pensions, in combination with Social Security, became a way to remove older workers from the labor force while still providing a means of support (Graebner, 1980).

## Military Retirement

There are two rationales for the military retirement system. First, the role of youth and vigor is the more prominently discussed objective of the military retirement system. It is argued that it is imperative to keep the forces young and vital and to allow for continuous opportunities to gain and use experience at all levels and ranks. The second argument is that military retirement functions as a benefit, which aids recruitment and retention in military service (Goldich, 1983).

The definition of "military retirement" is really a subset of retirement. It begins with the concept that one can exercise the option to retire after 20 years of active military service, for that is the time when vestment in the pension begins. There are also medical and disability retirements that can occur with less than 20 years of service, as well as retirement from the reserve forces or National Guard. In addition, with the reductions in force starting in the early 1990s, several early retirement options have been authorized by Congress and implemented by the services. The focus here will be those military members who have completed 20 or more YOS. This means that someone as young as 37 years old could be "retired" from military service.

Although not an integral part of the definition, it is important when describing military retirement to understand the context within which the military member retires. The military retiree receives a different color identification card and is placed in retired status, but may still be subject to recall in times of national emergency. The basic benefits are as follows: 50 percent of base salary at retirement after 20 years with 2½ percent increments for each subsequent year served, up to a maximum of 75 percent of base pay. There have been some changes in this aspect of the military retirement system since 1980, changes that many now see as a diminishment of overall military retirement benefits. When one retires from the military, he or she receives commissary and exchange privileges, medical benefits at military medical treatment facilities (MTFs) on a space available basis, and medical insurance (TRICARE). The recent changes to the entire military medical delivery system, though, have resulted in increased cost to military retirees and their families, especially those who have to rely solely on that system for their medical care. Another change is the closure or decreased capabilities of many MTFs used by military retirees and their families. This can create increased cost if they return to the civilian medical system or increased travel time if they choose to remain in the military system. Eligibility for use of the military medical system is also negatively impacted when the retiree reaches the age when he or she becomes eligible for MEDICARE.

### History of Military Retirement

Formal military retirement was really the first government-sponsored retirement program. It predates Bismarck's pension program by some 27 years and the Social Security system by almost 75 years. All of the legislation creating and modifying the military retirement system has had the intent of compensating those who have served in the military, and their families, for the injuries and/or hardships they have incurred during a military career. Since 1948 there has been a high degree of equity in the system in that the same criteria are applied to all, regardless of rank.

As early as the American Revolution, those disabled during conflict have received some type of compensation from the government. This has been in the form of a pension, usually 50 percent of their monthly pay for life. Until the Civil War, pensions were enacted only for disabled veterans of specific conflicts. The first nondisability retirement benefits were enacted in 1861 to retire Army officers who were no longer able to carry out the rigorous duties of command necessitated by the Civil War. In 1870, the first voluntary retirement benefits based on longevity were enacted, allowing officers to retire after 30 YOS at 75 percent pay upon approval of the president. In 1885, a system paralleling the officers' was enacted for enlisted personnel. The Fleet Reserve was created for Navy personnel in 1916 along with the pay formula basing retirement pay on 2.5 percent of monthly pay times YOS up to a maximum of 75 percent. The current military retirement system was created in 1948 when the 20 YOS minimum became the standard. Since 1948 there have been many attempts to modify this system, and in the 1980s two changes were actually made. The first major change occurred in 1980 when the determining factor in retirement pay was changed from the terminal base pay to the average of the highest three years of base pay for those who joined the military after September 8, 1980. The second change came in 1986 with the revision of the reimbursement schedule whereby the pay at retirement for all those joining the military after July, 31 1986 be reduced by 1 percent for every year short of 30 years when they retire after 20 YOS. This is a simplification of a complex formula that also affected cost-of-living allowances and deferment of other payments until the retiree reaches 62 years of age. These most recent changes in the retirement system, as well as a lengthy period of low unemployment, have reduced the attractiveness of retirement benefits in the 1990s. As a result, the military has experienced difficulty retaining some highly trained specialists who have crossover skills highly valued in the current civilian labor market. The most obvious examples are pilots, who are leaving to take advantage of a pilot shortage in the airlines, and those with computer or information technology skills and training. In response, a congressional commission included this issue as part of its charter (Report, 1999), and internal Department of Defense (DOD) papers suggest a number of alternatives to rectify the problems created by the 1986 changes. These changes would make the entire military retirement system more equitable and in line with corporate/civilian retirement plans (Faires, Whitley, & Wilson, 1998). As this book goes to press, there are bills in

Congress that should have a significant impact on the future of the military retirement system.

There is an impressive array of services offered by the Department of Veteran's Affairs (DVA) that are available to eligible military retirees and many veterans. The retiree may be rated with a service-related disability, which, depending on the percentage of the rating, may make that percentage of their pension tax-free, provide a stipend to eligible family members, and also entitle them to care in the DVA medical system. There are also possible educational benefits, vocational rehabilitation programs, employment assistance, and home loans. It is important for those providing services to military retirees to encourage them to connect with DVA to ensure that the they are receiving all the benefits to which they are entitled.

## ROLE TRANSITIONS: PROVIDING A THEORETICAL FRAMEWORK FOR RETIREMENT

It is helpful to discuss psychosocial aspects within the context of role. Role transition, especially the issue of role discontinuity, explains the activity of moving from the military to the civilian world, in particular the change in job roles.

### Role Transition

Role problems are often the context within which role theorists apply their theory. These role problems define how the person in a role may behave, thus providing the impetus for analyzing the interaction between the person and the role (Biddle & Thomas, 1966). The key element that defines the problem is the stress created by a change in position, a change in behavior, or the interaction of the two. The most obvious explanation of the "military retirement syndrome" (within the context of role theory) is "role discontinuity" where one moves, in a longitudinal fashion, from one role into another. The best example of this is the natural growth from childhood to adolescence to adulthood.

The symptoms of military retirement syndrome occur during the preretirement phase and often become more intense as the separation from the military becomes more imminent. The complaints are as follows: "anxiety, irritability, apprehension, job ineffectiveness, loss of interest, increases alcohol intake, depression, somatic complaints for which no physical basis can be found, and even over psychotic illness. Somatic complaints frequently center around the gastrointestinal tract or cardiovascular system" (McNeil, 1976, p. 251). When these problems manifest themselves there is a natural ripple effect in the family.

The military retiree leaves a role in a culture that has been a dominant factor in his or her life for at least 20 years. This aggregate role or culture is highly structured with myriad regulations and rules governing almost all aspects of life. The family has followed the military member wherever the military decided to send them. Upon retirement the decision on where to live is up to the service member, in consultation with the family. For the first time the decision is entirely theirs. In addition, there is the conformity of the uniform as well as the many courtesies and traditions (e.g., saluting, saying "sir" or "ma'am," parades or retreat ceremonies) that accompany the military life. The rank structure is the most obvious method of defining one's position within the military. If the family was heavily involved and reliant on the military community, they too took on the status of the military member, and they too may feel the loss when they move into a community where that status has little or no meaning. At the same time, the paternalism and the fostering of reliance blur the individual role by the cultural role group through the rewarding of unquestioning obedience. Taking all this into consideration, the individual role within the military is generally very clear, especially over the span of a career.

The military lifestyle also tends to shape one's nonmilitary role. First, the military lifestyle is very transient, with numerous moves over a 20-year career (Bellino, 1970; Frank, 1993). Second, there are often separations from family for varying lengths of time as a result of military duties (Pollock, 1987). There are extended family separations from supports for the military family because of the above-mentioned transience (Janowitz, 1971). Third, there may be varying exposures to the civilian community depending on assignment and where the family resides (Hunter & Pope, 1981; Hunter & Sheldon, 1981). Last, the sense of patriotic bond of actively participating in the defense of the country and the potential danger involved in "carrying out the mission" have an impact on how one views his or her role in life (Janowitz, 1971). These characteristics reinforce identification with the cultural role (the military) regardless of one's individual role within that culture. As a result, the cultural role becomes more prominent than the individual role. Therefore, friendships are often made primarily within the military community, and many retirees settle near military installations to maintain that identity with the group or culture.

"Role discontinuity" provides the longitudinal perspective that is crucial to this problem because it involves a lengthy transition process. The following are some of the more obvious problems the military retiree may encounter in making the role transition from military to civilian life. First, there is a loss of status. This is true for both officers and enlisted personnel. The latter group may have significant managerial and supervisory responsibilities that would be difficult to duplicate in a civilian setting. In the civilian world, military rank has little or no meaning and no formal clout. Second, there may not be the equivalent level of responsibility, leadership, or management in civilian employment (McNeil & Giffen, 1965b). Third, there often is a need to continue to work for both financial and emotional reasons. Problems arise when skills learned in the military are not easily transferable to the civilian labor market. Fourth, in that job market, the military retiree, who is middle aged (37-55 years old), often must compete with younger job applicants (Dunning & Biderman, 1973; McNeil, 1976). Fifth, the retiree must adapt to a more open, less clearly defined civilian environment that may not understand or appreciate the military experience (McNeil & Giffen; 1965a; 1965b). This becomes even more of a problem as fewer and fewer citizens have experience in the military. Sixth, because of the transient lifestyle, many military retirees do not have strong civilian community roots or role identifications, so they are not readily reintegrated into the civilian community where they retire unless there are other military retirees who may have paved the way (Bellino, 1970). Finally, family dynamics are often changed. While the military retiree is most likely playing a much larger and often different role in the family, the family too may be changing. Children may be leaving home for college, a job, or the military. The spouse may be more actively pursuing a career, and there may be the need or desire to relocate. The military retiree may be at home more than when on active duty. Even if the military retiree continues to work after leaving the military, most civilian jobs do not require the same type of separations from the family that a military job may have demanded. While on active duty, more time may have been spent performing military duties than being actively involved with the family (Frank, 1993; McNeil, 1976; Pollock, 1987).

The military pension provides an income cushion if the military retiree and/or the spouse are well employed but the family may have to make some financial adjustments. Another relocation may be required or desired, which may cause children to change schools one more time and to resettle once again. For the first time, the military member and his or her family will have to make decisions based on a different set of priorities. For example, do they stay in the area where the military member leaves the service and try to establish themselves there because the spouse has employment? Or do they move because either the military retiree or the spouse has employment elsewhere, or is there another set of circumstances driving these decisions?

## Similarity and Dissimilarity to the Civilian World

There have been marked changes in the military culture, which has had an important impact on the military role, especially since World War I. These changes have tended to mitigate some of the role discontinuity faced by the military retiree. As Lasswell noted, "the specialists on violence will include in their training a large degree of expertness in many of the skills that we have traditionally accepted as part of modern civilian management" (Lasswell, 1941, pp. 457-458). This is recognized as the seminal work describing the "civilianization" of the military as a result of the increased emphasis on technology. For Lasswell, this technology was exemplified by aerial warfare. The military role was examined extensively in Janowitz's *The Professional Soldier*, which further emphasized declining differences between the military and civilian life: "The narrowing difference in skill between military and civilian society is an outgrowth of the increasing concentration of technical specialists in the military" (Janowitz, 1971, p. 9). Moskos (1977) sees the military moving from an institutional to an occupational model. Others see an increasing convergence as it relates directly to civilian employment after military retirement (Biderman & Sharp, 1968; Sharp & Biderman, 1967). This increased similarity to the civilian world is graphically demonstrated by current recruitment advertisements. These hightech advertisements extol the virtues of the training, especially technical training. They highlight financial support for a college education offered by the armed forces and the Department of Veterans Affairs as an avenue to a better postmilitary life.

There are increasing similarities between the military and the civilian world, and there may be parallels between the transition from the military to the civilian work place at age 42, with the transition at the same age for a management level worker who is "outplaced" as a result of corporate changes. At the same time, there are several fundamental differences that make military retirement unique. Unlike private corporations, or even other government jobs, the fundamental purpose behind the military is the patriotic duty of defending the nation. The military has its own legal system to which its members are accountable as well as the existing civilian legal system. It is this legal system that legitimizes the myriad regulations that govern almost every aspect of life in the military. Although other organizations in the government and civilian world have rules and regulations, the scope of their social control is not as extensive as in the military. Another difference is the manner in which military personnel gain their duty positions. For the majority, they are more or less ordered to perform specific duty positions. Although individuals may try to maneuver to obtain the most desirable position possible, they do not apply or interview for that job, nor do they have much say as to where they will perform that job. Even though these are hardships that may be faced in the current corporate world, the military member does not generally have the option that the civilian employee has to simply quit and seek employment elsewhere. To leave the military prior to the end of an existing contract is generally a complicated extrication process (at least until they have 20 YOS and can retire), and when they do leave early they typically lose their vestment in the retirement system.

### Work Role Socialization

Successful socialization in any organization or institution involves the three processes of learning, social interaction, and communication mentioned by Goodman (1985a & 1985b). These processes are evident whether the setting is an institution whose purpose is to socialize or resocialize, or the organizations (work settings) which those institutions prepare one for, or an institution, such as the military, that both socializes and resocializes and at the same time provides a work setting. Schools and universities are institutions, that are meant to socialize—a positive impact—while jails and mental hospitals are intended to resocialize—a negative connotation. It could be argued that when people change jobs the process of being socialized into the new job might in fact be resocializing if they have to unlearn some aspect of their previous jobs or if they require additional training. Nevertheless, the military is an institution that performs both the socialization and resocialization functions.

On an individual level, the military recruit learns, through "basic training," new skills, social interactions, and communication techniques; at the same time he or she must unlearn previously learned skills, social interactions, and communication techniques. In a more general sense, the military acting as a socializing agent is exemplified by the recent advertisements touting the educational and training benefits of the military. Examples of the military as a potential resocialization institution are demonstrated by the judge who gives the juvenile offender the option of jail or joining the "army," or the parent who encourages their out-of-work, out-of-school, and "drifting" child to join the "service" to straighten out his or her life. The military is seen as a means of resocialization for those whose socialization, up to this point, is viewed as being flawed or deficient. It is this dual emphasis on socialization and resocialization, but particularly the high socialization expectations that are instilled early in a career military member, that defines the military. On the one hand, it is these traits that create potential difficulties in socialization (and possibly the need for resocialization) when military personnel retire and return to civilian life and the civilian work setting. On the other hand, in the current environment of low unemployment, the work ethic developed in the military is a valued trait for many civilian employers.

When one enters the world of work, one becomes involved in organizational socialization. Van Maanen defines this as the "process by which a person learns the values, norms and required behaviors which permit him to participate as a member of the organization"(Van Maanen, 1976, p. 67). This involves both formal and informal (covert) processes. The organization may have formal training and clearly spelled out rules and regulations for employees. At the same time the new employee must learn the informal or covert expectations of the others who make up the organization. Turner identifies the three activities of organizational socialization as "adjustment to the work environment, development of work skills, and culture and values of the organizational setting" (Turner, 1981, p. 3).

Because adult socialization is a lifelong process, one of the aspects of organizational socialization is the transition, and subsequent socialization (or resocialization), when a worker leaves one occupational setting and goes to another. This may occur voluntarily or involuntarily and may be frequent or happen only once at the end of a career. For the military retiree, generally the transition from the military to civilian life happens just once (though military retirees may not remain in the same civilian occupational setting until they finally retire from the workforce).

### Preretirement Planning

The last term that needs to be defined in this chapter is "preretirement planning." This term encompasses several types of programs and efforts. These programs can range from brief individual or group meetings that outline the benefits for which the future retiree is eligible, to elaborate programs taking several days. This latter type of program often includes other family members and covers a broad range of subjects relevant to the adjustment to retirement (Slover, 1982).

*History and theory of preretirement planning.* There is limited literature about the preretirement planning done by the military retiree, and much of what is written centers on second career issues or focuses on "normal" retirement. Even though there are some similarities between civilian and military retirement, because both require role transition, this literature tends to emphasize issues pertinent to the end of a career.

To get a flavor of the breadth of interest in this comparatively new field, it should be noted that the literature on preretirement planning falls into three general professional arenas: (1) gerontology; (2) adult education; and (3) personnel management and business. Although there is some overlap, each area has its own distinct focus. It is the gerontology literature that is most relevant, but it is important to briefly mention the other two areas.

The personnel management and business literature generally looks at preretirement planning within the context of company-sponsored formal programs and not informal, individual activities. This point of view is from an organizational perspective, especially how these programs benefit the organization. Although there is concern for the emotional well-being of the employee expressed in this literature, the general focus is on the structure of the programs and the companies' concerns and interests (Arnone, 1982; Levine, 1982). This literature tends to focus on the white-collar, upper-level management employee—that is the one most likely to receive company-sponsored preretirement planning programs and substantial retirement benefits (Bradford, 1979).

The adult vocational education literature tends to evaluate the different approaches or models used in presenting the programs, the settings for the programs, and the general types of educational theories and curriculum applied to presenting effective pre-retirement programs (Dennis, 1984, Keahey & Seaman, 1974; Tiberi, Boyack, & Kerschner, 1978).

Most of the research on preretirement planning or preparation appears in the gerontology literature and focuses on "normal" retirement. Much of this research on preretirement preparation involves formal programs or counseling situations. For example, Ash (1966) looks at attitude toward retirement and the change in attitude after pre-retirement counseling. Researchers have explored the preretirement life-style as it influences the degree of planning (McPherson & Guppy, 1979), preretirement attitudes and the relation to post-retirement life satisfaction (Streib & Schneider, 1971), the effectiveness of group preretirement preparation programs versus individual programs in facilitating the transition to retirement (Glamser & DeJong, 1975), and the positive correlation between pre-retirement planning and postretirement self-esteem (Reitzes, Mutran, & Fernandez, 1996). Finally, an early study relates general retirement planning to favorable preretirement attitude and accurate preconception of retirement (Thompson, 1958).

However, there have been four studies that related degree of preretirement planning and postretirement life satisfaction or adjustment, using samples of military retirees. The first (McNeil, 1964) was exploratory in conception. McNeil interviewed 46 Air Force officers and viewed planning in the general areas of employment, residence, and finances and categorized the retirees as active or passive planners, procrastinators or nonplanners He looked at their adjustment by age, rank, and whether their retirement was mandatory or voluntary but reported no significant findings. The second study (Stanford, 1968) used the open-ended concept of anticipation without looking at specific areas of preretirement planning and found a correlation between rank, education and job skill, and anticipation. Drawing from a large sample (over 700) of Army enlisted and officer retirees, Stanford found that increased anticipation correlated positively with increased postretirement morale. The third study (Fuller & Redfering, 1976) examined the relationship between rank and years retired in addition to degree of preretirement planning. Of the three variables, only the degree of preretirement planning was found to be significantly related to life satisfaction. Unfortunately, the individual activities that made up the planning scale (financial, recreational, benefits, health, housing/living, and employment) were not examined individually or in relationship to their degree of importance (Fuller, 1972). The final study (Wolpert, 1989) analyzed survey responses form 360 Air Force retirees as to the relationship between preretirement planning and postretirement job and life satisfaction. This study matched samples of retirees who attended a three-day transition workshop with those who did not attend the workshop and prepared for their retirement on their own. To place the results in a proper context, this study was done before 1990 when transition workshops became a universal benefit. The most important finding was that the positive correlation between the amount of preretirement planning in the concrete areas of employment, living arrangements, financial arrangements and medical care led to increased postretirement life satisfaction.

*Military preretirement programs.* There was limited assistance provided to separating or retiring service members prior to Project Transition, which was started by the Department of Defense (DOD) in 1968 at the urging of President Johnson, to help the Vietnam veteran make the transition from military service to the civilian world. Although this was a DOD-wide program, each branch of service administered its own version of the program. The objectives of this program were threefold: first, to insure that all who were separating from the military were informed of benefits available in both the civilian community and the military; second, to provide those participating with information and counseling on careers, education and training opportunities, as well as job placement assistance; and third, to enable those eligible to obtain a skill marketable in the civilian job sector before leaving the military (Eastlack, 1973). All personnel within six months of voluntary separation were eligible for Project Transition, but those with the enlisted rank of E-7 or below who did not have marketable job skills were given the highest priority. This program consisted of opportunities for training, either in the classroom or on the job, during the last six months prior to separation from the military (Traudt, 1974). Although Project Transition was intended to assist the separating Vietnam-era veteran, the retiring military member was also included.

The other program developed by DOD, which was designed specifically to help retirees, was Project Referral. This program, lasting two years from 1970 to 1972, was an offshoot of Project Transition. It combined counseling with a computerized program that matched the participating military retiree's experience with jobs requested by the civilian sector (Traudt, 1974). Members were eligible to register in the program six months before they retired, and their name was kept in the computer for six months after they retired. The computer portion of this program ended in 1972 due to lack of funding (Eastlack, 1973), but the counseling remained as part of Project Transition.

From the 1970s until 1990 there were some pilot transition programs offering assistance to separating and retiring service members. In 1990, after the fall of the Berlin Wall and the end of the Cold War, the "downsizing" of the military began. Congress provided the armed services the authority to offer a number of benefits and programs to facilitate this reduction in force that lasted throughout the 1990s. Included in this legislation was the authority for each branch of service to offer certain members the ability to retire after 15 YOS. At the same time, each service implemented a Transition Assistance Program (TAP) (National Defense Authorization Act for Fiscal Year 1991) for all those separating or retiring. The primary focus of these programs was to assist transitioning service members in developing the necessary job search skills to obtain civilian employment. The Department of Labor (DOL), in conjunction with the Department of Defense, devised a three-day workshop which is coordinated with military installation TAPs and Department of Veterans Affairs officials. The content of these workshops includes basic job search skills such as resume writing, interviewing, and dressing in civilian clothes. It also includes briefings on the wide variety of benefits offered by the DVA such as the Montgomery GI Bill, housing loans, and medical benefits.

Each service branch now has a TAP, (the Army calls theirs the Army Career Alumni Program [ACAP]) that expands on the topics covered in the three-day workshop. The staff of these programs provides individual counseling, facilitates the use of a variety of computer-based resources that focus on the job-search process, and provides access to a wide variety of job-search mechanisms. These programs have the ability to refer retirees to a wide variety of resources that can provide information to the retiree in the following areas: relocation assistance, financial planning, spouse employment, and family life education.

The mandatory retirement briefing is given regularly at installation level to active-duty personnel retiring from that installation. The duration of the briefing varies, but it is generally less than one day. It is usually led by personnel specialists and includes information about DVA benefits, veterans' life insurance, survivor benefit plans (SBPs), educational benefits from the GI Bill, rules governing employment with the federal government, and other general information about retirement benefits. The effectiveness of these briefings varies from installation to installation and depends upon the emphasis placed on this briefing by personnel and the relative number of men and women retiring from that installation each year.

## SUMMARY AND IMPLICATIONS

The civilian provider working with the military retiree and his or her family should be sensitive to the variety of issues raised by the uniqueness of military retirement. For those not yet retired, there is, an opportunity to work preventively to decrease the stress and anxiety of the transition and to encourage the use of the many programs and services available that specifically address many of the issues that arise during this transition. For those recently retired, the human service provider should assess how well the military retiree and the family have prepared for this change. Many of the programs and services that were available before retirement are still there to provide assistance. The provider should be aware of the changes in role for the retiree both within the family and in the world of work. There is a loss that needs to be acknowledged after leaving something with which the retiree and his or her family have been closely associated for 20 years or more. There is a definite change in status from being the military member to becoming a military retiree. Table 7.1 provides the civilian human service provider with a summary of the issues that should be considered in every needs assessment involving military retirees and their family members (including those approaching retirement status).

Above all, the civilian human service provider should remember the importance of treating the military retiree and his or her family with great respect and dignity. Despite the trials and triumphs of a military career, they have sacrificed much in the defense of their country, and they have persevered to this point of arriving at a very important life transition.

**Table 7.1**
**Issues to Remember when Providing Services to Military Retirees**

| Issue | Positives (Strengths) | Negatives (Weaknesses) |
|---|---|---|
| **Employment** | • May have easily transferable skill<br>• May have job lined up before retiring<br>• Has history of strong work ethic which is very marketable<br>• May have learned and is practicing good job search skills | • May not have transferable skill<br>• May not be mentally prepared for job search process<br>• May have unrealistic expectations about civilian job<br>• May have to take a job that does not have status or responsibility of previous military positions |
| **Spouse employment** | • Spouse may already be well employed<br>• Spouse may become the lead worker in family as planned | • Spouse may be forced to work to make up for lost income<br>• Military retiree may feel shame or inadequate if relying on spouse for bulk of financial support |
| **Relocation** | • Been there, done that – have a lot of experience moving and setting up house<br>• May have planned ahead for "final" move; is a positive event because it is the family's choice, not the military's | • May be forced to move because living on installation<br>• May be disruptive to older children in school or spouse with job to follow military retiree who moves for employment reasons<br>• Tired of moving, wants to settle down |
| **Finances** | • Has pension and benefits as a cushion<br>• May have planned well and invested appropriately in anticipation of retirement | • May be forced to work sooner than desired to ensure financial stability<br>• Has not made realistic assessment of how much pension will provide<br>• May have increased expenses with children in college |

**Table 7.1 (continued)**

| Issue | Positives (Strengths) | Negatives (Weaknesses) |
|-------|----------------------|------------------------|
| Change in status/role | • May feel free of constraining factors of the military<br>• May be energized by new challenge and different responsibilities<br>• Also may relish more active presence in the family | • Rank not very meaningful to civilian world<br>• May have to start new job supervised by younger, less experienced person<br>• May not be primary breadwinner any more |
| Family changes | • Military member home more and greater participant in family life<br>• No longer constrained by military rules that may have impacted family | • Spouse may be main breadwinner<br>• Spouse and military member may have to redefine roles and responsibilities within family |

## REFERENCES

Arnone, W. (1982, October). Pre-retirement planning: An employment benefit that has come of age. *Personnel Journal*, 760–763.

Ash, P. (1966, June). Pre-retirement counseling. *The Gerontologist*, 6, 97–128.

Atchley, R. C. (1976). *The sociology of retirement*. New York: Halstead/Wiley.

Baum, M., & Baum, R. C. (1980). *Growing old: A societal perspective*. Englewood Cliffs, NJ: Prentice-Hall.

Bellino, R. (1970). Perspectives of military and civilian retirement. *Mental Hygiene*, 54, 580–583.

Biddle, B. J., & Thomas, E. J. (1966). *Role theory: Concepts and research*. New York: Anchor Books.

Biderman, A. D., & Sharp, L. M. (1968, January). The convergence of military and civilian occupational structures: Evidence from studies of military retired employment. *American Journal of Sociology*, 73, 381–399.

Bradford, L., P. (1979, November–December). Can you survive your retirement? *Harvard Business Review*, 103–109.

Busse, E. W., & Kreps, J. M. (1964, September). Criteria for retirement: A re-examination. *The Gerontologist*, 4, 115–120.

Dennis, H. (Ed.). (1984). *Retirement preparation: What retirement specialists need to know*. Lexington, MA: Lexington Books.

Department of Defense. (1984). *Fifth Quadrennial Review of Military Compensation*.

Dunning, B. B. & Biderman, A. D. (1973, Spring). The case of military "retirement." *Industrial Gerontology*, 18–37.

Eastlack, R. J. (1973). An analysis of the Air Force transition program. Unpublished master's thesis, Auburn University, Auburn, AL.

Faires, J., Whitley, J. & Wilson, B. (1998). Military retirement–is it time to change? Unpublished research paper, U.S. Army War College, Carlisle Barracks, PA.

Frank, R. A. (1993). Military retirement in the post-cold war era. In F. W. Kaslow (Ed.), *The military family in peace and war* (pp. 214–240). New York: Springer Publishing Company.

Fuller, R. L. (1972). *A comparison of retirement adjustment between military officers and enlisted personnel on measures of years retired and pre-retirement planning.* Unpublished master's thesis, University of West Florida, Pensacola, FL.

Fuller, R. L., & Redfering, D. L. (1976, November). Effects of pre-retirement planning on the retirement adjustment of military personnel. *Sociology of Work and Occupations, 3*, 479–487.

Glamser, F. D., & DeJong, G. F. (1975, September). The efficacy of pre-retirement preparation programs for industrial workers. *Journal of Gerontology, 30*, 595–600.

Goldich, R. L. (1983, Fall). Military nondisability retirement reform. 1969-1979: Analysis and reality. *Armed Forces and Society, 10*, 59–85.

Goodman, N. (1985a). Socialization I: A sociological overview. *Studies in Symbolic Interaction,* Supplement 1, 73–94.

Goodman, N. (1985b). Socialization II: A developmental view. *Studies in Symbolic Interaction,* Supplement 1, 95–116.

Graebner, W. (1980). *A history of retirement: The meaning and function of an American institution, 1885-1978.* New Haven, CT: Yale University Press.

Hunter, E. J., & Pope, M. A. (1981). *Family roles in transition in a changing military.* San Diego, CA: United States International University, Family Research Center.

Hunter, E. J., & Sheldon, R. (1981). *Family adjustment to geographic mobility: Military families on the move.* San Diego, CA: United States International University, Family Research Center.

Janowitz, M. (1971). *The professional soldier: A social and political portrait.* New York: The Free Press.

Keahey, S. P., & Seaman, D. F. (1974, Spring). Self-actualization and adjustment in retirement: Implication for program development. *Adult Education, 24*, 220–226.

Lasswell, H. D. (1941, January). The garrison state. *American Journal of Sociology, 46*, 455–468.

Levine, H. Z. (1982, May-June). Consensus: Pre-retirement planning and other retirement issues. *Personnel, 59*, 4–11.

McNeil, J. S. (1964). *Adjustment of retired Air Force officers.* Unpublished doctoral dissertation, University of Southern California, Los Angeles, CA.

McNeil, J. S. (1976). Individual and family problems related to retirement from military service. In H. I. McCubbin, B. B. Dahl, & E. J. Hunter (Eds.), *Families in the military system* (pp. 237–257). Beverly Hills, CA: Sage Publications.

McNeil, J. S., & Giffen, M. B. (1965a, January). Military retirement: Some basic observations and concepts. *Aerospace Medicine, 36*, 25–29.

McNeil, J. S., & Giffen, M. B. (1965b, April). The social impact of military retirement. *Social Casework, 46*, 203–207.

McPherson, B., & Guppy, N. (1979, March). Pre-retirement life-style and the degree of planning for retirement. *Journal of Gerontology, 34*, 254–263.

Moskos, C. C., Jr. (1977, Fall). From institution to occupation: Trends in military organization. *Armed Forces and Society, 4*, 41–50.

National Defense Authorization Act for Fiscal Year 1991 (PL 101-510) (November 5, 1990). 104 STAT 1551.

*Oxford English Dictionary, Compact Edition.* (1979). Oxford, England: Oxford University Press.

Pollock, W. W. (1987, October-November). Military retirement: At ease, or stressed attention? *Modern Maturity*, 54–59.

Reitzes, D. C., Mutran, E. J., & Fernandez, M. E. (1996). Pre-retirement influences on post-retirement self-esteem. *Journal of Gerontology, 51B*, S242–S249.

Sharp, L. M., & Biderman, A. D. (1967, January). Out of uniform: The employment experience of retired servicemen who seek a second career. *Monthly Labor Review, 90*, 15–21.

Slover, D. (1982). Preparation for retirement: The impact of pre-retirement programs. In N. J. Osgood (Ed.), *Life after work: Retirement, leisure, recreation and the elderly*. New York: Praeger.

Snyder, W. P. (1994, Summer). Military retirees: A portrait of the community. *Armed Forces and Society, 20,* 581–598.

Stanford, P. I. (1968). *Anticipation of retirement by military personnel*. Unpublished doctoral dissertation, Iowa State University, Ames.

Streib, G. F., & Schneider, C. J. (1971). *Retirement in American society: Impact and process*. Ithaca, NY: Cornell University Press.

Thompson, W. E. (1958, Issue 2). Pre-retirement anticipation and adjustment in retirement. *Journal of Social Issues, 14,* 35–45.

Tiberi, D. M., Boyack, V. L., & Kerschner, P. A. (1978, October-December). A comparative analysis of four pre-retirement education models. *Educational Gerontology, 3,* 355–374.

Traudt, R. H. (1974). *The Air Force retiree's need for assistance in obtaining a second career*. Unpublished research paper, Air Command and Staff College, Air University, Maxwell Air Force Base, AL.

Turner, C. M. (1981). Socialization into organizations. *Coombe Lodge Working Paper* (ED249138).

Van Maanen, J. (1976). Breaking in: Socialization to work. In R. Dubin (Ed.), *Handbook of work, organization, and society* (pp. 67–130). Chicago: Rand McNally.

Wolpert, D. S. (1989). *Planning for military retirement: A study of the career transition program, general pre-retirement activities, and their effect on job and/or life satisfaction.* Unpublished doctoral dissertation, University of Pittsburgh, Pittsburgh, PA.

**Part II**

# Some Unique Aspects of Military Family Life

# Chapter 8

# Wartime Stress and Family Adaptation

*Leora N. Rosen, Doris B. Durand, and James A. Martin*

## INTRODUCTION

This chapter discusses the many stressors and stress mediators that affect military spouses during wartime separation as illustrated by the results of a study conducted during the Persian Gulf War. The chapter examines the various stressors which spouses were exposed to during the Persian Gulf War period and highlights the formal and informal social support and personal characteristics that helped spouses to cope during this conflict. Factors affecting the psychological well-being of spouses and specific issues affecting families with multiple problems are described.

The large mobilization of military service members during World War II and the need to understand their potential military effectiveness, spurred social scientists at that time to begin systematic collection of data on service members' adjustment to military life. It was around that time that a seminal study was conducted by Reuben Hill on the impact of war on military spouses (Hill, 1949). Hill focused on personal and family background characteristics that made for good or poor adjustment to separation—an approach which was adopted about a quarter of a century later by McCubbin and his colleagues in their study of the wives of Vietnam veterans (McCubbin et al., 1975). The philosophy that the military services were in any way responsible for the well-being of the military spouse was not yet well established in the early to mid-1970s, yet researchers were beginning to suggest that programs be developed for the benefit of military family members (Bey & Lange, 1974).

This concept of institutional commitment to the well-being of the military family took root with the adoption of the All-Volunteer Force (AVF) in 1973 and an increase in the number of married service members over the following decade (Morrison et al., 1989). As military leaders began to recognize the linkages between family issues and military readiness and retention in the late 1970s and 1980s, programs such as Family Support Groups and targeted family services became popular.

In October of 1990, within a few weeks of the announcement that U.S. troops were being deployed to the Persian Gulf in response to an Iraqi occupation of Kuwait, a task force of several Army agencies was assembled under the Deputy Chief of Staff for Personnel. This task force was commissioned to study the impact of the deployment on soldier and family well-being and the effectiveness of Army and military community resources in assisting and supporting families. This study was similar in concept to the above-mentioned work of earlier decades—it involved the examination of stress, coping, and adjustment of soldiers' spouses during wartime. In addition, this study provided an opportunity to evaluate the efficacy of numerous family support programs that the Army had set in place to assist families during wartime.

The study began with site visits to several Army installations, and selected Army Reserve and National Guard units in various locations around the United States. Informal individual and group interviews were conducted with spouses, Family Support Group leaders and volunteers, rear detachment personnel, garrison leaders, and local Army program and service providers. Questions were aimed at identifying family stressors related to the deployment, as well as stress mediators such as social supports and coping skills.

A subsequent systematic study of stress, support, and coping was conducted in which questionnaires were administered to spouses of soldiers from active component Army units representative of those that had deployed to the Persian Gulf. This self-administered questionnaire included items intended to measure and quantify variables that had emerged as relevant during earlier site visits. This chapter describes the results of this study. It helps to clarify both the nature of the deployment experience for family members and the effectiveness of various formal and informal social support initiatives. A separate study was conducted of reserve and National Guard component spouses (Rosenberg, 1992).

Most of the questionnaires in this study were mailed to survey participants. Some were distributed at briefings to ensure an adequate sample because rapidly changing events threatened to limit the time frame for reasonable data collection by mail. Response rates ranged from 37 percent to 65 percent for mailed questionnaires and 75 percent for those distributed at the briefings.

## DESCRIPTION OF THE SAMPLE

A total of 1,274 spouses completed the questionnaire. Only nine of these respondents were male spouses. All participants were living in the continental United States (CONUS). Thirty one percent of the sample was comprised of spouses of junior enlisted soldiers; 54 percent were spouses of noncommissioned officers; and 15 percent were officers' spouses. Seventy two percent were white, 15 percent were black, and 13 percent belonged to other ethnic groups. Ten percent of spouses were under 20 years of age, 53 percent were between 20 and 30 years of age, and 32 percent were between 30 and 40 years of age. Thirty five percent of spouses had a high school diploma or a General Equivalency Diploma, 40 percent had some college, and 18 percent had a college degree. Only 7 percent had not completed high school. Seventy-six percent had at least one child living at home, 30 percent had two children, and 16 percent had three or more children living at home. Most spouses lived off post. Only 29 percent lived on post.

## STRESSORS

Parting from a loved one and knowing that he or she may be going into a dangerous situation for an indefinite period would be considered a major stressor by most people. Indeed most of these military spouses found it so. However, there were many other, perhaps less obvious events and conditions associated with the deployment that were also very stressful experiences for these spouses. Three stressors were identified during the site visits as being potentially relevant to spouses' emotional well-being. They were emotional stressors; deployment-related events and general life events.

### Emotional Stressors

The first type of stressor was the emotional impact of those aspects of the deployment that were beyond the spouses' control, and which affected all or most spouses—for example, missing the soldier, problems with communication, concern about the soldier's safety and living conditions, and uncertainty about the length of the deployment. Problems with mail were frequently mentioned. Many soldiers did not receive their mail for long periods of time, even though their spouses were writing every day. Eventually they would receive mail, but often it was weeks or months old. At first, telephones were not available, but later, as the military infrastructure was built up in the war zone, many soldiers were able to phone home. Initially, the overwhelming demand required limiting calls to 10 minutes at a time.

Concern about the soldier's safety was another major emotional stressor. One woman said the scariest part of the deployment for her was when she heard that her husband's unit had been attached to the Marines. Her concern was the Marines' reputation for charging into danger. She tried to confirm this rumor, but local military officials would neither confirm nor deny it. Later General Schwartzkopf, the overall theatre commander, confirmed the rumor in a TV briefing. She remained frightened.

### Deployment-Related Events

The second type of stressor involved specific events or problems associated with the deployment, affecting some spouses, but not others. Examples included problems managing the household budget, confusion over military entitlements, getting repairs done, increases in childcare costs, and problems exercising power of attorney.

A great deal of stress was experienced during the standby period when families were constantly being told that the soldiers would leave the next day or the next week, and then found that they did not. Wives mentioned headaches, diarrhea and loss of appetite as a result of this stress. The emotional distress of the deployment was compounded by these kinds of events.

Financial management issues cropped up fairly frequently. A rear detachment commander explained that the most common financial problems were among young inexperienced spouses adjusting to a new situation: "The wife is finding out for the first time how to pay the bills and how the system works. These are mostly growing pains, and the solution is to get information to the wives." Money problems also arose, he said, as a result of soldiers going out and buying extra gear and equipment. For example, while two sets of combat fatigues were issued, some soldiers felt that they needed more, or in some cases a larger rucksack to fit their gear.

Banks varied in their acceptance of powers of attorney. Spouses said that they needed general power of attorney as opposed to special, but those interviewed agreed that some spouses may abuse this, buying cars or taking out loans. An official from the military finance office explained that some of the problems encountered were due to wives trying to use their husbands' power of attorney for everything. To cover bills and living expenses, he said, soldiers needed to set up a reliable way of getting money to their spouses, such as, direct deposit into a joint checking account, support allotments, or direct deposit pay.

Changing allotments could be complicated. One spouse told us that she ran into a problem when she wanted to stop a monthly allotment that had been paid in full, but her limited power of attorney did not enable her to do this. She was going to have to arrange for her husband to sign a special allotment form in Southwest Asia and send it back to her.

Another complaint often heard was that community businesses were taking advantage of spouses because they knew that their husbands were gone. One spouse said, "Recently my car broke down and I had to take it on my own to be fixed. I did not know how to tell if the mechanic was ripping me off."

**General Life Events**

The third type of stressor was general life events that had occurred in the previous year. Some of these events were directly related to increased stress levels during the deployment. For example, financial difficulty was often exacerbated by deployment. Cases were mentioned of couples that had moved into the area only weeks or days before the deployment, and the wife had not yet had a chance to settle in before the soldier departed. This was particularly difficult for wives who were unfamiliar with the military or who did not speak English.

Preexisting marital difficulties were another important issue. A Chief of Social Work Services at one post told us that he had seen 16 cases of couples with marital difficulties who came for help because they felt they needed closure before the deployment. In some instances divorce was contemplated or had already been decided on.

Our survey revealed that emotional stressors caused great to moderate amounts of distress for most spouses. For example, 91 percent of spouses missed their husbands and felt anxiety about the soldiers' safety and well-being. Specific events affected fewer spouses, although a substantial proportion of spouses experienced certain stressful events. For example 70 percent reported straining their budget through buying extra military equipment and paying long distance phone bills, 24 percent reported that they had not had a chance to say goodbye to their spouses before the unit departed, and 33 percent reported confusion over military entitlement. With regard to recent events prior to the deployment, 30 percent had experienced a permanent change of station (PCS) move, 24 percent had been pregnant, 18 percent had recently given birth, and 30 percent reported problems paying bills. All of these can be considered significant life stress events.

Although emotional stressors were mostly attributable to the deployment itself, deployment-related events contributed to the degree of distress experienced (Rosen, Westhuis, & Teitelbaum, 1993). The spouse's prior military experience significantly relieved emotional stress. This included the spouse having served on active duty or in the National Guard or reserves. The major predictors of deployment-related events were prior events. However, fewer events were experienced by those who felt comfortable dealing with Army agencies and who experienced good unit support for families after the alert.

## STRESS MEDIATORS

### Relocation to Be with Family of Origin

We were informed that a large number of young spouses had left the vicinity of the military installations where they had been residing and had gone to live with their own parents or other extended family members for the duration of the deployment. Our survey revealed that overall, 20 percent of the spouses left, and a further 30 percent had considered moving. Those who left tended to be younger (an average age of 24 compared with 29 for those who did not leave). Sixty-one percent of those who left were junior enlisted spouses compared with 23 percent of those who did not leave. Though 70 percent of those who left had children, compared with 77 percent of those who remained, the average age of the eldest child was four for those who left and eight for those who stayed.

The most common reason given for moving was to be near relatives or friends. Forty-four percent of those who moved gave this as a reason. Other reasons included financial difficulties (33 percent), and lack of support from the Army community (18 percent). Some spouses who did not move away from the military community would have preferred to move but were unable to do so for various reasons. A common reason for older spouses was not wishing to disrupt their children's schooling. The main reason given for wishing to move was to be near family and friends, which was mentioned by 53 percent of the spouses in this "wishing to move" category. Financial difficulty was mentioned by 30 percent and lack of support from the Army community by 25 percent.

About half of the spouses neither moved, nor considered moving. The main reason given for not wishing to move was to be near the military installation as a source of information on their soldier-husband. This reason was mentioned by 93 percent of those who did not move. Other reasons were "feeling supported by the Army community" (73 percent); "wishing to keep a job" (31 percent); "not wishing to disrupt their children's schooling" (51 percent); and "feeling that people outside the Army did not understand their feelings" (48 percent).

Young, inexperienced spouses who returned home seeking support from family and friends were not necessarily satisfied with the support they received.

Betty Smith was the 17-year-old wife of a specialist with a one-year-old child. Prior to the alert for Operation Desert Shield, they had orders for Germany, so they had given up their apartment on post, but then he received orders to deploy to the Persian Gulf. Betty found another apartment in the area, but after two months she decided to go home to her parents. "It was hard," said Betty. There were no military wives in her hometown. "My cousin's husband was a major, but she didn't want to hear anything." Her church was also not supportive. An important source of support was her company commander's wife who called her once a month in the beginning and then more often as the time drew closer for her husband to come home. "Next time," she said, "I don't want to go home."

Some older spouses also went home.

Jane Brown was a captain's wife and had a 10-year-old son. She had a severe emotional reaction to the deployment, and went home to stay with her mother. "I became real reclusive. The stress was always there. When he deployed, I was in total denial. I cried myself to death till I was sick. When the war started, I went through it again. I kept busy, trying to relieve stress. My mom took me to lunch." Because Jane's son was school age, she had to enroll him in a new school. Instead of returning to the base after the troops returned, she remained in her mother's town so that her son could finish the school year without changing schools again.

Not all spouses who returned to live with family were dependent and in need of care. Some were proactive in family support activities in their civilian communities.

Maria Smith started a support group called "Operation Homefront," saying that she needed to give of herself to others. Without any training or prior experience, she coordinated support to 2,000 spouses of service members from all branches of the service in her local area. "Some people just wanted somebody to listen," she said. Maria received a congratulatory phone call from President Bush, and got to present two T-shirts to Vice President Quayle.

On the other hand, some young spouses opted to remain in the military community despite hardship and lack of experience.

Sandy Jones was the 19-year-old wife of a specialist. They had been married approximately six months before he received orders to deploy. However, they had barely lived together during that time. Following their marriage in March of 1990, she and her husband lived separately while he went to Advanced Individual Training and she completed high school. Three days after they arrived at the Army base where he was to be stationed, he received orders to go to the Persian Gulf. Sandy stayed on at the base. "It was my first time alone in my entire life. I felt like I had been dumped in a foreign country." Nevertheless, she managed to make a go of things, and developed a sense of stability. "My security," she said "was my house." Things were also made bearable for her by her church and support from another military wife. While she did not participate in Family Support Group activities, phone calls from the group helped her cope.

Some spouses mentioned that children were a factor in their considering moving back home. "My daughter cries for her daddy. She needs her uncle who loves her," explained one woman. Some spouses told us that they would have left the area to go home if they could have afforded it, while for others the dilemma of whether or not to go home was a major issue. In one focus group, all the women interviewed said they knew someone who had gone home. However, one woman knew another spouse who had gone home and then returned to the post almost immediately. She missed her family support group and found that her civilian relatives were not understanding.

Uncertainty was a factor in the dilemma of whether or not to return home. As one woman said: "I would like to go home to my family in Chicago, but not knowing what's going to happen makes this decision difficult. What happens if I go home for Christmas and he comes back?"

### Social Support for Those Who Did Not Relocate

Previous studies had shown that informal support from other spouses in the soldiers' unit buffered the stress of separation experienced by young spouses during field exercises when soldiers were away for anywhere from a few days to several weeks (Rosen & Moghadam, 1988; Rosen & Moghadam, 1990). However, when the soldiers initially deployed to the Persian Gulf War, the length of the deployment was open-ended. Spouses did not know when the soldiers would come back or *if* they would come back. Social support became critically important. We examined three major support categories during our interviews:

- informal support, such as friends, neighbors, and community groups; and
- formal support such as that provided by Army agencies and Army service providers
- unit-level support, which included the unit commander or his representatives and the Family Support Group.

*Informal Sources of Support.* Informal sources of support included friends, neighbors, members of the local community, church groups, and extended family. In the survey we found that most spouses could count on their extended families for support (81 percent) and more than two-thirds could count on friends and neighbors. Employers were mentioned as a source of support. Some employers extended themselves to be supportive to spouses, and others did not. For example, one woman's request to change work hours so that she could spend more evening hours with her children was turned down, as was her request for time off to attend a predeployment picnic. She subsequently quit this job.

Groups within the community provided support.  In one community the American Legion offered to provide housing maintenance to spouses of deployed soldiers.  Many churches and community groups had support programs that spouses found helpful.

*Formal Sources of Support.*  For spouses who needed assistance with specific problems, services were provided through formal agencies such as Army Community Services (ACS) or the Family Assistance Center (FAC).  Only 26 percent said that they could count on an Army staff person, suggesting that most spouses may rely upon informal sources of support more than formal sources.  The proportion of spouses that actually used specific services during the deployment was relatively small.

Twenty-two percent of spouses noted that their use of services increased during the deployment.  In some instances, however, service providers saw this increase as stemming from needs that really require informal support.  A primary care emergency room physician told us that more young first-time mothers were bringing their children in for inconsequential complaints and that the spouses most likely to come in with trivial complaints were younger wives with no extended families to help.  She noted that the hospital staff had been supportive in helping to plug them into Family Support Groups, and she had personally made calls on behalf of these patients.

Chaplains were an important source of support, but unit chaplains deployed with their units.  Very few chaplains were available after the military units departed.  One spouse noted that the best thing that happened to her was the chaplain's briefing a few weeks before her husband left.  The chaplain warned them that the separation would be similar to the grieving process involving denial, anger, depression, and finally "picking yourself up and moving on."

*Unit Support for Families.*  The unit chain of command played a very important role in creating an environment that was supportive of families.  This included being sensitive to family members and to soldiers' family needs, and encouraging the development of family support groups.  We were interested in spouses' perceptions of military leaders' concern for families before and after the deployment alert, and the rear detachments' concern for families during the deployment.  While 69 percent said that military officials provided adequate information following the alert, roughly half agreed that rear detachment staff provided adequate support for families during the deployment.  Our survey results showed that *prealert unit climate for families was the major predictor of postalert unit climate for families, and of the rear detachment support for families during the deployment* (Rosen, Teitelbaum, & Westhuis, 1993).

After the units were alerted, but before they deployed, the commander's ability to get timely and adequate information to the spouses and to link them to Family Support Groups became critical.  Some commanders encouraged attendance at predeployment family support briefings by letting troops off early so that couples could attend.  Noncommissioned officers (NCOs) were seen as playing a vital role in communicating the importance of Family Supports Groups to soldiers.

The level at which information was communicated seemed important. Large battalion-level or brigade-level briefings (often more than 100 families) were too impersonal, particularly for younger spouses.

A soldier who remained behind told us: "There was some command emphasis on family support groups but not enough. Young couples need to be briefed on a one on one basis by the platoon sergeant or section chief. NCOs and chaplains should play a greater role. Section chiefs should be given a greater role. It is better for each section chief to talk to three wives than for the battalion commander to talk to 300 wives. Briefings on family support groups should be pushed down to a lower level." One sergeant said his wife went to a brigade-level briefing and came away with nothing. "A large group was present, and a big packet of information was given out. The problem was that the telephone numbers of the people in the chain of concern were flashed on a screen, but there was not enough time to write them down before they were removed."

Commanders also had to find creative ways to get spouses to attend these events, since spouses cannot be ordered to do anything. Soldiers, however, can be ordered so one commander told his soldiers that they all needed to attend a family briefing and 90 percent of their wives also showed up.

Command climate was judged by the timeliness and accuracy of information provided to families, and rumor control. In one location spouses complained that they had been lied to by unit commanders about what was going on. Though they understood the need for security, and that much of the information about the deployment had to be classified, they nevertheless felt insulted about being told deliberate untruths.

Commanders were responsible for the quality of people they left behind in the rear detachment to assist unit families. Many of those left behind in the rear detachment were in a nondeployable status because of health conditions or personal problems, and, as judged by unit spouses, many were not effective in their family support role.

### Family Support Groups.

Family Support Groups (FSGs) are mandatory unit-level, volunteer-based organizations specifically developed to provide support to spouses during deployments. We asked whether spouses were aware of the presence of these groups prior to the deployment and whether the groups had been active. We also asked about spouses' levels of participation, about changes that occurred in the FSGs after the alert, and about the leadership of FSGs. Six FSG functions were examined: the telephone tree, the newsletter, informational meetings, emotional support, recreational activities, and emergency assistance.

There was a dramatic rise in active FSGs from about 42 percent before the alert to about 82 percent after the alert. Level of FSG participation also increased but not as dramatically. For spouses who gave information on FSG activities, these activities were judged to work well in 40 percent to 60 percent of cases.

*Formation of Family Support Groups.* Family Support Groups that were already in existence had a smoother transition to the deployment phase than those that only formed during the alert period.

The successful formation of FSGs depended heavily on the interface between Family Support Group volunteers and unit leaders. One spouse tried to start a group in her husband's company prior to the deployment but had difficulty getting information out to spouses because the unit leaders were not encouraging the soldiers to get the messages home to their wives. Another spouse described a paranoid response from her husband's first sergeant when she tried to obtain a list of spouses' names and addresses. "He kept saying that this went against the Privacy Act, so we consulted the JAG [Judge Advocate General, who offers legal assistance to military families], and were told it was OK to use names and addresses as long as this was for the benefit and welfare of families."

Leaders' demonstrated support for families was important even if FSGs were not active before the deployment. Prior contact with families facilitated better communication between leaders and family members when the time came to swing into action.

Lack of prior communication between unit commanders and FSG leaders was noted to be a problem. "Prior to deployment the company commander never used to get together with the key people in the support group. Before the deployment he held one meeting with the support group in which he did all the talking. He did tell us a lot of important things, but he should have saved some time for the support group. For example, they wanted to know how they could get hold of a roster."

Even when units are in garrison, FSG volunteers and unit leaders seemed to have difficulty keeping track of unit wives, particularly the junior enlisted spouses. "Keeping track of wives is a problem. Young enlisted couples move a great deal, and change phones, or phones get cut off because they fail to pay the bill."

*Family Support Group Functions.* While 63 percent of spouses participated regularly or less frequently in FSG activities, up to 70 percent of spouses had sufficient knowledge of FSG activities to provide an opinion on their efficacy. Social activities usually included regularly scheduled meetings, for example a monthly meeting for company wives, with additional meetings sometimes scheduled for platoon spouses. Other activities included potluck suppers, organized outings, inviting guest speakers on topics of interest, and get-togethers on special occasions such as Thanksgiving or Christmas. One FSG leader had all the women over to her house for Christmas and videotaped them, then sent the video to their husbands in the Persian Gulf. She and other enthusiastic leaders were sometimes disheartened by the fact that some wives refused to participate in social activities. Of those who had knowledge of their FSGs, 38 percent rated fun activities as working well and 53 percent of spouses were satisfied with the emotional support they received.

Some FSGs came under criticism for being "cliquish." "There was so much jealousy and bickering among the wives. I have always been involved in wives' clubs before, but not here." In other cases, spouses raved about the FSG and its leaders. "The company commander's spouse was tremendous." "In our unit, all the key spouses worked full time including the battalion commander's wife, the sergeant major's wife, and the company commander's wife"; "They were committed to the women in the unit and the support was there."

Some spouses specifically said they were not interested in the social aspects of FSGs but relied on them mainly for their informational role. Forty-nine percent of spouses rated informational meetings as working well, 55 percent rated the telephone tree as working well, and 42 percent rated the newsletter as working well. The informational function of the FSG depended on teamwork and cooperation among volunteers at different hierarchical levels of the organization, sometimes referred to as the "chain of concern," and this support was sometimes not there.

A commander's wife described how she would spend several hours in meetings with higher ups and come away with piles of papers that she would copy and pass on to six deputies. However, if one of them failed to carry the ball, the information would stop flowing. "Information is not getting through from our key person. I get my information from wives from other units. I wanted to know if our husbands had arrived, and if they were OK and getting fed." On the other hand, an overworked volunteer complained: "I have called every girl in the platoon twice, but I have not yet had a chance to write my husband." A battalion commander's wife attributed many of these problems to the method of selecting FSG volunteers: "Soldiers volunteered their wives based on rank, and the wives resented it. Each unit recruited leaders differently. In some cases, when the husbands are gone, the wife steps out of her leadership role and doesn't have the courage to give this over to someone else. Such a person then cannot be found when needed to contact her people. In some family support groups calling chains are rotated and lists are switched to spread the burden."

Many FSG leaders made efforts to keep in contact with spouses who had left the area. Some leaders only kept in contact with spouses who had left post but who lived in the local area because it was too expensive to make long distance calls. Others made occasional long distance calls to spouses who were out of the area.

Emergency assistance was rated as working well by 60 percent of spouses, even though only 55 percent felt knowledgeable enough to rate this function. FSG volunteers, on the other hand, sometimes found themselves over their head with serious problems. A company commander's wife described how one of her "young ladies" had her phone and lights cut off and was without food. Her church helped her out. "She just didn't know how to budget."

A small number of volunteers did most of the work, such as providing rides to wives who lacked transportation. Sometimes demands became excessively burdensome and unreasonable.

*Leadership of Family Support Groups.* One-third of the spouses believed that FSG leadership was run along egalitarian lines, while another third believed that senior spouses were in control. The last third did not know or gave no information. Among those who were aware of the type of FSG leadership in their unit, higher ratings were given to FSG functions in egalitarian-led groups as compared with senior-spouse-led groups. A perception among some of the nondeployed soldiers that we interviewed was that wives who had no experience with deployments should not be high level people in the chain of concern. Spouses of older soldiers, particularly senior NCO spouses, were seen as more suitable for this role. A soldier commented: "Officers' wives were given key person positions even if they didn't want to do it. Enlisted wives who volunteered for these positions were ignored. Key person positions involve a lot of work. Even those that volunteer sometimes find they can't do it."

A battalion commander's wife told us of the difficulty of being a working battalion commander's wife and an active FSG leader. Many battalion wives were calling her directly even though they were supposed to call people lower down the chain of concern. She felt she was neglecting her own family due to spending so much time on the phone. She noted that many younger officers' wives (particularly captains and below) were choosing not to get involved in FGS matters, and the Army had made it clear that they could not be forced. Ultimately, she said, "it is the battalion commander's responsibility to ensure that FSGs are established."

### Personal Characteristics

Our site visits identified several personal characteristics as helpful in providing individuals with the skills required for coping with the stress of a deployment. In addition to obvious demographic characteristics—spouses' age, education, and soldiers' rank—other characteristics included previous experience with deployment, having grown up in a military family, previous special training for deployment, realistic expectations of what the military could provide for families, and comfort dealing with Army agencies. Soldiers' efforts to keep their spouses informed about the Army were a critical factor in spouses' successful coping with the stress of deployment and separation.

We were told during our interviews with spouses that some husbands deliberately kept their wives helpless, even to the extent of taking their military dependent's ID cards with them when they went into the field. A battalion commander's wife told us that: "Some husbands don't want their wives involved in Army activities such as FSGs, and give their unit wrong phone numbers so their wives will not be contacted to participate in activities."

A different problem involved spouses who had excessively high expectations of what the military could and should do for families. We were told that in some cases rear detachment staff and family support group leaders were being called upon to provide transportation to wives who had previously relied exclusively on their husbands to take them places.

Spouses who wished to return home turned to the Army for help, and many expected the Army to pay for the cost of moving them. In some cases the Army was able to do this. A housing official explained that commanders could, under certain circumstances, authorize the movement of household goods, for example if the neighborhood was deemed unsafe. He said the government would pay for the move in certain cases.  However, the government could not break leases, and several people wanting to move had come to housing and expected him to break leases for them.  The government would also not pay to move them again after the soldier returned home.

Perhaps the most unrealistic expectation was held by spouses who did not see that the Army had a right to send their husbands on a deployment.  Despite efforts on the part of service providers, leaders, and family support volunteers, these women could not be appeased.  One spouse described a predeployment briefing: "The captain and first sergeant were great with families, but I was ashamed at the outbursts of some of the wives at the briefing.  The leaders gave out information and handouts, and were as supportive as they could be.  But some of the wives didn't realize why their husbands were in the military.  One wife was completely out of control."

### Coping

Spouses were asked to rate their levels of coping with regard to their daily household tasks and with regard to their job performance for those who were employed outside the home.  Most spouses reported coping reasonably well with these activities.  About 10 percent said that they were coping poorly or very poorly.  Some women were stoical and emphasized that whatever their problems during the deployment, they would not communicate these to their husbands for fear of causing their husbands additional concern.  One woman mentioned that she had passed a gallstone during the standby period, while her husband was still in the United States waiting to leave, but she had not informed him of this.  She packed her kids in the car and took herself to the emergency room at 2:00 a.m.

## FAMILY ADAPTATION

### Spouses' Emotional Well-Being

Though many study variables demonstrated a statistical relationship with spouses' emotional well-being, only three emerged as important overall predictors of well-being—emotional stressors, deployment-related events, and FSG informational meetings (Rosen, Teitelbaum, & Westhuis, 1993).  FSG informational meetings were the only support variable in the study to emerge as a significant predictor of overall well-being.  While an increase in the number of deployment-related events did increase the impact of emotional stressors, high rear-detachment support and prior military experience appeared to reduced the impact of these stressors.  Certain social supports were related to a lower number of deployment-related events.  These included comfort dealing with Army agencies, support from extended family, and support from unit leaders after the alert.

### Families with Special Problems

An important recurrent theme that surfaced during the site visits was that while most spouses were coping with the stress of the deployment, a few spouses were having serious difficulty. These spouses presented themselves to FSG leaders, Army service providers, and rear detachment personnel with multiple complaints and frequently failed to cope despite efforts to help them. They consumed a disproportionate amount of the resources provided for families, and left help-providers with feelings of burnout and a sense of having failed to accomplish what the Army had promised. Bell and Schumm discuss these families in the next chapter of this book (Chapter 9).

Our analysis of the study data suggested that there were two groups of spouses with multiple problems (Rosen, Westhuis, & Teitelbaum, 1994). The first included young spouses all under the age of 30, over half of whom were married to NCOs, the remainder being junior enlisted spouses. They tended to have high expectations of the Army and were dissatisfied with service providers. The second group was an older, predominantly NCO cluster. More than 60 percent were over 35. This group contained the highest proportion of employed spouses and the lowest proportion of homemakers. They had high levels of stress, poor coping, and low support. Though a large proportion were dissatisfied with the services they had received, they had average to low expectations of the Army.

## SUMMARY AND PRACTICE GUIDELINES

Most spouses experienced moderate to high levels of distress during the deployment, but the vast majority coped well with their daily lives. Preexisting problems, such as financial difficulties, exacerbated the stress related to the deployment, and many events that arose during the deployment, such as difficulty managing a budget, were probably due to the inexperience of young spouses. Some spouses experienced chronic problems such as lack of transportation, and some of these spouses became excessively dependent on service providers and volunteers, who themselves experienced frustration and burnout.

A preexisting command climate that was favorable to families was an important factor in ensuring that unit-level support for families was in place and operational during the deployment. Even where formal FSGs were not in place at the time of the alert, prior contact between leaders and spouses facilitated better communication and more effective formation of FSGs during the deployment. Most spouses relied on informal sources of emotional support, but Family Support Groups played an important informational role, and worked better when leadership was perceived to be egalitarian.

Accurate and timely information was important in facilitating good adjustment among spouses during the deployment. Soldiers played an important role in this regard. Spouses who had been kept well informed about the Army by their husbands were more likely to cope effectively with the stress of the deployment than those who were ill informed.  It is important to note that information provided to spouses by unit leaders was more effectively absorbed when briefings occurred at a lower organizational level, for example at the company or platoon level rather than at the battalion or brigade level.  Mass meetings were not effective.

Human service providers need to be aware of the valuable role installation and unit-based formal and informal supports can play in helping military family members cope with wartime stress.  Whenever possible, civilian providers need to encourage and help sustain family member participation in these programs and unit-based relationships.  At the same time, it is critical to recognize that some family members will have needs that cannot be met by these support systems.  In these cases, it is important for civilian human service providers to work cooperatively with military installation and unit representatives to ensure the safety and well-being of these military family members.  As in many aspects of effective delivery of human services, having positive, preexisting relationships within the client's community is an important ingredient for successful interventions.

## REFERENCES

Bey, D. R., & Lange, J. (1974).  Waiting wives: Women under stress.  *American Journal of Psychiatry, 131*(3), 283–286.

Derogatis, L. R., Lipman, R. S., Rickels, K. Uhleahuth, E. H., & Covi. L. (1974). The Hopkins Symptom Checklist (HSCL): A self-report symptom  inventory. *Behavioral Science, 19*(1), 1–15.

Hill R. (1949).  *Families under stress: Adjustment to the crises of war separation and reunion.* New York: Harper & Row (reprinted by Greenwood Press, Westport, CT, 1971).

McCubbin, H. I., Dahl, B. B., Lester, G. R., & Ross, B. A. (1975). The returned prisoner of war: Factors in family reintegration.  *Journal of Marriage and the Family, 37*(3), 471–478.

Morrison, P. A., Vernez, G., & Grissmer, D. W. (1989).  *Families in the Army: Looking ahead.* Santa Monica, CA: Rand Arroyo.

Rosen, L. N., & Moghadam, L. Z. (1988).  Social support, family separation and well being among military wives. *Behavioral Medicine, 14*(2), 64–70.

Rosen, L. N., & Moghadam, L. Z. (1990).  Matching the support to the stressor: Implications for the buffering hypothesis. *Military Psychology, 2*(4), 193–204.

Rosen, L. N., Teitelbaum, J. M., & Westhuis, D. J. (1993).  Children's reactions to the Desert Storm Deployment: Initial findings from a survey of Army families.  *Military Medicine, 158*(7), 465–469.

Rosen, L. N., Westhuis, D. J., & Teitelbaum, J. M. (1993).  Life events, social supports, and psychiatric symptoms among spouses of soldiers deployed to the Persian Gulf during Operation Desert Shield/Storm.  *Journal of Applied Social Psychology, 23*(19), 1587–1593.

Rosen, L. N., Westhuis, D. J., & Teitelbaum, J. M. (1994).  Patterns of adaptation among Army wives during Operations Desert Shield and Desert Storm. *Military Medicine, 159*(1), 43–47.

Rosenberg, F. R. (1992). *Spouses of reservists and national guardsmen: A survey of effects of Desert Shield/Storm.* Unpublished manuscript, Walter Reed Army Institute of Research, Washington, DC.

Chapter 9

# Providing Family Support During Military Deployments

*D. Bruce Bell and Walter R. Schumm*

## INTRODUCTION

Helping military families to cope with the stresses of large-scale military deployments requires knowledge of the stresses families face, how they attempt to cope, and how they can improve their coping skills. The U.S. military has built an extensive literature on these topics. This chapter examines what service providers need to know to enhance family adaptation to the stresses of deployments. The chapter highlights some of the important family support documents developed by the military services and details how human service providers can access these documents.

The extent to which family members can successfully adapt to the conditions of military life has been shown to be related to retention, morale, and job performance (Segal & Harris, 1993). Segal (1988) lists five demands that military life places on families:

- Risk of injury or death to the service member.
- Geographic mobility.
- Periodic separation of the service member from the rest of the family.
- Residence in foreign countries.
- Normative role pressures placed upon family members because they are members of the military community.

This chapter reviews what is known concerning the adaptation of military families to two demands that are especially prominent during military deployments: physical risk and family separation. Some family separations occur without an overseas deployment, such as separations related to training activities at U.S. military training sites and operational deployments related to domestic emergencies (e. g., floods and hurricanes). The research that provides the basis of this chapter typically involved Army units and their involvement in overseas military operations where at least 500 service members deployed for at least six months to another country to accomplish a nontraining mission. Most of these deployments involved danger or at least the perceived threat of danger.

Much has changed in the armed forces since the fall of the Berlin Wall in 1989. Before this historical event, large numbers of our military forces were forward deployed primarily at permanent military bases in Europe, South Korea, Turkey, and Japan. As described in Chapter 1, today U.S. forces are primarily based in the United States and remain on call for rapid deployment for military missions around the globe. In recent times, these forces have been deployed to locations such as Hungary, Cuba (Guantanamo), Somalia, Macedonia, Haiti, Rwanda, the Sinai, and Kuwait, and most recently in Bosnia and other countries in the area of the Balkans. The end result is time away from home and loved ones. In fact, according to the latest Army figures, the number of nights soldiers spend away from home base has increased 300 percent since 1989 (Reimer, 1997). This increase is true for all the services. The reduction in the size of U.S. forces in the 1990s and corresponding increases in missions to be accomplished means that family separation is, and will continue to be, a fact of life for all service members and their families during the foreseeable future.

## FAMILY STRESS ACROSS THE PHASES OF DEPLOYMENTS

A deployment is a condition that combines family separation with increased danger, even in purely training situations, and deployments have long been known to be stressful for families (Alderks, 1998; Bell, Stevens, & Segal, 1996; Hill, 1949; Lewis, 1984). The kinds of stressors that a spouse faces while the service member is preparing to deploy, during deployment, and even after the service member returns home are reviewed here.

### Predeployment

What spouses want to know right after a deployment is announced is: (1) Where is my spouse going? (2) How long will he or she be gone? (3) Is he or she in danger? and (4) How do I get in touch with him or her if I have an emergency? The inability to obtain accurate answers to any of these four basic questions greatly increases spouse distress (Lewis, 1984; Martin, Vaitkus, Johnson, Mikolajek, & Ray, 1996).

During the predeployment period, the military community leaders try to get families ready to function during the service members' absence. Initial efforts often focus on the need for wills, powers of attorney, and financial arrangements. Most (82 percent to 98 percent) of the spouses whose soldiers deployed to Somalia in 1992 either had, or quickly acquired, the legal and financial mechanisms that they needed for the deployment—that is, a will from the soldier, a power of attorney, a dependent identification card, and direct bank deposit of the soldier's pay. Fewer spouses had at least two weeks of pay in savings (63 percent) or a pay allotment to meet expenses (32 percent). Likewise, relatively few spouses (59 percent) said that they understood the Army's casualty notification system (Kerner-Hoeg, Baker, Lomvardias, and Towne, 1993). Family members needed considerable time together to be both psychologically and logistically ready for the deployment. The fact that time always seems quite compressed around the start of a deployment is partly why many families typically complain that there is not enough family time prior to a deployment (HQ, USAREUR, 1991).

Predeployment is difficult for many families. Family members want to be close to one another but often need to distance themselves from one another to defend against the pain of the pending separation. The tensions between parents, the need for the parents to prepare for the deployment, the parents' reluctance to discuss the deployment with the children all add to the stress children feel, often leaving them even more upset than they would otherwise be (Amen, Jellen, Merves, & Lee, 1988).

### During Deployments

The reasons why deployments are stressful for the nondeployed spouse are fairly obvious. Among other factors, most spouses miss their husbands (or wives in the case of deployed female military members). Spouses left behind miss the companionship. They miss the assistance with daily household tasks (e.g., home repairs, childcare, yard work, and transportation). They miss the intimacy. Many fear that their deployed partner will not be faithful. They fear that they or their partners will somehow change during the separation and that these changes will wreck their marriages. They may resent the fact that they will not be able to share some once-in-a-lifetime events (e.g., a first Christmas together, a child's birth, and a baby's first steps). As described in Chapter 8, the non-deployed spouses may find that they have to accomplish various domestic tasks on their own, tasks such as balancing a checkbook or repairing a car, tasks that were previously done by the military member. Many spouses find that deployments create financial difficulties. Young spouses, particularly, may need the support of their parents or a friend back home. They may incur substantial long distance telephone charges. Some spouses find that the deployed service members need to call them and that these long distance calls may strain the family's budget.

More than 80 percent of the spouses of soldiers that have been sent to the peacekeeping mission in Bosnia have said that they experienced sadness and loneliness at least once a week during the deployment. Over half the spouses have reported that they experienced other stress symptoms at least once a week—sleep problems, trouble getting going, trouble concentrating, experiencing everything as an effort, and/or an inability to "shake the blues" (Bell, Bartone, Bartone, Schumm, Rice, & Hinson, 1997). About half the spouses of soldiers who had deployed to Bosnia for Operation Joint Endeavor reported a negative effect of the deployment on themselves (56 percent) and/or their military spouses (49 percent). While only 19 percent of the spouses reported an adverse effect on their marriage, the drop in marital satisfaction was larger than that seen for previous deployments (Schumm, Hemesath, Bell, Palmer-Johnson, & Elig, 1996) or for previous unaccompanied tours (Bell, Bartone, Bartone, Schumm, Rice, & Hinson, 1997, p. 16). While their financial difficulties appeared to be lower than those experienced during the Persian Gulf War, stress symptoms were equivalent, and marital adjustment may have been more adversely affected (Bell & Schumm, 1998). However, marital satisfaction bounced back when soldiers returned home (Bell & Schumm, 1998; Bell, Bell, Bartone, Bartone, Schumm, Rice, & Hinson, 1997). Nevertheless, reduced marital satisfaction of service members or their spouses can affect attitudes toward the military and job performance (Schumm, Bell, Segal, & Rice, 1996).

In studies of soldiers deployed to Bosnia, those spouses who felt more prepared for the deployment were much more supportive of the mission, a result that was not an artifact of rank (Bell, Bartone, Bartone, Schumm, & Gade, 1997). However, the spouses' worry about "mission uncertainty" was related to a host of important variables, including spouse stress, support for the mission, retention attitudes, and perceived adverse effects on the family, even controlling for rank, education, and age.

Research has shown that certain features of deployments can add to the stress. Rapid call-ups result in lack of time for families to get their physical and emotional affairs in order. Poor scheduling of the troop transportation results in missed opportunities to say good-bye or in multiple good-byes that are even more stressful. Open-ended return dates have also proven to be a problem. Families do not know what kinds of strategies to employ if they do not know how long they are planning for. Open-ended deployments also raise questions of equity. Most post–Vietnam War military deployments have involved a relatively small portion of the force. While it may not be a fact, it often appears to families that there are plenty of substitutes for those deployed. Families, therefore, wonder why specific dates for their own service member's return cannot be set.

There is substantial research showing that living a great distance from where military social services are being delivered contributes to stress. However, the effect is somewhat dependent upon the reason why the families are residing where they are (Bell, Stevens, & Segal, 1996; Bell, Schumm, Segal, and Rice, 1996).

Another source of stress for families is scarce or contradictory information about the deployment. Command-sponsored information is usually accurate at the time it is gathered. However, the need to avoid rumors by having all information verified and sent through official channels means that the command information may not be as current as what an individual spouse may have just heard via the telephone or e-mail from his or her deployed spouse. Rumors are generally available and tend to center upon what is most important to the families and for which they have the least amount of good information (e.g., when the unit is coming home).

Information from "home" can be a problem for the service member. Getting called to the phone can pull the service member away from his or her mission. It can remind him or her of the good things he or she is missing or that he or she cannot solve family problems from a distance, particularly if they require a timely intervention.

### Rest, Recuperation, and Reunions

Very little research has been done on the problem of how to conduct what is called "Rest and Recuperation" or R&R leave during a deployment. However, R&R was studied during a recent peacekeeping deployment to Bosnia. Researchers found the following: spouses favored having a home leave/R&R program, but they felt that the time should be "compensatory" rather than "charged" leave, given the long duty hours demanded by the deployment. Spouses wanted some say in when leave was granted, but that decision was largely a function of the needs of the unit. Although appreciated, leave was often experienced as a stressful time since it disrupted newly established family routines, required another painful good-bye, and was associated with increased depression in the spouses and soldiers after the soldier returned to Bosnia. There was some evidence that selection of service members for leave status (including leave back to home station) was due to previously existing family problems. Often these problems had not been resolved prior to the deployment (Bell, Bartone. Bartone, Schumm, & Gade, 1997; Bell; Bartone, Bartone, Schruum, Rice, & Hinson, 1997).

Although researchers have long known that reunion is a problem area, most soldiers and families assume it will be easy (Boulding, 1950; Hill, 1949; Segal, 1986). The service member, the spouse, and even the children often fantasize about how perfect the reunion will be, even though reality seldom lives up to advanced billings. Children can become upset and clingy, roles may have changed, and needs for personal freedom and space come into play.

Wood, Scarville, and Gravino (1995) interviewed wives in detail about all phases of their husbands' deployment to the Sinai in 1987. They found separation and reunion to be stressful but that most wives adjusted well to both phases. When the marriage had more problems than usual, reunion adjustment was relatively poor. Effective reunion appears to require that spouses and service members renegotiate their roles and levels of independence, which may be more difficult for some than for others—particularly in those marriages where the nondeployed spouse has become more independent (Bartone, Harris, Segal, & Segal, 1993; Gravino, Segal, & Segal, 1993).

Hill (1949) and Boulding (1950) found among World War II veterans and their families that families that kept the absent father as a part of the family's emotional life suffered more during his absence but actually did better at reunion than did those families that "closed ranks" and tried to ignore the absent father. McCubbin (1980) expanded on the idea that the behaviors that help families cope during deployments may actually prove detrimental during reunion. He isolated six separate behavioral patterns that Navy wives said were useful coping tools during an eight- month deployment: (1) maintaining family integration and stability, (2) believing in God, (3) trusting and building relationships, (4) living up to military expectations, (5) establishing independence and self-sufficiency, and (6) keeping active in hobbies and interests. Pattern 3, trusting and building relationships, proved to be positively related to husband-wife reintegration during the reunion. Patterns 1, 2, 4, and 6 proved to be negatively associated with husband-child reintegration. The remaining pattern, number 5, was not related to either measure of family integration.

During the Persian Gulf War, Durand (1992) found many spouses reporting that during reunion they or their soldier-spouse had changed. The most frequently mentioned areas of change included: a greater feeling of closeness (68 percent), greater independence in the nondeployed spouse (47 percent), and soldiers doing more household chores (35 percent) and childcare (27 percent).

## WHAT HELPS FAMILIES ADAPT

One of the recurring themes in deployment literature is that spouses adapt better if they adopt positive attitudes about the deployment and concentrate upon those things that they can control. Bell (1991) summarized what appears to be a winning strategy:

- Develop individual and family goals. Use them to develop/maintain family routines.
- Accept the lack of control over deployment events.
- Concentrate on what you can control: today, yourself, your family, your job, etc.
- Become or remain active: get a job, volunteer, or take up a hobby.
- Seek relevant information about the mission, the Army, and helping agencies.
- Seek social support from friends, relatives, Family Support Groups, and the families of other deployed soldiers.
- Communicate with your soldier, and open channels of communication within your own family.
- Check out rumors, and don't believe everything you hear.

Another consistent finding from deployment research is that friends and relatives are more likely to be utilized and seen as "helpful" during a deployment than any of the formal social services offered by the military (Bell, 1993; Bell, Schuum, Segal, & Rice, 1996; Kerner-Hoeg et al., 1993). This finding is not surprising given that spouses are more likely to need the kinds of services (e.g., free childcare on demand) that friends and relatives typically provide rather than those services normally provided by the military community.

The fact that spouses are less likely to use military services than friends or relatives does not mean that military community services are not useful or needed. Many of the programs offered by the military community (e.g., housing, programs for newcomers, and Family Support Groups) help families to acquire friends, which in turn leads to needed support. Furthermore, most military social programs are aimed at specific segments of the military population. It is more important that these programs serve their intended clients than that they reach a large number of families.

Junior enlisted families, in particular, are quite likely to leave the installation during a lengthy deployment and "go home" to get additional help from their relatives. Although they are generally successful in getting the support they are looking for, such as reduced housing costs, emotional support, and help raising small children, Peterson (1992) showed that these spouses were less likely to be adapting well to service life.  However, additional analyses have shown that poor adaptation is more a function of family characteristics than the fact that they have moved out of the local Army's support network (Schumm, Bell, Knott, & Rice, 1997).  Thus, more of an effort is required to teach families good coping skills rather than trying to prevent them from going "home."

Peterson (1992) found that the majority of Persian Gulf War spouses reported that readjusting to their marriages was easy during the first few months. However, 9 percent of these spouses reported that they were still having a difficult or very difficult time adjusting to their marriages seven months after the soldiers had returned.  Marital adjustment seemed to be less of a problem during the Somalia deployment (Bell, Teitelbaum, & Schumm, 1996) and during a recent U.S. peacekeeping rotation to the Sinai (Bell, 1998).

Different deployments do have unique features that help or hinder the families.  The Persian Gulf War enjoyed a higher level of public support than did either Somalia (Bell & Teitelbaum, 1993; Bell, Teitelbaum, & Schuum, 1996) or Bosnia (Bell, 1997).  Higher levels of public support were related to more visible, public help for military families such as free childcare, space for meetings, and free advice on car maintenance (Bell, Stevens, & Segal, 1996).

A related asset is the ability of spouses to believe in the purposes of the mission.   It appears that spouses were more supportive of the overall deployment during the Persian Gulf War than during either the Somalia or initial Bosnia deployments.  According to McCubbin and Patterson (1983), "belief in the mission" made it easier for families to justify making sacrifices to support the service member and the deployment.  During both of the Somalia and Bosnia deployments, support for the mission was found to be positively associated with spouse adaptation (Bell, Bartone. Bartone, Schumm, & Gade, 1997; Kerner-Hoeg et al., 1993).

For whatever reason, the level of spouse support for the mission was higher for Somalia than for Bosnia (Bell, Bartone, Bartone, Schuum, & Gade, 1997a).  In their comments to the Army researchers, spouses gave the following reasons for not supporting the initial military mission to Bosnia: it was too long, it was not likely to be successful, or Americans should be using their resources to solve American problems.

## WHICH FAMILIES ADAPT WELL TO DEPLOYMENTS

The vast majority of military families can and do adapt to the stresses of deployments.  A study conducted during the height of the Persian Gulf War found no difference between the ability of "deployed" and "nondeployed" spouses to meet the demands of daily life.  Eighty-five percent of both groups said they were able to meet the family, work, and social demands that they faced (HQ, USAREUR, 1991).

Families with the most social, financial, and emotional resources are the ones who tended to adapt best to deployments.  Thus, studies found that those who did best were better educated, older (experienced) spouses who were married to senior NCOs and officers (Bell, Stevens, & Segal, 1996).  They were tuned into military channels of communication; they were more supportive of the mission; and they experienced fewer stress symptoms (Bell, Bartone, Bartone, Schumm, & Gade, 1997).  The fact that it was the older, more experienced spouses who were doing well was partly due to self-selection.  Those who cannot cope with the stresses of separation—or are unwilling to try to cope—help convince their service members to get out of the military (Segal & Harris, 1993).

Recent interviews with family service providers have led to the description of four types of families that not only do not adapt well to deployments but also create a disproportionate amount of work for both volunteer and professional family service providers.

- The multiple problem family exhibits problems and is known to the "family service community" well before the deployment starts.  Their problems often get much worse once the service members leave.
- The excessively dependent spouse is often someone young and inexperienced who does well as long as the service member is present but is unprepared to cope alone.
- The overly demanding spouse expects that the military will step in to fill the void created by the service member's departure and is critical of any resistance or slowness in responding to a stream of demands.
- The families who are scheming to get their service members an early return are particularly frustrating.  They will create crises but then refuse to have the crises resolved unless the soldier's return is part of the solution.  A fuller description of these families and suggested ways of dealing with them is detailed elsewhere (Bell, Bartone, Bartone, Schumm, & Gade, 1997; Bell, Stevens, & Segal, 1996).

Although the public associates deployments with high divorce rates, there is no direct evidence that deployments cause divorce.  Divorce rates fall during deployments because those desiring a divorce cannot act on their wishes until the service members return.  Divorce rates rise after a deployment because service members get the divorces they wished to get earlier.  Service members with weak marriages before a deployment are much more likely to get divorces afterward.  Preliminary analyses done at the U.S. Army Research Institute showed that deploying a soldier with a weak marriage, rather than leaving him or her in garrison, is associated with an increased likelihood of a subsequent divorce.  Another apparent trend is that those with weaker marriages may be more likely to volunteer for a deployment, especially an overseas deployment.  Those with weaker relationships may anticipate a lower psychological cost to being separated.  Accordingly, any relationship between deployments and subsequent divorce may be an artifact of self-selection or predeployment conditions.  Nevertheless, most studies document some postdeployment divorces among soldiers or spouses who thought that they had stable marriages prior to the deployment.  One of the current areas of research for the Department of Defense is making a thorough assessment of the impact on divorce rates of military service in the Persian Gulf War.

## FAMILY SERVICES PROGRAMS AND RESOURCE MATERIALS

Operation of various aspects of the military family support system has been greatly improved by a wide variety of resource materials that have come into being in the 1990s. These include books, pamphlets, videotapes, and teaching materials. The best place to find these materials is to contact the Military Family Resource Center (located at 4040 N. Fairfax Drive, Room 420, Arlington, VA 22033-1635, 703-696-9053) or the headquarters of the family support agency for any of the military services. While most of these training materials have not been subjected to systematic evaluation, some of the more useful materials currently available include:

- *Family Support Group Leaders Handbook* (Schumm, Bell, Milan, & Segal, 2000);
- *Leaders' Wives Speak Out* (U.S. Army War College, 1984);
- *Who Cares? We Do!!* (U.S. Army War College, 1992);
- *Navy Ombudsman Program Manual* (Department of the Navy, Bureau of Naval Personnel, Navy Family Ombudsman Program, 1994);
- *Army Family Team Building: Levels I, II, and III* ( U.S. Army Community and Family Support Center, 1995);
- *The good ideas handbook* (DOD Office of Family Policy, Support and Services, 1995);
- *How to support families during overseas deployments* (Bell, Stevens, & Segal, 1996b); and
- *Operation Ready* (U. S. Army Community and Family Support Center, 1994).

## SUMMARY AND IMPLICATIONS

This chapter has highlighted information that service providers need to know about family adaptation to the stresses of deployments from the literature. The principal reasons most families experience deployments as stressful are that they combine two well-known stressors: family separation and potential harm to the service member and/or his or her family. These stresses can be increased by uncertainty, inability to communicate with the deployed service member, or any number of difficulties that arise out of the deployment or are exacerbated by it (e.g., task overload, fears about the marriage, child rearing difficulties, or financial problems).

Although the majority of spouses experience stress symptoms during deployments, most are able to cope. That is, they meet the demands that daily life places upon them, and they readjust to the service members' return with a few relatively short-lived difficulties. Spouses often have to become more independent during a deployment and some couples do experience some adjustment difficulties when the service member returns (i.e., couples must renegotiate their new roles or go back to the way they were, and a shift in either direction can be stressful).

Families are known to use a variety of coping strategies during deployments. The most successful ones seem to involve adopting a positive attitude, being active, and cultivating and using a social support network. Spouses are much more likely to turn to friends and relatives for help than to use military helping agencies. This fact is not necessarily a problem. Most of the help being requested (e.g., free, short-term childcare) is not what military agencies are designed to provide. The human services that are used by the spouses of deployed soldiers are more likely to be those that provide information than more direct social services, per se. Agencies and leaders provide a structure that will help families if they do manifest need for services. Examples of what military leaders and human service providers do to help include: leader briefings to keep families informed, and rear detachment commands and Family Support Groups to help pass information between the deployed unit and the unit's families.

Tables 9.1 through 9.3 highlight the three related but distinct phases of a deployment. These figures identify the major stressors at each deployment phase, the helpful actions family members can take to deal with the stressors associated with that phase, and how unit leaders and community human service professionals can help at each phase. These figures are not meant to be a comprehensive guide; rather they suggest some of the more frequent and often most important issues to consider.

**Table 9.1**
**Relieving Family Stress—Predeployment**

| Major Stressors | Helpful Family Behaviors | Helpful Leadership and Service Providers' Actions |
|---|---|---|
| Difficulty predicting deployment date (1,2,a,b)* | 1. Accept lack of control over deployment events | a. Keep families informed of deployment dates |
| Multiple and missed "good-byes" (1,a) | 2. Seek information about the mission, the military branch of service, and helping agencies | b. Affirm commitment to family support |
| Worry about mission uncertainty (1-3, a-c) | 3. Seek information about deployment stressors and coping strategies | c. Encourage public support of mission |

\* Specific family, leadership, and service provider actions that relate to each problem.

**Table 9.2**
**Relieving Family Stress—Deployment**

| Major Stressors | Helpful Family Behaviors | Helpful Leadership and Service Providers Actions |
|---|---|---|
| Stress symptoms: -Depression (1,5,6) -Loneliness (1,5-7,d) -Anxiety (2,6,b) -Loss of sleep (2,6,b) | 1. Maintain positive attitude 2. Concentrate on what you can control 3. Develop individual and family goals | a. Focus on intended clients b. Provide accurate and timely information on the deployment and mission |
| Strain on marriage (1,7,d) | | |

**Table 9.2 (continued)**

| Major Stressors | Helpful Family Behaviors | Helpful Unit Leadership & Service Providers Actions |
|---|---|---|
| Strain on marriage (1,7,d) | 4. Maintain family routines | |
| Financial difficulties (4,6,7,a,d) | 5. Become and remain active | c. Monitor and control rumors |
| Worry about mission uncertainty (1,2,6-8,b,c,d) | 6. Seek social support from friends, relatives, FSGs, and families of other deployed members | d. Provide rapid, reliable, inexpensive means of communication between service member and their families |
| Fears about service member safety (1,2,7,b,d) | 7. Communicate with your service member and open channels of communication within your family | |
| Rumors about service member return date (7,8,b,c) | | e. Encourage public support of the mission |
| Problems handling daily tasks* (3,4,6,e) | 8. Check out rumors, don't believe everything you hear | |
| Scarce and contradictory information about the deployment (7,8,b,c) | | |

* Daily tasks include activities such as snow removal, getting household or automobile repairs, managing finances, and transportation issues.

**Table 9.3**
**Relieving Family Stress—Rest and Recuperation and Reunion**

| Major Stressors | Helpful Family Actions | How Commanders and Service Providers Help |
|---|---|---|
| Rest-and-Recuperation (R&R) effects* (a) | 1. Maintain positive attitude | a. Teach families about R&R and reunion stresses and how to cope with them |
| Preexisting marital problems (1,2,b) | 2. Maintain open communication within the family | b. Provide leave and time off as needed |
| Renegotiating family roles (2) | | |
| Renegotiating levels of independence (2) | | |

* R&R effects include disruption of newly established routines, another painful goodbye, and subsequent increase in depression.

As noted in Chapter 1 (and reinforced in Chapter 17), in the twenty-first century it is likely that military family life will increasingly take on the characteristic of episodic separations. Some will be very routine and uneventful, but many will be dangerous. The overall quality of life for military members and their families will depend on successful adaptation to this uniquely stressful lifestyle. The lessons learned by individual families, by unit leaders, and by community human service providers have become critical to developing a successful military culture and community support system for sustaining military family life and promoting military readiness during deployments.

## REFERENCES

Alderks, C. E. (1998). *PERSTEMPO: Its effect on soldiers' attitudes*. Alexandria, VA: U.S. Army Research Institute for the Behavioral and Social Sciences.

Amen, D. G., Jellen, L., Merves, E., & Lee, R. E. (1988). Minimizing the impact of deployment separation on military children: Stages, current preventive efforts, and system recommendations. *Military Medicine, 153*(8), 441–446.

Bartone, J. V., Harris, J. J., Segal, D. R., & Segal, M. W. (1993). Paratroopers' wives. In D. R. Segal & M. W. Segal (Eds.), *Peacekeepers and their wives: American participation in the multinational force and observers* (pp. 129–139). Westport, CT: Greenwood Press.

Bell, D. B. (1991, November). The impact of Operation Desert Shield/Storm on Army families: A summary of findings to date. Paper presented at 53rd Annual Conference of the National Council on Family Relations, Denver, CO.

Bell, D. B. (1993, December). Spouse support during peacekeeping missions: Lessons learned from Operation Restore Hope. Paper presented at the 9th Annual NATO Stress Workshop, San Antonio, TX.

Bell, D. B. (1997). *USAREUR family support during Operation Joint Endeavor*. Unpublished manuscript, U S. Army Research Institute for the Behavioral and Social Sciences, Alexandria, VA.

Bell, D. B. (1998). *Findings from the 28th MFO rotation during unit formation, deployment, and 18 months after return*. Unpublished manuscript, U.S. Army Research Institute for the Behavioral and Social Sciences, Alexandria, VA.

Bell, D. B., Bartone, J., Bartone, P. T., Schumm, W. R., & Gade, P. A. (1997). *USAREUR family support during Operation Joint Endeavor: Summary report* (Special Report 34). Alexandria, VA: U.S. Army Research Institute for the Behavioral and Social Sciences.

Bell, D. B., Bartone, J., Bartone, P. T., Schumm, W. R., Rice, R. E., & Hinson, C. (1997, October). Helping U.S. Army families cope with the stresses of troop deployment in Bosnia-Herzegovina. Paper presented at the 1997 Inter-University Seminar on Armed Forces and Society Biennial International Conference, Baltimore, MD.

Bell, D. B., & Schumm, W. R. (1998, May 7). Supporting the families of Army peacekeepers: What we learned from two recent deployments. Paper presented at the Fourth Annual Joint Service Family Readiness Matters Workshop, Portland, OR.

Bell, D. B., Schumm, W. R., Segal, M. W., & Rice, R. E. (1996). The family support system for the MFO. In R. H. Phelps & B. J. Farr (Eds.), *Reserve component soldiers as peacekeepers* (pp. 306–408). Alexandria, VA: U.S. Army Research Institute for the Behavioral and Social Sciences.

Bell, D. B., Stevens, M. L., & Segal, M. W. (1996). *How to support families during overseas deployments: A sourcebook for service providers* (Research Report 1687).

Alexandria, VA: U.S. Army Research Institute for the Behavioral and Social Sciences.

Bell, D. B., & Teitelbaum, J. M. (1993, October). Operation Restore Hope: Preliminary results of a survey of Army spouses at Fort Drum, New York. Paper presented at the Inter-University Seminar on Armed Forces and Society Biennial Conference, Baltimore, MD.

Bell, D. B., Teitelbaum, J. M., & Schumm, W. R. (1996). Family support "lessons learned" in Operation Restore Hope (Somalia): An Army mission other than war. *Military Review, 76*(2), 80–84.

Boulding, E. (1950). Family adjustments to war separations and reunions. *Annals of the American Academy of Political and Social Sciences, 60*(2), 59–67.

Department of Defense Office of Family Policy, Support and Services. (1995). *The good ideas handbook.* Washington, DC: Department of Defense.

Department of the Navy, Bureau of Naval Personnel, Navy Family Ombudsman Program. (1994). *Navy Ombudsman Program Manual.* Washington, DC: Author.

Durand, D. B. (1992, August). The redistribution of responsibilities and power in Army families following Operation Desert Shield/Storm reunions. Paper presented at the Section on Sociology of Peace and War at the 87th annual meeting of the American Sociological Association, Pittsburgh, PA.

Gravino, K. S, Segal, D. R., & Segal, M. W. (1993). Lightfighters' wives. In D. R. Segal & M. W. Segal (Eds.), *Peacekeepers and their wives: American participation in the multinational force and observers* (pp. 140–156). Westport, CT: Greenwood Press.

Hill, R. (1949). *Families under stress: Adjustment to the crises of war separation and reunion.* New York: Harper & Row (reprinted by Greenwood Press, Westport, CT, 1971).

HQ, U.S. Army Europe (1991). *USAREUR personnel opinion survey 1991: General findings report, Vol. 1 (Family)* (USAREUR Pamphlet 600-2). Heidelberg, Germany: HQ, USAEUR.

Kerner-Hoeg, S., Baker, S., Lomvardias, C., & Towne, L. (1993). *Operation Restore Hope. Survey of Army spouses at Fort Drum, New York: Survey methodology and data book.* Fairfax, VA: Caliber Associates.

Lewis, C. S. (1984). *Grenada waiting wives.* Unpublished manuscript, Department of Military Psychiatry, Walter Reed Army Institute of Research: Washington, DC.

Martin, J. A., Vaitkus, M. A., Johnson, M. D., Mikolajek, L. M., & Ray, D. L. (1996). Deployment from Europe: The family perspective. In R. J. Ursano & A. E. Norwood (Eds.), *Emotional aftermath of the Persian Gulf War: Veterans, families, communities, and nations* (pp. 227–250). Washington, DC: The American Psychiatric Press.

McCubbin, H. I. (1980, Winter). Coping with separation and reunion. *Military Chaplains' Review,* DA Pamphlet 165-124, pp. 49–58.

McCubbin, H. I., & Patterson, J. M. (1983). The family stress process: The double ABCX model of adjustment and adaptation. *Marriage and Family Review, 6*(1-2), 7–37.

Peterson, M. (1992). *1991 survey of Army families II: Final summary.* Unpublished manuscript, U.S. Army Research Institute for the Behavioral and Social Sciences, Alexandria, VA.

Reimer, D. J. (1997). *Leadership and change in a values-based Army.* Washington, DC: Office of the Chief of Staff of the Army.

Schumm, W. R., Bell, D. B., Knott, B., & Rice, R. E. (1997). *Does "going home" help families to cope with overseas deployments?* Unpublished manuscript, U S. Army Research Institute for the Behavioral and Social Sciences, Alexandria, VA.

Schumm, W. R., Bell, D. B., Milan, L. M., & Segal, M. W., (2000). *Family Support Group Leaders' handbook*, (Technical Report). Alexandria, VA: U.S. Army Research Institute for the Behavioral and Social Sciences.

Schumm, W. R., Bell, D. B., Segal, M. W., & Rice, R. E. (1996). Changes in marital quality among MFO couples. In R. H. Phelps & B. J. Farr (Eds.), *Reserve component soldiers as peacekeepers* (pp. 385–408). Alexandria, VA: U.S. Army Research Institute for the Behavioral and Social Sciences.

Schumm, W. R., Hemesath, K., Bell, D. B., Palmer-Johnson, C. E., & Elig, T. W. (1996). Did Desert Storm reduce marital satisfaction among Army enlisted personnel? *Psychological Reports*, *78*(3), part 2, 1241–1242.

Segal, M. W. (1986). The military and the family as greedy institutions. *Armed Forces and Society*, *13*(1), 9–38.

Segal, M. W. (1988). The military and families as greedy institutions. In C. C. Moskos & F. R. Wood (Eds.), *The military: More than just a job?* (pp. 79-98). Washington, DC: Pergaman-Brassey's International Defense Publishers, Inc.

Segal, M. W., & Harris, J. J. (1993). *What we know about Army families* (Special Report 21). Alexandria, VA: U.S. Army Research Institute for the Behavioral and Social Sciences.

U.S. Army Community and Family Support Center. (1994). *Operation R.E.A.D.Y.* Alexandria, VA: U.S. Army Community and Family Support Center.

U.S. Army Community and Family Support Center. (1995). *Army family team building: Levels I, II, and III*. Alexandria, VA: U.S. Army Community and Family Support Center.

U.S. Army War College. (1984). *Leaders' wives speak out*. Carlisle Barracks, PA: U.S. Army War College.

U.S. Army War College. (1992). *Who cares? We do!! Experiences in family support, U.S. Army War College Class of 1992 spouses and students*. Carlisle Barracks, PA: U.S. Army War College.

Wood, F. W., Scarville, J., & Gravino, K. S. (1995). Waiting wives: Separation and reunion among Army wives. *Armed Forces and Society*, *21*(2), 217–236.

Chapter 10

# Marital Adjustment Following Deployment

*Leora N. Rosen and Doris B. Durand*

## INTRODUCTION

This chapter examines different patterns of adaptation to reunion following prolonged deployment. One year after the return of troops from the Persian Gulf War, a survey was conducted among spouses of soldiers who had deployed. Five types of marital adaptation were noted among these spouses: (1) distance, in which the soldier and spouse grew more distant from one another; (2) closeness, in which the soldier and spouse grew closer together; (3) role sharing, in which the soldier and spouse adopted more egalitarian roles; (4) independence, in which the spouse became more independent; and (5) dependence, in which the spouse became more dependent on the soldier. Demographic and psychosocial characteristics of spouses in these five categories are presented, and case histories are used to illustrate the different types of adaptation.

Marital adjustment after military service members return from war has interested social scientists since the end of World War II, when Hill (1949) conducted his comprehensive study of the family reunion process. Following the Vietnam conflict, studies on reunion were conducted by Pearlman (1970), Bey and Lange (1974), and McCubbin and colleagues (McCubbin, Dahl, Lister and Ross, 1975). Attempts have been made by scholars to develop models for explaining differences in patterns of reunion adjustment. Hill (1949) for example, suggested three patterns of adjustment. The first was related to what he called the "closed ranks" adaptation of the family to wartime separation. According to this pattern, the soldier's role in the family was assumed by other family members, and when he returned, he was excluded from the family. The second was the "open ranks" adaptation in which the soldier's place in the family was kept open during the deployment. However, this resulted in a great deal of anxiety experienced by family members during the deployment, followed by anger during the reunion phase. The third and best kind of adaptation according to Hill was the "partially open ranks" adaptation in which the soldier's place in the family was kept partially open during the deployment.

A subsequent attempt to develop a model of reunion adjustment was made by Vormbrock (1993) who drew on "attachment theory" pioneered by Bowlby (1969) and later developed by Ainsworth and colleagues (Ainsworth, 1979; Ainsworth & Bell, 1970; Ainsworth, Blehar, Waters & Wall, 1978). According to attachment theory there are three types of reunion adaptation: avoidant-detached adaptation; anxious-ambivalent adaptation; and successful adaptation.

The avoidant-detached pattern is similar to what Hill (1949) described as the "closed-ranks" adjustment, in which reunion is difficult because the returning soldier and his spouse are involved in separate emotional cliques. The anxious-ambivalent pattern is similar to Hill's "open-ranks" adjustment, which involves feelings of overdependency and anger on the part of family members towards the returning soldier. The successful adaptation is closest to Hill's "partially open" adjustment in which the soldier's place in the family is kept partially open during the separation. One problem with this model is that it makes no allowance for growth and development either on the part of the spouse or soldier, particularly with regard to renegotiation of roles, rights, and responsibilities in the marriage. Hill's model assumes that there is only one healthy, positive outcome—a return to the status quo, but what if the status quo was one in which the wife was helpless, needy, dependent, or submissive? These issues were addressed in a study of marital reunion among Gulf War spouses described below.

## THE GULF WAR FAMILY STUDY

During the Persian Gulf War, the Walter Reed Army Institute of Research conducted a study of family adjustment to wartime stress in collaboration with other Army agencies under the sponsorship of the Deputy Chief of Staff of Personnel (Rosen, 1992). The study included two phases. The first, which is described in Chapter 8, involved a study of stressors, stress mediators, coping, and well-being among spouses of deployed soldiers during the Gulf War. The second phase, described in the present chapter, involved a follow-up study dealing with marital reunion and psychological adjustment among the same spouses who participated in phase one.

The follow-up study of Gulf War spouses was conducted in the spring of 1992, one year after the soldiers returned from the Gulf War deployment. We were able to reach more than 1,100 of the original 1,274 spouses who had participated in the earlier survey, and we received 776 questionnaires back. The questionnaire dealt with marriage and reunion issues following the soldier's return, children's issues, spouse's psychological well-being, current stress, and attitudes toward the Army specifically with regard to future deployments. In addition to the follow-up survey, we conducted site visits to several Army installations from which soldiers had deployed, and we interviewed groups of individual soldiers and their spouses, as well as numerous couples.

## OVERVIEW OF SPOUSES' MARITAL SITUATIONS

Following the Gulf War deployment, the media were filled with stories about the disruptions in military families' home life, spouses' infidelity while service members were away, and marital break-ups.  One CBS news report alleged that the divorce rate for soldiers at a certain Army post had increased by 300 percent.  The findings from our survey suggest that these media accounts were greatly exaggerated.  Of those spouses who responded to our follow-up questionnaire, 93 percent were still married to the same soldier who had deployed a year earlier, while the rest were separated, divorced, or remarried. Spouses were asked to describe how their marriages had been going since the soldiers returned from the deployment to the Persian Gulf.  Forty percent said there were no problems; 35 percent said there were a few problems at first but that these were solved; 13 percent had some unresolved problems; 7 percent had serious unresolved problems; and 4 percent said that their marriages were going very poorly.  There was, however, a significant increase in the percentage of spouses who were considering divorce at the time of the follow-up survey (14 percent) as compared with the percentage who had considered divorce in the year prior to the deployment (5 percent).  We also interviewed groups of soldiers, spouses, and couples regarding marital adjustment and reunion issues following the deployment.  Subjects told us not only about their own problems and experiences, but also what they perceived to be problems facing other soldiers and spouses in their social or work environments.

## RESULTS FROM THE FOCUS GROUPS

### Soldiers' and Spouses Views' on Adultery and Divorce

Many of the soldiers that we interviewed believed that a number of marriages in their units were breaking up as a result of the deployment, although there were no precise statistics.  In one group of soldiers, most believed that much of the trouble was due to the fact that many younger soldiers got married right before the deployment. One soldier noted that of the four married men in his unit, two were splitting up with their wives.  He recounted that one of the divorcing soldiers had met the girl in a bar on Monday, married her on Thursday, and deployed on Saturday.  No one in the group mentioned that his own marriage was in trouble.

Among the soldiers and spouses that we interviewed, most had heard rumors of wives having affairs while the soldiers were deployed.  Some claimed personally to know individuals who had affairs, but for the most part this was second- or third-hand information, although we heard claims such as "50 percent of the wives were having affairs."  Claims like these could not be substantiated by our research because we did not ask spouses directly if they had had affairs. However, only 10 percent of spouses who participated in our survey said that there was "suspicion and mistrust" between soldier and spouse, while 67 percent described greater feelings of closeness.  Therefore widespread extra-marital affairs seem unlikely to have occurred in this sample.  Informants did suggest a number of interesting reasons why other wives allegedly had affairs.  One opinion was that affairs were the result of young women not having faith in their marriages. Women in the youngest age group in particular, we were told, felt insecure about their relationships surviving the deployment, believing that their husbands would either be killed or leave them. These women were particularly vulnerable to advances by predatory men in the local community, especially reservists and National Guardsmen who had moved into the area as "back-fill" for the deployed troops and who were single or married but unaccompanied by spouses and children.

The wives mentioned that sexual harassment by National Guardsmen and reservists was commonplace. One woman described them as a "pain." "They would just hang all over you even in stores." Another described them as "a nasty-looking bunch"; "they were a joke." However, it was believed that some women succumbed to them.

In other cases, our informants said, women took the attitude "this is my chance" (to fool around). One spouse claimed to have a neighbor who picked up boys at the local high school. Another said she heard women talking about partying and having a good time while standing in line waiting for free items being given away to Gulf War spouses.

"Some didn't want their husbands back. Some just didn't want to get caught," said one informant. Another claimed to have heard women say, "I hope he dies over there," and "I'm having a good time. I don't want him to come back."

Some wives were suspected of having affairs when they were observed arriving in cars with strange men to pick up their husbands' leave and earning statements from the rear detachment office once a month. Our informants claimed to know that at least some of these affairs were resulting in divorces or marital discord, and even violence against the spouse and her boyfriend. However, one case was mentioned of a woman living on post with three small children who spent all her time in the noncommissioned officers' (NCO) club during the deployment. She had two or three boyfriends, and mismanaged the household finances to the extent that "everything was repossessed." But when her husband returned he forgave her, and they were still together.

According to these informants, there are certain women who prior to the Gulf War deployment routinely went around in groups to nightclubs when their husbands were away on field duty. They did not regard this as wrong and simply hoped not to get caught. The men they met typically tried to pick them up using flattery and waited for reaction, or tried to create doubts in their minds about their marriages, asking questions like: "Are you happily married? Is he treating you right? Are you sure?" During the Gulf War this kind of behavior escalated because of the length of time the soldiers were away. This was exacerbated by rumors that some of the husbands were having affairs in the desert. "Letters were going back and forth as to who was doing what. " One informant described these as "love-hate" marriages. "Spouses would take the attitude 'He's doing his thing, so why shouldn't I? In one case, when a wife found out, she packed her bags and left."

From the soldiers' perspective we heard that some problems got started as a result of husbands not receiving letters for a long time, and then, assuming willful neglect on the part of their wives, they would respond by writing nasty letters home. Some romances started by mail, as a result of single women sending soldiers letters and their pictures. Soldiers who started affairs in the desert, they said, felt that they didn't have a future. "They felt wounded and vulnerable, and fell victim to affairs," said one soldier. "I had faith in God, but some gave up on life."

Another problem was leadership. One sergeant told us that there were males and females in his unit "seeing each other." Some even later divorced their spouses as a result of these liaisons, he claimed. Leadership in his unit was poor, and leaders made no effort to stop what he perceived as flagrant fraternization. Males and females were intermingling in the tents and having sex in the showers, he said, but there was no point in complaining to the chain of command. "The company commander was single. He was doing the same thing."

## RESULTS OF THE SURVEY

### Types of Marital Adjustment

Spouses were asked to indicate whether they had experienced any of 19 marital adjustment events listed in Table 10.1. The most common events were positive. In 80 percent of marriages, the soldiers were pleased with the spouses' running of the household and finances. In 68 percent of marriages the soldier and spouse felt closer to one another. However, in 17 percent of cases the soldier and spouse felt more distant, and in 10 percent of cases there were feelings of suspicion and mistrust. We conducted a statistical analysis (factor analysis) of the 18 events and found that they were grouped into five factors:

1. Distance: The soldier and spouse felt more distant from one another, and there was increased suspicion and mistrust.
2. Closeness: The soldier and spouse felt closer to one another, and the soldier was pleased with the way the spouse handled the household and family finances.
3. Role-sharing: The soldier adopted a more egalitarian role, doing more chores and caring for children, and new arrangements were worked out regarding control of the finances.
4. Independence: The spouse felt more independent and made more decisions.
5. Dependence: The spouse felt more dependent on the soldier and resented his new friends, while the soldier needed more time alone.

Three of these five types are similar to the three types of adjustment described by Hill (1949) and Vormbrock (1993)—distance, closeness, and dependence. We have described two additional types of adjustment that involve growth and change in the marriage—independence and role sharing.

*Distance.* In our statistical analysis of these data, the strongest predictor of distance was consideration for divorce prior to the deployment. Other predictors included stressful life events during the Gulf War, the spouse's dissatisfaction with her role, and the absence of Family Support Groups during the deployment. The following case illustrates some of the factors associated with distance, including preexisting marital difficulties, stressful events during the deployment (financial difficulties), lack of family support, and a discontent with the prospect of juggling the responsibilities of motherhood and paid employment.

**Table 10.1**
**Reunion Events**

| Type of Adjustment | Percentage of Spouses Reporting This Experience |
|---|---|
| Soldier was pleased with spouse's running of finances | 81 |
| Soldier pleased with the spouse's running of household | 78 |
| There were greater feelings of closeness of the couple | 68 |
| Spouse became more independent | 48 |
| Soldier became more helpful with chores | 36 |
| Soldier became more involved with childcare | 26 |
| Spouse participated more in decisionmaking | 23 |
| Soldier needed more time to be alone | 22 |
| Spouse and soldier felt more distant from one another | 17 |
| Changes in authority regarding children | 16 |
| Soldier adopts new roles | 15 |
| Soldier felt left out of the family | 14 |
| New agreement about control of finances | 14 |
| There was suspicion or mistrust between spouse and soldier | 10 |
| Spouse became more dependent on soldier | 9 |
| Soldier critical of spouse's handling of finances | 8 |
| Soldier resents spouse's new friends | 7 |
| Spouse resents soldier's new friends | 5 |

Kristin was the wife of a sergeant. She had two sons aged five years and 18 months. In her questionnaire completed during the deployment, she indicated that she and her husband had experienced marital difficulties in the year prior to the Gulf War deployment. During the reunion phase, we interviewed her to find out how things were going. Kristin's marital problems had clearly been exacerbated by deployment-related events. These difficulties continued into the reunion phase. She characterized her husband as controlling and suspicious. She had difficulty getting him to provide her with a power of attorney before he deployed. "He didn't want to give it to me. He thought I would spend all his money," she said.

For the first month after his return, she claimed that everything was fine. Then he went home to Texas to visit his family, while she stayed behind. After that everything changed. While in Texas, he redid his life insurance policy, renaming his niece as beneficiary. Since his return, he moved out of the house to spend several weeks in the barracks. "He just doesn't seem committed. He wants to be with his buddies," said Kristin. However, she described him as "confused." Some days he wanted out of the marriage, and other days he wanted to come home.

They had been to a marriage counselor for a while but "he just won't talk" she said. Two weeks prior to the interview he had filed for divorce. "I've lost 15 pounds in the last two months and I'm suffering from migraines," said Kristin. "He was angry with me because I hadn't saved, but we had no more money than before. It cost me $150 a month to send him stuff. It cost me a dollar a pound just to send him cookies. He claims I used him while he was gone." She denied that he was abusive to her, but described mild physical violence. "He may push or shove, but he won't hit.

Among their current difficulties was her husband's suspicion that she may have had an affair in his absence. Yet Kristin claimed to have led a relatively isolated existence during the deployment. She said: "In no way would I have an affair. I stayed in the house the whole time he was gone so that people wouldn't have anything to talk about.

My only contact was with the first sergeant's wife, and later my friend Mary." Marital stress was further exacerbated by current financial problems resulting from car repairs. Kristin noted that her husband was upset because the kids don't respond like soldiers. They don't do what he wants immediately.

Kristin was also confronted with insecurity about her future role. Her husband had been supporting the family financially, but the question on her mind was how long he would continue to do so. She was considering looking for a job, but noted that babysitting would cost her $400 per month so that even if she could find a job, it probably wouldn't be worth it.

*Closeness.* The strongest predictor of Closeness was the level of marital satisfaction before the deployment. In addition, we found that spouses who remained on the post during the deployment, who experienced fewer stressful life events, and who were kept informed about the Army by their soldier-husbands were likely to experience more closeness upon reunion. Thus, the strongest predictor of the two main types of reunion adjustment was the state of the marriage prior to deployment, however levels of stress and the presence of social supports also played a role. Spouse's moving away from post during the deployment may have placed an additional stressor on the couple in that they both had to adjust to returning home after the deployment. Both soldiers and spouses who felt they had grown closer gave as their main reason their deeper appreciation of the relationship. "He is more affectionate and secure," said a spouse. "We don't take each other for granted. We live more for each moment." "He has a more serious side now. But I'm so glad to see him. I tell him I'll sit in a mud puddle with you," "She appreciates me more," said one soldier. A newly married young wife who had waited till after the deployment to marry her boyfriend of eight years said: "He seems more calm, more mature. He looks at things different." Others said that strong faith in God, and dedication to the Bible and to church helped keep their marriages secure during the deployment.

*Role-Sharing.* Role-sharing following reunion was associated with increased visits to counselors, increased life events after the deployment, and spouse's difficulty coping with a job during the deployment. Spouses who felt overburdened with responsibilities during the deployment, or who experienced stressful events following the deployment, made efforts to renegotiate the distribution of tasks and responsibilities in the marital relationship. The success of this pattern of adjustment varied: in some cases it led to a stronger relationship, in other cases it led to trouble in the relationship. One soldier who took a positive attitude noted that his wife's ways had changed and that the challenge was "to make both our ideas into one." Some soldiers welcomed taking on new responsibilities in the home, particularly with regard to their children whom they had missed during the deployment.

Sergeant "S" admitted that he was adjusting to his wife's new independence, noting that she was now driving the car and had taken charge of paying the bills. "Men who are possessive," he said, "create problems." He, on the other hand, felt that he had to do more for his children. He was trying to spend more time with them because he had missed some of their milestones while he was away. His children had written him letters and were responding well to the reunion. His older daughter, who had reached school age, was now wearing glasses and had started to read. His 15-month-old daughter didn't recognize him initially, but on the second day she was beginning to warm up to him.

In a separate interview, Mrs. "S" told us that she had grown accustomed to doing everything according to her schedule while her husband was away. When he came back, he was more laid back than she would have preferred him to be. She pampered him at first, but after a while the novelty wore off. She wanted to give him tasks like grass cutting or washing the car, and he would say, "we'll get to that." She noted that she had become used to running the home, whereas he expected her to go back to the role of the "submissive wife." They had some growing, maturing and adjusting to do. There were little spats, but things were starting to improve.

*Independence.* Increased independence following the deployment was associated with spouses' reports of increased medical visits during the deployment. Younger spouses also tended to become more independent following the deployment.

"Betty" was the 17-year-old wife of a specialist, and the mother of a two-year-old daughter, "April." During the deployment she returned home to stay with her parents. She and her husband had to make major adjustments after his return home. "I became more independent and he doesn't like it. He feels like an outsider. He did everything before he left. Now I do it. He is very possessive with April and me."

During the deployment, Betty was able to save $1,000 of her husband's pay—a remarkable accomplishment considering he was only a private first class (E3) at the time. She said "I plan on doing something with my life," which in the immediate future meant getting a driver's license, but down the road she was thinking of a college education. Betty admitted that she was driving around without a license. The reason: "When I first got down here I was 16. I couldn't get one then because I had to be in school or 18." Her husband, she said, was not eager for her to be driving. He was also upset with her for not informing him during the deployment about a medical problem she was having. Betty had not informed him that precancerous cells had been discovered on her cervix. She didn't want to worry him while he was in the Gulf.

Another young wife was pregnant when her husband deployed and had the baby during the deployment. She was having difficulty getting adjusted to the reunion and letting her husband share the daughter he had never seen. "You grow that independence and then you have people telling you what to do."

Serious problems arose when the husband could not accept a wife's increased independence, and efforts to negotiate reassignment of responsibilities were absent or unsuccessful.

Sergeant "D" has been married for 12 years, and has a son and daughter aged 10 and 11. During the deployment the children's grades in school went down and, in his words, "their attitude went down." It was harder, he said, for his son than for his daughter. He described his wife as strong and dependable, but the stress of anticipating the deployment was causing her to have "a nervous breakdown," according to Sergeant D. He noted that during the deployment, her problems continued. His children told him that while he was away, his wife went out two or three times a week, got drunk, and sometimes did not return till 4:00 a.m.

At the end of the Gulf War deployment, Sergeant D's unit was among those provided with classes on reunion issues.

"We were told 'don't change things when you get home.' 'Don't assert authority.' General M. gave us a long talk, about one and a half-hours. He said 'when you get back things are going to change.' I thought he was talking nonsense." He thought that everything was going to be the same. It really came as a big surprise to find that this was not the case. "My wife was doing everything. I couldn't do anything. She was doing it. She was taking so much away from me. Before I left, because we were both working, she cooked and cleaned windows and I did everything else. After I got back, she did it all."

Disciplining the kids was a frequent problem for Sergeant D.

"She would correct the kids and they would move. They ignored me. I was like a piece of furniture and that hurt. I wanted things the way they used to be. I love my wife and kids depending on me 100%. I want to be part of the family again." At a certain point the problems escalated to the level of physical violence. "There was a lot of bickering for two weeks and then the big one. I blew off the handle. We weren't talking divorce, but my wife told me that I needed help. I just couldn't understand the feelings I was having. She was a completely different woman. She was completely self-sufficient. I felt she didn't need me anymore. I got uncontrollably mad. I wanted to hurt someone. I left fingerprints on her arm. Hurt so badly. I went for a walk—found myself cursing. My wife really worried about me."

Sergeant D's violent behavior was also directed at his children. He admitted being "hard on the kids mentally and physically." "I started spanking them on the butt." But when he drew back his fist at one of the children, he knew he was in trouble. He and his wife started talking more, and he began working out at the gym.

*Dependence.* Increased dependence, like independence, was associated with spouses' younger age. It was also associated with the soldier not keeping the spouse informed about the Army.

"Cheryl" worked as a floral assistant in a town two hours away from a large Army post. She had dated Bill, a divorced sergeant with a child from a previous marriage for whom he paid child support. They dated for a whole summer and married in mid-September. He deployed a month later. Cheryl did not move to the post after her marriage but lived with her parents. Though Bill claims he gave her name and address to his unit leaders more than once, nobody contacted her. Later in the deployment a videotape was made for the soldiers of all the wives in the unit—except for Cheryl.

Bill complained that members of his unit received unfair treatment in the Gulf. Only selected people had access to phones, and promises to make phones accessible to more soldiers were broken. On returning he and Cheryl faced financial problems. Their car needed a new transmission, and they had to go to Army Emergency Relief (AER) for a loan. Bill felt bitter that despite working hard day after day, he had nothing to show for it. Their financial situation was expected to improve since Cheryl now had a new job at a video store near the base. However, they were having problems in the relationship. Because she knew no one at the post, he was most important to her. Bill on the other hand wanted to distance himself from her. He admitted, "I just don't feel the same way about her since I got back. She says I don't show her that I care. She says sometimes she feels I am treating her like a private. I just like to go home and watch TV. She gets bored."

Cheryl had negative attitudes toward the Family Support Group, but had never actually made contact with them, and simply repeated stories she had heard from others. When Bill's unit finally returned from the Gulf War deployment, she was not contacted by the unit but heard the news from the media. Somehow she was misinformed about where to meet him, and when he finally arrived, she was not there but was waiting some place else. Their reunion, therefore, got off to a bad start, which was related to the fact that Cheryl was out of touch with information about Bill's unit.

Younger spouses experienced the greatest changes with regard to independence and dependence, some becoming more independent, and others becoming more dependent. Soldiers who failed to keep their young spouses "informed about the Army" were likely to facilitate greater dependency. Increased medical visits among the Independent spouses may indicate that that they were dealing with their dependency needs through help-seeking behavior. It may also indicate that they became more independent through being forced to deal with medical emergencies on their own.

### Family Adaptation and Retention

How did spouses feel about the Army after the Gulf War? Did the deployment affect their commitment to military life, and did they feel that the Army had come through for them? There were suggestions that some spouses' expectations of the Army had been too high and that they were unreasonable in what they believed the Army should have done for them.

In the follow-up questionnaire, we asked spouses to state their opinions regarding their commitment to Army life, and the Army's supportiveness towards families. It is noteworthy that almost all spouses (97 percent) believed that they should be prepared to take full responsibility for running the household and family matters while the soldier is away, and 94 percent accepted that their soldiers could be called upon at any time to serve their country. However, less than half said that they would actually want their husbands to deploy again. Only 40% believed that the Army takes good care of families, and over half did not feel that the Army gave soldiers enough time to be with their families. This was a sore contentious issue with soldiers and spouses, and frequently emerged in our interviews.

Soldiers and spouses spoke out against command policies that they believed did not give them enough family time. At one post, soldiers claimed their commanding general had promised 21 days of free leave and five months of recovery following the redeployment, when in fact there was no free leave, and they began to train immediately upon returning. "We can't get back with our wives because we don't have the time," was a frequent complaint. In addition, the general put a block leave policy into effect but left its implementation to individual commanders. In those units where block leave was implemented, soldiers missed opportunities to spend time with their families because children were in school at the time or spouses were working and could not take leave. In one group, a specialist noted that his commander had a 5 percent leave policy in which 5 percent of the unit could be on leave at any time. The others remarked on what a caring commander he must have. Many said they were getting out of the Army because they were "fed up" with the way they had been treated. Despite these negative comments, 65 percent of spouses said that they wanted their husbands to stay in the Army until retirement. We were interested in factors that influenced spouses' long-term commitments to the Army. We were also interested in factors that may have influenced soldiers to actually leave the Army. At the time of the follow-up survey, of the 776 spouses who participated, 85 had left the Army, and we were able to examine predictors of actual reenlistment (Rosen & Durand, 1995).

For junior enlisted couples, we found that the strongest predictor of having left the Army by the second survey was the spouse's belief during the deployment that the Army was responsible for solving all the problems of spouses of deployed soldiers. Other predictors included more years as a military spouse, consideration of divorce prior to the deployment, and perceived lack of support from the rear detachment commander during the deployment. For noncommissioned officers, the spouses' wish for her husband to get out of the Army at Time 1 was the strongest predictor of the couple having left the Army by Time 2. Other predictors included consideration of divorce and fewer years as a military spouse.

We also examined predictors of reenlistment intention for those spouses whose soldier-husbands were still in the Army. Among junior enlisted spouses, the strongest predictor was the Army/Family Interface scale, which measured the perceived fit between Army life and family life. The scale asks spouses, for example, to assess how well the Army takes care of families, and the kind of family life they can have in the Army. Another predictor was how well the soldier kept the spouse informed about the Army. Among noncommissioned officer spouses, the strongest predictor of reenlistment intention was the soldier's rank, followed by the spouse's wish at Time 1 for the soldier to stay in or get out of the Army, and the adequacy of Family Support Group informational meetings during the deployment (Rosen & Durand, 1995).

These results serve to underscore the importance of Army spouses regarding the soldiers' career decisions and retention. Junior enlisted soldiers with more years in the Army were more likely to leave than those with fewer years because they were at the end of their reenlistment period and did not wish to make a further investment of time in the organization. Failure to get promoted may have been a factor. Noncommissioned officers with more years in the service had already made a significant investment and were more likely to stay in the Army. However, for junior enlisted couples, the spouse's higher expectation of what the Army should do for families was a stronger predictor of actually leaving the Army than years in the service. If the wife was disappointed with the Army, the couple was likely to leave. Among noncommissioned officers, spouse's opinion about retention at Time 1 was the strongest predictor of reenlistment at Time 2, indicating the importance of spouses' long-term career goals for their husbands.

## SUMMARY AND IMPLICATIONS

Media accounts of marital disruption following the Gulf War were greatly exaggerated. However, there was a small increase in the number of marriages undergoing difficulty after the deployment compared to before the deployment.

Our follow-up survey indicated that while some marriages ended following the deployment, a large part of the problem in these marriages occurred before the deployment. The majority of marriages actually appear to have been strengthened by the deployment, even though in some cases there were initial adjustment problems.

It is important for counselors and human service providers to note that there are different patterns of adjustment among couples after prolonged deployments and that while most couples will experience some changes in their relationships, only a small number will experience serious ongoing difficulties. Predeployment counseling for couples experiencing marital difficulties may help to alleviate some of these stresses. Reunion briefings and advice booklets provided to couples prior to reunion should take into account the differences in reunion patterns, and need to target high-risk couples for special attention.

This study showed that young, dependent spouses can become empowered during a deployment and develop important life skills that lead to growth in the marriage. However, this study did not address the issue of the longterm impact on marriages of multiple deployments over the course of an entire military career. Since the Gulf War, the number of military deployments has increased, and couples are likely to be facing frequent repeated separations over the course of the service member's military career. These may become increasingly burdensome on a marriage as time progresses. Future research should examine the effects of repeated deployment on military marriages, and human service providers should be aware of the additional stress that these may place on a couple's marital adjustment and psychological well-being.

## REFERENCES

Ainsworth, M.D.S. (1979). Infant-mother attachment. *American Psychologist, 34*(10), 932–937.

Ainsworth, M.D.S., & Bell, S. M. (1970). Attachment, exploration and separation: Illustrated by the behavior of one-year-olds in a strange situation. *Child Development, 41*(1), 49–67.

Ainsworth, M.D.S., Blehar, M. C., Waters, E., & Wall, S. (1978). *Patterns of attachment: A psychological study of strange situations.* Hillsdale, NJ: Lawrence Erlbaum.

Bey, D. R., & Lange, J. (1974). Waiting wives: Women under stress. *American Journal of Psychiatry, 131*(3), 283–286.

Bowlby, J. (1969). *Attachment and loss: Volume I. Attachment.* New York: Basic Books.

Hill, R. (1949). *Families under stress: Adjustment to the crises of war separation and reunion.* New York: Harper & Row (reprinted by Greenwood press, Westport, CT, 1971).

McCubbin, H. I., Dahl, B. B., Lister, G. R., & Ross, B. A. (1975). The returned prisoner of war: Factors in family reintegration. *Journal of Marriage and the Family, 37*(3), 471–478.

Pearlman, C.A. (1970). Separation reactions of married women. *American Journal of Psychiatry, 126*(7), 946–950.

Rosen, L. N. (1992). Stress and coping on the homefront: Family adaptation during operation Desert Storm, Unpublished manuscript, Walter Reed Army Institute of Research, Washington, DC.

Rosen, L. N., & Durand, D. B. (1995). The family factor and retention among married soldiers deployed to operation Desert Storm. *Military Psychology, 7*(4), 221–234.

Rosen, L. N., Durand, D. B., Westhuis, D. J., & Teitelbaum, J. M. (1995). Marital adjustment of Army spouses one year after Desert Storm. *Journal of Applied Social Psychology 25*(8), 677–692.

Vormbrock, J. K. (1993). Attachment theory as applied to wartime and job-related marital separation. *Psychological Bulletin, 114*(1), 122–144.

# Part III

# Family Advocacy Issues

# Chapter 11

# Understanding Spouse Abuse in Military Families

*Stephen J. Brannen and Elwood R. Hamlin II*

## INTRODUCTION

Over the past several years there has been a heightened interest in the issue of domestic violence in the United States. Several studies have suggested that military families experience higher levels of aggression than families in the civilian sector because the military either attracts aggressive men or that the culture and training promote aggression. This chapter provides an overview of the issue of domestic partner abuse both within the general population and the military services. It discusses the structure of the Department of Defense (DOD) programs aimed at treating domestic violence, and it provides a synopsis of the interventions commonly used to combat this major social issue.

Based upon national samples, it has been estimated that between 10 and 20 percent of all couples report some type of physical abuse toward women (Straus & Gelles, 1986). A review of the relevant literature shows that in the United States, one woman is physically abused every 12 seconds (Stark, Flitcraft, & Frazier, 1979), raped every 46 seconds (Kilpatrick, 1992), and murdered by a partner every six hours (ACOG, 1992). In the 1985 National Family Violence Survey, a nationally representative sampling conducted by Straus and Gelles, 16 percent of respondents indicated some type of violence had occurred between spouses in the past year and 28 percent reported violence at some prior point in their marriage (Gelles & Cornell, 1990). A comparison between the two National Family Violence Survey samples conducted in 1975 and again in 1985 showed a 21.8 percent decrease in the reported rate of male-female violence. In the civilian sector, the rates of abuse perpetrated by males against their female partners appears to have decreased or at least stabilized over the years (Straus & Gelles, 1990).

Although some studies report that violence by women toward their partners is as prevalent as that of men toward women (Straus, 1980) this body of research fails to take into account the differing contexts in which men use violence as opposed to women (Stordeur & Stille, 1989). Saunders (1988) reported that, most often, women who resorted to violence within the relationship did so only in self-defense. Nonetheless, it is important to note than men can also be abused within the context of intimate relationships (Saunders, 1988).

Within the military services, the incidence of spouse abuse is estimated to be even greater than that in the civilian sector. Neidig (1988) found that one in three military spouses had been abused at some point during their marriage. It should be noted that this analysis was conducted comparing the 1985 National Family Violence Survey (Straus & Gelles, 1990) rates to the Army rates without controlling for demographic differences between the two populations. A recent reanalysis of the Neidig data controlling for the key demographic variables of age and race demonstrated that the spousal aggression prevalence rates in representative U.S. Army and civilian samples were very comparable for the mild to moderate categories. Higher rates of aggression were shown in the severe physical aggression category (Heyman & Neidig, 1999).

In 1995, the Air Force administered a modified Conflict Tactics Scale (CTS) to a random sample of military personnel and civilian spouses throughout the United States, Europe, and Korea. The reported prevalence rates for all types of abuse were 147 per 1000 for active duty personnel and 168 per 1,000 for civilian spouses. These rates are fairly comparable to rates found in studies with civilian samples (Straus & Gelles, 1990).

Recent Department of Defense (DOD) data suggest that as many as 19 wives per 1000 of Air Force and Navy personnel have been abused in the past year while over 21 Army wives per thousand have been abused by their spouses. Marine Corps data are consistent with that of the Army (Caliber, 1996). Certainly, no one can minimize the impact this has on our military services as well as our society as a whole. Unfortunately, there is no national sample with which to compare the DOD data with the civilian rates.

## DEPARTMENT OF DEFENSE FAMILY ADVOCACY EFFORTS

Within the DoD, organized efforts at identifying and treating cases of spouse abuse have been in existence since the early 1980s. The Office of the Under Secretary of Defense for Personnel and Readiness (OUSD[(P&R]), Personnel Support, Families, and Education (PSF&E) is the responsible agent for all programs related to Family Advocacy. The Family Advocacy Program, Standards and Self-Assessment Tool (DoD, 1992) provides guidelines for implementation of spouse abuse intervention programs within each of the services. These guidelines state that educationally based programs or combination educational/psychotherapy must be provided to abusers and victims of abuse. These programs are generally provided in groups and address issues of: stress management, anger management, interpersonal communications, and power and control issues. Specific topics and activities involved in educationally based programs include:

- Understanding the dynamics of violence and the cycle of violence.
- Self-observation of individual "behavior cycles" that precede, occur with, and follow violent events.
- Identification of stresses in interpersonal relationships and the military environment that may stimulate anger reactions.
- Cognitive restructuring of irrational belief systems and faulty thinking styles.
- Recognizing and combating destructive anger-producing self-talk styles.
- Developing an understanding of the differences of learned responses to stress of males and females.
- Skills training in developing alternatives to violent behavior.
- Developing constructive communication patterns.
- Training in relaxation techniques.
- Recognizing the difference between aggressiveness and assertiveness.
- Utilizing an "anger log or diary" to record behavior and reactions to stress and anger-producing situations.

Specific programs within each of the Services (Army, Navy, Air Force and Marine Corps) were mandated in 1981 by DoD Directive 6400.1. By direction, all contain essential elements including prevention, identification and mandatory reporting, assessment, command involvement, treatment, coordination with local authorities, and follow-up.

Health care providers are mandated by regulation to report all incidents of spouse and child abuse to the appropriate authority. Although incident reporting is standardized across all four services, each has developed programs to best fit its organization structure and needs. For example, the Army has split the program responsibilities between its command (line) and medical department assets, with overall program responsibility being assigned to the command (personnel) side. The Navy and Marine Corps have located their programs totally on the line side, while the Air Force has chosen to locate its FAP assets within its medical department.

Army Community Service (ACS) has overall responsibility for the Army's Family Advocacy Program at the installation level. The Army FAP manager is responsible for primary prevention efforts, coordination between military community and civilian resources, and liaison with the installation commander. The medical treatment facility (MTF) commander is responsible for providing treatment services. Functional responsibility is normally delegated to the Chief of Social Work Service. The Chief of Social Work Service chairs the Family Advocacy Case Review Committee (CRC) and coordinates treatment initiatives which may involve MTF resources, Army Substance Abuse Program (ASAP) personnel, and/or local civilian social service workers.

The Air Force FAP is managed from the Air Force Office of the Surgeon General. This program involves three components: outreach, family maltreatment, and the Exceptional Family Member Program (EFMP). On each Air Force base, the MTF commander is responsible for the FAP, although a social work officer is normally assigned as the Family Advocacy Officer (FAO) with day-to-day functional responsibility for the program. Like the Army, the Air Force treatment services may include MTF resources or off-base services. The Air Force FAP includes a research component to study treatment efficacy.

The Navy assigns overall program management of the FAP at the installation (base) level to the director of the Family Service Center (FSC). Navy MTFs appoint a Family Advocacy Representative (FAR) who coordinates all programs and treatments. Treatment services may include military mental health care providers, social workers, civilian service providers, chaplains, and alcohol and drug abuse treatment programs. The Navy FAP as well as the Army FAP offers a variety of innovative prevention programs such as the New Parent Support Teams, which provide home visitor services.

In the Marine Corps, the FAP is a major component of the Marine Corps Family Program. At the installation level, the FAP is managed at the Family Service Center (FSC). The Marine Corps utilizes an innovative approach termed the Coordinated Community Response in managing cases of child and spouse abuse. The approach emphasizes the sharing of information among the numerous community organizations involved in the identification and treatment of family abuse. The Marine Corps FAP places a special emphasis on the role of the commander at each stage of the FAP case management process, from initial report through final disposition. The Marine Corps FAP, like the Navy and Army FAP, employs the New Parent Support concept to provide home visitor prevention services to new parents.

## RESPONDING TO CASES OF ALLEGED SPOUSE ABUSE IN THE MILITARY

In 1992, the DOD developed a set of uniform program standards for responding to abuse incidents, from receipt of the initial report of abuse and opening a case through case closure. While each service's program is structured slightly differently to best serve its population, the process is nonetheless consistent across each. Once a referral to the FAP for spouse abuse has been made, a FAP case manager will conduct an initial investigation and assessment. During this preliminary work, the case manager gathers evidence of the alleged abuse and develops a safety plan with the victim. Generally, as part of this process, the service-specific Central Registry is queried to determine if there have been any previous incidents involving this family. A recommended case or service plan is developed by the case manager and presented to the CRC within 30 days of the initial referral.

The CRC, tasked with substantiating or unsubstantiating cases, consists of social workers, case managers, chaplains, physicians, military police, lawyers, alcohol and drug specialists, the Family Advocacy Program Manager (FAPM), and unit representative (for each specific case) and is chaired by the Chief of Social Work Service. Some cases, while not substantiated, are designated "high risk" and are referred for further evaluation and assistance. Those cases that are substantiated are assigned a case number and are reported to the Central Registry. An individualized treatment plan is developed and implemented. Cases are reviewed monthly and remain open until all treatment recommendations are completed or the case is determined to be unresolved. Resolved cases are those in which all treatment recommendations have been met and there have been no further episodes of violence for at least 12 months. Cases are designated as unresolved if:

- The abuser has not complied with treatment plan.
- The command does not order the abuser into treatment.
- The abuser is not able to comply with treatment due to deployments.
- The abuser separates from the military before completion of treatment; or there continue to be abuse even though the individual has completed the treatment plan.

## PARTICIPANT CHARACTERISTICS OF MILITARY FAP SPOUSE ABUSE PROGRAMS

Caliber Associates (1996) conducted a survey of a randomly selected sample of 96 couples engaged in one of the service's FAP programs. They found that 82 percent of the families included an active-duty husband and civilian wife, 7 percent included an active-duty wife and civilian husband, and 10 percent were dual-military couples. The mean ages were 26 (males) and 25.5 (females) respectively. Over 98 percent were enlisted service members, with the vast majority of personnel below the grade of E-4. The majority of male-initiated abuse was reported as minor physical abuse. Females were more likely to report using severe physical violence than minor violence.

More than half of the abusers had been deployed on temporary duty during the past year. The average length of deployment was 110 days. However, over half of the respondents indicated being absent from the home for less than 60 days. As might be expected, the most frequently cited stressor on the couples was separation due to military service (39 percent of husbands, 21 percent of wives). Other major stressors included relocation (32 percent of husbands, 21 percent of wives) and stress in the marriage (29 percent of husbands, 25 percent of wives).

## THEORIES OF INTERVENING IN SPOUSE ABUSE

With the increasing development of treatment programs designed to assist both abusers and their victims, it is critical to examine theory as it relates to practice in order to provide an understanding of both the theoretical and practical issues underlying the various treatment approaches. Gondolf (1989) maintains that a program's identity, direction, and purpose are built on its theoretical foundation.

### Individual Psychopathology

Rounsaville (1978) found that individual psychopathology, although frequently cited as a possible causal agent of abuse, was not a factor in the vast majority of cases he studied. In addition, it is estimated that only about 3 percent of people involved in abusive relationships experience any diagnosable mental disorder (Straus, 1978). Throughout the 1980s, several researchers attempted to find the "typical profile" of the batterer, only to find that the group is very heterogeneous (Hamberger & Hastings, 1986). However, Rounsaville (1978) did find certain characterological indicators of men who were abusive. These include impulsiveness, being violent in a number of situations, and abuse of alcohol and/or drugs. Abusive men also are likely to be jealous and highly possessive of women. Tolman & Bennett (1990), in a review of programs for batterers, suggested that in attempting to use psychopathology as a causal factor in abusive relationships, care must be taken due to the fact that in several studies there exist major inconsistencies in the results. Alcohol, however, has consistently been cited as a correlate and "clearly needs further exploration, because alcoholic men show more severe psychopathology and the presumably nonalcoholic battering samples may be confounded by the presence of undetected alcohol problems" (Tolman & Bennett, 1990, p. 89).

Aside from the theoretical considerations, there has been little reported in the professional literature concerning interventions focused on individual psychopathology in batterers. Consensus remains, however, that working individually with batterers is not an effective means of primary intervention. The primary drawback of working individually with batterers is that the social context of the group is lost. Social support, feedback, confrontation, and modeling that take place in groups are absent when working with individuals. Also, it would seem that denial of individual responsibility for abusive behavior is easier to maintain when dealing with only a single counselor when compared to a group of peers. As a result, individual treatment has been limited to an adjunct to other means of primary treatment (Edleson & Tolman, 1992).

### Feminist Theory–Based Interventions

Although there is no single, feminist position concerning domestic violence, there are certain commonalties found in the literature. In general, the feminist intervention philosophy envisions battering as a purposeful tool used by men to impose their will on women rather than as part of any relationship difficulties. Within a sociopolitical context, power and control are seen as the fundamental issues. Consequently, interventions are aimed at providing education directed toward assisting both women and men about gender politics with the ultimate goal of eliminating all behaviors on the part of the batterer that "serve to undermine the woman's rights as an individual and as a partner (Caesar & Hamberger, 1989, p. 8).

Feminist interventions initially focus on ensuring the safety of the women. Many programs espouse a safety theme and offer interventions aimed at assisting women in terminating their abusive relationships rather than terminating abuse within the relationship. Of those who go to shelters, most choose to stay for only a brief period and then return to their spouses (Caputo, 1988). Rubin (1991), in a study of outreach groups for battered women, suggested that despite the abundance of programs aimed at assisting battered women, no well-controlled outcome studies have been conducted to test the efficacy of these programs. He concluded that this underscored the importance of evaluating services to battered women, a field of service delivery that has virtually no rigorous empirical outcome evaluation.

Safety plans for men often include ensuring that the men fully comply with court orders, eliminate drug and/or alcohol usage if it is accompanied by violent behavior, and cease intimidating tactics aimed at their partners. Once safety issues are resolved, these programs begin a process of educating both men and women about the effects of abusive behavior and directly confront men with their attempts to minimize or deny responsibility for their abusive behavior. Men, in addition to accepting responsibility for their abusive behavior, are expected to become community advocates for change (Adams, 1988).

Strategies employed in these intervention programs often include psychoeducational or cognitive-behavioral approaches. The vast majority of programs are influenced by social learning theory, which holds as its basic premise that violence is a socially learned behavior and self-reinforcing (Edleson & Tolman, 1992). In addition, most programs provide specific intervention techniques aimed at assisting the batterer in such specific areas as anger management, stress control, conflict containment, and communications skills (Caesar & Hamberger, 1989).

Recent studies of group treatment for batterers provide some support for the effectiveness of structured, time-limited programs (Tolman & Bennet, 1990; Edleson & Syers, 1991). Despite the optimistic findings, a limitation of these programs is that they involve interventions involving only male batterer groups. An obvious disadvantage of working only with the batterer is that if the spouse "victim" is not involved and kept well informed of the social skills component of the treatment, the abuser's first attempts to communicate in a positive fashion will receive negative reactions from their partners.

Evaluation efforts of feminist programs "have been limited by the unavailability of comparison groups and difficulty in locating subjects at follow-up" (Pence, 1989, p. 48). Nonetheless, it should be pointed out that in her evaluation of the Duluth program, Shephard (1992) reported a 70 percent reduction in physical violence at one-year follow-up. Edleson and Syers (1991) report that 64 percent of the men attending an education-only group remained nonviolent, 62 percent of those attending a combined educational and therapeutic group remained nonviolent, and 79 percent of those men attending self-help groups remained nonviolent at 18-month follow-up. Nonetheless, the fact still remains that studies of interventions focused on working with batterers' groups have reflected serious theoretical and methodological weaknesses (Eisikovits & Edleson, 1989).

## Interventions Based on Family Systems Theory

Probably the most viable outcome data reported thus far have been provided concerning the effectiveness of approaches utilizing a family systems approach (couple's group interventions). Proponents of the family systems perspective argue that abuse occurs in the context of a dyadic relationship with violence considered one manifestation of a dysfunctional relationship.

Proponents also argue that if treatment is to be effective in reducing the incidence of violence, it must be done in the context of the marital relationship (Brannen & Rubin, 1996). Proponents of this perspective adhere to Walker's (1984) concept of the "cycle of violence." Using a social learning/behavioral perspective,

Walker discusses a cycle of violence that appears to have three distinct phases: the tension phase, the explosion or acute battering incident (violent episode), and the calm (reconciliation period). The cycle is not constrained by time, but rather can consist of a very long tension-building phase, followed by an acute episode and then a period of remorse and reconciliation on the part of the batterer. It also can be very rapid cycling when abuse is frequent. In fact, in most violent relationships, both types of cycles will be present (Walker, 1984). Research (Hotaling & Sugarman, 1986) has demonstrated that many abusers and victims alike were either abused as children or were witnesses to familial violence. Among others, Geffner, Mantooth, Franks, and Rao (1989) suggest that the violence perpetuates itself through intergenerational transmission of violence. This cycle of violence and the "mutual interaction of abuse" have been supported by other recent research (Hamberger & Hastings, 1986).

Family systems theorists argue that the marriages of abusive couples are marked by dissatisfaction of the marital relationship, decrease in communication between the dyad, a rigid adherence to sex-role stereotyping, and an increase in expectations and projection of hostility (Neidig & Friedman, 1984). Cook and Frantz-Cook (1984) identified several themes that have emerged from the literature on spouse abuse:

- Violence follows a cyclical pattern and is very resistant to change unless treated.
- Violence and the spouse's response to it are, at least in part, learned behavior.
- Men can learn to control their violent behavior.
- Couples can be taught methods of reducing anger and violence in their relationships.
- Change requires not only working on controlling individual behavior but also interventions that will help break the cycle that maintains the violence.

Family systems interventions are highly structured. They last 10 to15 weeks and utilize a cognitive-behavioral/social learning theory framework. The focus of these models is the cessation of abuse using specific skill-building techniques to enhance communications skills, assertiveness skills, conflict tactics, marital and family relations, and anger management. Much like their feminist counterparts, family systems approaches emphasize the need for the abuser to assume responsibility for his personal violent behavior and to contract to eliminate this behavior.

Several studies have been conducted that support the effectiveness of interventions based on a family systems/learning theory model. For example, a quasi-experimental study conducted by Lindquist, Telch, and Taylor (1985) demonstrated significant decreases in physical aggression along with reductions in anger and jealousy and increases in marital satisfaction and assertiveness at the end of treatment. Unfortunately, due to methodological considerations, the study had limited generalizability.

Neidig, Friedman, and Collins (1985) claimed to have obtained excellent preliminary success in working with a military population. They suggested that "about 8 out of 10 program participants remained violence free for the post-program period of time (6 months) they were followed" (p. 7). However, a problem with this study is that there is no clear delineation as to who was contacted to provide data or how recidivism was determined (Edleson & Tolman, 1992). Brannen and Rubin (1996), when comparing couples' group and gender-specific group interventions, found that over 90 percent of men assigned to both interventions remained violence free at six-month follow-up. Still, this six-month follow-up provides a very limited view of an abuser's likelihood to recidivate. Perhaps a more appropriate follow-up would be to evaluate at 6-month, 12-month, 18-month, and 24-month intervals.

The provision of couples' treatment for spouse abuse is highly controversial. Opponents argue that the use of couples' groups:

- shifts the blame from the husband to the wife, thus making her culpable for her own abuse;
- raises volatile issues in treatment settings that can lead to further expression of violence on the part of the batterer against the victim; and may inhibit the wives from expressing their true feelings due to the presence of their abusive partner in treatment (Tolman & Bennett, 1990).

Proponents of couples' treatment argue that it is effective when the couple requests it, the abuse is categorized as minor or mild, there are no significant psychiatric problems, violence has been more expressive than instrumental, and there are no lethality indicators.

Yet despite all the controversy, the success rates of couples' group studies appear comparable to those for men-only groups (Brannen & Rubin, 1996). However, much like studies conducted in the gender-specific groups, several methodological concerns are raised concerning the reporting of outcome data. Nonetheless, as evidenced by the initial studies, couples' treatment may be a viable alternative to gender-specific batterers' and victims' groups.

### A Synopsis of the Major Interventions

There appears to be some optimism for the major approaches to intervention in this very difficult arena. For example, Shupe, Stacey and Hazelwood (1987) compared three treatment programs located in Texas. All three programs focused on anger control, communications, and sex-role issues. One of the programs provided services to batterers in mens' groups, one worked with couples' groups, and the third worked with individual couples. Shupe and associates (1986) reported that all three programs were successful in reducing or eliminating violence, and there did not appear to be any differences in the success of the various formats. Unfortunately, this study was an uncontrolled program evaluation in which the results were based on a subsample of program participants and spouses who could be reached after treatment had been terminated. Brannen and Rubin (1996) found that both couples' groups and gender-specific groups appear to reduce the level of violence in couples who have indicated a desire to remain in the relationship. They found that the group to which a couple was assigned had little effect on the level of marital satisfaction and communication ability evidenced as a result of treatment. In fact, they found that at posttest, both approaches helped to reduce the level of marital dissatisfaction from pretest scores and increased the level of communication within the dyadic relationship. Brannen and Rubin (1996) were not able to demonstrate statistically significant differences between therapy groups in the amount of physical violence and severe physical violence experienced by the couples at posttest. They did show that for those abusers who had a history of alcohol abuse, assignment to the couples' group appeared to be more effective.

After reviewing the literature, it seems the major differences between the approaches are basically philosophical and relate more to the origins and etiology of spouse abuse. When the actual application of treatment is assessed, however, the paradigms are very similar. The philosophical differences seem to center around the profeminist sociopolitical context of abuse as being an attempt of male dominance in a patriarchal society by the use of force whenever necessary, as opposed to a family systems perspective of a dysfunctional marriage that contains reciprocating reinforcement for the abusive behaviors. Interestingly enough, despite all the philosophical differences, both adhere to a social-learning theory perspective that emphasizes that the abuse is learned, albeit for different reasons.

Stordeur & Stille (1989), in discussing the profeminist perspective, assert, "Wife assault is thought to be sanctioned by the society and maintained by political, social, and economic factors within our society" (p. 31). The profeminists attribute a well-designed, well-implemented political motive for the abuse, the subjugation of women and children by the men in this society. Within this broader context, they consider abuse to be only one of many tools used by men to oppress and subjugate women (Bograd, 1988; Edleson & Tolman, 1992; Stordeur & Stille, 1989). On the other hand, the family systems theorists suggest that the abuse is a learned behavior, which is reinforced in certain types of marital and family relationships. In this context, violence is a relationship issue, with the violence being a symptom of a dysfunctional or pathological relationship (Neidig & Friedman, 1984).

Although the perspectives from which the treatment programs are developed are quite different, the treatment approaches themselves are not. In most studies, both the feminist and family systems camps have utilized a cognitive-behavioral approach to treatment. This approach emphasizes the development of specific skills. They include anger management; assertion and communications training to enable men to express feelings more appropriately, including anger; and problem-solving using techniques such as cognitive restructuring with an emphasis on self-talk, teaching couples to observe cues to violence or stressors in their lives, thought stopping, modeling, role play, and behavioral assignments (Eisikovits & Edleson, 1989).

In assessing techniques frequently used in groups for batterers, Eisikovits & Edleson (1989) liken the voluminous approaches to a "patchwork of procedures" (p. 394), the largest number being cognitive-behavioral. They suggest that "the sheer number of techniques employed in the men's groups makes it difficult to interpret what, if any, procedures are critical to the success of treatment" (p. 394). A thorough review of the literature reveals that the same can be said of interventions focused on working with couples' groups. Considering the heavy reliance placed upon cognitive-behavioral approaches by both the profeminist and family systems/social learning theorists, it appears that when all is said and done, the only major difference between the major intervention strategies is the use of gender-specific versus couples' groups.

In sum, there have been numerous attempts to alleviate the problem of spouse abuse in this country since the development of early programs in the mid-1970s. Despite all the efforts to provide empirical data regarding the effectiveness of the various approaches, to date "there is little information about the relative effectiveness of one approach over another" (Caesar & Hamberger, 1989, p. xxviii). Finally, despite the growing body of empirical literature on both the approaches dealing with batterers' group and couples' group interventions, there remains a lack of studies focused on the victims (Rubin, 1991).

## TREATMENT OPTIONS WITHIN THE RESPECTIVE SERVICES

While each of the armed services offers a slightly different array of treatment alternatives, there is a similarity among them. In their study of 94 military couples, Caliber Associates (1996) found that the range of treatments varied from individual, couples and/or family therapy and group counseling in single-gender and mixed groups. The three most common forms of treatment were men's group (55 percent of respondents), individual counseling (45 percent), and women's support group (41 percent). Most families received multiple treatments, with the most common combination being gender-specific group and individual counseling. Active duty men were twice as likely to participate in men's groups (56 percent) than individual counseling (28 percent), and almost three times more likely than couple counseling (20 percent). Mutual spouse-abuse couples were almost two times more likely to receive couple counseling (83 percent) than single-offender couples (44 percent). Most of the interventions were received on base (83 percent). In most cases, those treated off base were civilian male abusers. Only 4 percent of the couples did not receive any interventions, and these represented a select group that were separated from the service via retirement, administrative discharge, courts-martial, or normal separation.

Command involvement with the FAP has been consistently high. About 98 percent of the abusers' commands were involved in the treatment planning process, while 90 percent of the victims' commands were involved. In addition, 63 percent of commanders reported providing counseling for abusers at the unit level.

## SPOUSE ABUSE RESEARCH WITHIN THE MILITARY SERVICES

Although research has been conducted to assess the effectiveness of interventions, to date no study has been conducted within the DOD to directly compare the effectiveness of the two primary approaches to intervention in cases of spouse abuse. Nonetheless, there are several ongoing research initiatives within the services. The Air Force is conducting a pilot study investigation of the effectiveness of a prevention program for at-risk families, the Home-Based Opportunities Make Everyone Successful (HOMES) program, as well as conducting a program-wide study examining changes in marital satisfaction over the course of FAP treatment. The Marine Corps is evaluating the effectiveness of their community-based initiative based upon the Duluth model's program. The Navy has several initiatives related to spouse abuse. The first, which has been met with some severe criticism, is named the San Diego Spouse Abuse Intervention Study. This study is a four-year study comparing the effectiveness of four interventions commonly used in the Navy to treat spouse abuse. While the final results have yet to be released, Dunford (1997) presented data suggesting that the most effective intervention was the command monitoring of substantiated cases. A second Navy study is assessing the effectiveness of the New Parent Support Program. Finally, the Navy recently completed a study addressing the interrelationships among personal history of family violence, family violence outcomes, job performance, and attrition from the Navy using a sample of Navy recruits.

The Army has undertaken several recent initiatives. McCarroll and associates (1999) recently completed a study reporting the distributions and characteristics of spouse abuse victims and offenders based upon data stored in the Army Central Registry. Brannen and associates at the Uniformed Services University of the Health Sciences (USUHS) are conducting an evaluation of the effectiveness of batterers' groups versus couples' groups with intact couples referred from the FAP, using random assignment of couples to groups. The studies discussed above should contribute to the body of information we have concerning the effectiveness of spouse abuse treatment efforts in the military. These efforts will assist the military community and the treatment community as a whole in identifying what works for whom and under what conditions. The military, with its immense, stable population, offers a setting for the conduct of research in spouse abuse that is available in no other sector of society.

## SUMMARY AND IMPLICATIONS

Civilian practitioners benefit by understanding the unique environment in which military domestic violence programs operate and the relationship between the military family and the military work place. Military domestic violence programs are staffed primarily by civilian social workers. Civilian social workers employed or contracted by the Department of Defense understand the military environment and can serve as a bridge between community/agency social workers and the military social service, health care, and law enforcement communities located on military installations. For example, all the military services have established Family Service Centers, which house a variety of programs and services to support military families. Among them are relocation assistance, victim advocacy services, information, and referral and follow-up services. These programs and services recognize the special needs of military families.

The relationship between the military family, military and civilian social workers, and the military work place is unique. Social workers within the Department of Defense do not have privileged communication with domestic violence clients. Only chaplains and lawyers have privileged communication. Military unit leaders enjoy a special relationship with service members and their families. Based on the uniqueness of the military occupation, its mission, readiness, and deployment requirements, unit leaders are in a special position to assist families in need of domestic violence services. They can support families in many situations to include the provision of time off to ensure that families receive necessary services. They can hold perpetrators accountable for their actions and when appropriate support treatment recommendations.

Civilian practitioners can establish meaningful partnerships with military and civilian domestic violence social workers to assist military families. Such partnerships require the identification of primary, secondary, and tertiary prevention programs available in each community, military and civilian, and connect those helping resources to meet the identified needs of military families.

## REFERENCES

Adams, D. (1988). Treatment models of men who batter: A profeminist analysis. In K. Yllo & M. Bograd (Eds.), *Feminist perspectives on wife abuse* (pp.176–199). Newbury Park, CA: Sage.

American College of Obstetricians and Gynecologists (ACOG). (1989). *The battered woman*. Technical Bulletin Number 124. Washington, DC.

Caliber Associates. (1996). *The study of spousal abuse in the armed forces: Analysis of spouse abuse incidence and recidivism rates and trends*. Fairfax, VA: Caliber Associates.

Bograd, M. (1984). Family systems approach to wife battering: A feminist critique. *American Journal of Orthopsychiatry, 54*, 558-568.

Brannen, S. J., & Rubin, A. (1996). Comparing the effectiveness of gender-specific and couples groups in a court-mandated spouse abuse treatment program. *Research on Social Work Practice, 6*(4), 405–424.

Caesar, P. L., & Hamberger, L. K. (Eds.). (1989). *Treating men who batter: Theory, practice, and programs*. New York: Springer.

Caputo, R. (1988). Managing domestic violence in two urban police districts. *Social Casework, 69*, 498-504.

Cook, D. R., & Frantz-Cook, A. (1984). A systemic approach to wife battering. *Journal of Marital and Family Therapy, 10*(1), 83–93.

Department of Defense (DOD). (1992). *Department of Defense Regulation 6400.1. The Family Advocacy Program*. Washington, DC: The Pentagon.

Dunford, F. W. (1997, June). The research design and preliminary outcome findings of the San Diego Navy Experiment. In J. Breiling (chair), *Partner abuse: An experimental comparison of interventions for Navy couples*. Symposium conducted at the Fifth International Family Violence Research Conference, Durham, NH.

Edleson, J. L., & Syers, M. (1991). The effects of group treatment for men who batter: An 18-month follow-up study. *Research on Social Work Practice, 1*(3), 227–243.

Edleson, J. L., & Tolman, R. M. (1992). *Intervention for men who batter: An ecological approach*. Newbury Park, CA: Sage.

Eisikovits, Z. C., & Edleson, J. L. (1989). Intervening with men who batter: A critical review of the literature. *Social Service Review, 63*, 384–414.

Geffner, R., Mantooth, C., Franks, D., & Rao, L. (1989). A psychoeducational, conjoint therapy approach to reducing family violence. In P. L. Caesar & L. K. Hamberger (Eds.), *Treating men who batter: Theory, practice, and programs* (pp. 103–133).

New York: Springer.

Gelles, R. J., & Cornell, C. P. (1990). *Intimate violence in families* (2nd ed.). Newbury Park, CA: Sage.

Gondolf, E. W. (1989). Foreword. In P. L. Caesar & L. K. Hamberger (Eds.), *Treating men who batter: Theory, practice, and programs* (pp. ix–xiii). New York: Springer.

Hamberger, L. K., & Hastings, J. E. (1986, August). Personality characteristics of spouse abusers: A controlled comparison. In L. K. Hamberger (Chair), *The male batterer: Characteristics of a heterogeneous population.* Symposium conducted at the annual meeting of the American Psychological Association, Washington, DC.

Heyman, R. E., & Neidig, P. (1999). A comparison of spousal aggression prevalence rates in U.S. Army and civilian representative samples. *Journal of Consulting and Clinical Psychology, 67*(2), 239–242.

Hotaling, G. T., & Sugarman, D. B. (1986). An analysis of risk markers in husband to wife violence: The current state of knowledge. *Violence and Victims, 1*(2), 101–124.

Kilpatrick, D. (1992). *Rape in America: A report to the nation.* Washington, DC: The National Victim Center and the Crime Victims Research and Treatment Center at the Medical University of South Carolina.

Lindquist, C. U., Telch, C. F., & Taylor, J. (1985). Evaluation of a conjugal violence treatment program: A pilot study. *Behavioral Counseling and Community Intervention, 3,* 76–90.

McCarroll, J. E., Newby, J. H., Thayer, L. E., Norwood, A. E., Fullerton, C. S., & Ursano, R. J. (1999). Reports of spouse abuse in the U.S. Army central registry (1989-1997). *Military Medicine, 164*(2), 77–84.

Neidig, P. H. (1988). *High rate of physical violence among courting and newly married: Support for premarital counseling in new findings.* Washington, DC: Department of the Army Publications: MDC Acc#5143.

Neidig, P. H., & Friedman, D. H. (1984). *Spouse abuse: A treatment program for couples.* Champaign, IL: Research Press.

Neidig, P. H., Friedman, D. H., & Collins, B. S. (1985). Domestic conflict containment: A spouse abuse treatment program. *Social Casework, 16* (4), 195-204.

Pence, E. (1989). Batterer programs: Shifting from community collusion to community confrontation. In P. L. Caesar & L. K. Hamberger (Eds.), *Treating men who batter: Theory, practice, and programs* (pp. 24–50). New York: Springer.

Rounsaville, B. J. (1978). Theories in marital violence: Evidence from a study of battered women. *Victimology: An International Journal, 3,* 11–31.

Rubin, A. (1991). The effectiveness of outreach counseling and support groups for battered women: A preliminary evaluation. *Research on Social Work Practice, 1*(4), 322-357.

Saunders, D. G. (1988). Wife abuse, husband abuse or mutual combat: A feminist perspective on the empirical findings. In K. Yllo & M. Bograd (Eds.), *Feminist perspectives on wife abuse (*pp. 99–113*).* Newbury Park, CA: Sage.

Shephard, M. (1992). Predicting batterer recidivism five years after community intervention. *Journal of Family Violence, 7*(3), 167–178.

Shupe, A. D., Stacey, W. A., & Hazelwood, L. R. (1987). *Violent men, violent couples: The dynamics of domestic violence.* Lexington, MA: Lexington Books.

Stark, E., Flitcraft, A., & Frazier, W. (1979). Medicine and patriarchal violence: The social construction of a "private" event. *International Journal of Health Services, 9,* 461–493.

Stordeur, R. A., & Stille, R. (1989). *Ending men's violence against their partners: One road to peace.* Newbury Park, CA: Sage.

Straus, M. A. (1978). Wife beating: How common and why? *Victimology: An International Journal, 2,* 443–458.

Straus, M. A. (1980). Victims and aggressors in marital violence. *American Behavioral Scientist, 23,* 681–704.

Straus, M. A., & Gelles, R. J. (1986). Societal change and change in family violence from 1975 to 1985 as revealed by two national surveys. *Journal of Marriage and the Family, 48,* 465-479.

Straus, M. A., & Gelles, R. J. (Eds.). (1990). *Physical violence in American families: Risk factors and adaptations to violence in 8,145 families.* New Brunswick, NJ: Transaction; William Morrow.

Tolman, R. M., & Bennett, L. W. (1990). A review of quantitative research on men who batter. *Journal of Interpersonal Violence, 5,* 87–118.

Walker, L. E. (1984). *The battered woman syndrome.* New York : Harper & Row.

# Chapter 12

# Responding to Child Maltreatment Involving Military Families
*Albert L. Brewster*

## INTRODUCTION

This chapter provides the civilian human service provider with an overview of child maltreatment interventions within the Department of Defense (DOD). An understanding of the unique nature of the military and military family life is a prerequisite for appreciating the military's response to child maltreatment. Incidence data from national sources reveals distinct differences in the frequency of substantiated child abuse and neglect between military and civilian populations. This chapter explores these differences and offers possible explanations for these variations. Resources available on most military installations and effective roles for networking in child maltreatment interventions are discussed. Tips for working successfully within the military culture and references for additional information for civilian human service providers are included throughout the chapter.

This chapter is intended for experienced human service providers who may be new to working with military families or new to working in concert with military community resources. Those new to the field of child maltreatment will also find this information useful. The Department of Defense (DOD) has published a series of documents providing overall guidance for its Family Advocacy Program (DODI 6400.1). In addition there are DOD documents on "Child and Spouse Abuse Reporting" (DODI 6400.2), and documents describing the role and function of the Department of Defense Family Advocacy Command Assistance Team (FACAT) (DODI 6400.3). Human service providers working with military families regarding family violence issues need to be familiar with these documents. They will also benefit from the development of a working relationship with the installation Family Advocacy Officer and members of the FACAT.

Civilian human service providers will find a comprehensive review of the professional literature in the area of partner violence on the Internet at www.nnfr.org/research/pv/. The National Network for Family Resiliency maintains this Internet site and features information on the networking between Air Force and civilian clinician/researchers in the specific area of domestic violence. Of particular interest is information on prevention and the impact of domestic violence upon children. Additional practice information is provided by Mannarino and Cohen (1990), Kaufman and Rudy (1991); Kolko (1992); Mollerstrom, Milner, and Patchner (1992); and Mollerstrom, Patchner, and Milner (1995).

## NATURE OF THE PROBLEM

One of our civilization's most persistent problems is child maltreatment. The leading cause of death to children less than one year of age in this country is physical abuse. This fatal abuse of infants is usually in the form of either severe shaking, leading to intracranial hemorrhage, or intra-abdominal injuries caused by blows from a parent's clenched fist (Brewster, Nelson, Hymel, Colby, Lucas, Milner, & McCanne, 1998; Walker, Bonner, & Kaufman, 1988). Whether fatal or not, child maltreatment has a widespread and often lasting impact on the victims, other family members, and even the community.

While child maltreatment has only been scientifically studied for the last 30 or so years, history is rich with examples indicating that children have probably been abused both in public and "behind closed doors" since families began (Radbill, 1974; Straus, Gelles, & Steinmetz, 1980). Suggestions for gentler ways of teaching children are known as far back as 400 b.c. when the Greek philosopher Plato advised "train children not by compulsion but as if they were playing" (Radbill, 1974, p. 174). Largely credited with being among the first to bring the issue effectively to the attention of the medical community and public policy makers, Kempe and colleagues' (1962) observations of the factors related to child battering are interesting and significant historically.

Kempe's work was essentially qualitative, and it was not until recently that data from the U.S. Department of Health and Human Services (1998); were available to understand child maltreatment from a quantitative perspective. Trends in these data suggest that child maltreatment is either steadily rising or at least being more frequently reported. For example, the latest report, covering 1996 data, from the U.S. Department of Health and Human Services (1998) observes that compared to 1990 the number of children substantiated to have been abused or neglected increased by 18 percent to approximately 1 million children. More alarming are the reports of scholars (e.g., Finkelhor, 1993) who support the notion that the published rates of child maltreatment underestimate the true nature of the phenomenon. Support for this argument comes from the observation that as maltreatment has become subject to increasing legal sanction and public awareness (e.g., Gelles & Loseke, 1993) the number of child maltreatment reports has risen suggesting a gradual uncovering of the extent of the problem. Following the nation's struggle to come to grips with the issue (Buzawa, Buzawa, & Inciardi, 1996; Costin, 1973), the U.S. military has increasingly focused resources toward child maltreatment prevention, intervention, treatment, and research (McNelis, 1987; Mollerstrom et al., 1992; Mollerstrom et al., 1995; Brewster et al., 1998).

## Comparison of Military and Civilian Rates of Child Maltreatment

The annual incidence of child maltreatment in military families appears to differ from child maltreatment in civilian communities nationwide. These differences between military and civilian families have not been systematically examined, so there are no definitive explanations at this time. When comparing DOD data with data collected from states, there are usually only slight variations in the definitions of abuse and neglect. The DOD definition follows federal definitions contained in the Child Abuse Prevention and Treatment Act of 1974. States are required to set equivalent definitions to be eligible for child abuse grants from the Department of Health and Human Services. The criteria used by many family violence researchers (Straus, 1979; Straus, Gelles, & Steinmetz, 1981; Straus, 1992; Straus & Gelles, 1990; Straus & Smith, 1990) to investigate the prevalence of child maltreatment are often more stringent and therefore more likely to identify certain behaviors as child maltreatment (e.g., being spanked or witnessing spouse abuse) than either current state and federal definitions. In addition, depending upon the resources available to investigate reports, the thresholds for substantiating maltreatment will vary. Policies and procedures governing the receipt and investigation of reports therefore differ among agencies. There are always the issues of missing data in any data set and quality control of data entry that will shape the reliability and validity of data analysis. McCarroll, and colleagues (1996) not only provide a good overview of some of the military data routinely collected and the limitations of military data in general but also give examples of data that are available for use by clinicians or administrators in every DOD Family Advocacy Program. There is a growing body of state-level and DOD data suggesting differences between civilian and military communities that are worthy of consideration when working in a military setting. The following explanatory view of the differences is, without any pretense of methodological rigor, provided to give the reader a cogent way of understanding some of the differences between child maltreatment in civilian families and that in military families.

Before looking at the data, it is important to examine some underlying assumptions. The first assumption is that the availability of child maltreatment prevention, investigation, and treatment resources in a given state or military agency will influence the ability of that agency to prevent, investigate and treat child maltreatment. The second assumption, widely reported (Reid, 1995; McCurdy & Daro, 1994), is that civilian Child Protective Services (CPS) workers are frequently overworked and underpaid, experience a high staff-turnover rate, and are often inadequately trained. All are factors that adversely impact the ability of civilian agencies to investigate reports let alone actively prevent or provide treatment services. A third assumption is that DOD military family advocacy programs are, relative to civilian CPS agencies, adequately staffed and trained. This assumption gains support when one considers that the investment by the Congress and, subsequently, the Department of Defense in Family Advocacy Programs has been increasingly strong since Congress passed the Child Abuse Prevention and Treatment Act of 1974. Indeed, today, every military installation with command-sponsored families has personnel assigned to prevent, intervene when necessary, and treat family violence.

With the above assumptions in mind, consider the fact that nationwide child maltreatment (physical, emotional, sexual, or neglect) impacts about 15 of every 1,000 children every year according to data collected by the National Center on Child Abuse and Neglect Data System (U.S. Department of Health and Human Services, 1998). Considering the limited resources in most states, this is probably a very conservative estimate of the extent of child maltreatment. Assuming that the actual rate of child maltreatment in the military is at least equal to the civilian rate, with relatively greater resources available to investigate and treat military families, one would predict that the military would be reporting a rate of child maltreatment substantially higher than civilian agencies. However, the DOD annual incidence rate of child maltreatment has remained between 6.2 and 7.3 per 1,000 children since 1989, less than half the national rate (Brewster, 1997). While the reasons for this disparity are unclear, a deeper look at the national and DOD data does offer some clues.

Information about the extent of child maltreatment nationwide is available through the Clearinghouse on Child Abuse and Neglect Information. An annual report describing child maltreatment data collected from all 50 states is available by phone at 1-800-FYI-3366 and has great utility for any clinician in the field. The latest report available (U.S. Department of Health and Human Services, 1998) provides analysis of data from calendar year 1996 and is the source for the following comparison of military to civilian statistics. Of particular importance are the sections dealing with military-specific data because these, when contrasted with data descriptive of the nation as a whole, provide some insight into the similarities and differences between military and civilian families and the disparate systems of service delivery.

Allegations of sexual abuse are usually vigorously investigated in both military and civilian settings. Consequently, differences in the investigative resources available may be less likely to distort the annual incidence data on sexual abuse. If the incidence data are accurate, other derived statistics should also be valid. Indeed, when looking at substantiated sexual maltreatment within the universe of all substantiated maltreatment in both populations, the results are similar (14 percent for DOD versus 12 percent for the U.S. population). This convergence of the two data sets suggests confidence that the military is not only accurately identifying instances of sexual abuse within its population but that it is possible to view the rest of the military data with some confidence.

There are other differences between military and civilian maltreatment data sets. The military is usually more likely to substantiate that maltreatment has occurred than are civilian social service agencies (48 percent of DOD cases versus 33 percent of cases nationwide). This difference may reflect the relatively greater resources available for, and a consequential lower threshold for, substantiating maltreatment in the military community. DOD case management teams have substantiated physical abuse when children have been publicly slapped on the mouth without bruising by a parent. DOD teams have also substantiated child neglect in cases where parents had left a well-nourished infant locked in a car seat in an automobile parked in front of the post office while the parent was gone for a matter of a few minutes to gather mail from their post office box. It is doubtful that many state child protective service agencies would substantiate neglect in similar circumstances.

Two main areas of difference between civilian and military maltreatment data are neglect and physical abuse. Neglect, including its root causes and possible avenues for treatment, is a complex topic worthy of extensive study. Nationwide, it is the most prevalent form of child maltreatment. DePanfilis (1996) provides a good review of models to assess and intervene in neglect cases. Forty-two percent of military child victims experienced neglect versus 58 percent nationwide. The lower proportion of child neglect in the military may be explained in part by the fact that military families have at least one steady paycheck and ready access to health care.

Thirty-six percent of the substantiated military reports were for physical abuse versus 22 percent of the civilian substantiated cases. With easy access to health care, and the requirement that all family members are seen by a health care provider at certain times (for example prior to a move to an overseas location), military families may be more likely than civilian families to be seen by a health care provider. The increased surveillance by military health care providers may partially explain the larger proportion of physical abuse observed in military versus civilian families.

Military data indicate that 17 percent of military substantiated cases were for emotional abuse versus only 6 percent in the civilian data set. This disparity may be a function of the relative differences in resources and consequent increased sensitivity to all forms of maltreatment in the military. The dynamics of emotional maltreatment make it difficult and time consuming to treat. Because of its effect on self-esteem, injuries from emotional abuse may last a child's lifetime and may also interfere with parenting in the next generation. Although, of all the types of maltreatment, emotional maltreatment may have the most impact in the long term, it may simply not obtain constrained civilian treatment resources when competing for those resources with cases of broken bones and sexual abuse. Many military case review committees, not so severely resource-constrained as their civilian counterparts, may be making the clinically logical link between physical and emotional abuse and substantiating for both, leading to relatively higher proportions of both physical abuse and neglect.

The military services hope that by investing a considerable portion of Family Advocacy resources into primary and secondary prevention efforts, they will be able to enhance the resilience and coping skills of military families. The services hope to encourage early help-seeking behavior and thereby decrease the severity of every type of maltreatment. Early reports from the Air Force suggest that this strategy is working. Military measures of severity of maltreatment at initial case opening show a steady decline over the past few years. Reports indicate that people who have participated in Air Force Family Advocacy Programs report high levels of customer satisfaction with the services they received (Brewster, 1996).

In summary, these data suggest that child maltreatment in the military is less frequent and less severe than child maltreatment in the civilian sector. Far more rigorous examination of the data is required before definitive conclusions are made about the relative differences between military and civilian populations. However, the clinician that practices within a military network with military families as clients should know that military families, as a whole, do enjoy certain attributes that may build resilience to stress and other factors that have been linked to risk for abusive behavior. Prior to examining the stressors and protective factors unique to military families, a very brief overview of the military child maltreatment prevention, investigation, and treatment process is in order.

## AN OVERVIEW OF THE DOD RESPONSE TO CHILD MALTREATMENT

### Prevention

All branches of the service have robust child maltreatment prevention resources. These range from a preventionist assigned to provide community-wide primary prevention education and consciousness-raising information to public health models with home visiting nurses and social workers geared toward secondary prevention efforts with high-risk families. The hard lessons, learned during the implementation of the federal 1964 Community Mental Health Centers Act, about the difficulty of protecting prevention resources from being turned into treatment assets were apparently heeded by some of the services. The Air Force, for example, generally forbids preventionists from being credentialed to provide treatment services. This prohibition precludes the tendency to turn preventionists into clinicians and ensures the dedication of resources to primary and secondary prevention.

### Managing Child Maltreatment Reports

The military has uniformly high standards for responding to reports of abuse or neglect. Typically, medical records are reviewed and arrangements made to interview collateral contacts and family members within 72 hours of receiving a report. If the child is in the emergency room, or there is reason to suspect imminent danger, an immediate response may be both appropriate and expected. Depending upon the nature of the report (e.g., sexual abuse) special criminal investigators may need to be consulted and arrangements made both to maximize the collection of information that can be used for prosecution and to minimize the emotional trauma of unnecessarily redundant questioning of a child victim. The military legal offices and criminal investigators of the installation served should be consulted before handling any reports to agree upon general procedures (e.g., Will interviews be video taped? Who will interview young children? How will treatment services be delivered if families are in the process of a criminal investigation or prosecution?). A very controversial question is, Under what circumstances, if any, will a clinician read a family member his or her rights? Some attorneys, unable to distinguish a clinical investigation from a criminal investigation, will say "always"; some clinicians prizing the therapist-patient alliance and privilege will say "never." The best bet is to work these questions out long before there is a case requiring a smooth, coordinated response.

### The Family Maltreatment Case Management Team

Each military installation has its own version of a case management team that comes to a clinical determination about whether or not there is sufficient "information" (not evidence) to substantiate abuse or neglect. This differentiation between clinical "information" and legal "evidence" is crucial for successful team management. Members of the team have to understand fully the intent of the DOD regulations. If the clinical case management team degenerates into a quasi-administrative legal panel, treatment and prevention may quickly take a back seat to legal machinations. The fact is that in some severe cases a court of law will have to make a legal finding on a case, but the clinical process of treatment and prevention needs to continue independent of the legal process. Like any other health problem, abuse and neglect require treatment that ethically cannot wait while the courts determine whom, if anyone is legally responsible. A clinical case review committee substantiation of abuse or neglect does not necessarily equate to a legal judgment, and, in the interest of prevention and treatment of abuse and neglect, the two processes should be kept separate.

Case management teams meet regularly. The frequency of meetings is dependent upon the caseload. The installation commander usually appoints the members of the team, although this responsibility may be delegated to the military hospital commander. The membership usually includes a pediatrician, a clinical social worker, a civilian child protective services representative, a chaplain, a military legal representative, a military special criminal investigator, and often the commander or senior enlisted supervisor of the active-duty member responsible for the family being discussed. Each member has a specific role in bringing forth information that will be useful to the committee in making a clinical determination about whether abuse or neglect is substantiated. The commander or senior enlisted supervisor (first sergeant, gunnery sergeants or chief petty officer, depending upon branch of service) is usually relied upon for both information pertinent to the specific report and as a potential ally in encouraging compliance by the active-duty member in any recommended treatment plan. The presence of command representatives underscores one of the unique aspects of the military Family Advocacy system—the critical importance of command involvement and support.

### Cooperation Between the Military and Civilian Community

The quality of the relationship between the military Family Advocacy Program (FAP) and the local civilian Child Protective Services (CPS) agency is critical. Usually there are memorandums of understanding (MOUs) between the installation and the local civilian child protection agency outlining the responsibility for case finding and service delivery. These arrangements are often a function of the nature of the "jurisdiction" in which the reported abuse or neglect allegedly occurred. For example, if the report alleges that abuse or neglect occurred in a government housing unit, that home may fall under any one of three jurisdictions: local, exclusive federal, or joint.

An MOU, or similar memorandum of agreement (MOA), between the military authorities and the civilian authorities should specify the type or types of jurisdictions relevant to that specific military installation. It also needs to spell out clearly out both civilian and military agency responsibilities for reporting cases to each other, determinations of maltreatment, and provision of services. It is common for resources to be shared on a case where both agencies agree that abuse or neglect is substantiated (e.g., anger management group treatment provided by military FAP and intense in-home family counseling by state CPS). It is common for the civilian agency to "unsubstantiate abuse" while the military case review team "substantiates." With differing definitions, case loads, thresholds, and resources, it is not surprising that there will be differences between civilian and military agencies.

With good coordination and communication the military and civilian agencies can, and often do, compliment each another. Since the relationship between the civilian community and the military installation usually has such high visibility and wide interest, it is a good idea for the local Child Protection Service (CPS) to be invited to participate in any installation-level committees that focus on policies related to the prevention and treatment of abuse and neglect. Through exposure to these military-specific committees, both local CPS workers and military-specific child maltreatment prevention and treatment professionals will have the opportunity to network as they exchange ideas and resources.

## NETWORKING FOR SUCCESS ON A MILITARY INSTALLATION

Human service providers new to a military installation or just beginning to work with military families in their civilian practice should quickly make the acquaintance of others in positions of responsibility for the health of military families. Each branch of service (Army, Navy, Marines, and Air Force) has a somewhat different organizational structure for Family Advocacy. The goal is to develop "synergistic networking". This is the process of cultivating relationships with other professionals who share a common interest or goal in order to expedite action through the social system. In synergistic networking the whole is greater than the sum of its parts.

There are two types of networks found on any military installation: the informal, or naturally occurring network, and the formal network operating under law or military regulation. The informal networks include kinship and family groups, work groups, neighborhoods, and spiritual or religious networks that may exist either in the local area or even in a virtual dimension on the Internet.

### Informal Networks

Covey (1990) reminds us to "seek first to understand—then be understood." This advice is excellent for a civilian human service provider working on a military installation. Accessing informal networks requires a willingness to attend installation activities and important military social events. This may not be comfortable for the civilian human provider, especially if he or she has very little prior military experience. But the payoff can be substantial. While some activities are by invitation only, most sporting events, commander's calls, and recognition ceremonies with civilian and military awards are open to anyone. A regular appearance at these events is worth the time and effort. This participation can lead to informal discussions with the very people who can smooth the way toward increased referrals, better cooperation from commanders, enhanced teamwork on investigations, increased participation in case management meetings, and stronger military support for prevention and treatment recommendations. Participation can be an opportunity to get informal program advice from the installation legal officer, invite the installation commander and spouse to a community prevention workshop or bounce an idea for a newspaper article off the installation public affairs officer (who also publishes the installation paper). Networking in local professional association meetings that include military and/or DOD civilian employee members can also be helpful. Time spent engaged in this sort of networking can have a tremendous payoff.

Civilian human service providers need to make a habit of observing basic military customs such as stopping their cars and standing at attention during the playing of the national anthem when the flag on the installation is retired each night. Providers can attend events like the installation's annual Prisoner of War/Missing in Action (POW/MIA) ceremonies to feel the depth of emotion shared by the profession of arms. The same is true for participation in the installation Black History Month and Asian/Pacific or Latino heritage functions. Joining in the celebration at military retirement, promotion, or award ceremonies allows the civilian human service provider to become a military cultural anthropologist and will help in gaining an appreciation of the rich and varied texture of military life.

### Formal Networks

On every military installation there are formal agencies required to cooperate with the FAP program. For example, the Child Development Center will depend upon FAP personnel for consultation, and FAP members may even be asked to sit on a staff selection board or train new child development staff about child maltreatment prevention and identification. The military police and investigative services cooperate with the FAP on various committees. Forensic investigators, in particular, can become very good allies in child maltreatment intervention efforts. They are of special importance in the investigation of alleged sexual abuse. The local schools on the installation are often closely allied to the installation Family Advocacy Program activities.

*Military Leaders.* Military leaders, both officers and noncommissioned officers (NCOs), are critical to the success of any military child maltreatment prevention and treatment program. Unit leaders are much more than just employers. They have a pervasive role in the life of any military member and in turn a critical responsibility for the health and well-being of members and their families. The support and cooperation of unit leaders are invaluable to human service providers in their efforts to assist military families. One formal group that is typically vital to human service efforts in any military community is composed of the senior enlisted members of the units on the installation. Depending on the branch of service, this group may be called the first sergeants, chiefs, or top three group. These senior enlisted members can be a vital source of referrals. They can usually be counted among the human service providers' strongest advocates on the installation. Civilian human service providers can get invited to their gatherings by calling upon the installation commander's senior enlisted advisor (SEA). Providers should explain their interest (i.e., civilian clinician newly hired on the installation or a civilian provider serving military families in a community setting) and ask for help in getting to know other essential enlisted leaders. With support from unit leaders, civilian human service providers will greatly enhance their ability to help military families.

*Various Aid Groups.* Each military service has its own agency responsible for providing a variety of material aids to military members and their families. Air Force Aid, Army Emergency Relief, Coast Guard Mutual Assistance, and Navy Marine Corps Relief, all with somewhat different models of service delivery, are agencies that the human service provider will come to rely upon when dealing with military families. Each provides emergency loans and grants in situations ranging from deaths of family members to need for crisis assistance with housing, food, transportation, and utility costs, as well as respite care for special needs families.

## SUMMARY AND IMPLICATIONS

This chapter highlights information on the nature and management of child maltreatment within a military community. It provides basic information that civilian human service providers can use to enhance their impact through networking activities within the military community. A few of the important support networks that exist in a military community are highlighted. There are many more. The critical issue for the civilian human service provider is to reach out, participate, and become part of the military community. Most providers will be pleasantly surprised by the positive reception that they will receive from all members of the military community. For those whose professional role involves direct participation in child maltreatment prevention and/or treatment, the installation Family Advocacy Officer and the installation's Family Advocacy Program staff represent important and willing partners in the provision of services to military families.

## REFERENCES

Brewster, A. L. (1996, July 23). USAF Family Advocacy Program. Paper presented at the Department of Defense Conference on Domestic Violence, Alexandria, VA.

Brewster, A. L. (1997, July). Research that you can use. Briefing presented at the USAF Family Advocacy Prevention Conference, San Antonio, TX.

Brewster, A. L., Nelson, J. P., Hymel, K. P., Colby, D. R., Lucas, D. R., McCanne,T. R., & Milner J. S. (1998). Victim, perpetrator, family, and incident characteristics of 32 infant maltreatment deaths in the United States Air Force. *Child Abuse and Neglect, 22*(2) 91–101.

Buzawa, E. S., Buzawa, C. G., & Inciardi, J. A. (Ed.). (1996). *Domestic violence: The criminal justice response* (2nd ed.). Thousand Oaks, CA: Sage.

Costin, L. B. (1972). Protecting children from abuse and neglect. *In Child welfare policies and practice* (pp. 253–296). New York: McGraw-Hill.

Covey, S. (1990). *7 habits of highly successful people*. New York: Simon & Schuster.

DePanfilis, D. (1996). Social isolation of neglectful families: A review of social support assessment and intervention models. *Child Maltreatment 1*(1), 37–52.

Finkelhor, D. (1993). The main problem is still underreporting, not overreporting. In R. J. Gelles & D. R. Loseke (Eds.), *Current controversies on family violence* (pp. 273–288). Newbury Park, CA: Sage.

Gelles, R. J., & Loseke, D. R. (Eds.). (1993). *Current controversies on family violence*. Newbury Park, CA: Sage.

Jasinski, J. L., Williams, L. M., Brewster, A. L., Finkelhor, D., Giles-Sims, J., Hamby, S. L., Kaufman Kantor, G., Mahoney, P., Weaver, T. L., West, C. M., & Wolak, J. (1997). Partner violence: A 20 year review and synthesis. A 341-page, 8-chapter review of the domestic violence literature with implications for clinical practice supported by the United States Department of Agriculture, Cooperative Research Education and Extension Service Cooperative Agreement No. 95-EXCA-3-0414; the University of Missouri; and the United States Air Force. HYPERLINK http://www.nnfr.org/research/pv/ w w w .nnfr.org/research/pv/

Kaufman, K. L., & Rudy, L. (1991). Future directions in the treatment of physical child abuse. *Criminal Justice and Behavior, 18* (1), 82–97.

Kempe, C. H., Silverman, F. N., Steele, B. F., Droegmueller, W., & Silver, H. K. (1962). The battered child syndrome. *Journal of the American Medical Association, 181* (July 7), 17–24.

Kolko, D. J. (1992). Characteristics of child victims of physical abuse: Research findings and clinical implications. *Journal of Interpersonal Violence, 7*(2), 244–276.

Mannarino, A. P., & Cohen, J. A. (1990). Treating the abused child. In R. T. Ammerman & M. Hersen (Eds.), *Children at risk: An evaluation of factors contributing to child abuse and neglect* (pp. 249–266). New York: Plenum Press.

McCarroll, J. E., Ursano, R. J., Norwood, A. E., Fullerton, C. S., Newby, J. H., Dixon, S., Vance, K., & McFarlan, K. (1998). Initial Reports on Child Abuse and Neglect from the U.S. Army Central Registry (1975-1995). Analysis conducted by the Family Violence and Trauma Project, Department of Psychiatry, F. Edward Hebert School of Medicine, Uniformed Services University of the Health Sciences, Bethesda, MD, 20814-4799.

McCurdy, K., & Daro, D. (1994). Child maltreatment: A national survey of reports and fatalities. *Journal of Interpersonal Violence, 9*(1), 75–94.

McNelis, P. J. (1987). Military social work. *Encyclopedia of Social Work* (17th ed., pp. 154–160). Washington, DC: National Association of Social Workers.

Mollerstrom, W. W., Milner, J. S., & Patchner, M. A. (1992). Family violence in the Air Force: A look at offenders and the role of the Family Advocacy Program. *Military Medicine, 157*(7), 371–374.

Mollerstrom, W. W., Patchner, M. A., & Milner, J. S. (1995). Child maltreatment: The United States Air Force's response. *Child Abuse and Neglect, 19*(3), 325–334.

National Research Councile. Panel on Child Abuse and Neglect. (1993). *Understanding child abuse and neglect*. Washington, DC: National Academy Press.

Radbill, S. X. (1974). A history of child abuse and infanticide. In S. K. Steinmetz & M. A. Straus (Eds.), *Violence in the family* (pp. 173–179). New York: Harper & Row.

Reid, T. (1995). CAPTA, Basic protections for children, in danger despite vigorous advocacy. *American Professional Society on the Abuse of Children Advisor, 8*(4), 2.

Straus, M. A. (1979). Measuring intrafamily conflict and violence: The Conflict Tactics (CT) scale. *Journal of Marriage and the Family, 41*(1), 75–88.

Straus, M. A. (1992). Children as witnesses to marital violence: A risk factor for lifelong problems among a nationally representative sample of American men and women. Paper presented at the Twenty-third Ross Roundtable on Critical Approaches to Common Pediatric Problems. (September 21-23, Washington, DC).

Straus, M. A., & Gelles, R. J. (1990). How violent are American families? Estimates from the national family violence resurvey and other studies. In M. A. Straus & R. J. Gelles (Eds.), *Physical violence in American families: Risk factors and adaptations to violence in 8,145 families* (pp. 95–112). New Brunswick, NJ: Transaction.

Straus, M. A., Gelles, R. J., & Steinmetz, S. K. (1981). *Behind closed doors: Violence in the American family*. Garden City, NY: Anchor Press.

Straus, M. A., & Smith, C. (1990). Family patterns and child abuse. In M. A. Straus & R. J. Gelles (Eds.), *Physical violence in American families: Risk factors and adaptation to violence in 8,145 families* (pp. 245–261). New Brunswick, NJ: Transaction.

U.S. Department of Health and Human Services, Children's Bureau. (1998). *Child maltreatment 1996: Reports from the states to the National Child Abuse and Neglect Data System.* Washington, DC: U.S. Government Printing Office.

Walker, C. E., Bonner, B. L., & Kaufman, K. L. (1988). *The physically and sexually abused child: Evaluation and treatment*. New York: Pergamon Press.

Chapter 13

# Transition into Parenthood for High-Risk Families: The New Parent Support Program

*Martha Salas and Leasley Besetsny*

## INTRODUCTION

The Air Force Family Advocacy Program (FAP) offers a range of maltreatment intervention and prevention programs to active duty and family members. The New Parent Support (NPS) program is targeted to military families who are preparing for the birth of a child or who have recently experienced the birth of a child. It is a home-based visitation program with services delivered by community health nurses. This chapter describes the development, implementation, and expansion of the program. Service interventions are also detailed, with an emphasis on the role of the father. The authors conclude by giving recommendations to civilian human service providers how to link with military providers and Air Force personnel participating in the program.

In 1986 the Air Force Family Advocacy Program (FAP) made a commitment to design, implement, and support a primary and secondary outreach prevention program component targeting families at risk for abuse, with the specific goal of reducing intrafamilial violence. This prevention focus started with strategically placed outreach programs at most Air Force bases. The purpose of this initiative was to operationalize a proactive outreach approach of early intervention before abuse occurred. The program was staffed by Air Force social workers referred to as Outreach Managers. Their role consisted of assessing community needs, developing prevention service plans, marketing Family Advocacy Program services, planning and coordinating key prevention initiatives, developing community partnerships, and enhancing Air Force community protective factors through activities that heighten awareness of abuse. Prevention efforts by Outreach Managers were highly successful and well integrated in the FAPs across the Air Force. Their role became a core component of Air Force Family Advocacy prevention efforts.

In an effort to expand the prevention component, a working group of Air Force social workers was convened in 1989 to revise the FAP. Two major outcomes resulted: first, an effort to expand the scope of prevention activities, and second, an initiative to design a program evaluation component to measure intervention effectiveness. These actions were designed to augment and expand the continuum of Air Force Family Advocacy services and establish evaluation as a major component of Air Force FAPs. Today, program evaluation is a hallmark of the Air Force FAP.

In response to the decisions of the working group, the FAP director of research designed a maternal child home-visitation program to prevent child abuse, linking the best practice on child abuse prevention programs and home visits. Findings from the 1986 study by Olds, Henderson, Chamberlin, and Tatelbaum, and the "Hawaii Healthy Start" (Department of Health, State of Hawaii, 1992) home-visit programs influenced the design and development of services targeted toward new parents in the Air Force, called the First Time Parents (FTP) Program. This revolutionary program recognized that parenting is extremely demanding for all families. It sought to enhance protective factors within an Air Force environment where social support systems can be limited and the lack of community linkages can be challenging and stressful for young military families.

A report published by the U.S. General Accounting Office (GAO) in 1990 validated the home-based prevention focus the Air Force was taking. In their report, the GAO concluded that home visitation is an effective service delivery strategy and provided a framework for improving the program within the Air Force. They recommended the use of home visitation as an effective method to improve the health and well-being of families and children. Their analysis determined that home-visited families had fewer low-birthweight babies, higher immunization rates, more age-appropriate child development, and less reported cases of child abuse and neglect. The following year, the U.S. Advisory Board on Child Abuse and Neglect (1991) published a report that recommended the federal government phase in a national universal home-visiting program for children during the neonatal period. Their recommendations were based on the social and economic impact of child abuse and the rapidly increasing focus and awareness of this phenomenon.

The Air Force pilot-tested the FTP program at eight Air Force bases. This voluntary home-based program was staffed with professional community health nurses, called Family Advocacy Nurses (FANs). They targeted first-time parents who had not experienced a child abuse incident but were at risk for abuse. FANs were strategically placed between the Family Advocacy Outreach Program, maltreatment program components, and military medical services. The goals of the program were to prevent child abuse and neglect among Air Force families, improve family life skills, and enhance military readiness by providing psychosocial and maternal child educational health needs to young parents during this stage of family life.

## FIRST-TIME PARENTS PILOT TEST RESULTS

The Child Abuse Potential (CAP) Inventory was administered as a measure of program effectiveness. The CAP was administered prior to offering services, preferably in the prenatal period. The CAP Inventory was administered a second time when services were completed. The CAP Inventory is comprised of

160 items in an agree/disagree format.  Scores obtained include overall abuse potential and ego strength scores and six factor scores: Distress, Rigidity, Unhappiness, Problems with Child and Self, Problems with Family, and Problems with Others (Milner, 1986).  Both parents were requested to complete the CAP Inventory to assist in program evaluation.  Preliminary analysis conducted in 1992 of the data indicated that prevention interventions were highly successful in decreasing abuse potential and levels of distress, while improving self-esteem of participants.  Clients who scored above the abuse potential cut score of 166 had the greatest reduction in scores postinterventions.  Clients in the moderate and low categories experienced smaller decreases in abuse potential scores.  As a result of these early successes, the FTP program was expanded in 1993 to 65 additional locations.  Currently, the Air Force FAP has programs at seventy-six Air Force bases worldwide.

## FIRST-TIME PARENTS PROGRAM

The FTP is a voluntary prevention program.  Participating families include those with a first pregnancy; pregnant, single, active-duty service members; multiple births; unwanted pregnancies; and mothers with postpartum depression.  Also, new parents with military stressors such as frequent deployments and isolation factors that can impact family stability are also targeted.  Home-visit interventions start prenatally and continue through the postpartum period, up to the child's first year of life.  Factors such as client motivation, developmental readiness, and frequency of contact with providers offer a window of opportunity for FANs to present educational and supportive interventions in the areas of effective positive parenting skills, bonding attachment, and infant and family health issues.

### Program Entry

Expectant families are referred to the FTP program from a variety of sources.  The top referral sources from a group of 1,172 mothers were from the obstetrics department in military medical facilities, accounting for 59 percent (see Figure 13.1).  The second highest source, accounting for 21 percent, was self-referrals.  Such a large percentage of self-referrals indicates the success of this program among military families.

### Home Visits as the Primary Service Modality

The literature on early intervention home-visitation programs for at-risk families documents positive outcomes.  Studies show that interventions provided by registered nurses in the area of improving maternal child health in pregnant women reduced the incidence of child abuse and neglect (Olds et al., 1986).  Both social support and health information provide a full continuum of services that are required during this life cycle development of parents expecting their first child so that families' attainment of positive health and social outcomes in

**Figure 13.1**
**FANS Data Referral Sources**

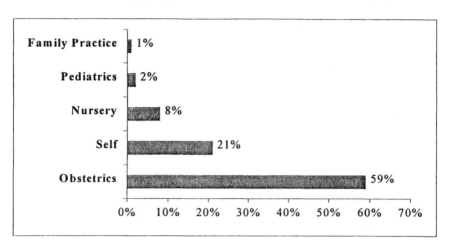

family management can be accomplished. In addition, the literature on prenatal families and families with children supports an ecological model. This model is a blend of both social support and public health models addressing the importance of health-related behaviors and social support during pregnancy and subsequent care of the child in his or her early years (Olds & Kitzman, 1990). The philosophical view of delivering services in the home ties to the empowerment, enablement, and enhancement of the parents (Wasik, Bryant, & Lyons, 1990). Parents are empowered by their ability to closely guide the development of their personal objectives and goals they wish to fulfill through program participation.

Nurses provide families with information about child health, infant care, information, and support in managing military family life events in general with the goal of preventing child abuse. Home-based interventions are diverse and tailored for each family as they adapt to parenthood, focusing on the prevention of child abuse. While in the home, the nurse has many teachable moments and opportunities to provide support, anticipatory guidance, education, and linkage of families to available community services.

**Fathers and the New Parents Support Program**

Another important focus of the NPS Program is to provide opportunities to actively engage fathers in their new parenting role. The focus in most home-visit child abuse prevention programs is centered on the mothers. Interventions consist of providing them with education and information in the areas of prenatal health, care of newborn, parenting skills, and nutritional family needs. Engaging fathers is important as the literature indicates that most child death perpetrators are male. The Air Force FAP conducted a study on child death due to maltreatment (Brewster, Nelson, Hymel, Colby, Lucas, McCanne, & Milner, 1998). The deaths of thirty-two infants, one year of age or less, that occurred between 1989 and early 1997 were evaluated. Eighty-one percent of the perpetrators were male. Brewster and colleagues (1998) identified the following risk factors in the majority of deaths: perpetrator males were alone with the infant in 86 percent of the incidents, the event was triggered by the infant crying in 58 percent of the cases, and 47 percent of the deaths occurred on weekends. This study provides a focus for preventionists to develop and include the fathers in child abuse prevention strategies. Programs should include and emphasize calming a crying fussy baby, understanding the newborn language, and the prevention of Shaken Baby Syndrome.

## ROLE OF THE FAMILY ADVOCACY NURSE (FAN)

In 1991, the U.S. Advisory Board on Child Abuse and Neglect reported that interventions with new parents, especially young families having their first child, afford an opportunity to teach good parenting skills and avoid the development of destructive parenting patterns. The literature indicates that child abuse prevention programs do have an impact on the prevention of child abuse (Olds & Kitzman, 1993) and that new parents are like "sponges" and want to learn as much as possible about their new baby (Donnelly, 1992).

The FAN provides prevention services to the whole family as a system. The level and intensity of services vary, and interventions are diverse and tailored for each family as they adapt to their new parenthood role prenatally, postpartum, and during the child's first year of life. Child abuse interventions are woven throughout the nurse's interventions and provide focus in their delivery of services. Home visits provide the FAN with important additional information that cannot be captured in an office setting and offer many opportunities for the nurse to find teaching opportunities in the families' own environment. Information and support on how to utilize civilian and base agencies are provided to the family for the purpose of empowering them to access base and community support services. In addition, the nurse collaborates with military and civilian agencies linking families to available services that support families (see Figure 13.2).

## CHILD ABUSE PREVENTION INTERVENTIONS

Unique military factors, such as frequent job-required separations, living a great distance from extended family, and frequent moves that disrupt the establishment of social support networks, can lead to stress among young military family members expecting their first child. This program offers an important resource to these new parents by offering interventions to families who are experiencing challenges that are magnified by these unique factors.

The specific child abuse interventions that nurses address are very diverse. They are driven by family and individual needs. Education and information regarding maternal health, family, and individual psychosocial issues are common intervention issues. Positive parenting coping skills, growth and development, and role changes are issues the nurses address most frequently with families. Other more specific child abuse prevention intervention activities deal with

**Figure 13.2**
**FANS Data Sources of Support**

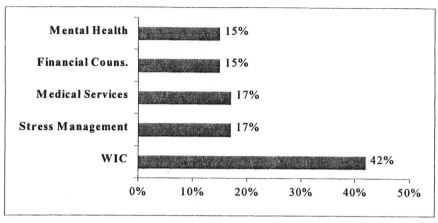

care of the newborn, calming a crying fussy infant, infant attachment and bonding, nutrition, environmental preparation for infant, at home safety, prevention of Shaken Baby Syndrome, and sudden infant death syndrome (SIDS) prevention. These are important areas for education and information provided by the nurse. Other important factors include psychosocial issues such as body and emotional changes impacting self and relationships with partner and family.

During the period that the FANs provide services, they have an opportunity to assess for risk factors such as acceptance of the pregnancy, birth, family role transition and appropriate bonding behaviors, ineffective coping of stress, and other family issues impacting family functioning that may need to be referred to other services or agencies. Maternal health issues addressed by the FAN include the importance of prenatal visits, family health, and the avoidance of alcohol and smoking during pregnancy. During this period families are eager to learn as much as possible about the three trimesters of pregnancy, family role transition into parenthood, and engaging fathers into the birth experience.

**THE FIRST-TIME PARENT (FTP) FAMILY**

An example of an FTP family that might benefit from prevention services is provided in the following vignette:

Jan is 32 weeks pregnant. She and her husband Dave recently moved to Peak Air Force Base in Ohio four months ago. They are geographically separated from extended family and friends and do not have a social support system established at their new base or in the local civilian community where they are now living. Dave is an Airman first class (a junior enlisted service member) and currently deployed to a remote assignment for six weeks. Jan is at home in an unfamiliar military and civilian environment. Dave's new assignment will require him to be away from home often. Jan feels isolated (new base, new to military, separated from family and friends). She has expressed her concern that Dave is not as interested in the baby as she is. She worries that he may not feel that this is the right time to have a baby. Dave says that he is excited about the pregnancy, but he has also said that he is concerned about how he will hold up in the delivery room. Dave hopes he will be on base when the baby arrives and not deployed away from home. He says that he just cannot get as excited as his wife about this expectant child. He is concerned about the financial responsibility associated with having a baby. He is fearful about what the baby will mean to the marriage—he fears being displaced. Dave is also very concerned about the health and safety of his wife and infant.

## FAN INTERVENTIONS

Most families rely on health professionals for guidance in parenting and child rearing. Helping professionals can support and facilitate effective parenting skills with families identified as being at risk for maltreatment. Important efforts include:

- Recognition of the father as an equal parent. This will boost the father's self-esteem and foster his feelings of accomplishment.
- Teach fathers to recognize newborn behavior and language so that the father is able to interpret the newborn cues that lead him to calm a crying fussy infant. His ability to accomplish this task enhances his competence and reduces family stress.
- Include fathers when teaching infant care and provide education on the prevention of Shaken Baby Syndrome.
- Assist mothers to understand that it takes fathers longer to process the infant as a reality and that reality is not concrete until he sees the infant at birth. Strategies that contribute to the infant's reality for the father before birth are to have fathers hear the unborn heartbeat, see the unborn on ultrasound, feel the in-utero movement, and participate in gathering baby supplies and equipment.
- Assure fathers that when the baby is born, he will be more involved and see the newborn as a reality.
- Provide special classes for fathers that provide a forum to express their concerns and fears.
- Linkage into the military and civilian community resources and support services will help new parents lower their stress from being geographically separated from family and close friends.

The family can benefit from participating in the program at several different levels. At the individual parent level we would like to see an increase in positive father involvement in childcare. At the couple level, interventions should decrease couple stress and increase appropriate use of referred community resources. At the family level, positive parent-child interaction can be seen.

## SUMMARY AND IMPLICATIONS

The Air Force's NPS home-based visitation program seeks to empower new parents with skills and education at a time when these individuals are most open to improved parenting techniques—a "plastic" time where they can be positively shaped.

Civilian human service providers can play a large role in supporting Air Force families enrolled in the NPS program. Early discharge from American hospitals, military and civilian, acts as a constraint for hospital staff to provide education on parenting a newborn and prevention of child abuse. Helping professionals need to provide this support, especially in the prevention of child abuse and neglect. Unfortunately, many human service professionals lack the training and knowledge in caring for and understanding newborn behavior and its role in the prevention of abuse. One specific training program developed to meet this need is *Keys to Caregiving* (Sumner, 1990). This program was developed to teach professionals and parents about newborn behavior and appropriate interventions. For example, *Keys to Caregiving* addresses newborn cycles of sleep and wakefulness. This cycle must be understood because an infant that is in a "quiet sleep state" will not suck or swallow well. Therefore, it is important to know that the infant must be in an "awake state" for successful feeding to occur. Infant state modulation is another important newborn cue that parents need to identify so they can soothe a crying fussy baby. Knowledge of such issues helps to reduce parental stress and reduce the potential for abuse. Also, according to the theory of self-efficacy (Bandura, 1977) strengthening the parents' mastery of successful parenting practices becomes a cycle where the parents' confidence grows in coping with parenting issues and reduces stress. The service provider can play a strong role in this cycle. It is very important that the home visitor promotes the parents' healthy caregiving behavior through positive reinforcement and role-modeling activities. So, it quickly becomes evident that service providers must increase their knowledge concerning issues related to new parents and parenting practices.

Helping the male identify his role as a new father is critical. Frequently health care professionals see the father as a mate or co-worker, but not as a co-parent. This perception leads to the father feeling removed and detached from the child. The mother plays an important role in helping the male bond with the baby. Whereas bonding for the mother begins early during pregnancy, the male generally does not begin this process until after birth. It is very important that the "mother focus" of most home visitation programs be expanded to more successfully include the father. Mercer (1998) identified four areas of concern that helping professionals should address: performance, security, relationship, and existential fears. Fathers can become anxious about the additional financial and emotional responsibilities that result from a growing family. He can be at a loss concerning the changes in his wife and unborn/newborn health and care issues. With the shifting of mother's focus from the father to the newborn, he can be at risk for feelings of exclusion or replacement. Additionally, a new father frequently grapples with concern about his future welfare and what would become of his family should something happen to him.

This prevention program provides nurses with a unique opportunity to intervene and support fathers as they transition into their parenting role as well as reinforces positive parent-child interaction specifically in the area of child abuse prevention.

## NOTE

Each branch of the military has an intervention program to support new parents at risk for child maltreatment. Civilian human service providers can obtain additional information by contacting their local military installation public information office.

## REFERENCES

Bandura, A. (1977). Self-efficacy: Toward a unifying theory of behavioral change. *Psychological Review, 84*(2), 191–215.

Brewster, A. L., Nelson, J. P., Hymel, K. P., Colby, D. R., Lucas, D. R., McCanne, T. R., & Milner, J. S. (1998). Victim, perpetrator, family, and incident characteristics of 32 infant maltreatment deaths in the United States Air Force. *Child Abuse and Neglect, 22*(2), 91–101.

Department of Health, State of Hawaii. Report to the Sixteenth Legislature State of Hawaii. (1992). On House Bill No. 139, C.D.1 requesting review and recommendations from the Director of Health on the Healthy Start Program. Report prepared by Personal Health Services Administration, Family Health Services Division, Maternal and Child Health Branch.

Donnelly, A. C. (1992). Healthy families America. *Children Today, 21*(2), 25–28.

Mercer, R. T. (1998). *Transitions to parenthood.* Sunnyvale, CA: NurseWeek Publishing.

Milner, J. S. (1986). *The Child Abuse Potential Inventory: Manual* (2nd ed.). Webster, NC: Psytec.

Mollerstrom, W. W., Patchner, M. A., & Milner, J. S. (1995). Child maltreatment: The United States Air Force's response. *Child Abuse and Neglect, 19*(3), 325–334.

Olds, D. L., Henderson, C. R., Chamberlin, R., & Tatelbaum, R. (1986). Preventing child abuse and neglect: A randomized trial of nurse home visitation. *Pediatrics, 78*(1), 65–78.

Olds, D. L, & Kitzman, H. (1990). Can home visitation improve the health of women and children at environmental risk? *Pediatrics, 86*(1), 108–116.

Olds, D. L., & Kitzman, H. (1993). Review of research on home visiting for pregnant women and parents of young children. In R. E. Behrman (Ed.), *The future of children—Home visiting* (pp. 53–92). Los Altos, CA: The David and Lucile Packard Foundation.

Sumner, G. (1990). *Keys to caregiving: Self instructional series.* Seattle, WA: NCAST Publications.

U.S. Advisory Board on Child Abuse and Neglect. (1991). *Creating caring communities: Blueprint for an effective federal policy on child abuse and neglect.* Washington, DC: U.S. Government Printing Office.

U.S. Department of Health and Human Services, Childrens Bureau. (1998). *Child maltreatment 1996: Reports from the states to the National Child Abuse and Neglect Data System.* Washington, DC: U.S. Government Printing Office.

U.S. General Accounting Office (GAO). (1990). *Home visiting: A promising early intervention strategy for at-risk families* (GAO/HRD Publication No. 90-83). Washington, DC: GAO.

Wasik, B. H., Bryant, D. M., & Lyons, C. M. (1990). *Home visiting: Procedures for helping families.* Newbury Park, CA: Sage Publications.

**Part IV**

# Children and Adolescents in the Military

Chapter 14

# Young Children's Adaptation to a Military Lifestyle

*Henry K. Watanabe and Peter S. Jensen*

## INTRODUCTION

Children growing up in the military environment experience unique stresses. Throughout the years, concerns have been raised about the potentially pathological effects of these stresses on children in military families. In this chapter, the authors review the research literature concerning the prevalence of psychosocial dysfunction in military children. They examine available research concerning specific risk factors that may impact on the well-being of military children, including the authoritarian military structure, father absence, geographic mobility, cross-cultural families, war, combat stress and retirement. The authors discuss variables that mediate the effects of these risk factors, they describe preventive principles and approaches, and they clarify issues requiring further investigation.

Anecdotal evidence from previous military family literature suggests that military families suffer from greater psychosocial difficulties than the general population (La Grone, 1978; Wertsch, 1991). Other early evidence suggests that family problems can affect the military member's duty and combat performance (Rosen, Moghadam, & Vaitkus, 1989; Steiner & Neuman, 1978), the risk of going AWOL (absent without leave) (Hartnagel, 1974), and may lead to retention difficulties (Nice, 1981; Jensen, Lewis, & Xenakis, 1986). These studies also raise concern about the potentially high levels of psychopathology in children of military families. In general, the early literature on military family life, and specifically on the psychological well-being of military children, was problem focused and provided a definite negative perspective. This chapter examines both previous and current research in an attempt to provide a more balanced view.

## BACKGROUND

### Stereotypes

The military community has generally not enjoyed the admiration and respect of the larger society. On occasions, the military community has been the object of ridicule and disdain. In the context of antimilitary sentiment, military children have sometimes been the recipients of prejudices or stereotyping. The military child has been perceived to suffer from either too much or too little authority. Parental absence, frequent moves, and the lack of family and environmental stability have been blamed for upsetting the child who has been called a poor student, undisciplined, or a "military brat" (Wertsch, 1991).

### The Military Family Syndrome

The term "Military Family Syndrome" (LaGrone, 1978; Wertsch, 1991) has been used pejoratively, typically to describe a family characterized by an authoritarian father, a depressed mother, and out-of-control children. This description was based on anecdotal evidence from poorly drawn samples rather than from scientific studies examining the nature and extent of psychopathology in military families (Jensen, Xenakis, Wolf, & Bain, 1991; Wertsch, 1991). Studies conducted over the past three decades actually indicate that military children function better than their civilian counterparts. Kenny (1967) found that children of military parents had a higher median intelligence quotient, a better school achievement record, fewer emotional disorders, and a lower incidence of juvenile delinquency.

Morrison's (1981) research on military children indicates that levels of conduct and behavioral disorders may actually be lower among military children than among children in the civilian community. Recent studies have confirmed that the levels of psychopathology in military children are at or below levels reported in epidemiological studies of the general civilian population (Jensen et al., 1991; Jensen, Watanabe, Richters, Cortes, Roper, & Liu, 1995; Jensen, 1992). Research evidence does not support the notion of a "Military Family Syndrome" or indicate significantly increased levels of psychopathology in military families (Fernandez-Pol, 1988). In fact, the relatively low incidence of conduct and oppositional defiant disorder among children in military families stands in stark contrast to prevailing stereotypes. The lower rates of severe conduct problems among military children may be due to the higher degree of external control and authority as well as the closer familial observation of these children and the absence of parental unemployment (Jensen et al., 1986).

### Authoritarian Military Structure

It has been hypothesized that the organizational structure of the military creates difficulties for military families because of the relative lack of autonomy, the rigid hierarchy, and the "second-class citizen" status of wives and children. However, evidence to support this assumption tends to be anecdotal (e.g., Wertsch, 1991). Research actually indicates that children of military parents have positive images of their military fathers' roles as fathers (McIntire & Drummond, 1978). Military adolescents view their life in the military as not particularly unique compared to civilian adolescents (Darnauer, 1976; Eastman, Archer, & Ball, 1990). Children's perceptions of their fathers' and mothers' expressions of love and authority toward them are comparable to those of nonmilitary parents (Crain & Stamm, 1965; Shaw, 1979; Watanabe, 1985). Not all reports have reached the same conclusion. Some modest evidence exists that adolescents' reports of parental spousal violence is higher in youth from a military family background than those from civilian backgrounds (Cronin, 1995).

Regardless, according to a study of self-image (Watanabe, 1985), growing up in a military environment does not seem to deter the adolescent from developing a healthy self image. This study indicated that in the area of impulse control, military adolescents exceed their nonmilitary counterparts. This was considered to reflect the attitude toward discipline in the military. The military adolescent also scored well on the vocational and educational goal scale. This may reflect the positive value placed on education by military parents since advancement in the military is highly dependent on one's level of training and education.

### Characteristics of the Military Child

Children in military families experience the same general developmental and motivational processes as other children. They experience unusual developmental pressures imposed by the unique demands of the military environment, including father absence, relocations, and an authoritarian structure. The unusual demands of military life influence each developmental stage of childhood. These demands can become disruptive to normal childhood development. For example, with the military adolescent, the authoritarian military structure may frustrate the development in independence and self-reliance. Teenagers in military families may feel that they are under frequent surveillance due to the closeness and structure of the military community. Despite these pressures, as noted above, systematic subsequent studies of military families do not provide evidence for support of the notion that the amount or form of psychopathology in military youth differs from that in their civilian counterparts (Jensen et al., 1991; 1995).

## FACTORS AFFECTING CHILDREN'S ADAPTATION TO MILITARY LIFE

### Rank and Economic Status

When attempting to understand the prevalence of psychopathology in military children, an important consideration involves the military member's rank and the associated family socioeconomic status. In the past officers' children were reported to be more well-adjusted and less likely to come from dysfunctional homes than children from lower-ranking enlisted soldiers' homes (Kenny, 1967). This finding was probably related to the fact that officers and noncommissioned officers (higher ranking enlisted personnel) reported more life and career satisfaction. Lower ranking enlisted soldiers' families experienced more stressors partly as a function of low income. In addition, the military member's rank provided some ability to influence assignments, educational advances, and work situations. All of these factors are still true today (Rosen et al., 1989; Rosen & Moghadam, 1989). Therefore, any attempts to understand the extent of psychopathology among military children must take into account the military member's rank and economic status, ongoing family stressors, and the stress unique to the military setting and lifestyle (Jensen et al., 1991).

Rank is associated with commitment to the military and identification with the military community. When the parents identify positively with the military and are sensitive and understanding of the unique stresses imposed upon their children, the stresses are significantly mitigated. When they do not, this imposes greater stress on family members including reciprocal effects upon parents and their children (Watanabe, Jensen, Rosen, Newby, Richters, & Cortes, 1995b; Jensen, Bloedau, Degroot, Ussery, & Davis, 1990; Rosen & Moghadam, 1989).

For career personnel, the military remains a relatively secure employer. As a result its career "employees" typically display a high level of commitment to the service. Available medical care ensures that families are protected from financial losses associated with severe injuries, chronic conditions, and expensive medical procedures and treatments. The availability of social support systems and peers with similar values, life experiences, and socioeconomic status likely provides additional psychological supports and buffers stressful periods of military family life (Jensen et al., 1991; 1995). The majority of military families cope reasonably well with the demands of military life. This tends to insure family stability. However, satisfaction does vary as a function of rank, income, and housing, as well as other military lifestyle factors (Watanabe et al., 1995a; 1995b).

### Unique Life Stressors Associated with Military Family Life

*Parent Absence.* Some findings from military literature about the effects of father absence and reunion on military families are quite variable. Overall results from this literature indicate that absences of less than one year are associated with temporary behavioral and emotional symptoms in family members, particularly in wives and sons (Bach, 1946; Tiller, 1958; Lynn & Sawrey, 1959). Absences of greater length, frequency, or under combat or wartime conditions may exert more persistent effects. Extensive absences during a child's early years may exert cognitive effects, with a shift in relative verbal-math abilities, such that verbal skills are increased, while math scores are decreased. Absence effects are apparently mediated by preexisting father-family relationships; the age, sex, and order of siblings; the meaning of the absence to the family; the extent of danger to which the father is exposed; and how the mother copes with the father's absence (Carlsmith, 1964; Hillenbrand, 1976; Jensen et al., 1990). Some studies have shown fewer problems for girls, but the possible delayed effects on girls are not known (Jensen, Martin, & Watanabe, 1996). In some instances, father absence may mediate negative effects on children. Possibly, in families where absences occur with some predictable regularity (especially Navy families), family functioning may improve after the father's return to sea (Jensen et al., 1986).

Father-absence and reunion effects on children may be partly mediated by the mother's responses. After World War II, an investigator documented that fantasies of children whose fathers were absent due to military assignment were significantly related to how the mother talked about the father in his absence–"father-typing" (Bach, 1946). In a more recent study relating the psychiatric disturbances of children to the length of father-absence, it was found that father-absence difficulties were related to maternal psychopathology (Pedersen, 1966). Pedersen (1966) noted that father-absence in a stable home setting was associated with better adjustment on several measures, suggesting that in the more normal ranges of psychological adjustment, some degree of father-absence may lead to increased coping and "hardiness" in children (Jensen et al., 1986). Most recently, investigators have documented the impact of parent functioning as an important determinant of child outcomes during and after parental absence (Jensen et al., 1989; Jensen et al., 1996; Medway, David, Cafferty, & Chappell, 1995; McCurry, Jensen, & Watanabe, 1998).

The circumstance surrounding a given separation may be more relevant to the question of untoward effects on the child than the simple separation itself. In the case of separations where there is a lack of adequate preparation of the child, the effects may be quite different from instances where separations occur with adequate preparation. Interestingly, longer absences have actually been associated with better child adaptations, suggesting that with increasing lengths of father absence, children (and possibly wives) are able to develop partially compensatory adaptive strategies to cope with the separation (Hillenbrand, 1976).

Families' responses to reunion have indicated that good marital adjustment prior to separation predicts good reunion adjustment. Families that only partially "closed ranks" (i.e., kept the absent father's role and importance central to the family emotional environment) suffered more during his absence but did better at reunion than those families that "closed ranks" completely (Hill, 1949; Boulding, 1950).

There have been other findings indicating that separation can result in severe marital problems, disagreements between spouses over child discipline, poorer father-son relationships and more severe child discipline by fathers. Stoltz (1954) found that children suffered from worse peer relationships and increased anxiety as a result of separation. These early studies suggest that separation and reunion have differential effects. A good response to separation may bode an ill response to reunion, and vice versa, while other families may cope poorly with both.

The recent increase of families with two military parents and an increase in single female active-duty parents pose special problems for the child. A recent publication (Pierce & Buck, 1998) reported that children whose mothers deployed during the Persian Gulf War experienced a number of social and psychological stressors associated with this life disruption. Despite this experience during the deployment, these children typically did not show evidence of lasting effects.

Based on both previous and current research, it appears that parent absences have variable effects on military children. The effects, however, tend to be temporary, especially when the remaining family situation remains stable. When problems do develop, other family stress factors are typically present.

*Relocation and Geographic Mobility.* Within the military establishment, family members expect relocations to another military base or to an overseas area every three to four years. Although relocation continues to be a part of the military lifestyle, Department of Defense and the armed forces have recently attempted to decrease the frequency of family moves. The responses of children to relocations are highly dependent on their age and developmental stage. The most vulnerable group seems to be early school- age children, due in part to the separation conflicts and the breaking up of peer group activities. Adolescents encounter similar disruptions. There is no evidence that military children encounter significant emotional and behavioral problems as a result of periodic family relocation. In fact, children generally tended to report a positive experience associated with relocation (O'Connell, 1981; Jensen, 1992).

While relocations do not appear to cause psychopathology, the disruptions associated with moves may exacerbate the difficulties of families with preexisting psychosocial dysfunction. Parental attitudes and perceptions do have a significant impact on the child's attitude and perceptions. When mothers are accepting of the relocation and when both parents display a strong identification with the military community, military children generally experience little or no difficulty with relocation (Pedersen & Sullivan, 1964).

Studies of children in military families have consistently failed to find any predictable relationship between emotional and behavioral problems and the frequency of family moves (Shaw, 1979). For some children, the frequency of mobility and the constant interruptions of friendships may result in an impaired capacity for intimacy. Geographic mobility may present challenges for both military children and parents, but associated difficulties are typically time-limited (Jensen, 1997). The challenges associated with relocations may actually represent growth opportunities for most military families.

*Living Overseas.* American children who grow up overseas may experience stresses that are quite different from children who spend all of their lives in the United States. The overseas experience may either negatively impact on the military child's development or it may enhance development.

In most overseas areas, military children live within or near to a military base. They typically attend a DOD school that is structured much like a public school in the United States. The school is usually located within the military base and staffed by DOD civilian personnel. When the family relocates from the United States to an overseas area, the child finds little difference in the school system and is not likely to encounter very many difficulties in the transition.

In addition to the problems a child would normally experience moving into a new community in the United States, children overseas face some unique challenges. For example, the child must adjust to a different culture, language, and customs. The structure of the family overseas may be quite different from the structure that existed in the United States. Typically, families living overseas do not have the support of relatives and the accustomed closeness of the extended family. In addition, when the military member is away on assignments, the family is put in a much more stressful position due to a greater degree of isolation (Jensen, 1997).

*Cross-Cultural Families.* There is an increasing number of cross-cultural families in the military. This includes families where a spouse may speak English as a second language. Children in these families face special challenges. Among other issues, these children are likely to experience conflicts over identity and culture (Waldron & McDermott, 1979). In an intercultural marriage for example, every developmental stage of the child has the potential to produce stress between the parents or between the parent and child. Issues of dependency, autonomy, power, values, educational expectations, and peer relations create conflicts when the culturally different parent adheres to practices intended to achieve the desired culturally based behaviors. Both parents may feel undermined, and conflicts may arise as a result of their different child-rearing practices and beliefs. Which developmental stage will become problematic depends on the interplay of many factors including the cultural mix, the intensity of either parent's, adherence to tradition, the parents' personality structure, and the family's integration in the social environment.

Women in cross-cultural marriages have been reported to have more regrets about marriage, more sexual dissatisfaction, and poorer marital communication than women in other families in the military (Orthner, 1980). Such marital conflict impacts significantly on the well-being of children.

The loss of cultural identity is a significant issue for racially mixed children. They experience a greater incidence of self-doubt, confusion about identity, and increased difficulties during father absences (Cottrell, 1978). Furthermore, it is not uncommon that the racially mixed child tends to be hypersensitive, to be excessively self-conscious, to feel inferior, and to be defensive or overly obsequious. As adolescence is a particularly critical period for identity formation, these children may experience a serious conflict about themselves during this period. These military cross-cultural families and children may constitute a high-risk group.

*Parental Deployments.* Earlier reports on the effects of wartime separations on children suggest intensification of emotional problems (McDonald, 1943), increased delinquency (Gardner & Spencer, 1944), and a significant increase in anxiety symptoms (Milgram & Milgram, 1975). In a more recent study (Jensen et al., 1996) of the reaction of children during the Persian Gulf War, the combat deployment was evaluated in terms of its direct effects on the child (child psychopathology) and the influence of family responses to the child. Concerning children's responses, deployment was related to a modest increase in children's symptomatology, generally more in internalizing symptoms known principally to the child (e.g., children's self-reports of depression). However, the symptoms were mild, and many did not reach a clinical threshold.

According to parental reports, more than one-half of the children (aged 3 to

12 years) experienced sadness and/or home disciplinary problems, symptoms presumably related to the deployment. Boys and younger children appeared to be especially vulnerable to the deployment effects.

Although families of deployed personnel reported significantly more intervening stressors compared with children and families of nondeployed personnel, deployment per se rarely provoked pathological levels of symptoms in otherwise healthy children. Previous research has identified a number of factors that may mediate children's response to the effects of parental deployment. These factors include preexisting family relationships, the child's age and sex (with younger males being somewhat more vulnerable than females and older males), the family's perception of the situation, and the remaining parent's coping strategies. For children showing more persistent or pervasive psychopathology, factors other than simple deployment (with or without combat duty) should be considered, such as the responses of the remaining caretaker and the vulnerabilities of children with special needs (Jensen et al., 1986).

Children's reactions to deployment are very closely related to family responses. Therefore, awareness of the difficulties that parents experience during deployment is necessary in order to understand children's functioning. In this context, children's difficulties during deployment are best understood as a family problem. Deployed personnel's children who have increased psychological or behavioral symptoms are likely to have caretaking parents with their own increased symptoms, as well as greater family stress levels. Because the differences in outcomes among deployed personnel's children are related to family stressors and levels of parental symptomatology, assistance to such children requires assistance to the whole family. The caretaking parent does not cause his or her child's increased symptoms during deployment of the service member parent; rather, the functioning of the parent at home and the functioning of the children are closely intertwined and may be most effectively dealt with by addressing the family's multiple needs.

On occasion, there are discrepancies between parents' and children's perspectives. Examination of the potential discrepancies between parents' and children's reports is essential to understand fully the potential impact of deployment on children and families. Such discrepancies do not necessarily indicate the lack of a deployment effect. Thus, some children, recognizing the high levels of stress faced by their parents, may hide their feelings in order to keep from further upsetting the family. Clinicians commonly observe that when a child feels unsafe or threatened (for example, during times of marital conflict, family dissolution, etc.), he or she may only display covert signs of depression or anxiety, or none at all. Only when pressures decrease and life returns to "normal" do such children "let off steam" and manifest overt behavioral problems and symptoms. Potentially, parents in wartime studies might underreport the effects of the deployment on their children because of their preoccupation with their own problems.

Deployment is considered to affect certain children more than others. Certainly, age and developmental factors may set important limits on children and adolescents to respond adaptively to war crisis. The young child lacks the cognitive capacities available to the adult. Young children's theories of causality are egocentric, and they may be unable to talk about frightening experiences. Unable to transform internal conflicts and feelings into words, the child may express such feelings in action, play, or aggressive behaviors or activities. In contrast, the older child and adolescent may have a wider repertoire of adaptive responses and coping capabilities. Perhaps younger children may be at greater risk for later consequences of war stress because of their increased preponderance of idiosyncratic and egocentric thoughts. Young children tend to attribute blame associated with their inner feelings. Long ago, Freud and Burlingham (1943) suggested that very young children must be protected from war and violence not because the horrors are strange and traumatic but because the outer violent circumstances may parallel the children's inner experiences. Under such conditions the normal processes of sublimation and suppression are made more difficult.

When considering the role of war stressors on children and adolescents, it should be noted that the war traumas might unmask latent psychopathology or perhaps more commonly serve as stimulation for more normal developmental fears. In this sense, the war events may serve as a focus for the child to express normal developmental anxieties.

One possible explanation for boys' greater vulnerability during a parent's deployment could be that the great majority of deployed parents have been fathers. As others have suggested (Blount, Curry, & Lubin, 1992), boys in particular may be vulnerable to the loss of a male figure in the home. Similarly, research in other areas (e.g., studies of the effects of divorce on children) has suggested that younger boys in particular (compared with older or female children) may be most susceptible to the effects of divorce (and loss of the father's presence).

In addition to gender, younger children seem more vulnerable to the deployment impact. Related studies of children during wartime have yielded similar information that may clarify the reasons why younger children may be more vulnerable than older children may. Weisenberg, Schwarzwald, Waysman, Solomon, & Klingman (1993) reported that younger children more commonly utilized problem-focused coping, compared with older children, who relied on emotion-focused coping. Furthermore, children who used problem-focused coping experienced more anxiety-related difficulties than did children who used emotion-focused coping. It is possible that this factor could explain the differences in younger versus older children's functioning in response to deployment.

Several aspects unique to military life and families must be considered to understand fully the limited effects of wartime deployment on children. A number of factors likely buffer the family and, in turn, insulate these children. Many families experience routine parental absence for training, temporary duty, and overseas deployments. These families typically move every few years as a function of military operational needs and individual career progression. Even peacetime military training often entails an elevated level of risk that civilian families do not face. Thus, many military families learn to cope with many stresses just short of war, and as a result they may be better prepared to deal with a combat deployment than children whose parents are rather suddenly called up and deployed overseas as a result of reserve status.

In summary, the combat deployment may provoke a wide variety of symptoms in children and their parents. To a lesser extent deployment for peacekeeping missions has the same effects on family members. Although our findings indicate that parental combat deployment is related to elevated depressive symptoms in children, the deployment per se rarely provokes pathological levels of symptoms in otherwise healthy children. However, boys and younger children appear to be especially vulnerable, and increased monitoring of these children is warranted. The factors shaping the differential outcomes among children of deployed personnel do not differ from the variables affecting outcomes of children of nondeployed parents (e.g., family stressors, parental psychopathology, and the presence or absence of community and family supports) (Jensen et al., 1990). Because children's distress may not always be apparent, health professionals and parents must remain vigilant during deployments. Adequate treatment of the child likely requires support and treatment of the effects of the deployment on other family members. Mothers are especially important. Typically the mother must cope with both her own distress as well as the emotional needs of her children. For many military spouses this deployment experience occurs without the immediate availability of extended family members as sources of support. Unless the family has been well integrated into the unit and community, the spouse is facing these challenges alone.

## THE MILITARY SYSTEM AND SPECIAL NEEDS CHILDREN AND FAMILIES

### The Chronically Ill Child

The chronically ill or handicapped child in the military family is no different in terms of needs and the care that must be given than a child with a similar disorder in the nonmilitary setting. The difficulties that parents experience are much like those of other parents in similar situations. The difference is that the access to care in the military setting has been greatly enhanced to support these parents so that the mission of the military may be accomplished in as undisrupted a manner as possible.

The DOD Exceptional Family Member Program (EFMP) assists families with children with handicapping conditions that require intensive and specialized medical care. This program attempts to locate these families in areas in the continental United States where military or civilian facilities are readily available. In addition, the educational and other community supports that are necessary in the total care of the child are taken into consideration in the assignment process. Along with the medical services, mental health services for the child as well as for the family are made accessible.

Remission and exacerbation are common aspects of chronic illnesses. Thus there are developmental interferences in all areas including social, emotional, and cognitive areas of development. Appropriate supportive interventions must be available in assisting these children and their families. Furthermore, chronically ill children experience mourning due to their sense of loss and failure as well as the possibility of death.

Other common problems faced by chronically ill children and their families include the need for continuity of care. When families are situated where the child can receive the necessary care, the military member may be given or request an unaccompanied overseas assignment rather than moving his family with him. There are times, however, when the family does move to another location. This requires a system of care capable of meeting their needs. These disruptions are difficult for the chronically ill child as well as for the family. They pose significant stress on everyone concerned. In the civilian sector, families may have a greater choice of moving or not. In the military the family may not have a choice in the relocation decision. It is often necessary and required that the parent take another assignment in order to meet the needs of the service and/or to enhance career advancement. Getting started in another community and with a new set of health care and educational providers may be disconcerting or at times even discouraging for the chronically ill member and the family. This is usually due to the fact that at the last location, they had everything in place and now they must start all over again.

## Effects of Children's Chronic Illness on the Parents

Family concerns, attitudes, and responses significantly impact on the child. In the case of a disabled child, the situation is greatly aggravated. The well-being and especially the progress of the child in attaining his or her potential are closely interwoven with parental supports and resources.

In a study (Watanabe et al., 1995b) of psychological functioning of military parents with a handicapped child, the service member parents with handicapped children showed significantly higher depressive symptoms, including lower scores on coping, fewer favorable perceptions of their military skills and abilities, and more pessimistic attitudes about their long-term military career options. These parents reported high levels of satisfaction with the military educational and medical support programs, and perceived social supports played a significant role in buffering the effects of stress on families with a handicapped child. Interestingly, the stress of having a handicapped child did not affect marital adjustment significantly. This finding, which is contrary to other studies indicating that parents of chronically ill children are at risk for marital difficulties, might possibly be attributed to the medical support. The availability of military medical and family support services may alleviate family stresses that might otherwise accumulate in the face of caring for the chronically ill child.

Some of the difficulties and effects on the parent of caring for a chronically ill child may result not just from the child's illness per se but from the effects of the illness on the child's adjustment, which in turn affects the parents' well being. Generally, it seemed that the degree of medical stressors that the family experienced greatly influenced their attitude and outlook concerning their careers. The pessimism that the military member felt with regard to his career may be related to his sense of vulnerability to involuntary separation because of assignment limitations—that is, that the family must be located in areas where adequate medical resources are available.  The enduring effect of stress on parents is indefinite because the illnesses are chronic in nature.

## SUMMARY AND IMPLICATIONS

Although the majority of military children experience one or more of the potential risk factors outlined above, relatively few children appear to be overtly dysfunctional.  This may occur because a potentially supportive military network attenuates these risk factors and because severely dysfunctional service members (and, therefore, their families) tend to be screened from the services.

Future research on the effects of military service on children should control for or at least examine a number of factors.  These include: childhood age and sex; marital stability; coping style of the children and adults; the role of the father in the family; preexisting individual, family, and marital functioning levels; and individual and family identification with the overall service organization's needs and goals.  It is important to examine war and combat stress, specific problems of cross-cultural families, and changes occurring over time to the soldier and family.  Preventive approaches are most likely to be useful when specific segments of the military population who may be at risk are approached, utilizing active outreach strategies.  Rich opportunities exist in the military setting to study longitudinally the complex interactions between persons, environmental stressors, and social supports while controlling a broad number of variables that are often elusive in civilian research settings.  Longitudinal epidemiologic research is urgently needed on the prevalence of psychiatric disorders and family dysfunction, as well as delineation of effective supportive interventions for military families.

In working with military children and families, the provider is often asked to evaluate behavior outside of the limited context of his or her own personal social system and background.  The provider who is familiar with the experiences of a group of people he or she is dealing with and who understands the impact of the group values on individual behavior will certainly have an advantage.  The more closely the provider is able to identify with the family member of a military family, by either his or her own experiences or situation, the more successful the encounter will be.

Trust may be more difficult to establish between persons of different situations and social backgrounds.  Establishing trust is influenced by the degree of awareness and concern about such issues of the individual at a given time.  Another factor is the personal experience of the given patient.  The provider may not have had the personal experiences of any of his or her patients.  But a provider who is nonjudgmental, fair, interested, and naturally empathetic and not influenced by social attitudes has the best chance of establishing a trusting relationship with any patient.

Establishing trust is generally easier when the provider has some familiarity with the people, places, and experiences of the patient.  Children have less concern about revealing their thoughts and the events in their lives when they sense that the provider knows about and respects their personal experiences.  Many of them may be particular to the military life.

Aside from providing psychological services to military children and their families, reconnecting them to supportive services and personnel in the military installation can be helpful. Here, knowledge about resources and means of accessing them is extremely useful.

Finally, in dealing with children, as the incongruity between children's symptoms and parental reports cannot always be reconciled, the health care provider must not rely solely on parental reports when evaluating the well being of a child or family. Additional information from children, teachers, or other knowledgeable informants is necessary to determine the nature and extent of the child's disorder.

## REFERENCES

Bach, G. R. (1946). Father-fantasies and father typing in father separated children. *Child Development, 17,* 63–80.

Blount, B. W., Curry, A., Jr., & Lubin, G. I. (1992). Family separations in the military. *Military Medicine, 157*(2), 76–80.

Boulding, E. (1950). Family adjustments to war separations and reunions. *Annals of the American Academy of Political and Social Sciences, 60*(2), 59–67.

Carlsmith, L. (1964). Effect of early father absence on scholastic aptitude. *Harvard Educational Review, 34,* 3–21.

Cottrell, A. B. (1978). Mixed children: Some observations and speculations. In E. J. Hunter & D. S. Nice (Eds.), *Children of military families: A part and yet apart* (pp. 61–81). Washington, DC: U.S. Government Printing Office.

Crain, A. J., & Stamm, C. S. (1965). Intermittent absence of fathers and children's perceptions of parents. *Journal of Marriage and Family, 27,* 344–347.

Cronin, C. (1995). Adolescent reports of parental spousal violence in military and civilian families. *Journal of Interpersonal Violence, 10*(1), 117–122.

Darnauer, P. (1976). The adolescent experience in career Army families. In H. I. McCubbin, B. B. Dahl, & E. J. Hunter (Eds.), *Families in the military system* (pp. 42–26). Beverly Hills, CA: Sage Publications.

Eastman, E., Archer, R. P., & Ball, J. D. (1990). Psychosocial and life stress characteristics of Navy families: Family Environment Scale and Life Experiences Scale findings. *Military Psychology, 2*(2), 113–127.

Fernandez-Pol, B. (1988). Does the military family syndrome exist? *Military Medicine, 153*(8), 418–420.

Freud, A., & Burlingham, D. T. (1943). *War and children.* New York: Medical War Books, Ernst Willard.

Gardner, G., & Spencer, H. (1944). Reactions of children with fathers and brothers in the Armed Forces. *American Journal of Orthopsychiatry, 14),* 36–43.

Hartnagel, T. F. (1974). Absent without leave: A study of the military offender. *Journal of Political and Military Society, 2*(2), 205–220.

Hill, R. (1949). *Families under stress: Adjustment to the crises of war separation and reunion.* New York: Harper & Row (reprinted by Greenwood Press, Westport, CT, 1971).

Hillenbrand, E. D. (1976). Father absence in military families. *The Family Coordinator, 25*(4), 451–458.

Jensen, P. S. (1992). Military family life is hazardous to the mental health of children:

Rebuttal. *Journal of the American Academy of Child and Adolescent Psychiatry, 31*(5), 985–987.

Jensen, P. S. (1997). Foreign culture, geographic mobility, and children's mental health. In J. Noshpitz & N. Alessi (Eds.), *Handbook of child and adolescent psychiatry, Volume 4, Varieties of development* (pp. 504–509). New York: Wiley.

Jensen, P. S., Bloedau, L., Degroot, J., Ussery, T., & Davis, H. (1990). Children at risk: I. Risk factors and child symptomatology. *Journal of the American Academy of Child and Adolescent Psychiatry, 29*(1), 51–59.

Jensen, P. S., Grogan, D. G., Xenakis, S. N., & Bain, M. W. (1989a). Father absence: Effects on child and maternal psychopathology. *Journal of the American Academy of Child and Adolescent Psychiatry, 28*(2), 171–175.

Jensen, P. S., Grogan, D. G., Xenakis, S. N., & Bain, M. W. (1989b). Zero divorce rate--too good to be true (reply)? *Journal of the American Academy of Child and Adolescent Psychiatry, 28*, 618.

Jensen, P. S., Lewis, R. L., & Xenakis, S. N. (1986). The military family in review: Context, risk, and prevention. *Journal of the American Academy of Child and Adolescent Psychiatry, 25*(2), 225–234.

Jensen, P. S., Martin, D., & Watanabe, H. K. (1996). Children's response to parental separation during Operation Desert Storm. *Journal of the American Academy of Child and Adolescent Psychiatry, 35*(4), 433–441.

Jensen, P. S., Watanabe, H. K., Richters, J. E., Cortes, R., Roper, M., & Liu, S. (1995). Prevalence of mental disorder in military children and adolescents: Findings from a two-stage community survey. *Journal of the American Academy of Child and Adolescent Psychiatry, 34*(11), 1514–1524.

Jensen, P. S., Xenakis, S. N., Wolf, P., & Bain, M. W. (1991). The "military family syndrome" revisited: "By the numbers." *Journal of Nervous and Mental Disorders, 179*(2), 102–107.

Kenny, J. A. (1967). The child in the military community. *Journal of the American Academy of Child Psychiatry, 6*(1), 51–63.

LaGrone, D. A. (1978). The military family syndrome. *American Journal of Psychiatry, 135*(9), 1040–1043.

Lynn, D. B., & Sawrey, W. L. (1959). The effects of father-absence on Norwegian boys and girls. Psychology *Journal of Abnormal and Social Psychology, 59*, 258–262.

McCurry, L. J., Jensen, P. S., & Watanabe, H. K. (1998). Children's reponses and recovery following parental military deployment. Scientific Proceedings of the Annual Meeting of the American Psychiatric Association, Toronto, p. 98.

McDonald, M. W. (1943). Impact of war on children and youths: Intensification of emotional problems. *American Journal of Public Health, 33*, 336-338.

McIntire, W. J., & Drummond, R. J. (1978). Familial and social role perceptions of children raised in military families. In E. J. Hunter & D. S. Nice (Eds.), *Children of military families: A part and yet apart* (pp. 15–24). Washington, DC: U.S. Government Printing Office.

Medway, F. J, David, K. E., Cafferty, T. P., & Chappell, K. D. (1995). Family disruption and adult attachment correlates of spouse and child reactions to separation and reunion due to Operation Desert Storm. *Journal of Social and Clinical Psychology, 14*(2), 97–118.

Milgram, R., & Milgram, N. (1975, January). The effects of the Yom Kippur War on anxiety level in Israeli children. Paper presented at the International Conference on Psychological Stress and Adjustment in Time of War and Peace, Tel Aviv, Israel.

Morrison, J. (1981). Rethinking the military family syndrome. *American Journal of Psychiatry, 138*(3), 354–357.

Nice, D. S. (1981). The course of depressive affect in Navy wives during family separation. *Military Medicine, 148*(4), 341–343.

O'Connell, P. V. (1981). *The effect of mobility on selected personality characteristics of ninth and twelfth grade military dependents.* Unpublished doctoral dissertation, University of Wisconsin, Milwaukee.

Orthner, D. K. (1980). *Families in blue: A study of married and single parent families in the U.S. Air Force.* Air Force Contract F33600-79-CO423, Office of the Chief of Chaplains, United States Air Force, Bolling Air Force Base, Washington, DC.

Pedersen, F. A. (1966). Relationships between father-absence and emotional disturbance in male military dependents. *Merrill-Palmer Quarterly, 12)*, 321–331.

Pedersen, F. A., & Sullivan, E. J. (1964). Relationships among geographic mobility, parental attitudes, and emotional disturbance in children. *American Journal Orthopsychiaty*, 34, 575–580

Pierce, P. F., & Buck, C. L. (1998). Wartime separation of mothers and children: Lessons from Operation Desert Shield and Desert Storm. *Military Family Issues: The Research Digest, 2*(2), 1–4.

Rosen, L. N., & Moghadam, L. Z. (1989). Can social supports be engineered? An example from the Army's Unit Manning System. *Journal of Applied Social Psychology, 1989* (15, part 1), 1292–1309.

Rosen, L. N., Moghadam, L. Z., & Vaitkus, M. A. (1989). The military family's influence on soldiers' personal morale: A path analytic model. *Military Psychology, 1*(4), 201–213.

Shaw, J. A. (1979). The child in the military community. In S. I. Harrison (Ed.), *Basic handbook of child psychiatry*, Vol.1 (pp. 310–315). New York: Basic Books.

Steiner, M., & Neuman, M. (1978). Traumatic neurosis and social support in the Yom Kippur War returnees. *Military Medicine, 143*, 866–868.

Stoltz, L. M. (1954). *Father relations of war-born children: The effect of postwar adjustment of fathers on the behavior and personality of first children born while fathers were at war.* Palo Alto, CA: Stanford University Press.

Tiller, P. O. (1958). Father-absence and personality development of children in sailor families. *Nordisk Psyko Monogr, 9*, 1–48.

Waldron, J., & McDermott, J. F. (1979). Transcultural considerations. In S. I. Harrison (Ed.), *Basic handbook of child psychiatry*, Vol. 3 (pp. 443–456). New York: Basic Books.

Watanabe, H. K. (1985). A survey of adolescent military family members' self image. *Journal of Youth and Adolesence, 14*(2), 99–107.

Watanabe, H. K., Jensen, P. S., Newby, J., & Cortes, R. M. (1995a). The Exceptional Family Member Program: Perceptions of active duty enrollees. *Military Medicine, 160*(12), 639–643.

Watanabe, H. K., Jensen, P. S., Rosen, L. N., Newby, J., Richters, J. E., & Cortes, R. (1995b). Soldier functioning under chronic stress: Effects of family member illness. *Military Medicine, 160*(9), 457–461.

Weisenberg, M., Schwarzwald, J., Waysman, M., Solomon, Z., & Klingman, A. (1993). Coping of school age children in the sealed room during Scud missile bombardment and postwar stress reactions. *Journal of Consulting and Clinical Psychology, 61*, 462–467.

Wertsch, M. E. (1991). *Military brats: Legacies of childhood inside the fortress.* New York: Harmony Books.

Chapter 15

# The Strengths and Vulnerabilities of Adolescents in Military Families

*Dorothy J. Jeffreys and Jeffrey D. Leitzel*

## INTRODUCTION

This chapter presents results from a 1996-1997 survey of over 6,000 military adolescents. Areas addressed in this chapter include physical and mental health, antisocial behavior, drug and alcohol use, educational experiences, peer relations, family satisfaction, and military-related perceptions and experiences of these adolescents. The results are generally consistent with comparable findings from civilian populations. Despite a high rate of residential disruption, these youth reported generally positive educational experiences, peer relations, and involvement with daily life activities. Their physical and mental health, and family satisfaction indices were comparable with civilian normative groups. They reported relatively low levels of antisocial and substance use/abuse behaviors. Relevant literature is reviewed and implications and recommendations for human service providers are presented.

Adolescence is the stage during which an individual makes the transition from childhood to adulthood. The unique challenges of adolescence result from developmental changes at both the individual and the social environmental levels. Adolescents who have an active-duty parent are faced with the additional challenges of family relocation and the possible deployment of the military member. This chapter addresses what is known about adolescence in general and compares this information to adolescents who live in a military family. The comparison data came from 6,382 military adolescents 10 to 18 years of age whose parent(s) were stationed worldwide. The installations and the respondents from the United States were randomly selected. At selected sites outside of the United States all adolescents where asked to participate. The respondents completed a self-report questionnaire, in group settings, during the latter part of 1996 and the first half of 1997. The areas addressed in this chapter are the adolescents': (1) physical and mental health status and well-being; (2) antisocial behaviors including use of drugs and alcohol; (3) recreational and leisure time activities; (4) educational experiences and perceptions; (5) experiences with peers; (6) relationship with their family; (7) unique experiences as part of a military family; and (8) perceptions about military life.

## Physical and Mental Health Status and Well-Being

The majority (approximately 70 percent) of adolescents in the United States report their physical health to be good, with very few reporting a handicapping condition (e.g., Udry, Baurman, Billy, Blum, Grady, Harris, Jaccard, Resnick, & Rowe, 1997). Brandenburg, Friedman, and Silver (1990) reported that only 14 percent to 20 percent of children in the United States suffer from psychiatric disorders. This includes the 7 percent who are severely disturbed. However, a research study of adolescents from Air Force families found that 77 percent of females and 59 percent of males reported feeling so sad or problem ridden that nothing was worthwhile at least once during the past month. Comparison of the Air Force and civilian youth in this sample revealed that civilian females were slightly less likely to have had such feelings more than once during the past month (41 percent for female civilians and 52 percent of females for the Air Force, respectively). Approximately 30 percent of both the civilian and military males reported similar feelings (Orthner, Giddings, & Quinn, 1987). A study (Connelly, Johnston, Brown, Mackay, & Blackstock, 1993) found that the prevalence of depression reported by high school students is influenced by the stress and anxiety that result from increasing demands of school life, social adjustment to peers, and new experiences of independence from the family. Self-esteem, the most widely studied facet of well-being (Epstein, 1990), has strong associations with depression and anxiety disorders. Social anxiety, lack of social skills, and loneliness have also been found to be associated with low self-esteem (Inderbitzen-Pisaruk, Clark, & Solano, 1992).

In terms of physical health status, 91 percent of the military adolescents surveyed reported their overall health to be good or excellent. A small percentage of youths did report having either a serious orthopedic handicap, long-term health problem, or some other health impairment (12 percent). In examining health-enhancing and compromising behaviors, the majority of the participants stated that they engaged in regular exercise three or more times per week (57 percent) while 11 percent reported not exercising at all. A small percentage of these adolescents reported that they had used cigarettes or chewing tobacco: occasionally (9 percent) or regularly in the past or now (6 percent). This sample of military adolescents was less likely to smoke cigarettes than the sample of adolescent surveyed by Johnston, O'Malley, & Bachman (1995).

Respondents' mental health was assessed with a number of instruments. These included assessment of self-esteem (Rosenberg, 1965), depressed mood (Carey, Lubin, & Brewer, 1992), and trait anxiety (Spielberger, Gorsuch, Lushene, Vagg, & Jacobs, 1983). (See Table 15.1.) The scores of these military adolescents were similar to normative and civilian data. The average optimism

**Table 15.1**
**Comparison of Military Adolescents with Civilian Adolescent Data for Mental Health Measures**

| Measure | Military Adolescents | Civilian Data | Source of Comparison Data |
|---|---|---|---|
| Self-Esteem | 3.19 (s.d. = .55) | 3.06 | O'Brien et al. (1996) |
| Anxiety | 2.04 (s.d. = .51) | 2.03 | Speilberger et al. (1983) |
| Depressed Mood | 5.25 (s.d. = 4.30) | 4.92 | Carey, Lubin, & Brewer (1992) |

reported by these youths was high. An Index of Psychological Well-Being (IPW) (a composite mental health index composed of self-esteem, depressed mood [reverse coded], trait anxiety [reverse coded], and optimism) showed only 4 percent of the respondents are severely at risk for experiencing psychological difficulties.

### Antisocial Behaviors and Drug and Alcohol Use

Juvenile delinquency is conceptualized as a wide range of socially unacceptable behaviors that occur in childhood. These may range from relatively harmless disobedience to violent and destructive illegal behaviors. Despite legislation prohibiting alcohol use by minors, alcohol use is the most frequent drug problem for adolescents (Merril & Fox, 1994). According to Johnston and colleagues (1995), alcohol has been consumed by 56 percent of eight grade students, 71 percent of tenth grade students, and 80 percent of high school seniors. Studies have found that adolescent drinking is most common among males and whites (Johnson et. al., 1995). Additionally, national data indicate that males begin to drink at an earlier age, drink more often, and drink more per session than females. Alcohol use has been found to increase with age and results in a decrease in academic performance (Escobedo, Chorba, & Waxweiler, 1995). Youths who drink alcohol are eight times more likely to use other drugs (Merril & Fox, 1994).

The PRIDE survey (Parents Resource Institute for Drug Education, 1996) reported 30 percent of adolescents in grades 6 through 12 used an illicit drug. The most often-used illicit substance among adolescents is marijuana (Johnston et. al., 1995). Use of this drug has increased in recent years. A troublesome increase has also been found in the use of inhalants by eighth graders (Heyman, Adger, Anglin, Fuller, Jacobs, Shah, & Tenenbein, 1996).

The majority of the military adolescents in this sample had not engaged in any of the mild to moderate antisocial behaviors (e.g., gambling, shoplifting, vandalism, or carrying a weapon). A sizable number of them reported having once bet money (20 percent); stolen something from school, a teacher, or a student (15 percent); and had police contact (13 percent). The most frequent behaviors occurring more than once were betting money (22 percent), breaking the law, uncaught (17 percent); and shoplifting (15 percent). Most of the adolescents stated that they had not engaged in any serious antisocial behaviors. However, 11 percent said that they had hurt someone badly, 8 percent had been convicted of a crime, 4 percent had been given a ticket for something besides speeding, and 7 percent had been arrested. Comparisons with available civilian data revealed that these military adolescents were slightly more likely than their civilian counterparts to have damaged property on purpose but less likely to report that they had hurt someone badly enough that they needed medical attention. In all other areas the two groups reported similar behaviors.

Only 29 percent of the respondents reported that they had ever used alcohol or illegal drugs. Of those youths who reported ever using any substances, the drugs of choice were alcohol, marijuana, and inhalants. For those military adolescents reporting any drug use, 56 percent used alcohol during the past 30 days and 97 percent reported they had ever used alcohol. Marijuana use was reported by 20 percent of respondents during the past 30 days and 44 percent during their lifetime. Inhalants were used by 9 percent of respondents during the past 30 days (24 percent lifetime). Use of alcohol and drugs in the civilian population is significantly higher than what was reported by these respondents (Johnston et. al., 1995). Table 15.2 presents a comparison of the substance use patterns of these military adolescents and the respondents to Johnston and colleagues' (1995) survey.

### Recreational and Leisure Time Activities

The inclusion of activity in one's daily life is a trademark of good physical and mental health, increased self-esteem, and positive interpersonal relationships (Roth & Holmes, 1987). Activity assists in the creation of adolescents' personality and the construction of their identity. Adolescents utilize extracurricular activity to express themselves and to cultivate and discover their talents and creative capacities. Extracurricular activity is seen as an integral part of the educational process, providing students opportunities to develop interpersonal, social, and leadership skills. Students who become engaged in academic and extracurricular activities experience a sense of belonging that contributes to

Table 15.2
**Drug and Alcohol Use: Military Adolescents versus Civilian Adolescents**

| Substance | Group | Lifetime | | Past 30 days | |
|---|---|---|---|---|---|
| | | MFI % | MTF% | MFI % | MTF% |
| Alcohol | 8th Grade | 26.9 | 55.8 | 16.6 | 25.5 |
| | 10th Grade | 48.8 | 71.1 | 27.1 | 39.2 |
| | 12th Grade | 50.5 | 80.4 | 27.6 | 50.1 |
| Inhalants | 8th Grade | 9.3 | 19.9 | 5.1 | 5.6 |
| | 10th Grade | 7.9 | 18.0 | 3.1 | 3.6 |
| | 12th Grade | 5.3 | 17.7 | 1.3 | 2.7 |
| Marijuana | 8th Grade | 11.3 | 16.7 | 6.7 | 7.8 |
| | 10th Grade | 21.9 | 30.4 | 10.6 | 15.8 |
| | 12th Grade | 25.0 | 38.2 | 7.6 | 19.0 |

Note. MFI=Military adolescents, MTF=Civilian Adolescents (Monitoring the Future).

their integration within their school community (Benard, 1991). Such adolescent adjustment to environmental context is believed to contribute to a smooth progression through the developmental stages of puberty (Fenzel & Blyth, 1986), and greater participation in activities is linked with academic achievement (Voelkl, 1995). Rathunde (1993) conducted a study to learn which activities elicited the most adolescent involvement. The author concluded that maintaining extracurricular activities and encouraging adolescents to participate are crucial to positively influencing attitudes about school, which in turn leads to healthy development of adult roles. Finally, Steitz and Owen (1992) conducted a study of 212 sophomores and 230 juniors to understand the effects of school activities and employment on the self-esteem of adolescents. They found that adolescents who worked over 20 hours working per week had more negative experiences (i.e., drug or alcohol abuse, less participation in extracurricular activities, delinquent behavior, and negative views of employment) than those who did not work or who worked less than 20 hours. Therefore, it is evident that adolescent involvement in extracurricular activity plays a major role in all parts of their lives. The level of this participation influences peer and familial relationships, education, substance use or abuse, self-perception, and self-esteem. A report on adolescents of U.S. military families overseas (Williams-Scaife, 1994) found that adolescents who participate in extracurricular activities are less likely to use drugs, alcohol, or tobacco than students who do not participate in such activities.

While the military generally provides recreational and leisure activities on installations for youth, a higher percentage of the respondents reported using youth programs off base (67 percent) than those available on installations (42 percent). Military adolescents most often reported attending programs on the installation only for special events. Ten percent of respondents stated they did not participate in any of the activities listed on the survey during the last year (A similar item administered with a civilian sample found that 17 percent did not participate in any school activities, Udry et al., 1997). Participants were most often active in sports outside of school (41 percent), church activities (39 percent), band/chorus (38 percent), and athletic teams (37 percent). A large percentage of military youths participated weekly in sport activities.

The free-time activities most often reported by the respondents were hanging out with friends (85 percent), watching TV (83 percent), and doing homework (78 percent). While a large percentage of respondents reported doing volunteer work (64 percent) or working at a job (39 percent), only a small percentage stated that they frequently engaged in these activities (12 percent). Where comparison data were available for civilian populations in terms of school-time activities, these military adolescents were found to be quite similar to the general population. For example, the study by Udry and colleagues (1997) questioned frequency of a number of activities such as hanging out with friends (90 percent) and watching TV/videos (97 percent) once a week or more often.

## Educational Experiences and Perceptions

One of the most important factors that impacts on the well-being of adolescents in military families is their frequent changing of schools and the corresponding requirement to adjust to a new school culture (Humke & Schaefer, 1995). A school culture that integrates the adolescent into the activities of the school is thought to reduce the potential negative impact of school transitions. Various researchers have identified components of school culture that include student relationships with teachers, peers, and the administration (Paredes, 1993); practices responsive to the needs of adolescents (Epstein & MacIver, 1990); availability of resources (Ferreira, Bosworth, & Smith, 1995); safety (Meier, 1996); and warmth (Voelkl, 1995).

Classroom behavior is also related to school performance (Downs & Rose, 1991). Although some negative behaviors are expected, patterns of negative behaviors such as absences, tardiness, and vandalism as well as violent behaviors can jeopardize opportunities for academic success. Disruptive school behaviors have also been identified with peer group influence (Downs & Rose, 1991).

The number of schools attended by each military adolescent ranged from one to ten or more; the average was about five. The overall grade point average (GPA) of the respondents was 3.03 on a 0-4 point scale with 4 representing the highest GPA. The majority of adolescents reported positive interactions with teachers. A small percentage (18 percent) said that teachers "put down" students. The majority of participants agreed that there was a real school spirit that rules for behavior were strict, and that discipline was fair. A large percentage stated that other students disrupted class, disrupted learning, and often got away with their misbehavior. Negative school behaviors most frequently reported by respondents included being late for school and breaking rules. Receiving warnings about grades and behavior, as well as being sent to the office for misbehavior, were the most frequently reported consequences. Skipping classes, suspensions (in school or out of school), as well as transfers due to misbehavior were infrequently reported. The majority of these adolescents reported feeling safe at school; however, some agreed (19 percent) with the statement "I don't feel safe at this school." A large percentage of respondents indicated that their parents were actively involved in their education by checking homework, helping with homework, and rewarding good grades. However, three-fourths said that their parents limited privileges because of poor grades at some point in time.

## Peer Relations

Adolescence is a time when peers, particularly group members, become important social references (Youniss & Smollar, 1985). The peer group can serve as a bridge between childhood parental dependencies and a sense of autonomy and connection with wider social networks (Newman & Newman,

1991). Peer relations of equality and mutuality are said to be the basis for the development of moral understanding, consensual self-validation, and self-exploration (Youniss, 1980).

Lack of connection to a peer group may indicate that one is left without a source of social support during this period of physical, emotional, and social change (Coleman, 1980). Dunn and McGuire's (1992) study noted that research has examined the unique value of peer relationships in the development of so-cial-cognitive understandings. According to this view, peer social experiences are necessary for developing the skills to relate to others as well as attaining assertiveness, morality, fairness, and reciprocity. Lastly, Dunn and McGuire (1992) suggested that peer experiences may serve a moderating role in the experience of being supported by peers and may provide a buffer from trouble, whereas lack of support from peers may lead to loneliness, inadequacy, or resentment.

The majority of the adolescent respondents reported that they had good relationships with their peers. Many indicated that they were part of a large group, a small group, or both. A small percentage related that they were not part of any group. A high percentage of these adolescents identified with friends. The majority indicated having lots of friends, having someone to hang out with, and being liked by peers. Most did not relate that they felt lonely or alone. Many of the youths reported not dating or not currently dating, while a small percentage stated that they seriously dated.

## Family Satisfaction

Adolescents look to their parents for information about academic, voca-tional, moral, social, and family issues (Hunter, 1982). Family environment affects the development of psychosocial problems during adolescence (Ohan-nessian, Lerner, & Von Eye, 1994). A caring relationship with a parent or an-other adult, and low family stress are two factors associated with resiliency among adolescents (Blum, Harris, Resnick, & Rosenwinkel, 1989). If children have an emotionally supportive relationship with their parents, they are more likely to demonstrate high levels of self-esteem, healthy psychological devel-opment, and to incorporate parents' attitudes, values, and role expectations (Amato, 1990).

Research has found that a family climate that promotes participation in family decision making has positive implications for adolescent identity devel-opment and self-esteem (Eccles, Midgely, Wigfield, Buchanan, Reuman, Flan-nagan, & MacIver, 1993). These researchers found that adolescents who re-ported more opportunities to participate in the family's decision making were more likely than their peers to prefer challenges and independence in academic endeavors. Effective communication patterns within families facilitate family interaction (Olson, McCubbin, Barnes, Larsen, Muxen, & Wilson, 1983) and are associated with social competence in youth (Peterson & Leigh, 1990). Parental support, in particular, was found to be positively associated with a general sense of self-satisfaction among adolescents (Young, Miller, Norton, & Hill, 1995).

The adolescents in this sample reported reasonably good family relationships. Family satisfaction was significantly related to family structure. Adolescents living with one parent and one stepparent had the lowest family satisfaction followed by those from single-parent families and two-parent families. Slightly over one-quarter of these adolescents reported parental use of physical punishment. Of those adolescents who reported parental use of physical punishment, 30 percent indicated it occurred only once with 8 percent reporting it occurred often during the past year. Respondents' reports of family satisfaction were related to whether or not their parents used physical punishment. Satisfaction was highest among those who were not physically punished. Among those who were physically punished, family satisfaction was inversely related to frequency of such punishment.

### Military-Specific Experiences

Growing up in a military environment has both positive and negative aspects. Positive aspects include the opportunity to make friends in a variety of locations; fluency in another language; immersion in a new culture; and access to services, programs, and facilities to meet needs under various circumstances (Wuebker-Battershell, 1994). Wertsch (1991) noted strengths that may be gained from this lifestyle, including a strong sense of responsibility, excellent social skills, resilience, loyalty, willingness to take risks, discipline, tolerance, idealism, and the ability to handle crises. These same characteristics, when not in balance (e.g., excessive perception of responsibility for family well-being), may produce problems. Some of these problems may include a tendency to be overresponsible, to protect oneself from developing close friendships, to have difficulty taking a stand for one's own beliefs, and to have a tendency to move on rather than to stick with a situation and work through the problems (Wertsch, 1991).

Fewer youths reported living on base in military housing than living off base in nonmilitary housing. A very small percentage reported living in military housing off base or post. Sixty-six percent of active-duty fathers and 51 percent of active-duty mothers had been separated from their children during the past year. When parents were away, the most frequently reported duration was less than three months. Eleven percent of adolescents experienced residential displacement due to parental deployment during the preceding five years (e.g., Southwest Asia, Haiti, Somalia). When this occurred, it was generally due to their father's deployment, and the duration was often greater than one year. A large percentage of adolescents (64 percent) reported that they had lived overseas and many related that their last move was from overseas (48 percent). The average number of moves reported by these adolesents was five. While a large number of respondents perceived military family life as strict (37 percent), the largest percentage of youths felt that military family life was neither strict nor relaxed. About 80 percent reported feeling safe in their area of residence and were relatively unconcerned about the possibility of moving to an area with more violence and higher crime. The majority of these adolescents reported being happy with where they lived (51 percent), being happy with the military way of life (61 percent), and feeling that the military offered many opportunities for its members such as good money (52 percent), education/training (69 percent), and advancement (52 percent).

### Service Differences

Important differences were found in terms of adolescent health, antisocial behaviors, alcohol and drug use, recreational and leisure activities, and environmental factors among the various services. Air Force youths reported fewer risk factors, and Navy youths appeared to be most at risk. Adolescents living overseas were found to be more at risk than those living stateside. Youths living overseas seemed to have greater potential for obtaining support since they were more likely to live on base or post and/or participate in youth programs on the installation. The children of officers presented themselves as less at risk than the other two pay groups, while children of parents in the E7-E9 pay group appeared to be at greatest risk.

Air Force youths were least likely to have ever smoked cigarettes, used drugs or alcohol, or to report engaging in antisocial behaviors during the past year. Navy youths, on average, scored lower than the other three services on the index of psychological well-being. Air Force youths generally viewed their interactions with their teachers more positively than youth with a parent in one of the other three services. More Army families than other service families reported living in military housing on and off base/post, living overseas, and moving often. Army fathers were more often separated from their children than were those from other services. Air Force adolescents had the most positive perception of opportunities the military offers its members.

Military adolescents living overseas reported more moves, more safety in their place of residence, and greater concerns about moving to an installation with more violence and higher crime than those adolescents living stateside. Adolescents living overseas were more likely to report that they had engaged in antisocial behaviors. On the other hand, those youths living stateside reported happiness with where they lived and with the military family life more often than those living overseas. Adolescents living in the United States perceived their interactions with their teachers more positively than those living overseas. Youth living overseas reported more frequent separations from both their mothers and their fathers.

Officers' children, more often than youths with enlisted parents, reported moving often, feeling safe in their neighborhoods, feeling happy with where they lived and military life, and feeling that the military offers its members opportunities.

Fewer females than males reported their health as excellent, and females were also less likely than males to participate in weekly exercise and physical activities. On the other hand, females were more involved in academic endeavors than males were and reported fewer problems with school and fewer behavior problems. More males than females reported engaging in sports and antisocial behaviors. While there were no differences by gender in alcohol use, males were more likely to have used marijuana or inhalants at some point during their lives. Furthermore, females were having an easier time socializing with friends than males, but males reported greater family satisfaction than females. More females than males reported that they felt that military family life was strict and that they worry about moving to an installation with more violence and higher crime.

The younger rather than the older adolescents were more likely to report good to excellent health, engaging in activities (including activities at the youth centers on base or post), doing better at school, interacting with teachers, identifying with friends, and having better perceptions of their family and military family life. The youngest age group reported substantially higher levels of both psychological well-being and family satisfaction than either of the older age groups. More of those in the older two groups of participants reported engaging in sports programs and antisocial behaviors. As military youths aged, like the civilian population, they perceived themselves as having less support and thus were more at risk. Furthermore, it is problematic that as youths aged they were more likely to report feeling alone and lonely.

Older youths more often than younger adolescents viewed the military family life as strict, reported being unhappy with their place of residence, and reported that they were less happy with military family life. However, this older group was more likely than other groups to report that the military provided its members with opportunities.

## SUMMARY AND IMPLICATIONS

The preponderance of respondents to this survey reported being healthy, engaging in weekly exercise, participating in appropriate school and community activities, doing homework, and getting good grades in school. Furthermore, they recounted being happy with their school, home, and community environments. Comparisons with other studies, where available, revealed that military adolescents are doing at least as well as and in some cases slightly better than their civilian peers on most of the indicators measured.

Only a few respondents were at serious risk for mental health problems. These percentages appeared to be comparable to those in the civilian population. A large percentage of the adolescents surveyed related that they did not use alcohol, illicit drugs, or cigarettes. When they did use these substances, their drugs of choice during the past 30 days were alcohol, marijuana, and inhalants. These military adolescents reported substantially less alcohol and drug use than civilian youth. Furthermore, few respondents related that they engaged in antisocial behaviors.

A concern arising from these data is the adolescents' reports of discipline problems of other students. Many stated that their learning in school was disrupted because of the behavior problems of others and that few consequences were given for these behaviors. There were a number of youths who related questionable discipline patterns by one or both of their parents (e.g., the repeated use of physical punishment). While the majority declared that they did not engage in delinquent behaviors, a small percentage of youth were engaging in antisocial behaviors of a serious nature.

While most adolescents reported having friends, a small subgroup appeared to be having difficulties making new friends. Peer relationships can be problematic since these youths move and change schools often, thus enduring frequent exposure to disruption of their social networks.

The majority of the respondents reported that they felt safe at school and in their place of residence. However, the fact that some respondents felt unsafe is of particular concern since these feelings could lead to school and mental health problems (Jeffreys & Leitzel, 1997).

The rates of health problems in this military sample are close enough to those presented in the civilian literature to indicate that there are not substantial differences in the health status of military adolescents as compared to civilian youths. Recommendations from the general civilian literature with respect to improving adolescent health should be applied. For example, antismoking education programs (shown to delay the onset of use) should be implemented or expanded (Igoe, 1992).

In terms of mental health, a sense of belonging and family satisfaction accounted for a substantial proportion of the variance in well-being scores (Leitzel, Jeffreys, VanBelle, & O'Brien, 1997). Given the frequent moves that are encountered by military adolescents, well-being may be buttressed by assisting youths in quickly developing a sense of belonging with their peers. Programs should be developed to identify and ensure appropriate intervention for those youth that are most clearly at risk.

Family-friendly relocation processes, including outreach from youth and family support program staff, could have a positive impact in terms of both increased family satisfaction and greater levels of social belongingness. Mentoring programs should be developed with input and assistance from adolescents.

While the majority of respondents did not engage in antisocial behaviors or use alcohol and drugs, any level of involvement in these behaviors is problematic. The military should consider expanding programs (e.g., prevention/mentoring programs, such as the 12 pilot programs conducted DOD-wide, evaluated by Caulkins, Fitzgerald, Model, & Willis, 1994) that address various types of misconduct indirectly through modeling appropriate behavior and providing youth with relationships with caring, interested adults. It would be beneficial if these programs were implemented overseas as a higher percentage of youths living overseas reported using alcohol and engaging in antisocial behaviors. At-risk youths should be identified, prevention programs expanded, and intervention programs that have been successful in the military (e.g., Caulkins et. al., 1994) and civilian populations should be initiated or expanded.

Involvement in activities has been identified as a protective factor against negative outcomes during adolescence (Loesel & Bliesener, 1994). Higher self-esteem and greater well being is associated with appropriate activity involvement (Jeffreys & Leitzel, 1997). While 90 percent of the respondents reported participation in school or community activities, only 42 percent (58 percent of those living on installation and 31 percent of those living off installation) used military youth centers. Females and older youths participated in fewer activities than other adolescents. Therefore, efforts should be concerted to involve more youths, especially the most vulnerable populations, in activities on base, off base, and at school. These efforts might include increasing adolescent awareness of activities that are available to military youths on and off base and involving adolescents in the planning of activities to increase their interest and, therefore, their utilization. Activities on base should be coordinated and integrated, wherever possible, with school and community activities. Efforts to involve and to encourage females and older adolescents to be involved in athletics and other programs should be increased. These recommendations could be implemented at minimal cost with the involvement of adolescents.

Respondents' Grade Point Averages (GPAs) were generally high, school culture was generally viewed as positive, and parents were reported to be involved in respondent's schoolwork. However, the misbehavior of other students was reported to be disruptive and as interfering with learning. Involvement in school activities was associated with greater well-being and a positive school culture was associated with less antisocial behaviors (Jeffreys & Leitzel, 1997). Therefore, the military should investigate ways to encourage parents to become more involved with the school process in ways that will encourage adolescent involvement in school activities and foster a positive school culture.

Military parents should be encouraged to collaborate as much as possible with school personnel in the development of policies and procedures addressing rules and discipline. One example is parents assisting with the development of programs focused on handling misconduct in the classroom. Increasing adolescent awareness of the consequences of misbehavior in educational settings may have a significant payoff. Military personnel should be encouraged to participate in those school programs (academic and nonacademic) that foster student involvement. Military personnel should be made aware of service-wide policies, such as the Army's allowing time off from duty for volunteering. Since September 5, 1997, Army policy has allowed soldiers to spend up to one hour per week engaging in volunteer activity, mission permitting. This policy expands upon what individual commanders have been permitting for quite some time (Jowers, 1997). In 1996 at Fort Hood, Texas, 6,301 Army and Air Force personnel volunteered 41,180 hours in over 70 public schools in the area (Willis, 1997). Encouraging personnel to become more involved in schools and youth activities would accrue important benefits to all.

The majority of respondents reported satisfying relationships with peers. A small percentage did not report belonging to a group of peers and thus felt alone and lonely. Peer relationships were not associated with family, school, well-being, involvement in activities, or antisocial behaviors (Jeffreys & Leitzel, 1997). Military personnel might explore ways to help promote the development of friendships among youth. Peer mentors could be identified for adolescents when they move to a new base or post.

Most respondents reported generally high levels of satisfaction with military family life. While family structure was significantly related to level of satisfaction, whether or not they lived in military housing was not related to level of family satisfaction. While many respondents perceived military family life as strict rather than relaxed, the largest percentage of youths felt that military family life was neither strict nor relaxed. According to the literature and current data, family satisfaction is often linked to higher levels of satisfaction with peers, school, and the community as well as lower levels of delinquent behavior and alcohol and drug use (Eccles et al., 1993; Jeffreys & Leitzel, 1997).

Those youths who reported being physically punished by their parents reported lower family satisfaction. Therefore, the military should consider implementing and expanding parenting classes, especially for those with young children. Such programs should focus on the connections between family satisfaction, strictness, punishment, well-being, and antisocial behaviors. These programs can provide instruction in behavior modification techniques that could be utilized as an alternative to physical punishment.

The majority of respondents reported feeling safe in their place of residence and in their schools, but those who reported feeling unsafe were also likely to have reported more indicators of gang activity and greater exposure to violence against both themselves and others (Jeffreys & Leitzel, 1997). Public relations work regarding safety, violence, and crime on installations needs to be done with incoming families. If safety is an actual issue at a given site, efforts should be made to educate families regarding safety and security features and programs already in place. Coordination with schools and communities in the vicinity of installations is essential if these efforts are to be successful. In-depth investigations of safety and gang-related activities are needed.

We would like to conclude our chapter with a number of individual comments that adolescents wrote on the last page of their surveys. These comments address a number of the issues discussed in this chapter.

> I think that if we had more activities for the military children, we wouldn't have to worry about drugs, teen sex, and drinking as much as we have to.
>
> I think the military has done a lot for me. I'm better at school and I [am] very involved in sports and the community. I really like visiting new places and learning about different cultures.
>
> I think the different bases should have programs for teenagers who move to a new place so they can get to know the area a little better.
>
> I like being in the military because you can't get sick of a place, you move too much. I don't like the military because you lose friends.

I have lived overseas almost all of my life—I happen to like military life and plan on joining the Air Force. Living overseas gave me a chance to get to travel. However, there are some disadvantages. Like the amount of shopping and activities there are for teenagers to do. The services over here are limited. I feel much safer in a military DODDS [Department of defense Dependent' Schools] school and feel the education is adequate.

## REFERENCES

Amato, P. R. (1990). Dimensions of the family environment as perceived by children: A multidimensional scaling analysis. *Journal of Marriage and the Family, 52(3)*, 613–620.

Benard, B. (1991, August). *Fostering resiliency in kids: Protective factors in the family, schools, and community.* Portland, OR: Northwest Regional Educational Laboratory.

Blum, R., Harris, L. J., Resnick, M. D., & Rosenwinkel, K. (1989). *Technical report on the adolescent health survey* (Grant #MCH273460). Minneapolis: University of Minnesota.  .

Brandenburg, N. A., Freidman, R. M., & Silver, S. E. (1990). The epidemiology of childhood psychiatric disorders: Prevalence findings from recent studies. *Journal of the American Academy of Child and Adolescent Psychiatry, 29*(2), 76–83.

Carey, M. P., Lubin, B., & Brewer, D. H. (1992). Measuring dysphoric mood in preadolescents and adolescents: The youth depression adjective checklist (Y-DACL). *Journal of Clinical Child Psychology, 21*(4), 331–338.

Caulkins, J. P., Fitzgerald, N., Model, K. E., & Willis, H. L. (1994). *Preventing drug use among youth through community outreach: The military's pilot programs* (Rand/MR-536-OSD). Santa Monica, CA: Rand.

Coleman, J. C. (1980). Friendship and the peer group in adolescence. In J. Adelson (Ed.), *Handbook of adolescent psychology* (pp. 408–431). New York: Wiley.

Connelly, B., Johnston, D., Brown, I.D.R., Mackay, S., & Blackstock, E. G. (1993). The prevalence of depression in a high school population. *Adolescence, 28*(109), 149–158.

Downs, W. R., & Rose, S. R. (1991). The relationship of adolescent peer groups to the incidence of psychosocial problems. *Adolescence, 26*(102), 473–492.

Dunn, J., & McGuire, S. (1992). Sibling and peer relationships in childhood. *Journal of Child Psychology and Psychiatry and Allied Disciplines, 33*(1), 67–105.

Eccles, J. S., Midgely, C., Wigfield, A., Buchanan, C. M., Reuman, D., Flanagan, C., & MacIver, D. (1993). Development during adolescence. *American Psychologist, 48*(2), 90–101.

Epstein, J. L., & MacIver, D. J. (1990). *Education in the middle grades: National practices and trends.* Columbus, OH: National Middle School Association.

Epstein, S. (1990). *Cognitive-experiential self-theory.* New York: Guilford Publications, Inc.

Escobedo, L. G., Chorba, T. L., & Waxweiler, R. (1995). Patterns of alcohol use and the risk of drinking and driving among US high school students. *American Journal of Public Health, 85*(7), 976–978.

Fenzel, M. L., & Blyth, D. A. (1986). Individual adjustment to school transitions: An exploration of the role of supportive peer relations. *Journal of Early Adolescence, 6*(4), 315–329.

Ferreira, M. M., Bosworth, K., & Smith, J. (1995). The caring culture of a suburban middle school. Paper presented at the Annual Meeting of the American Educational Research Association, San Francisco, CA.

Heyman, R. B., Adger, H., Jr., Anglin, T. M., Fuller, P. G., Jr., Jacobs, E. A., Shah, R. Z., & Tenenbein, M. (1996). Inhalant abuse. *Pediatrics, 97(3),* 420–423.

Humke, C., & Schaefer, C. (1995). Relocation: A review of the effects of residential mobility on children and adolescents. *Psychology: A Journal of Human Behavior, 32*(1), 16-24.

Hunter, E. J. (1982). *Families under the flag: A review of military family literature.* New York: Praeger.

Igoe, J. (1992). Health promotion, health protection, and disease prevention in childhood. *Pediatric Nursing, 18*(3), 291–292.

Inderbitzen-Pisaruk, H., Clark, M. L., & Solano, C. H. (1992). Correlates in mid adolescence. *Journal of Youth and Adolescence, 21*(2), 151–167.

Jeffreys, D. J., & Leitzel, J. D. (1997). *Military adolescents: Their strengths and vulnerabilities.* Briefing at DOD, Office of Family Policy, Support and Services, Arlington, VA. Scranton, PA: Military Family Institute of Marywood College.

Johnston, L. D., O'Malley, P. M., & Bachman, J. G. (1995). *National survey results on drug use from the monitoring the future study, 1975-1994,* Volume I (NIH Publication No. 95-4026). Rockville, MD: National Institute on Drug Abuse.

Jowers, K. (1997, May 26). Charity begins on Base. *Army Times,* p. 24.

Leitzel, J. D., Jeffreys, D. J., VanBelle, S., & O'Brien, E. J. (1997, August). Correlates of psychological difficulties among military adolescents. Paper presented at the 105th Annual Convention of the American Psychological Association, Chicago, IL.

Loesel, F., & Bliesener, T. (1994). Some high-risk adolescents do not develop conduct problems: A study of protective factors. *International Journal of Behavioral Development, 17*(4), 753–777.

Meier, D. W. (1996). The big benefits of smallness. *Educational Leadership, 54(1),* 12–15.

Merril, J. C., & Fox, K. S. (1994). *Cigarettes, alcohol, marijuana: Gateways to illicit drug use.* New York: Columbia University, The National Center on Addiction and Substance Abuse at Columbia University.

Newman, B. M., & Newman, P. R. (1991). *Development through life: A psychosocial approach* (5th ed.). Pacific Grove, CA: Brooks/Cole Publishing Company.

O'Brien, E. J., Mensky, L., Jeffreys, D., O'Brien, J. P., & Marchese, M. (August 12, 1996). Gender differences in self-esteem of adolescents: A meta-analysis. Poster presented at the Annual Convention of the American Psychological Association, Toronto.

Ohannessian, C. M., Lerner, R. M., & Von Eye, A. (1994). Discrepancies in young adolescents' and their parents' perceptions of family functioning. Paper presented at the Society for Research on Adolescence, San Diego, CA.

Olson, D. H., McCubbin, H. I., Barnes, H., Larsen, A., Muxen, M., & Wilson, M. (1983). *Families: What makes them work?* Beverly Hills, CA: Sage.

Orthner, D. K., Giddings, M. M., & Quinn, W. H. (1987). *Youth in transition: A study of adolescents from Air Force and civilian families.* (Prepared under contract to Department of the Air Force Office of Family Matters, The Pentagon, Washington, DC). Athens: University of Georgia, Center for Work and Family Issues.

Paredes, V. (1993, April). School correlates with student persistence to stay in school. Paper presented at annual meeting of the American Educational Research Association, Atlanta, GA.

Parents Resource Institute for Drug Education. (1996). PRIDE survey 1996. <http://www.drugs.indiana.edu/drug_stats/pride>, October 1, 1997.

Peterson, G. W., & Leigh, G. W. (1990). The family and social competence in adolescence. In T. Gullota, G. R. Adams, & R. Montemayor (Eds.), *Advances in adolescent development: Social competence* (pp. 97–138). Newbury Park, CA: Sage.

Rathunde, K. (1993). The motivational importance of extracurricular activities for adolescent development: Cultivating undivided attention. Paper presented at the Annual Meeting of the American Educational Research Association, Atlanta, GA.

Rosenberg, M. (1965). *Society and the adolescent self-image.* Princeton, NJ: Princeton University Press.

Roth, D. L., & Holmes, D. S. (1987). Influence of aerobic exercise training and relaxation training on physical and psychological health following stressful life events. *Psychosomatic Medicine, 49*(4), 355–365.

Spielberger, C. D., Gorsuch, R. L., Lushene, R., Vagg, P. R., & Jacobs, G. A. (1983). *Manual for the state-trait anxiety inventory (Form Y).* Palo Alto, CA: Consulting Psychologists Press.

Steitz, J. A., & Owen, T. P. (1992). School activities and work: Effects on adolescent self-esteem. *Adolescence, 27*(105), 37–50.

Udry, J. R., Bauman, K. E., Bearman, P. S., Billy, J.O.G., Blum, R. W., Grady, W. R., Harris, K. M., Jaccard, J. J., Resnick, M. D., & Rowe, D. C. (1997). National Longitudinal Study of Adolescent Health. Carolina Population Center at the University of North Carolina, Chapel Hill. Internet Address located at <http://www.cpc.unc.edu/projects/addhealth /addhealth_home.html.>

Voelkl, K. E. (1995). School warmth, student participation and achievement. *Journal of Experimental Education, 63*(2), 127–138.

Wertsch, M. E. (1991). *Military brats: Legacies of childhood inside the fortress.* New York: Harmony Books.

Williams-Scaife, G. (1994). A report on the need for a strategic plan to address the problems of adolescents in U.S. military communities overseas. (Research Report Requirement). Department of Defense, Office of Dependents Education.

Willis, G. E. (1997, October 20). You can take time off to volunteer. *Army Times,* p. 9.

Wuebker-Battershell, R. (1994). The military lifestyle and children. *The Family Forum Library* (pp. 1–15). Huntington, NY: Bureau for At-Risk Youth.

Young, M. H., Miller, B. C., Norton, M. C., & Hill, E. J. (1995). The effect of parental supportive behaviors on life satisfaction of adolescent offspring. *Journal of Marriage and the Family, 57*(3), 813–822.

Youniss, J. (1980). *Parents and peers in social development: A Sullivan-Piaget perspective.* Chicago, IL: University of Chicago Press.

Youniss, J., & Smollar, J. (1985). *Adolescent relations with mothers, fathers, and friends.* Chicago, IL: University of Chicago Press.

# Chapter 16

# Beyond Adolescence: The Experiences of Adult Children of Military Parents

*Morten G. Ender*

## INTRODUCTION

Many Americans have grown up in and around the military and other agencies like the Foreign Service, missionary groups, and the international business community. They spent some or all of their childhood and/or adolescence sharing their organizational parent's career, including a lifestyle marked by mobility and foreign residence. This lifestyle sets them apart from their civilian peers. Their socialization in a family that was occupationally committed to a service organization has a long-term impact that is not yet fully understood. This chapter provides results from an ongoing study of this unique population and offers human service providers insight into the background and current characteristics of these men and women.

A small social movement has emerged among adult children from military and other kinds of organization-affiliated families such as, the State Department, international business, and missionaries. Among a number of similarities is a shared experience living abroad. The movement encompasses a loose network of ties among adult children from organization families, with the largest group from military families. "Military Brat"and "PK"( Preacher Kid) are some of the popular labels used by children, adolescents, youths, and adults from military and missionary families to identify themselves and by others to identify them.

Popular portrayals of growing up military or in a foreign service family are offered in such books as *Growing Up in Khaki: Life as a Service Brat* (Allingham, p. 309, 1998); *Hidden Immigrants: Legacies of Growing Up Abroad* (Bell, 1996); *APO San Francisco 96525: Growing Up in the Military* (Grubbs, 1988); *Notes from a Traveling Childhood: Readings for Internationally Mobile Parents and Children* (McCluskey, 1994); *Army Brat: A Memoir* (Smith, 1980); *Strangers at Home: Essays on the Effects of Living Overseas and Coming "Home" to a Strange Land* (Smith, 1996); *The Absentee American: Expatriates' Perspective on America* (Smith, 1994); *Brats: Children of the Military Speak Out* (Truscott, 1989); *Army*

*Brats: A Legacy of Military Family Life Inside the Fortress* (Wertsch, 1991); a popular magazine, *Nomad: The Brat Journal* (Ang, 1996); magazine articles (Long, 1986); comic strips (Army Times Publishing, 1997); and books made into films such as *The Great Santini* (Conroy, 1976). The label has also appeared in the names of associations such as Overseas Brats, Military Brats of America, Inc. Operation Footlocker, and the American Overseas Schools Historical Society and Military Brats, Inc. Adults from Foreign Service and missionary families have similar books and organizations (e.g., Global Nomads International).

The labels, popular media, and organizations denote the development of a social movement. In this sense, adult children from organization families share a collective form of behavior in which large numbers have organized to support and bring about awareness of their shared experience. The movement began with a few high school reunions, a recognition of a collective identity, the confirmation of a shared ethos that remains fairly constant across and within generations, and the establishment of formalized not-for-profit and for-profit associations.

Information technologies, including the Internet, e-mail, and other electronic forums, continue to propel the movement. Electronic resources provide a virtual community for a people who do not have a common geographic space. Instant worldwide communication provides access to a collective space for members of this "community" who are scattered throughout the world.

Appendix 16.1 provides a list of some of the on-line organizations and individual home pages, alumni associations, and school home pages, USENET groups, LISTSERVs and electronic discussion lists, for-profit companies on-line, and other not-for-profit electronic sites related to growing up in an organization family, especially growing up overseas. Home pages from such groups are being added to the Internet at a rate of approximately one to three per week.

The number of people who have experienced the organization lifestyle is impressive. For example, in 1990, when the downsizing effect of the U.S. military had not yet been substantial, the 2 million active duty military personnel had some 1,625,111 children under twenty-one years of age. One-fourth of these service members lived outside the United States. By the end of the Cold War in 1990, more than 5 million men and women were either on active duty, retired from, or in a reserve component of the U.S. armed forces (*Defense Almanac*, 1990).

This chapter highlights information from a study of adult children from primarily military families. The study also includes adult children whose parent(s) worked overseas, typically for US international companies and various religious or humanitarian organizations, for a period during their childhood and/or adolescence. While similar studies with large samples are available (Cottrell & Useem, 1994; Gerner, Perry, Moselle & Archbold, 1992; Salmon, 1988), the present study provides the largest single sampling of adult children from military families.

Human service providers will benefit from the research on this community of people whose formative years were spend in foreign countries scattered around the world. Foremost, human service providers will gain an appreciation for the diversity of experience that exists in military and other organization type families.

# RESEARCH DESIGN

## Sample

The participants in this study (a sample of 607 men and women) were surveyed between 1991 and 1997 from a variety of sources using a snowball sampling approach (one contact was used to locate another). Potential participants were solicited through: (1) undergraduate sociology courses at two eastern U.S. universities; (2) two Department of Defense Dependents Schools (DODDS) high school reunions in the Washington, D.C., area in 1992 and 1993; (3) an electronic chain referral sampling method via the Internet, NEWSGROUPS, LISTSERV, electronic bulletin boards, and electronic mail distribution lists; (4) print advertisements in the *Overseas Brats* magazine, which caters to adults who attended DODDS outside of the United States; and (5) two regional newspapers in the U.S. upper Midwest.

Some respondents volunteered to serve as "electronic" research assistants. Many respondents requested multiple questionnaires to distribute to others considered eligible to participate. These individuals provided questionnaires to family members, friends, and/or their alumni. Others provided additional participant contacts through siblings, friends, and acquaintances. Many of the sources were eventually cross-listed. For example, electronic bulletin board messages were downloaded and published in print media newspapers and newsletters.

## Measures

The original questionnaire used for the larger study is 11 pages in length and includes both forced response and open-ended questions. Forced response items include: (1) organization family history; (2) social history and demographics; and (3) present lifestyle. Two specific forced response scale items are an organizational lifestyle stress inventory based on the demands of the military lifestyle and a life satisfaction scale. Open-ended questions provide an opportunity for respondents to elaborate on their experiences.

## Procedure

After reading or hearing of the call for participants, potential respondents contacted me via regular mail, telephone, or electronic mail, and volunteered to participate or requested additional information about participating in the study. Each eligible participant received one or more copy(ies) of the 11-page questionnaire with instructions on how to complete and return it in the self-addressed stamped envelope. The survey was administered between 1991 and 1997. Potential respondents totaled 1,160 with 607 completing (response rate of 52 percent).

### Family History

The data in Table 16.1 show the frequency and percentage distribution of the respondents' parents' organizational affiliation service branch. Just over three-fourths of the sample (78.5 percent) came from military families (Army 34.4 percent; Air Force 36.4 percent, Navy 6.6 percent, Marine Corps 0.8 percent; or Coast Guard 0.2 percent). Of the military family respondents, parents were reported as either officer (60.7 percent) or enlisted (39.3 percent) service members. The remaining 21.5 percent of the respondents came from foreign service (3.9 percent), international business (1.5 percent), missionary (1.7 percent), civilian government employee (11.5 percent), or "other" (2.9 percent) agencies. Other occupations include international school educators, visiting professors, Red Cross workers, or other nongovernmental workers (NGOs) such as medical doctors.

Of those responding (n=590), most had siblings (95 percent). The average was two, with a range from none to seven or more. Almost three-quarters (73.3 percent) of the respondents reported that their parent had served in a major war during the 20th century. Most had served in Vietnam (33.3 percent) or World War II (23.6 percent). A small, but notable, number served in World War II, Korea, *and* Vietnam (13.4 percent).

Most of the parents of respondents had retired from service by the time they participated in the survey (90.5 percent). The respondents at the time of the parents' retirement ranged in age from 1 to 49 (their average age was about 21).

**Table 16.1**
**Frequency and Percentage of Adult Children by Parents' Branch of Service Affiliation**

| Branch of Service | f | % |
|---|---|---|
| Army | 203 | 34.4 |
| Air Force | 215 | 36.4 |
| Navy | 39 | 6.6 |
| Marines | 5 | .8 |
| Coast Guard | 1 | .2 |
| Foreign Service | 23 | 3.9 |
| International Business | 9 | 1.5 |
| Missionaries | 10 | 1.7 |
| U.S. Government Civilian | 68 | 11.5 |
| Other | 17 | 2.9 |
| *Total* | 590* | 100.00 % |

*Seventeen cases did not provide valid responses.

Almost all of those responding reported that their parents had retired in North America (96.1 percent). Of those providing valid responses, the five popular retirement states are, in order of popularity, Texas, California, Florida, Virginia, and Maryland. All other states and the District of Columbia are represented except Arkansas. These results parallel where former U.S. military service members generally retire (*Defense Almanac*, 1990).

## DEMOGRAPHICS AND SOCIAL HISTORY

At the time of the survey, the respondents ranged in age from 15 to 46. The average age was approximately 39. More women than men responded to the survey (58.4 percent). The vast majority lived in North America (96.6 percent) and over half reported living in large urban areas and suburbs near large cities (55.8 percent). Similar to where organization parents retire, most respondents report living in Virginia (14.8 percent), Texas (9.7 percent), California (9.3 percent), Maryland (9 percent), and Florida (5.1 percent) at the time of the survey. All states and the District of Columbia are represented with the exception of Rhode Island.

Of those responding, whites are overrepresented (90.5 percent). African (2.5 percent), Hispanic (1.5 percent), Asian (1.0 percent), mixed (1.7 percent), and other Americans (2.8 percent) are under-represented. African Americans are generally over represented in the U.S. military, especially in the lower and enlisted ranks, in contrast to their proportional representation in the larger U.S. society.

Most respondents reported being married at the time of the survey (61.9 percent), and the number of their children ranged from none to five or more. The average number of children was one, and most reported having no children (43.4 percent). Twenty-one percent of the married and divorced respondents met their spouse while they were overseas with their families.

The respondents reported significant educational achievement. Slightly more than 95 percent indicated at least some college and 29.1 percent possessed an advanced degree beyond baccalaureate. Occupationally, of those responding, most were either professionals (29.5 percent), in business management (16.2 percent), students (11.2 percent), or are spread across other categories including clerical work, skilled and unskilled labor, military, government employed, homemaker, unemployed, or other work situations at the time of the survey.

A small number of respondents reported to be currently serving in the military (5.7 percent) at the time of the survey, and a large proportion had prior military service (21.8 percent). Of those with military experience, most were in the enlisted ranks (57.4 percent). The majority served in the Army (45.7 percent), followed by the Air Force (34 percent), Navy (16 percent), and the Marine Corps (4.3 percent). Of those responding, most reported having served six years or less (61.3 percent). Among current servers, most were officers (63.3 percent) and serving in the Air Force (52.4 percent).

Among those reporting never serving in the military, slightly more than half said they had generally had no interest in serving (53.3 percent). The next largest coded category attributed not serving as a consequence of their gender, in particular being female (16.9 percent). Others said they did not like the regimented orientation or the lifestyle of the military. A handful reported to be pacifist. Political orientations were reported and were equally distributed on a five-point scale ranging from very conservative (7.9 percent) to very liberal (11.7 percent), with most reporting to be middle of the road.

Today, many adult children from organization-families report traveling outside of the United States. About half (44.3 percent) travel outside the United States once a year or more for leisure and fewer for business (13.2 percent).

The information in Table 16.2 shows the frequency and percentage of total moves in two move intervals between birth and their first relocation after completing high school. The average number of moves is eight. Adult children from Army families reported the most moves nine, followed by the Navy eight, Air Force eight, foreign service eight, the Marine Corps eight, missionary and others seven, international business seven, the Coast Guard six, and civilian government workers six.

Geographic mobility and foreign residence permeates the experience of the sample. While growing up in their organization families, virtually all respondents reported having spent time overseas between birth and completing high school. The range of time was from one to 20-plus years. The average number of years overseas was seven. The most frequent number of years spent overseas was four. For most, this meant spending at least one "tour" with their parents overseas. As a group, eight years was the average number of years overseas over the course of their lifetime. Some reported having returned overseas as adults to live and work.

Respondents were asked to identify one to three countries where they had lived while growing up. The vast majority listed residence in at least one foreign country (97 percent), fewer listed a second (63 percent), and still fewer listed a

**Table 16.2**
**Frequency and Percentage of Adult Children from Military and Other Organization Families by Number of Moves Between Birth and First Move After High School Graduation**

| Number of Moves | f | % |
|-----------------|------|----------|
| 1 to 2 moves | 24 | 4.0 |
| 3 to 4 moves | 50 | 8.3 |
| 5 to 6 moves | 122 | 20.3 |
| 7 to 8 moves | 174 | 29.0 |
| 9 to 10 moves | 136 | 22.7 |
| 11 to 12 moves | 66 | 11.0 |
| 13 or more moves | 28 | 4.7 |
| *Total* | 600* | 100.00 % |

*Seven cases did not provide valid responses.

third (31 percent). Seventy countries were represented in the sample, including the more obvious but notable places such as Germany, Britain, Italy, Thailand, and Japan and the less notable such as Senegal, Bahrain, Cuba, and Honduras.

More in-depth, respondents were asked to rank the degree to which they had mingled with the local populations in their host country. Almost two-thirds (65 percent) of the respondents reported that they had mingled between "often" and "totally" with people in their host country.

Finally, respondents were asked about second language acquisition while growing up. Twenty-five languages were reported, including an "other" category. A stunning 80.9 percent reported to have spoken one additional language other than English while growing up, 37.9 percent spoke two additional languages, and 14.3 percent reported speaking at least three. Among the one additional language group, about 57 percent reported their proficiency level to be moderate or proficient. The five most popular languages spoken were German, Spanish, French, Japanese, and Italian. Less frequently occurring languages include Farsi, Vietnamese, and Swahili.

## ATTITUDES AND OPINIONS

The information in Table 16.3 shows the average for levels of stress for each of nine organization lifestyle demands by the respondents' parents' branch of service affiliation. Two "Other" categories also are reported. Respondents were allowed to write in one or two stressful demands that they thought warranted reporting. The latter three columns in the table have parents' service affiliations aggregated. This is done because some respondent subgroups are fairly small. The scores on the item measure are 1= "Not at all," 2 = "Slightly," 3 = "A little bit," 4 = "Moderately," 5 = "Quite a bit," and 6 = "Extremely."

In comparing the subgroups of respondents, adult children of civilian government workers had the most variability in their answers. They experienced less stress with normative constraints of their organization, parental separation, and transition to civilian status, and slightly more stress with antimilitarism and residence in foreign countries than any other group. Adults from international business, foreign service, missionary, and other types of families varied somewhat as well. They reported less stress with organization-sanctioned machismo, personal antimilitarism, and risk of parental death or injury probably because they had much less exposure than others to the U.S. military. This latter group did report the highest stress of the five groups on parental shift-work. Within the demands, Navy, Marine Corps, and Coast Guard adult children reported the most stress on geographic mobility, normative constraints, and parental separation. Other uniformed services are also high on normative constraints (Army mean = 2.98 and Air Force mean = 2.89). Also noteworthy are that government civilians, and the international business, Foreign Service, and missionary, and others report lower risk of injury or death and transition to civilian status as stressful.

The two "Other" categories in the table are of special interest and are worth examination in greater detail. These two items are added to the scale on the questionnaire to allow the respondents to write in a stressful demand and report its level of stress. The first "Other" option had more write-ins (160) than the second (72). On both "Other" options, the responses varied. Three demands appeared to dominate. they include geographic mobility (41 percent and 39 percent respectively); foreign residence (27 percent and 36 percent respectively); normative constraints (13 percent and 10 percent); and a new category that was added and labeled "work and family" (6 percent and 8 percent respectively). Topics under this latter category dealt mostly with dysfunctional family situations related to the organization lifestyle. For example, one respondent wrote in "excessive drinking in the military" as extremely stressful. These items have the highest overall stress means levels.

Overall, the highest averages for all groups between the lifestyle demands are geographic mobility, normative constraints imposed by the organization, and parental separation. The overall least stressful demands are antimilitarism, living in a masculine-dominated culture, and potential shift-work.

Life-satisfaction-type questions were asked of these respondents. Life-satisfaction questions are standard questions asked of a random sample of Americans on the General Social Survey. Items query respondents about levels of satisfaction with life areas from "A very great deal" to "No" satisfaction in six areas of their life—family, friends, job, nonwork activities, health, and the place they live.

Since 1972, Americans in general have been fairly consistent in their responses to the scale. Family, friends, and health are reported to be the most satisfying, with work, nonwork activities, and place of residence still high in satisfaction, but less than the first three. In the present study, the top three areas of satisfaction (in order from highest to lowest satisfaction) are almost identical to the general U.S. population—family, friends, and nonwork activities, followed by job, health, and place of residence.

## DISCUSSION

Growing up in a military or other type of organization-family, such as Foreign Service or missionary, nestled in a work environment during the Cold War set people geographically and culturally apart from their "civilian" peers. Characteristics of their lifestyle growing up include: significant geographic mobility; risk of parental death or injury; family separation; parent's shift-work; constraints imposed by the organization and the host country; masculine-dominated employment subcultures; counterculture leanings; foreign residence; and transitions to civilian life. These occupational demands impinge on families. Many of these demands are found individually in the civilian society; however these demands are unique to military and other organization life.

**Table 16.3**
**Means* for Organization Lifestyle Demand Stresses by Parents' Service Affiliation (N=582)****

| Organization Lifestyle Demands | Total Sample (N=582) | Army (n=200) | Air Force (n=214) | Navy, Marines, & Coast Guard (n=42) | International Business, Foreign Service, Missionaries, & Others (n=58) | Government Civilians (n=68) |
|---|---|---|---|---|---|---|
| Geographic Mobility | 3.19 | 3.20 | 3.07 | 3.52 | 3.39 | 3.20 |
| Normative Constraints | 2.84 | 2.98 | 2.89 | 3.04 | 2.42 | 2.51 |
| Family Separation | 2.64 | 2.75 | 2.71 | 2.81 | 2.52 | 2.13 |
| Transition to Civilian Life | 2.45 | 2.62 | 2.73 | 2.12 | 1.57 | 1.91 |
| Parental Risk of Death/Injury | 2.07 | 2.35 | 2.14 | 1.95 | 1.49 | 1.55 |
| Foreign Residence | 2.04 | 2.12 | 1.83 | 2.24 | 2.12 | 2.29 |
| Parental Shift-work | 1.78 | 1.77 | 1.85 | 1.57 | 2.02 | 1.55 |
| Masculine Dominated Subculture | 1.53 | 1.64 | 1.52 | 1.59 | 1.15 | 1.52 |
| Personally Anti-Military | 1.39 | 1.3 | 1.37 | 1.54 | 1.23 | 1.62 |
| Other 1*** (n=160) | 4.89 | 4.77 | 5.09 | 4.91 | 4.74 | 4.76 |
| Other 2 (n=72) | 4.96 | 4.88 | 5.22 | 4.00 | 4.89 | 5.25 |

*Scaled responses range from 1 (not at all) to 5 (extremely) stressful.
**Twenty-five respondents did not provide valid responses.
***Both Other items are added to the scale to allow respondents to write-in any untapped demands of organization life and report the level of stress.

While the present study is not the largest sample of such a population to be collected (Cottrell & Useem, 1994), it is by far the largest sample of adult children from US military families collected to date. It should be noted that the present sample is by no means representative of the entire population of adult children from military or other organization families. Indeed, once I advertised for and located people to participate in this study, they inevitably self-selected themselves to participate. Nonetheless, until a random sample or significantly larger sample is collected, the present study provides a profile of the typical adult child from military or other organization families who came of age during the Cold War. This being duly noted, the typical respondent in this study can be described.

Today, a social movement has emerged among people from military and other organization families. A major feature of this social movement is reconnecting with people and legitimizing one's experience growing up mobile and abroad. This group is culturally rooted in a society that values individuality, family, community, and nationality. They have transported these values from new home to new home and even abroad. Today, these adults find themselves relatively settled and seeking to anchor their experiences of family separation from parents and extended kin, organization rules and regulations, geographic mobility, and living abroad. Information technologies are assisting them in their efforts and providing them with a collective consciousness in the form of virtual community. While rooted in the universal values of American culture, they have acquired shared experiences through organization life that set them apart from their civilian peers.

Adult children from organization-families appear diverse. Foremost, the social structure demands of the various organizations can vary. For example, missionary life requires extended tours in a particular country, generally isolated from other Americans. Military family life abroad almost always involves transferring American accoutrements such as movies, commissaries, and schools abroad. Second, their numbers vary. Adult children from military families make up the largest proportion within this population. Their numbers are followed by Foreign Service and missionary people. International business, civilian government workers, educators, and NGO workers comprise smaller numbers of the remaining groups. Third, some parents might work for more than one organization while their children are still living at home. For example, an army officer might retire from military service and begin work for a U.S. embassy abroad.

The typical respondent in the present study is different from their civilian peers and somewhat different from adult children of military families in general. He or she comes from an officer family, where the father is a war veteran. This number is somewhat skewed as most service members come from the enlisted service member ranks, where enlisted service members outnumber officers 70 to 1 (with the caveat that most of the enlisted soldiers are young, between 18 and 24 years of age, and in their first term of service). In the larger population, adult children from military and other organization families are found in all age categories, including when their parents retire. In the present study, 21 years is the average age. Further, the typical respondent probably lives near his or her retired parents in an urban or semiurban area—perhaps near a military installation with support services such as medical care, commissary, and post exchange privileges.

Yet, they may live anywhere in the United States or abroad. The respondent also is likely to travel abroad for work and play.

The typical respondent in this study probably grew up in a traditional house-hold—with the father as service member. However, the military is increasingly reflecting the changes in the larger U.S. society where a postmodern family is becoming normative. Military families are increasingly nontraditional—single mother or father, reconstituted families, dual-career families, and extended kinship families beyond the nuclear family (Segal, 1989). There is no reason to suspect other U.S. agencies are not being influenced by social trends in American families in the larger society and reflecting these trends as well.

In the present study, the typical respondent was 39 years of age, married, a professional with some military training, was a political moderate, and travels. Yet, ages of the respondents will continue to vary as U.S. military service members continue a trend of marrying and having children earlier than their civilian peers. The typical study respondent was highly educated. Many were working on an advanced degree beyond their undergraduate degree. This level of education reflected two attributes—a high value placed on education among service families and occupations of parents where credentialing played a significant role in career advancement. In addition, the highly educated may have played a role in skewing the sample for the present study. While the access to computers and the Internet are becoming more and more popular throughout American society, at the time of data collection for the present study, the more educated in society had greater access to information technologies and may have been more receptive to my electronic call for participants.

The data on geographic mobility and overseas tours reflect mobility in service organization families. In the present study, the typical adult child from an organi-zation family member moved about eight times before graduating from high school. He or she lived overseas, mostly in Germany, for at least four years. In contrast to popular perceptions of isolated American military communities in Germany and elsewhere, adult children reported to have interacted with people from their host countries, learned the language to varying degrees, and made friends. This finding supports earlier research in the 1970s and 1980s on military family adolescents overseas focused on second language acquisition (Rainey, 1978) and interactions with the local populations (Tyler, 1990).

Geographic mobility, normative constraints, and family separation are re-ported as the most stressful lifestyle demand experiences from adults growing up in an organization family. The stresses of mobility reported here by adults are consistent with research findings from the 1960s through the 1990s on children and especially adolescents (Hunter, 1982; Hunter & Nice, 1978; Steinglass & Edwards, 1993). No long-term follow-up studies of these groups were conducted. The present study does support earlier findings. Moreover, those early findings couple with the preliminary results reported here, that the experiences of growing up mobile has a long-term impact on the cohort of children from the Cold War.

The stresses of normative constraints are a new finding and contribution to the research literature on military families. Normative constraints are direct and indirect rules and regulations. They may diverge from civilian norms and are dictated by the host country and the organization. For example, curfews on bases might differ from locale to locale. They are directly imposed on the service member and their family members. Virtually no research has addressed normative constraints, and this area could benefit from further study. The data reported here suggest that normative constraints imposed on children and adolescents for their behavior have some stressful features, and they may be long-term.

Finally, military family separation studies are not new (Hill, 1949), nor are studies of children separated from their parents (Carlsmith, 1964). There is an increased interest in this area of research in recent years especially following experiences during the Persian Gulf War (Jensen & Shaw, 1996). These findings and others suggest some degree of long-term implication of growing up in a military or other organization, and the topic deserves continued focus on the part of social scientists and some concern among practitioners.

## SUMMARY AND IMPLICATIONS

This chapter presents results from a study of adult children from mostly military families and people whose parent(s) worked overseas for U.S. organizations for a period during their childhood, youth, and adolescence. It is one of the largest samples of data collected from adult children from military families. The chapter describes what might be the characteristics of the typical adult child from a military family while remaining grounded in the demographic, psychological, and historical research on this population.

Human service providers need to recognize the diversity of experience that exists within the population of adult children from organization families in general. This diversity is rooted in generational differences, varied household configurations, geographic residences, different organizational experiences, and, finally, a significant amount of mobility and experiences living abroad during their formative educational years. Few people have lived such a life.

This shared experience among a minority of Americans, including mobility and overseas experiences, sets them apart from their "civilian" peers. This shared sense of "otherness" has constructed an atypical socialization that they are only as adults beginning to appreciate. Increasingly policies are being implemented to help ease the social and psychological experiences of living under the demands of organization life, especially military family life (e.g., children of veterans, POWs, and MIAs). The paradox is that many adult children from military and other organization family situations feel their experience has provided them an unprecedented opportunity that not many people are afforded—extensive travel and living in new, different, and exciting places and cultures around the world. I believe such experiences can foster resilience, tolerance, and worldliness (Ender, 1996), characteristics essential for successful living in an increasingly diverse and global social and economic society. These experiences can also contribute to feelings of rootlessness (Cottrell & Useem, 1994). Some of the adults in this study recognize the positive and negative attributes associated with their early life experiences. The paradox is the social and psychological weight associated with geographic mobility juxtaposed with the awesome experiences gained once they have moved to and experienced a new and diverse place and culture. The approach to success appears to be reconciling the two organization lifestyle demands of moving and living.

Geographic mobility and foreign residence are likely to increase for Americans in the future as occupations become more fluid and economies become more international. Information technology and modern transportation have bridged the distance between American and foreign cultures. At the same time, separation may become more prevalent for future generations of adult children from military and other organization families. The demands of service life will not disappear; rather the intensity of the demands will simply shift.

## REFERENCES

Allingham, G. E. (1998). *Growing up in khaki: Life as a service brat.* Research Triangle, NC: Research Triangle Publications.

Ang, A. (1996, December 3). A magazine for nomadic military brats. *San Francisco Chronicle*, p. A9.

Army Times Publishing. (1997). Military brats. http://www.armytimes.com/bratpg.html.

Bell, L. (1997). *Hidden immigrants: Legacies of growing up abroad.* Notre Dame, IN: Cross Cultural Publications.

Carlsmith, L. (1964). Effect of early father absence on scholastic aptitude. *Harvard Educational Review, 34*(1), 3–21.

Conroy, P. (1976). *The great Santini.* Boston, MA: Houghton-Mifflin.

Cottrell, A. B., & Useem, R. H. (1994, March). ATCKs maintain global dimensions throughout their lives. *Newslinks: The Newspaper of International Schools Services,* pp. 1, 14, and 30.

*Defense Almanac.* (1990). Defense 90. Alexandria, VA: Armed Forces Information Services.

Ender, M. G. (1996). Recognizing healthy conflict: The postmodern self. *Global Nomad Perspectives Newsletter, 4*(1), 13–14.

Gerner, M., Perry, F., Moselle, M. A., & Archbold, M. (1992). Characteristics of internationally mobile adolescents. *Journal of School Psychology, 30*(2), 197–214.

Grubbs, J. (1987). *APO San Francisco 96525: Growing up in the military.* Springfield, IL: Independent Publishing.

Hill, R. (1949). *Families under stress: Adjustment to the crises of war separation and reunion.* New York: Harper & Row (reprinted by Greenwood Press, Westport, CT, 1971).

Hunter, E. J. (1982). *Families under the flag: A review of military family literature.* New York: Praeger.

Hunter, E. J., & Nice, D. S. (Eds.). (1978). *Children of military families: A part yet apart.* Washington, DC: Superintendent of Documents, U.S. Government Printing Office.

Jensen, P. S, & Shaw, J. A. (1996). The effects of war and parental deployment upon children and adolescents. In R. J. Ursano & A. E. Norwood (Eds.), *Emotional aftermath of the Persian Gulf War: Veterans, families, communities, and nations* (pp. 83–109). Washington, DC: American Psychiatric Press, Inc.

Long, P. (1986, December). Growing up military. *Psychology Today,* 31-37.

McCluskey, K. C. (Ed.). (1994). *Notes from a traveling childhood: Readings for internationally mobile parents and children.* Washington, DC: Foreign Service Youth Foundation Publication.

Rainey, M. C. (1978). Language learnings of internationally mobile military youth: Some third culture comparisons. In E. J. Hunter & D. S. Nice (Eds.), *Children of military families: A part yet apart* (pp. 83-100). Washington, DC: Superintendent of Documents, U.S. Government Printing Office.

Salmon, J. L. (1988). *The relationship of stress and mobility to the psychosocial development and well being of third-culture-reared early adults*. Unpublished doctoral dissertation, University of Florida, Tallahassee.

Segal, M. W. (1989). The nature of work and family linkages: A theoretical perspective. In G. L. Bowen & D. K. Orthner (Eds.), *The organization family: Work and family in the U.S. military* (pp. 3–36). New York: Praeger.

Smith, C. D. (1994). *The absentee American: Repatriates' perspectives on America and its place in the contemporary world*. Bayside, NY: Aletheia Publications.

Smith, C. D. (Ed.). (1996). *Strangers at home: Essays on the effects of living overseas and coming "home" to a strange land*. Bayside, NY: Aletheia Publications.

Smith, W. J. (1980). *Army brat: A memoir*. New York: Persea Books.

Steinglass, P., & Edwards, M. E. (1993). *Family relocation study, final report*. A report by the Ackerman Institute for Family Therapy for the Family Liaison Office. New York: United States Department of State.

Truscott, M. R. (1989). *Brats: Children of the military speak out*. New York: E. P. Dutton.

Tyler, M. P. (1990). American teenagers abroad: A view from one military community. *SOWI Socialwissenschaftliches Institute der Bundeswehr* Forum, IX, 13–17.

Wertsch, M. E. (1991). *Military brats: Legacies of childhood inside the fortress*. NewYork: Harmony Books.

**APPENDIX 16.1: Available Resources (Websites and Email Addresses are Accurate as of 1999)**

**On-line Organizations:**

*THE AMERICAN OVERSEAS SCHOOLS HISTORICAL SOCIETY* Homepage
> Webpage: http://www.cpcug.org/user/cwoodell/aosa.html
> Contact: Thomas T. Drysdale, Ed.D., President overseasschools@juno.com

*AMERICAN WORLD WAR II ORPHANS NETWORK*
> Contact: Annie Bennett Mix anniemix@aol.com

*CANADIAN AIR FORCE BRATS ASSOCIATION* Homepage
> Webpage: http://www.logicnet.com/alan.macleod/air.htm
> Contact: Alan McLeod alan.mcleod@bbs.logicnet.com

*CANADIAN FORCES BRATS* Homepage
> Webpage: http://fn2.freenet.edmonton.ab.ca/~cfbrat/cfbrat.html
> Contact: Taunja cfbrats@freenet.edmonton.ab.ca

*THE CANADIAN MILITARY BRAT LIST* Homepage
> Webpage: http://www.milbrats.net/
> Contact: Susan Minaker minaker@zoology.ubc.ca

*EXPAT FORUM*
> Homepage: http://www.expatforum.com
> Contact: webwiz@expatforum.com

*GLOBAL NOMADS INTERNATIONAL*
> Homepage: http://globalnomads.association.com
> Contact: info@gni.org

*MILITARY BRATS On-line*
> Homepage: http://www.lynxu.com/brats/index.html#top
> Contact and Page Owner: Vann Baker VannB@aol.com

*MILITARY BRATS Registry* Homepage
> Webpage: http://www.military-brats.com/
> Contact: Mike B. Adams usbrats@aol.com

*OPERATION FOOTLOCKER*
> Webpage: http://www.tckworld.com/opfoot/index.html
> Contact: Gene Moser opfoot@tckworld.com

*UNIVERSITY OF MARYLAND MUNICH GERMANY ALUMNI*
> Webpage: http://cpcug.org:80/user/cwoodell/
> Contact: Carlton Woodell cwoodell@cpcug.org

**USENET NEWS GROUPS**

> alt.culture.military-brats
> can.military-brats

**ELECTRONIC DISCUSSION LISTS**

*MILITARY BRATS DISCUSSION LIST* M-BRATS@LISTSERV.IUPUI.EDU
> Contact: Ann Holcombe aholcomb@indyunix.iupui.edu

# Chapter 17

# Afterword: The Changing Nature of Military Service and Military Family Life

*James A. Martin*

## INTRODUCTION

This final chapter highlights the changing nature of military service and military family life at the start of the twenty-first century. It discusses changes in military duties and careers, trends in family-related military quality of life entitlements, and the evolution of the concept of the military community. The chapter highlights advances in information technologies and discusses the application of these technologies in the delivery of human services for military members and their families. Finally, it encourages civilian human service providers to become part of a military-civilian partnership capable of supporting and sustaining the well-being of current and future military families.

The 25 years of the All-Volunteer Force have been a period of profound change for the U.S. military. Our military's combat success against Iraqi forces in the 1990-1991 Persian Gulf War is a tribute to a prolonged investment in high-technology weapons and the corresponding development of a well-trained and well led all-volunteer military.

In the 1990s, U.S. military forces demonstrated their capabilities in a variety of peacekeeping and peacemaking operations, and in support of numerous humanitarian missions around the globe. As evidenced by America's continued presence in Southwest Asia, a prolonged peacekeeping role in Bosnia, extensive humanitarian efforts in hurricane-torn Central America, and, most recently, air-combat operations in the Balkans, the trend in American foreign policy is for a greater, not lesser use of military forces. It is too soon to know if this trend will continue in the post-Clinton era. Regardless of which political party occupies the White House in the first decade of the twenty-first century, it is difficult to imagine that the United States will back away from its current role as the world's dominant democracy or its involvement in global humanitarian missions and other military actions intended to promote and sustain peace.

During this last decade of the twentieth century there have been moments of great military pride for Americans. For example, the homecoming parades that followed the Persian Gulf War and the military relief efforts after the 1999 hurricane and floods in Central America represent important moments of national pride in our armed forces. During the same timeframe there have also been moments of profound sadness and frustration as seen in the memorial services for the soldiers who were killed and whose bodies were desecrated during peacemaking operations in Somalia. Today, as this chapter is being written, Southwest Asia and the Balkans no longer provide daily front-page news, but American-led NATO military forces continue their dangerous activities in both locations. For military planners in the Pentagon these represent two more locations in a seemingly ever-expanding and never-ending list of military personnel and monetary requirements.

## A PERIOD OF PROFOUND CHANGE

This past decade represented a turning point in the size, composition, stationing, and deployment of U.S. military forces. The long feared "Armageddon" on the plains of western Europe evaporated with the collapse of the Soviet Union and the democratization of Eastern Europe. These events precipitated a profound change for our nation's military. Congress approved numerous base closures and force realignments at home and abroad, substantially reducing the number of military personnel and families stationed in Europe (and to some extent in Asia). At the end of the 1990s, the president recommended and Congress authorized the smallest armed forces since the adoption of the All-Volunteer Force concept. Many now wonder if this force is sufficient to carry out our world-wide military commitments.

### The Development of a Twenty-First Century Force

Today, the military services are undertaking efforts to develop a twenty-first century military capable of rapidly executing a broad range of missions around the globe. The vision of this twenty-first century military represents a relatively small force, a force whose success will be heavily reliant on advanced technology weapon systems. As currently envisioned, this military force will be primarily based in the United States, but it will maintain a high level of activity and operational responsibility around the globe (National Research Council, 1997). This force will rely heavily on the availability of a reserve component capable of a more involved and active operational role than at any previous period of our nation's history. Building this *total force* and ensuring the recruitment and retention of the required personnel presents a considerable challenge. Funding the required advanced technology research and the subsequent military procurement required to make this defense strategy work as intended may be an even greater challenge. Future military readiness will require the successful accomplishment of these recruitment and retention goals, and success in developing and procuring these new technologies.

Since the Persian Gulf War, each branch of the military has made substantial movement toward this smaller force and begun an investment in these future warfighting technologies. There are now fewer Army divisions, Air Force squadrons, and Navy ships and submarines, and overall substantially fewer soldiers, sailors, airmen, and Marines than at any time since the inception of the All-Volunteer Force concept. In addition to fewer units and people, a substantial part of the defense budget is now programmed for what is referred to as "modernization." While our current generation of advanced technology weapon systems may have been successful in the Balkans (a topic of considerable debate and disagreement among military leaders and defense consultants), most of our premier weapons systems are actually the products of the 1980s or earlier. Continual, often heavy use of these weapon systems in the 1990s has taken its toll. The demands made upon our military since the Persian Gulf War have seriously strained both people and equipment. Important questions about the well-being and continued capabilities of our armed forces are being raised within and outside of the Pentagon. These are issues and corresponding debates that will continue to dominate defense planning well into the first decade of this new century.

Despite profound changes in the size, composition, and stationing of our forces, many military experts believe that we actually posses too much military base infrastructure (Defense Science Board, 1996). As the United States enters the 21st-century more changes are likely to occur, including additional base closures and subsequent realignments of operational units to new locations within the United States. In the context of this movement, it is likely that we will continue to see the increased stationing of combat forces at major bases (megabases) on the East Coast, West Coast, and in a few southern states.

### Quality of Life in this Future Force

In this future military, members and their families will mark their service and careers not by the number of times they relocate, but rather by the amount of time the military member is deployed away from home and loved ones. The Air Force has aptly coined the term "An Expeditionary Air Force" as a descriptor of this twenty-first century military organization and its lifestyle. More permanent stationing may have some positive effects for families, spouses with careers, children keeping friends and having more continuity in school, and so on. Since the majority of these families will actually live in the civilian communities surrounding these installations, families may become more integrated into these local communities, putting down some roots and possibly making contributions not just as temporary residents but as citizens. To quote Dr. Jesse Harris, dean of the School of Social Work at the University of Maryland and a retired Army officer, "During my military career I often found myself planting annuals while my civilian neighbors were planting trees" (Harris, 1999). In the future, military families will have more opportunity to "plant trees."

The costs associated with the development and procurement of 21st-century military technologies are enormous. The personnel costs, including recruitment, pay and allowances, and retirement, will continue to pose serious challenges to military recruitment and retention goals. Faced with these economic realities, some senior advisors believe that these costs are unaffordable unless there are dramatic changes in the way the military services are structured and operated. Among the recommendations that are already being implemented are fundamental changes that impact directly on the nature of military life and careers (National Research Council, 1997). These changes include extensive privatization of programs and support services in military communities. They include important changes in the nature and delivery of health care, military housing, and retirement services as well as other aspects of military quality of life (Haskett, 1997).

## CHALLENGES IN BUILDING AND SUSTAINING THIS FORCE

### Recruitment

Military leaders recognize the severe challenge that they face in recruiting and retaining quality personnel for this evolving 21st-century force. Presently, recruitment is on the verge of becoming a national crisis (Moskos, 1999), and there are indications that this problem will get worse in the immediate future (Graham, 1999). The military services are competing with a prolonged healthy national economy and civilian employers who are aggressively seeking the same scarce human capital. Today, a record number of youths are entering college. In addition, there is diminished public support for military service as a useful transition into adulthood and a general lack of interest among eligible youths for the perceived rigors and demands associated with a military lifestyle. Military interventions in the 1990s, including the war in Southwest Asia and the conflict in the Balkans, have not stirred large numbers of young adults to volunteer for military service. Middle class and more affluent families are not encouraging their sons and daughters to volunteer for what might be described as "society's dirty work" (Hughes, 1971). Based on these factors, military leaders realize that the pool of technically qualified personnel available for military service is very small (Maze, 1999) and increasingly represents a rapidly growing population of ethnic minorities and young women interested the training and work experience opportunities offered by the military.

### Retention

Retention in a booming economy is a problem that will likely continue throughout this next decade, and current efforts to increase military pay are not likely to solve this problem (Ballard, 1999). For those with certain skills, such as pilots, the frequency of deployments that have marked the last half of the

1990s and the corresponding time spent away from home are noted as primary reasons for leaving military service (Maze, 1999). The reality of today's service life, especially the frequency of overseas deployment in response to crisis events and a seemingly never ending array of peacekeeping and peacemaking roles, has placed an enormous strain on all military members and their families (Bogdanowicz, 1996). For many, this is not the lifestyle they envisioned and signed on for and they are electing to leave for what they believe are numerous, well-paying, and more satisfying opportunities in the civilian sector (Matthews, 1999).

While time spent away from home is seen as the major stressor associated with military service, promotion opportunities, compensation, benefits, and entitlements are still recognized as important in the overall decision to stay or leave the service. Increasingly, military members (and their spouses) are making comparisons with the quality of life perceived to be available in the civilian society. Industry and business are aggressively seeking new employees with technological aptitudes and skills. These civilian employers recognize that the attitudes and personal qualities that are associated with good military performance are the same attitudes and qualities that they desire in their employees. Today, military members represent an important recruitment pool for business and industry.

## Meeting the Needs of Junior Enlisted Members and Their Families

The current debate over military compensation, as highlighted in a *Washington Post* editorial (1999), is focused on pay and retirement compensation, with somewhat limited discussion of other benefits such as housing and medical care. While officers and senior enlisted service members will see future increases in their income, it is unlikely that the most junior enlisted members will see their compensation advance much above a level associated with what is still considered by most economists and social scientists as low income employment. This level of compensation may be adequate for the young, single service member who is receiving free housing (albeit a shared barracks room) but for the married junior-enlisted member, it represents an income level often associated with economic distress. These married junior-enlisted service members often struggle to maintain a family in a situation where it is typically impossible to supplement one's income with a second job (either the regulations prohibit it or the reality of one's duty schedule makes a second job impossible). In addition, for these families spouse employment maybe difficult to obtain or prohibited by a lack of affordable childcare or the absence of adequate transportation to and from work. These factors, often combined with limited money management skills and the early assumption of parenthood responsibilities, increase the likelihood of economic distress among these junior enlisted military families.

### Other Compensation Considerations

As an increasing menu of employment compensation options become the standard in the civilian sector, military members maybe given some of the same opportunities.  For example, military members may find it possible to buy into selected personnel benefits packages.  This could include some form of a retirement savings account.  Even in this era of benefit choices, it can be expected that there will be considerable fiscal and political constraints on what are now often thought of as "entitlements of military service."  If current trends continue, military families will actually experience less, not more, in actual employment benefits.  Many programs and services that have traditionally been available in the military community, often at no or little direct cost to the service member and family, will no longer be subsidized by the military.  More and more, military families will encounter some form of "cost-sharing" in the provision of a broad range of community and other human services.  The demise of the traditional Officers' and Noncommissioned Officers' Clubs are examples of this trend that actually started a number of years ago.  Where programs and services continue to exist, facilities like fitness and recreation centers or health promotion programs, these services will often be provided via contractual arrangements with the private sector and users of these services and facilities will bare a substantial share of the cost.  At smaller installations, military families may have to rely totally on the local civilian community for many of these services and fully contribute to the user costs.

## MEETING MILITARY FAMILY HUMAN SERVICE NEEDS
## IN A TWENTY-FIRST CENTURY MILITARY

In the future, military families will increasingly encounter an institutional philosophy that focuses on prevention, self-help, and personal accountability across all aspects of personal and family life.  Dependency is a quality that will be actively discouraged in the 21st-century military community.  In this regard, emerging technologies will become an increasingly important part of how military families meet the challenges of military life.  These technologies are rapidly evolving and producing a "virtual military community."  In the future, military installations and the civilian community will increasingly blend together.  At smaller installations, especially installations dominated by logistical and personnel functions, the military facility will often be physically within the civilian community—businesses operating "within the gates."  They will cater to military requirements and military family service requirements and private sector contractors.  They will operate under a variety of arrangements and provide many (if not most) human services for military members and their families.

Many human services in this future virtual military community will be "electronically" based—an extension and evolution of what is currently called

Internet-based services. The area that we refer to as the informal military support system—families helping other families (the heart of the future "military community")—will require developing and maintaining "connections" among members and member families based on social-psychological interactions in an electronic universe rather than a physical community.

This vision raises concerns about the apparent isolation of the family in modern society. Even military communities are not exceptions. Homes are typically self-contained, people do not sit on their screened front porches anymore—in fact most new houses, and even townhouses, do not have functional porches or front stoops. Individuals in single family homes and townhouses spend their outdoor time in fenced-in backyard patios or on decks attached to the home's kitchen area, in many cases these spaces are physically and even visually separated from neighbors. Interestingly, those families living in apartment buildings that have common recreational areas, meeting areas, laundry, and play areas for young children, may be at an advantage in having more frequent opportunity to encounter their neighbors and establish social relationships.

While computers can connect people who are separated from one another geographically, some worry that computers are becoming a substitute for face-to-face interaction and relationships. This computer-based technology is here and it is a reality that will not go away—even in military communities. The challenge for the military is achieving universal access and developing and supporting its appropriate use.

## LIFELines: TWENTY-FIRST CENTURY INFORMATION TECHNOLOGY

Recently, the Navy took a major leap into this futuristic world with an Internet-based human service delivery system called LIFELines. The development of LIFELines highlights how the advances in information technology will benefit military members and their families in this next decade. The Navy has established a vision and method for electronically linking individuals with a collection of broadly defined quality-of-life services and programs. The LIFELines initiative provides an opening into an incredible array of information technologies now emerging in both the military and civilian sectors.

LIFELines was first envisioned as a joint partnership among the different service branches designed to deliver quality of life (QOL) services and programs to military members and their families using the Internet, teleconferencing, satellite broadcasting and cable TV. Today civilian partner organizations are adding their talents, information, and resources to help create a "High Tech – High Touch" system of care for military members and their families. Currently, this new human services delivery system supplements, but does not replace, the traditional QOL military community–based service delivery system. Like the current shift from wall-mounted phones to hand-held portable phones, and now to cell-phones, future human service programs will become heavily invested in this method of delivering services.

LIFELines represents a potential comprehensive QOL human service delivery system. It currently consists of two major components. The LIFELines Internet component is called the "Virtual QOL Mall." Individuals can "shop" at the mall to meet many of their QOL needs (e.g., find housing, register for school or a course, schedule and receive various counseling services, take a training course, go to the library, learn about the military lifestyle, get a loan, gain information about medical care, find out about job opportunities, buy uniforms, and much, much more). There is something at the QOL Mall for everyone—singles, families, active duty, reservists, retirees, civilian personnel, recruiters, even those at sea and in isolated, remote duty locations. Currently developed features of the QOL Mall include: adult education and distance learning; hosted chat rooms with QOL experts; hotlines; helplines; a QOL multimedia center and library; and electronic links to a variety of other community resources.

LIFELines is designed to overcome many traditional barriers to QOL service delivery in the military, issues such as transportation, childcare, geography, stigma of help seeking, privacy concerns, and work schedules. It meets the needs of service members and families in remote or isolated overseas areas as well as at sea. It even provides a central electronic gathering place for military members and their families.

The LIFELines broadcast component is called the "LIFELines QOL Network." It delivers QOL services and programs using real time, interactive teleconferencing, satellite broadcasting, and cable TV. In order to form this worldwide network, partner organizations have linked their broadcast facilities and equipment to make QOL programming more accessible at sea, ashore, and most important, in remote and isolated communities within and outside of the United States. Through this network, QOL programs and direct services will be available to the total force, in their homes, their workplaces, and a full range of community locations. Key features of the LIFELines QOL Broadcast Network include: desktop telecounseling and conferences; QOL teletraining broadcasts; electronic "home visits" for new parents; access to hard copies of video; CD-ROMs; QOL audio and video clips; electronic peer support groups; and satellite/teleconference academic skills and degree programs.

Electronic villages and new community support frameworks are emerging across the nation. LIFELines is one part of this evolving process. Within the military services, LIFELines is transforming current QOL programs into a multimedia service delivery system capable of reaching and supporting individuals in their homes, workplaces, and communities. It is impacting all age groups, from very young children in preschool settings to senior citizens living in retirement communities and even nursing care facilities. These programs provided an opportunity for human service linkages essentially free from the constraints of time and space. The primary drawback today is ease of access. As sources of electronic access expand for military members and their families, LIFELines will become this population's primary point of access to a broad range of QOL services. It is envisioned that human service providers in military, public, and private sector agencies, as well as individual civilian practitioners, will be important contributors to the services offered via these electronic links to military members and their families. The potential is virtually unlimited and human service agencies and providers need to be prepared to enter this electronic community. Likewise, the DOD and the various military services need to recognize the potential of these electronic resources and facilitate service member and family access to the Internet.

## SUPPORT AND SERVICES FROM THE CIVILIAN COMMUNITY

Much has been made of our society's apparent loss of connection and corresponding identification with the military (Califano, 1999). President Clinton's lack of military service, the rapidly diminishing presence of military service experience among members of Congress, and the obvious lack of societal representation in the current all- Volunteer Force speak to this concern. It is a mistake to believe that the burdens of military service were ever equally shared across all segments of our society. At the same time, our modern history has, until very recently, been one where most American's did in fact know someone, a father or mother, an uncle or aunt, a brother or sister, a cousin, or even just a friend, who wore the uniform.

As the Persian Gulf War parades demonstrated, there is still a sense of pride in our nation for the military. Individuals like General Colin Powell, former prisoners of war like Senator John McCain, the names listed on all the war memorials, and, for a few of us, the names of heroes etched in our hearts represent the best of our nation. Yet, this sense of connection to the military and its members is rapidly diminishing. Even the recent series of base closures and reduction in the size of the military has had the unintended effect of diminishing the public's connection to the military. As simple as it may be, military units are no longer available in many locations to participate in local holiday parades. Military bands are not as available for local celebrations, and military honor guards are not present at the funerals of many of our deceased combat veterans. These historical linkages between the general public and the military have been greatly diminished in this decade, and in some parts of our country, they cease to exist. It may be that the challenge for sustaining military quality of life rests in how we address this issue—the nature of the connection between the military and the nation it represents and defends—in simpler terms, how we avoid hiring "someone (else) to do our dirty work." Without this sense of connection, it is unlikely that military members and their families will receive the quality of life they need and deserve.

## SUMMARY AND CONCLUSION

As a recent National Research Council report (1997) suggests, a major task confronting the Navy Department (and all the other services) is the establishment of a duty, career, and personal life environment that increases retention, enhances readiness, and promotes performance. This chapter has highlighted many of the problems confronting the Department of Defense and the individual service branches in developing this environment. A Marine Corps quality-of-life study (Kerce, 1995) provides evidence of the causal relationship between military quality of life and behavioral outcomes, including readiness, reenlistment intentions, and military performance. These results support what military leaders have long believed, that quality of life investments have an important payoff in desired military outcomes (Defense Science Board, 1995). Positive perceptions of military life are critical in attracting and retaining qualified personnel, and quality-of-life factors in duty-related life domains have an important impact on morale and performance.

The changes in military service and service life described in this chapter represent trends that have emerged in the 1990s and are likely continue into the twenty-first century. They include: additional personnel reductions; greater reliance on reserve components to meet military requirements; substantial base realignments and closures; greater racial, ethnic, and gender diversity among recruits; an increasing proportion of military families residing in the civilian community; and radical shifts in the military's human service delivery system, including civilianizing, outsourcing, privatization of human services and various community functions (Defense Science Board, 1996) and the development of new Internet technologies designed to enhance the nature and accessibility of human services.

These actions will produce substantial change in the nature of military life and careers. They require a new conceptualization of what we mean by the concept "military community." The military "camp, post, station" that evolved after the World War II into the "military company town" of the 1970s and 1980s (Martin & Orthner, 1989), must take on a new form and new functions. It is apparent that there must be closer linkages between the military and civilian sector in order to meet the human service needs of military families.

Increasingly, civilian human service providers who live and practice in areas with military installations will find themselves involved with military families. Civilian human service providers who wish to engage these families will need to understand the unique nature and needs of the military family, and a corresponding appreciation of their military lifestyle. It is imperative for successful interventions with military members and their families that civilian human service providers enthusiastically engage local military unit and military community leaders. Even human service providers living in areas without large military bases will occasionally encounter the military spouse who has returned home to wait out a deployment with parents, or the military member and family serving in a recruiting assignment in the civilian community far from any military base. Families of reserve and national guard members are likely to increasingly surface in the human service providers caseload as these families experience the stressful consequences of the Department of Defense's increasing reliance on the reserves in support of many world-wide missions.

**Table 17.1**

**Assumptions about the Armed Forces in the 21st Century**

| |
|---|
| **The People:** |
| • Smaller percentage of "first-term" members, larger percentage in the 5 to 10 year cohort, more members staying 25 to 30 years. |
| • Better educated, older, more married force, more "community college-level" first-term service members. |
| • Whites no longer represent a majority of the force; Hispanics replace blacks as the largest minority group. |
| • A higher percentage of women enter and remain in the force. |
| • More senior and mid-level leaders are women and minority group members. |
| |
| **Their Duties:** |
| • A focus on combat roles—the private sector provides most support services, even in the operational environment. |
| • A focus on being "trained and ready" for a much wider array of missions. |
| • Fewer large-scale deployments of combat forces, more use of military technical expertise and resources for multinational and/or United Nations interventions. |
| • Individual training and small unit training "at home" in a simulated environment. |
| • Providing predictable personal/family time is a critical leadership challenge. |
| |
| **Their Careers:** |
| • Continued reduction in the number of personnel based overseas, and more reliance on rotation of forces to meet overseas commitments. As a consequence, fewer requirements for overseas tours and family relocation over a career. |
| • Use of home station internet-based education reduces relocation requirements. |
| • Use of partial and deferred retirement benefits encourage 10 to 15 year careers. |
| • More non-commissioned officers serving greater than 20 years. |
| • More economic incentives for personnel to complete 30 years of service. |
| |
| **Their Entitlements:** *21ˢᵗ-Century Welfare Capitalism* |
| • Rank continues to have its privileges—but more equality in non-pay benefits. |
| • Fewer entitlements and more opportunity for benefit selection. |
| • Increased use of civilian for-profit quality-of-life programs and services with required "co-payment." |
| • An increased focus on prevention, self-help, and personal accountability. |
| |
| **Their "Community":** *A Virtual Military Community* |
| • A few "megabases" representing the traditional concept of a military community. |
| • Most small installations more like a high technology, light industrial subdivision. |
| • In many cases these installation and the civilian community blend together. Some freestanding military facilities will be in the civilian community. |
| • Many (if not most) quality of life services will be provided within the private sector in a variety of fee-for-service reimbursement arrangements. |
| • Tomorrow's "military community" will require new models for developing and sustaining connections among members and member families—a social-psychological rather than a physical community—a virtual military community with increased reliance on electronic communication technologies. |

Table 17.1 provides a number of characteristics envisioned for the 21st century military. It offers the civilian human service provider a place to begin understanding the nature of the military, its families, the lifestyle, and stresses inherent in military service. Hopefully, human service providers will be encouraged to reach out and connect with military families in their community.

Enhanced quality of life for military families will require wider institutional encouragement and support. Innovative programs like LIFELines, which helps to build and to foster commitment and community among military families, should be encouraged. While necessary, these initiatives alone are not sufficient to sustain a competent and capable military force in the 21st century. The level of institutional concern required must be equal to the degree of commitment and sacrifice that the military demands of its members and member families. Anything less is a prescription for military failure and a betrayal of those who have previously served and sacrificed as military members.

# REFERENCES

Ballard, R. (1999, April 5). Pay gap between soldiers and citizens must be closed. *Army Times*, p. 54.

Bogdanowicz, R. (1996). *PERSTEMPO: A non-classified briefing prepared by the Joint Staff.* Washington, DC: The Department of Defense, Office of the Joint Chiefs of Staff.

Califano, J. A., Jr. (1999, April 6). When there's no draft. *The Washington Post*, p. A23.

Defense Science Board. (1995). *Task force on quality of life.* Washington, DC: Office of the Under Secretary of Defense for Acquisition and Technology, The Pentagon.

Defense Science Board, U.S. Department of Defense. (1996). *Achieving an innovative support structure for 21st century military superiority: Higher performance at lower costs.* Washington, DC: Office of the Under Secretary of Defense for Acquisition and Technology, The Pentagon.

Editorial. (1999, March 12). A wrong defense decision. *The Washington Post*, A32.

Harris, J. (1999). Personal communication.

Haskett, G. (1997). Privatization: Let the buyer be aware. *Military Family Issues: The Research Digest*, 2(1), 1–7.

Hughes, E.C., 1971. *The Sociological Eye.* Chicago: Aldine & Atherton.

Kerce, E. W. (1995). *Quality of life in the U.S. Marine Corps* (Report No. NPRDC TR-94). San Diego, CA: Navy Personnel Research and Development Center.

Martin, J. A., & Orthner, D. K. (1989). The "company town" in transition: Rebuilding military communities. In G. L. Bowen & D. K. Orthner (Eds.), *The organization family: Work and family linkages in the U.S. military* (pp. 163–177). New York: Praeger.

Matthews, W. (1999, April 5). Officials asked to consider shorter enlistments. *Army Times*, p. 8.

Maze, R. (1999, March 8). Painting a bleak picture of military life. *Army Times*, p. 12.

Maze, R. (1999, March 15). Recruiters lament: "It's the economy." *Army Times*, p. 11.

Military Family Resource Center. (1998). *Profile of the military community: 1997 demographics.* Arlington, VA: Military Family Resource Center.

Moskos, C. (1999, March 8). Short-term soldiers. *The Washington Post*, p. A19.

National Research Council. (1997). *Technology for future naval forces: The United States Navy and Marine Corps, 2000-2035 becoming a 21st century force*, Volume Number 4: Human resources. Washington, DC: National Academy Press.

# Index

# About the Contributors

JAMES A. MARTIN, Ph.D., B.C.D., is an associate professor of Social Work and Social Research at Bryn Mawr College, Bryn Mawr, Pennsylvania. Dr. Martin is a licensed clinical social worker with extensive background in behavioral science research. A retired colonel in the Army Medical Department, Dr. Martin's military career includes a variety of clinical, research, and policy assignments. Dr. Martin is the senior editor of *The Gulf War and Mental Health: A Comprehensive Guide* published in 1996 by Praeger. He was the creator and first editor of *Military Family Issues: The Research Digest*, a publication of the Military Family Institute of Marywood University. Dr. Martin has served on a number of Department of Defense study groups and was a member of the National Research Council panel that examined quality-of-life issues for the Navy and Marine Corps in the 21st century. His research and scholarly interests focus on stress and social support issues, quality of life, and work–family life adaptation.

LEORA N. ROSEN, Ph.D., is senior research scientist at the Department of Justice. Previously she served as a Research psychologist at the Division of Neuropsychiatry of the Walter Reed Army Institute of Research, Washington, D.C. Dr. Rosen was born and raised in South Africa, and immigrated to the United States in 1976. She completed her doctoral studies in Social Anthropology at Witwatersrand University and a subsequent Masters in Public Health Degree at Columbia University, specializing in psychiatric epidemiology. Dr. Rosen joined the Walter Reed Army Institute of Research as a social science analyst, and has worked in this capacity for the past 12 years. Her main areas of interest have involved the military family and women in the military. Dr. Rosen has co-authored a book on child sexual abuse in the civilian world based on her volunteer experience as a child advocate.

LINETTE R. SPARACINO, M.A., is a medical editor for the Textbook of Military Medicine Series being produced by the Borden Institute, a special project of the Office of the Surgeon General of the Army, Washington, D.C. Ms. Sparacino was one of the editors for *Military Psychiatry: Preparing in Peace for War* and *War Psychiatry*. She was a co-editor for *The Gulf War and Mental Health: A Comprehensive Guide*.

D. BRUCE BELL, Ph.D., is a social scientist in the Organization and Personnel Resource Research Unit of the U.S. Army Research Institute for the Behavioral and Social Sciences (ARI), Alexandria, Virginia. Dr. Bell has planned and carried out research on the adaptation of Army families to the stresses of the Operation Joint Endeavor in Bosnia, Operation Restore Hope in Somalia, and the Gulf War. His recent summary report, "How to Support Families during Overseas Deployments: A Sourcebook for Service Providers," is in wide use throughout the Department of Defense. Dr. Bell holds a B.A. and M.A. in psychology from the University of Texas at Austin and a Ph.D. in counseling psychology from Texas Tech University in Lubbock, Texas.

LEASLEY BESETSNY, M.A., is the research and data program manager for the Air Force Family Advocacy Program. He is actively engaged in child and spouse maltreatment and prevention research and program evaluation projects for the Air Force. He is also responsible for the automation of all data collection activities for maltreatment and prevention projects Air Force wide.

GARY L. BOWEN, Ph.D., A.C.S.W., is the Kenan Distinguished Professor in the School of Social Work at the University of North Carolina at Chapel Hill. He holds a joint appointment in the Department of Communication Studies. Dr. Bowen received his Ph.D. in Child Development and Family Relations in 1981 from the University of North Carolina at Greensboro; he received his M.S.W. in 1976 from the University of North Carolina at Chapel Hill. Dr. Bowen is co-author of the *Families-in-Blue* series that led to the development of Family Support Centers in the U.S. Air Force. Dr. Bowen is serving presently as consultant to the Family Advocacy Division, Office of the Surgeon General, United States Air Force. He is author of *Navigating the Marital Journey* (1991), co-editor of *The Work and Family Interface: Toward a Contextual Effects Perspective* (1995) with Dr. Joe F. Pittman, and co-editor of *The Organization Family: Work and Family Linkages in the U.S. Military* (1989) with Dr. Dennis K. Orthner.

STEPHEN J. BRANNEN, Ph.D., LTC, U.S. Army, is an assistant professor and director of research at the Department of Family Medicine, Uniformed Services University of the Health Sciences, Bethesda, Maryland. Dr. Brannen is a social work officer with more than 17 years of professional experience in a range of Army health and mental health settings. Dr. Brannen received a B.A. degree in social work from the University of Nebraska, Lincoln, an M.S.W.

from the University of Nebraska at Omaha, and a Ph.D. from the University of Texas. Dr. Brannen's major research interest is in the area of evaluation research, specifically family violence.

ALBERT L. BREWSTER, Lt. Col., U.S. Air Force, is a board certified clinical social worker. Currently he serves as Chief of Behavioral Medicine/Research in the Department of Family Practice at Andrews Air Force Base, and as assistant professor in the Uniformed Services University School of Medicine. His earlier experiences include being a Marine Corps rifleman in Vietnam; Child Protective Services casework aide; Family Advocacy Officer at both Eglin and Seymour Johnson Air Force Base; Chief of Mental Health and Director of Research—Headquarters Air Force Family Advocacy.

LEA M. DOUGHERTY, M.S.W., L.S.W., is a Pro Rate faculty member at Marywood University, School of Social Work, and is pursuing her Ph.D. in social work at Bryn Mawr College Graduate School of Social Work and Social Research. Ms. Dougherty is a licensed clinical social worker in Pennsylvania. She received both her B.S.W. and M.S.W. from Marywood College. Prior to her current teaching position, she served as research associate at the Military Family Institute, Marywood University, for four years. During that time she participated in and helped author two major Department of Defense supported technical reports: Health and Nutrition of Children in Military Families and Military Adolescent Study. She is author of a number of related journal articles now under development.

DORIS B. DURAND, Ph.D., is a senior research associate at the Henry M. Jackson Foundation for the Advancement of Military Medicine in Rockville, Maryland. Dr. Durand has a long history of involvement in military service and military family research. Her recent accomplishments include two major studies: "An Assessment of Burnout among Army Volunteers and Its Implications for Soldier and Family Readiness and Quality of Life" and "Assessment of the Impact of Pre-military and Military Trauma on the Physical and Psychological Well Being of Female Active Duty Soldiers."

MORTEN G. ENDER, Ph.D., is an assistant professor of Sociology in the Department of Behavioral Sciences and Leadership at the United States Military Academy, West Point, New York. Dr. Ender obtained both his master's degree (1991) and doctoral degree (1996) in sociology from the University of Maryland at College Park. His many research interests include family studies, military sociology, and applications of new communication media to a range of social science issues.

ELWOOD R. (Woody) HAMLIN II, D.S.W., is an associate professor at Florida Atlantic University. Dr. Hamlin is a retired colonel in the U.S. Army. He is a graduate of the University of Illinois (M.S.W.) and Catholic University of

America (D.S.W.). During his military career, he served as a clinician, supervisor, educator, program manager, consultant, and administrator of social work and behavior science programs. His areas of interest include social work practice activities in family and child welfare.

DOROTHY J. JEFFREYS, Ph.D., is a Professor at the School of Social Work, Marywood University, Scranton, Pennsylvania. Dr. Jeffreys served as the principal investigator of a recent Department of Defense–sponsored study entitled "Military Adolescents: Their Strengths and Vulnerabilities." Dr. Jeffreys is a licensed social worker in Pennsylvania. She has also served as a co-investigator on the Women Aboard Ship Study conducted by the Naval Health Research Center, San Diego, California. Dr. Jeffreys received her Ph.D. in Social Work and Developmental Psychology and her M.S.W. from the University of Michigan. She holds an M.A. in Developmental Psychology and a B.A. in Psychology from Oakland University.

PETER S. JENSEN, M.D., is the Chief, Developmental Psychopathology Research Branch, Division of Mental Disorders, Behavioral Research, and Aids at the National Institute of Mental Health (NIMH), Rockville, Maryland, and the associate director, Child and Adolescent Research, and Chief, Developmental Psychopathology Research Branch, of the NIMH. Formerly with the Walter Reed Army Institute of Research, Dr. Jensen joined NIMH in 1989. Dr. Jensen serves on a number of editorial and scientific advisory boards (including the C.H.A.D.D. Professional Advisory Board and the Tourettes Syndrome Association Scientific Board), is the author of over 100 scientific articles and chapters, and has edited two books on children's mental health research.

SUSAN KERNER-HOEG, M.S., is a Principal at Caliber Associates. She has over 25 years of experience in survey research and program evaluation for human services programs. She has worked with the Army, Navy, Air Force, and Department of Defense for over 20 years in assessing the effectiveness of military family programs and military recreation services. She has traveled extensively throughout the military community, conducting on-site interviews and focus groups with military members and their families. Ms. Kerner-Hoeg holds an M.S. in Statistics.

JEFFREY D. LEITZEL, M.A., is a research associate at the Military Family Institute of Marywood University, Scranton, Pennsylvania. Mr. Leitzel served as research associate on the "Military Adolescents: Their Strengths and Vulnerabilities" study at the Military Family Institute, Marywood University. Mr. Leitzel received his B.S. in Psychology from Pennsylvania State University and his M.A. in Psychology from Marywood University. He is an adjunct faculty member in the Counseling/Psychology and Nutrition and Dietetics Departments at Marywood. He is currently pursuing his Ph.D. in Human Development, Counseling Psychology Specialization, at Marywood University.

PEGGY MCCLURE, Ph.D., is senior scientist at the Military Family Institute of Marywood University. She received her BA in Sociology from Smith College and her doctorate in Sociology from the University of California at Berkeley. Her recent research has focused on community cohesion of military installations and dual-career military marriages. She has also worked on several large-scale survey research projects in the fields of mental health, occupational stress, and, recently, a qualitative study of people retiring from the military.

DOROTHY OGILVY-LEE, A.C.S.W., earned her master's degree from Washington University in 1967 and began her federal career in a VA mental health program in 1974. She began working with military families in Germany in 1977 and has been at the National Guard Bureau since 1984. Since that time she has planned, organized, trained, and directed the highly respected National Guard Family Program since its inception.

DAVID H. PRYCE, M.A., M.S.S.W., L.G.S.W., is a retired Army colonel with extensive experience as an educator and trainer. Since leaving military service, Colonel Pryce has transitioned from combat arms soldier to social worker. His first social work position was a four-year tenure as State Family Program Coordinator for the Hawaii National Guard. Colonel Pryce is a secretarial appointee on the Department of Veterans Affairs Advisory Committee on the Readjustment of Veterans, and also serves as executive director of the Alabama Chapter of the National Association of Social Workers.

JOSEPHINE G. PRYCE (aka KNOX), Ph.D., is on the faculty of the School of Social Work at the University of Alabama. She is the recipient of several awards for teaching excellence. Dr. Pryce has practiced in a variety of social work settings including the Department of Human Resources, Hospice, and in Air Force Mental Health Clinic in Izmir, Turkey. She has published research reports and articles on military families, HIV prevention, and human services for refugees. Dr. Knox is currently performing research in collaboration with the Office of Family Programs, National Guard Bureau.

BARBARA JANOFSKY RUDIN, Ph.D., is a social science research consultant with more than 10 years of consulting experience. She has worked extensively with the Air Force, Army, Navy, and Marines assessing the needs of families in many different areas including childcare, family advocacy, family support, and recreation services. Dr. Rudin has managed large-scale survey projects, as well as smaller, qualitative assessments. Dr. Rudin is a senior managing associate; she has been employed by Caliber Associates for over 10 years.

THERESA J. RUSSO, Ph.D., C.F.L.E., is an assistant professor at the Department of Family Studies, SUNY-Oneonta, Oneonta, New York. She received her Ph.D. from Kansas State University and was a postdoctoral fellow with the Military Family Institute at Marywood University, Scranton, Pennsylvania, in

1994-1995. She is certified as a Family Life Educator by the National Council on Family Relations.

MARTHA SALAS, R.N., M.B.A., serves as the Air Force Family Advocacy Program New Parent Support Manager for Air Force installations worldwide. In this role she develops, implements, evaluates, and manages New Parent Support Programs for the Air Force. She provides clinical nursing, program management consultation, and Family Advocacy training to Air Force Family Advocacy personnel, Department of Defense, and other military services. She participates in the collection of FAP data and research initiatives.

WALTER R. SCHUMM, Ph.D., is professor of Family Studies and Human Services at Kansas State University, where he has taught since 1979. Dr. Schumm earned his Ph.D. at Purdue University in family studies. He is also a colonel in the Army Reserve, with over 27 years commissioned service, and has frequently worked as a research consultant with a variety of federal, state, and private agencies.

HENRY K. WATANABE, M.D., FAPA, FAACAP is an associate professor and director of Child and Adolescent Service at the University of Nevada, Reno, Nevada. Dr. Watanabe is certified by the American Board of Psychiatry and Neurology in General and Child and Adolescent Psychiatry. He is a fellow of the American Psychiatric Association and the American Academy of Child and Adolescent Psychiatry. Dr. Watanabe retired from the U.S. Army Medical Corps in 1994. While on active duty, he served as the psychiatric consultant to the 18th MEDCOM and as Chief of the Department of Psychiatry at the U.S. Army Community Hospital in Seoul, Korea. He has served as a research psychiatrist and guest scientist at the Walter Reed Army Institute of Research in Washington, D.C., where he conducted research concerning Army families and children.

DAVID S. WOLPERT, Ph.D., Lt.Col., U.S. Air Force, Ret., spent twenty years as an Air Force social worker. His research has dealt with general mental health, family violence, and the Transition Assistance Program. His doctoral dissertation, at the University of Pittsburgh, looked at planning for military retirement. He received an M.S.S.W. from Columbia University. Dr. Wolpert was a VISTA volunteer and worked with children in New York City.